Rochester, N.Y. St. Peter's Church

Book of Worship in use in St. Peter's Church

of the Presbytery of Rochester City, New York

Rochester, N.Y. St. Peter's Church

Book of Worship in use in St. Peter's Church
of the Presbytery of Rochester City, New York

ISBN/EAN: 9783337291648

Printed in Europe, USA, Canada, Australia, Japan

Cover: Foto ©Lupo / pixelio.de

More available books at **www.hansebooks.com**

The

Book of Worship

in use in

St. Peter's Church,

of the

Presbytery of Rochester City,

New York.

Rochester:
E. Darrow & Brother.
1864.

STEAM PRESS OF CURTIS, BUTTS & Co., ROCHESTER.

Order

of

Divine Services.

THE REGULAR SERVICE

OF THE

LORD'S DAY.

MORNING SERVICE.

THE SALUTATION AND DOXOLOGY.

The Congregation standing, the Minister begins the service with a sentence of Salutation from the Scriptures.
After which the People chant with the Choir the Doxology:

GLORY be to the Father, and to the Son,
And to the Holy Ghost;
As it was in the beginning, is now, and ever shall be,
World without end. Amen.

THE PROFESSION OF FAITH.

All still standing, the People then, being invited by the Minister, say with him the *Apostle's Creed*, as follows:

I BELIEVE in God the Father Almighty, Maker of heaven and earth:
And in Jesus Christ his only Son, our Lord; who was conceived by the Holy Ghost, born of the Virgin Mary, suffered under Pontius Pilate, was crucified, dead, and buried; he descended into hell; the third day he rose again from the dead; he ascended into heaven, and sitteth on the right hand of God the Father Almighty; from thence he shall come to judge the quick and the dead.

I believe in the Holy Ghost; the holy catholic church; the communion of saints; the forgiveness of sins; the resurrection of the body; and the life everlasting. Amen.

The Invocation, and the Lord's Prayer.

The People then kneeling, or reverently bowing, the Minister offers the Prayer of Invocation; the Minister himself standing, both here and in all other prayers.

After the Invocation, the *Lord's Prayer* is said by the People, with the Minister, as follows:

Our Father which art in heaven, Hallowed be thy name. Thy kingdom come. Thy will be done in earth, as it is in heaven. Give us this day our daily bread. And forgive us our debts, as we forgive our debtors. And lead us not into temptation, but deliver us from evil: For thine is the kingdom, and the power, and the glory, forever. Amen.

The Reading of the Law.

The People then being seated, the Minister solemnly reads the *Ten Commandments*, with the Two Commandments wherein they are summed up by our Lord.

And the following Response is sung by the Choir:

> The Lord our God be with us;
> Let him not leave us, nor forsake us;
> That he may incline our hearts unto him,
> To walk in all his ways, and to keep his commandments.

The Invitation, and the Confession of Sin.

After this, the Minister reminds the People of their sins and exhorts them to confession, in some Scriptural sentences of Invitation.

Then, the Congregation kneeling or humbly bowing, the Minister offers the Prayer of Confession and Absolution.

THE HYMN.

After the Confession, the Congregation, standing, sing with the Choir one of the Hymns appointed in this book for this First Part of the service.

THE READING OF THE SCRIPTURES.

Then follows the reading of a portion of the Word of God by the Minister, the People sitting and devoutly attending.

The portion of Scripture for this reading is selected by the Minister according to his discretion; except that the Book of Psalms, being appointed for another part of the service, is not used here.

THE ANTHEM.

Then is sung by the Choir one of the Sentences appointed for this place on page 8 of this book.

THE READING OF THE PSALTER.

Then is read, by the Minister and People responsively, a lesson from the Psalter, as given in this book.

The lesson is selected by the Minister at his discretion. But the lessons are so arranged, that, if the Minister prefer, the whole Psalter may be read through in one year at the Morning and Evening Service of the Lord's day.

THE HYMN.

After the reading of the Psalter, the Congregation, standing, sing with the Choir one of the Hymns appointed in this book for this Second Part of the service.

THE COLLECTION.

Here is taken, on such days as may be appointed, the Collection of the Religious Offerings of the People; the Elders, Deacons, or other authorized persons, receiving the contributions, and placing them upon the Communion Table; the Minister meanwhile reminding the People, by suitable sentences from the Scriptures, of the duty and privilege of thus offering of their substance to the Lord.

THE GENERAL PRAYER.

The People then kneeling, or devoutly bowing, the Minister offers the Prayers of general and special Supplication, Thanksgiving and Intercession.

The Anthem.

Then is sung by the Choir one of the Anthems appointed for this place on page 10 of this book; or some like selection, under the direction of the Minister.

The Sermon.

The Minister here gives any public notices which may be required; and then preaches the Sermon.

The Closing Prayer and Doxology.

The Sermon being ended, the People kneeling or devoutly bowing, the Minister offers the Closing Prayer.

After which the Congregation, standing, sing with the Choir the metrical Doxology:

To God the Father, God the Son,
And God the Spirit, three in One,
Be honor, praise, and glory given
By all on earth and all in heaven.

The Benediction.

The People still standing, but reverently bowing the head, the Minister then pronounces upon them the Apostolic *Benediction*.

THE END OF THE MORNING SERVICE.

THE SENTENCES AND ANTHEMS
FOR THE MORNING SERVICE.

I. *The Sentences for the First Part of the Morning Service, after the Reading of the Scriptures, as directed on page 7.*

I.
Gloria.

GLORY be to thee, O Lord.

MORNING SERVICE.

II.
Sanctus.

HOLY, holy, holy Lord God of hosts! Heaven and earth are full of thy glory. Glory be to thee, O Lord Most High.

III.
Angelic Hymn.—Lu. II, 14.

GLORY to God in the highest, and on earth peace, good will toward men.

IV.
Revelation VII, 12.

BLESSING, and glory, and wisdom, and thanksgiving, and honor, and power, and might, be unto our God forever and ever. Amen.

V.
Luke XI, 28.

BLESSED are they that hear the word of God, and keep it.

VI.
From Psalm CXIX.

TEACH me, O Lord, the way of thy statutes,
And I shall keep it unto the end.

VII.
From Psalm XIX.

THE law of the Lord is perfect, converting the soul;
The testimony of the Lord is sure, making wise the simple.
The statutes of the Lord are right, rejoicing the heart;
The commandment of the Lord is pure, enlightening the eyes.
The fear of the Lord is clean, enduring forever;
The judgments of the Lord are true and righteous altogether.
Moreover, by them is thy servant warned;
And in keeping of them there is great reward.

VIII.
From Psalm LXXII.

BLESSED be the Lord God, the God of Israel;
Who only doeth wondrous things.
And blessed be his glorious name forever;
And let the whole earth be filled with his glory. Amen, and Amen.

II. *The Anthems for the Second Part of the Morning Service, after the General Prayer, as directed on page* 8.

I.

Te Deum laudamus.

WE praise thee, O God:
We acknowledge thee to be the Lord.
All the earth doth worship thee,
The Father everlasting.
To thee all angels cry aloud,
The heavens and all the powers therein.
To thee Cherubim and Seraphim
Continually do cry:
Holy, Holy, Holy, Lord God of Sabaoth;
Heaven and earth are full of the majesty of thy glory!
The glorious company of the apostles praise thee;
The goodly fellowship of the prophets praise thee;
The noble army of martyrs praise thee;
The holy church throughout all the world doth acknowledge thee,
The Father, of an infinite majesty; thine adorable, true, and only Son;
Also the Holy Ghost, the Comforter.
Thou art the King of Glory, O Christ;
Thou art the everlasting Son of the Father.
When thou tookest upon thee to deliver man,
Thou didst humble thyself to be born of a Virgin.
When thou hadst overcome the sharpness of death,
Thou didst open the kingdom of heaven to all believers.
Thou sittest at the right hand of God, in the glory of the Father.
We believe that thou shalt come to be our Judge.
We therefore pray thee, help thy servants,
Whom thou hast redeemed with thy precious blood;
Make them to be numbered with thy saints
In glory everlasting.
O Lord, save thy people, and bless thine heritage;
Govern them, and lift them up forever.
Day by day we magnify thee;
And we worship thy name ever, world without end.
Vouchsafe, O Lord, to keep us this day without sin.

O Lord, have mercy upon us, have mercy upon us.
O Lord, let thy mercy be upon us,
As our trust is in thee.
O Lord, in thee have I trusted;
Let me never be confounded.

II.

Venite, exultemus.—From Ps. XCV. and XCVI.

O COME, let us sing unto the Lord,
Let us heartily rejoice in the strength of our salvation.
Let us come before his presence with thanksgiving,
And show ourselves glad in him with psalms.
For the Lord is a great God;
And a great King above all gods.
In his hand are all the corners of the earth;
And the strength of the hills is his also.
The sea is his, and he made it,
And his hands prepared the dry land.
O come, let us worship and fall down,
And kneel before the Lord our Maker,
For he is the Lord our God;
And we are the people of his pasture, and the sheep of his hand.
O worship the Lord in the beauty of holiness;
Let the whole earth stand in awe of him.
For he cometh, for he cometh to judge the earth;
And with righteousness to judge the world, and the people with his truth.

III.

Bonum est confiteri.—From Ps. XCII.

IT is good thing to give thanks unto the Lord,
And to sing praises unto thy name, O Most Highest;
To tell of thy loving-kindness early in the morning,
And of thy truth in the night season;
Upon an instrument of ten strings, and upon the lute;
Upon a loud instrument, and upon the harp.
For thou, Lord, hast made me glad through thy works,
And I will rejoice in giving praise for the operations of thy hands.

IV.

Malachi I, 11,

FROM the rising of the sun even unto the going down of the same,
My name shall be great among the Gentiles;
And in every place incense shall be offered
Unto my name, and a pure offering;
For my name shall be great
Among the heathen, saith the Lord of hosts.

THE DOXOLOGY

AS IT IS CHANTED BY THE CONGREGATION

AT THE BEGINNING OF THE MORNING AND EVENING SERVICE.

Gloria Patri.

GLORY be to the }
    Father, and   } to-the | Son, | And | to-the | Ho-ly | Ghost;

As it was in the be- }   { shall | | with- }
ginning, is now, and } e - ver { be, |World| out { end. A- | men.

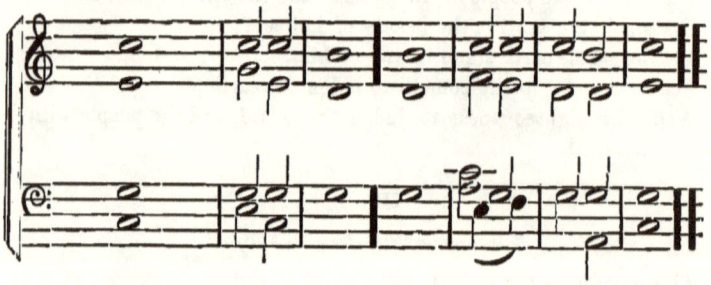

EVENING SERVICE.

The Salutation and Doxology.

The Congregation standing, the Minister begins the service with a sentence of Salutation from the Scriptures.

After which the People chant with the Choir the Doxology:

GLORY be to the Father, and to the Son,
And to the Holy Ghost;
As it was in the beginning, is now, and ever shall be,
World without end. Amen.

The Lord's Prayer.

The People then kneeling, or reverently bowing, say with the Minister the *Lord's Prayer*, as follows:

OUR Father which art in heaven; Hallowed be thy name Thy kingdom come. Thy will be done in earth, as it is in heaven. Give us this day our daily bread. And forgive us our debts, as we forgive our debtors. And lead us not into temptation, but deliver us from evil: For thine is the kingdom, and the power, and the glory, forever. Amen.

The Confession of Sin.

The People still kneeling or bowing, the Minister then offers the Prayer of Confession and Absolution.

The Hymn.

After the Confession, the Congregation, standing, sing with the Choir one of the Hymns appointed in this book for this First Part of the service.

The Reading of the Scriptures.

Then follows the reading of a portion of the Word of God by the Minister, the People sitting down and devoutly attending.

The portion of Scripture for this reading is selected by the Minister according to his discretion; except that the Book of Psalms, being appointed for another part of the service, is not used here.

The Anthem.

Then is sung by the Choir one of the Anthems appointed for this place on page 15 of this book; or some like selection under the direction of the Minister.

The Reading of the Psalter.

Then is read, by the Minister and the People responsively, a lesson from the Psalter, as given in this book.

The lesson is selected by the Minister at his discretion. But the lessons are so arranged that, if the Minister prefer, the whole Psalter may be read through in one year at the Morning and Evening Service of the Lord's Day.

The Hymn.

After the reading of the Psalter, the Congregation, standing, sing with the Choir one of the Hymns appointed in this book for this Second Part of the service.

The General Prayer.

The People then kneeling, or devoutly bowing, the Minister offers the Prayers of general and special Supplication, Thanksgiving and Intercession.

The Anthem.

Then is sung by the Choir one of the Anthems appointed for this place on page 17 of this book; or some like selection under the direction of the Minister.

EVENING SERVICE. 15

The Sermon.

The Minister here gives any public notices which may be required; and then preaches the Sermon.

The Closing Prayer and Doxology.

The Sermon being ended, the People kneeling, or devoutly bowing, the Minister offers the Closing Prayer.

After which the Congregation, standing, sing with the Choir the metrical Doxology:

> To God the Father, God the Son,
> And God the Spirit, three in one,
> Be honor, praise, and glory given,
> By all on earth and all in heaven.

The Benediction.

The People still standing, but reverently bowing the head, the Minister then pronounces upon them the Apostolic *Benediction*.

THE END OF THE EVENING SERVICE.

THE ANTHEMS FOR THE EVENING SERVICE.

I. *The Anthems for the First Part of the Evening Service, after the Reading of the Scriptures, as directed on page* 14.

I.
Gloria in excelsis.

GLORY be to God on high,
And on earth peace, good will towards men.
We praise thee, we bless thee, we worship thee,
We glorify thee, we give thanks to thee for thy great glory,
O Lord God, heavenly King,
God the Father Almighty.
O Lord, the only-begotten Son, Jesus Christ;

O Lord God, Lamb of God, Son of the Father,
That takest away the sins of the world,
Have mercy upon us.
Thou that takest away the sins of the world,
Have mercy upon us.
Thou that takest away the sins of the world,
Receive our prayer.
Thou that sittest at the right hand of God the Father,
Have mercy upon us.
For thou only art holy;
Thou only art the Lord.
Thou only, O Christ, with the Holy Ghost,
Art most high in the glory of God the Father.

II.

Benedictus.—Luke I, 68–71.

BLESSED be the Lord God of Israel;
For he hath visited and redeemed his people;
And hath raised up a mighty salvation for us,
In the house of his servant David;
As he spake by the mouth of his holy prophets,
Which have been since the world began;
That we should be saved from our enemies,
And from the hand of all that hate us.

III.

De profundis.—Ps. CXXX.

OUT of the depths have I cried unto thee, O Lord.
Lord, hear my voice;
Let thine ears be attentive
To the voice of my supplications.
If thou, Lord, shouldst mark iniquities,
O Lord, who shall stand?
But there is forgiveness with thee,
That thou mayest be feared.
I wait for the Lord, my soul doth wait,
And in his word do I hope.
My soul waiteth for the Lord

More than they that watch for the morning;
I say, more than they that watch for the morning.
Let Israel hope in the Lord;
For with the Lord there is mercy,
And with him there is plenteous redemption.
And he shall redeem Israel from all his iniquities.

IV.
Quemadmodum.— From Ps. XLII.

AS the hart panteth after the water-brooks,
So panteth my soul after thee, O God.
My soul thirsteth for God, for the living God;
When shall I come and appear before God?
My tears have been my meat day and night,
While they continually say unto me, Where is thy God?
When I remember these things, I pour out my soul in me.
For I had gone with the multitude; I went with them to the
    house of God,
With the voice of joy and praise, with a multitude that kept
    holy-day.
Why art thou cast down, O my soul? and why art thou disquieted
    in me?
Hope thou in God; for I shall yet praise him,
Who is the health of my countenance, and my God.

II. *The Anthems for the Second Part of the Evening Service, after the General Prayer, as directed on page* 14.

I.
Benedic, anima mea.—From Ps. CIII.

PRAISE the Lord, O my soul;
And all that is within me, praise his holy name.
Praise the Lord, O my soul,
And forget not all his benefits;
Who forgiveth all thy sin,
And healeth all thine infirmities;
Who saveth thy life from destruction,
And crowneth thee with mercy and loving kindness.

O praise the Lord, ye angels of his, ye that excel in strength;
Ye that fulfil his commandment, and hearken unto the voice of his word.
O praise the Lord, all ye his hosts;
Ye servants of his that do his pleasure.
O speak good of the Lord, all ye works of his, in all places of his dominion;
Praise thou the Lord, O my soul.

II.
Cantate Domino.— Ps. XCVIII.

O SING unto the Lord a new song;
For he hath done marvellous things.
With his own right hand, and with his holy arm,
Hath he gotten himself the victory.
The Lord declared his salvation;
His righteousness hath he openly showed in the sight of the heathen.
He hath remembered his mercy and truth toward the house of Israel;
And all the ends of the world have seen the salvation of our God.
Show yourselves joyful unto the Lord, all ye lands;
Sing, rejoice, and give thanks.
Praise the Lord upon the harp;
Sing to the harp with a psalm of thanksgiving.
With trumpets also and shawms,
O show yourselves joyful before the Lord the King.
Let the sea make a noise, and all that therein is;
The round world, and they that dwell therein.
Let the floods clap their hands, and let the hills be joyful together before the Lord;
For he cometh to judge the earth.
With righteousness shall he judge the world,
And the people with equity.

III.
Jubilate Deo.— Ps. C.

O BE joyful in the Lord, all ye lands;

EVENING SERVICE. 19

Serve the Lord with gladness, and come before his presence with
a song.
Be ye sure that the Lord, he is God;
It is he that hath made us and not we ourselves; we are his
people and the sheep of his pasture.
O go your way into his gates with thanksgiving, and into his
courts with praise;
Be thankful unto him, and speak good of his name.
For the Lord is gracious, his mercy is everlasting ;
And his truth endureth from generation to generation.

IV.

Deus misereatur.—Ps. LXVII.

GOD be merciful unto us, and bless us,
And show us the light of his countenance, and be merciful unto us ;
That thy way may be known upon earth,
Thy saving health among all nations.
Let the people praise thee, O God;
Yea, let all the people praise thee.
O let the nations rejoice and be glad ;
For thou shalt judge the folk righteously, and govern the nations
upon earth.
Let the people praise thee, O God;
Yea, let all the people praise thee.
Then shall the earth bring forth her increase;
And God, even our own God, shall give us his blessing.
God shall bless us;
And all the ends of the world shall fear him.

THE COMMUNION

OF

THE LORD'S SUPPER.

The Communion of the Lord's Supper is administered at such times as the Minister and Elders, in their discretion, appoint.

The service of Preparation for the Communion, at a convenient time before, follows the order of the Evening Service of the Lord's Day, with a suitable Sermon; or any other form which the Minister may prefer.

THE SALUTATION AND DOXOLOGY.

The Congregation standing, the Minister begins the service with a sentence of Salutation from the Scriptures.

After which the People chant with the Choir the Doxology:

GLORY be to the Father, and to the Son,
And to the Holy Ghost;
As it was in the beginning, is now, and ever shall be,
World without end. Amen.

THE PROFESSION OF FAITH.

All still standing, the People then, being invited by the Minister, say with him the *Apostles' Creed*, as follows:

THE COMMUNION.

I BELIEVE in God the Father Almighty, Maker of heaven and earth.

And in Jesus Christ his only Son, our Lord; who was conceived by the Holy Ghost, born of the Virgin Mary, suffered under Pontius Pilate, was crucified, dead, and buried; he descended into hell; the third day he rose again from the dead; he ascended into heaven, and sitteth on the right hand of God the Father Almighty; from thence he shall come to judge the quick and the dead.

I believe in the Holy Ghost; the holy catholic church; the communion of saints; the forgiveness of sins; the resurrection of the body; and the life everlasting. Amen.

THE INVOCATION, AND THE LORD'S PRAYER.

The People then kneeling, or reverently bowing, the Minister offers the Prayer of Invocation; the Minister himself standing, both here and in all other prayers.

After the Invocation the *Lord's Prayer* is said by the People with the Minister, as follows:

OUR Father which art in heaven, Hallowed be thy name. Thy kingdom come. Thy will be done in earth, as it is in heaven. Give us this day our daily bread. And forgive us our debts, as we forgive our debtors. And lead us not into temptation, but deliver us from evil: For thine is the kingdom, and the power, and the glory, forever. Amen.

THE READING OF THE LAW.

The People then being seated, the Minister solemnly reads the *Ten Commandments*, with the Two Commandments wherein they are summed up by our Lord.

And the following Response is sung by the Choir:

THE Lord our God be with us;
Let him not leave us, nor forsake us;
That he may incline our hearts unto him,
To walk in all his ways, and to keep his commandments.

THE COMMUNION.

The Invitation, and the Confession of Sin.

After this the Minister reminds the People of their sins and exhorts them to confession, in some Scriptural sentences of Invitation.

Then, the Congregation kneeling or humbly bowing, the Minister offers the Prayer of Confession and Absolution.

The Receiving of New Communicants.

Here takes place, according to the Order given on page 28, the solemn Receiving to the Lord's Supper of such persons as may have been admitted by the Session.

The Hymn.

After this service, or, if there be no persons to be received, then after the Confession, the Congregation, standing, sing with the Choir the Hymn "*My God accept my heart this day*" (the 274th of this book), or some like selection from the Hymns appointed for this First Part of the service.

The Reading of the Scriptures.

Then follows the reading of a portion of the Word of God by the Minister, the People sitting and devoutly attending.

The portion of Scripture for this reading is selected by the Minister according to his discretion; except that the Book of Psalms, being appointed for another part of the service, is not used here.

The Anthem.

Here the Elders and Deacons take their places near the Communion Table. And any Clergymen, or Elders and Deacons of other churches, who may be present in the congregation, are invited to take places with them.

Then is sung by the Choir the Anthem *Gloria in excelsis*, as follows:

GLORY be to God on high,
And on earth peace, good will towards men.
We praise thee, we bless thee, we worship thee,
We glorify thee, we give thanks to thee for thy great glory,
O Lord God, heavenly King,
God the Father Almighty.
O Lord, the only-begotten Son, Jesus Christ;
O Lord God, Lamb of God, Son of the Father,

That takest away the sins of the world,
Have mercy upon us.
Thou that takest away the sins of the world,
Have mercy upon us.
Thou that takest away the sins of the world,
Receive our prayer.
Thou that sittest at the right hand of God the Father,
Have mercy upon us.
For thou only art holy;
Thou only art the Lord.
Thou only, O Christ, with the Holy Ghost,
Art most high in the glory of God the Father.

The Reading of the Psalter.

Then is read, by the Minister and the People responsively, the Forty-fifth Lesson of the Psalter (Ps. lxxii.) as given in this book; unless the Minister for special reason prefer another.

The Hymn.

After the reading of the Psalter the Congregation, standing, sing with the Choir the Hymn "*Now at the Lamb's high royal feast*" (the 98th of this book), or some like selection from the Hymns appointed for this Second Part of the service.

The Collection.

Here is taken the Collection of the Alms and religious Offerings of the People; the Elders, Deacons, or other authorized persons receiving the gifts and placing them upon the Communion Table; while the Minister, in suitable words of Scripture, reminds the People of the duty and privilege of thus offering of their substance to the Lord, as a proper part of their offering of themselves to Him in the holy Communion.

The Exhortation.

The Minister here announces what persons, if any, have been received into this church by letters from other churches; and what persons have been now for the first time admitted to the Communion; also giving any other notices which may be required.

And all members of other churches, who may be present, and desire to partake of the Communion, are invited so to do.

Then the Minister begins the administration of the Communion with the proper Exhortation; reminding the People of the holy nature and benefits of the ordinance, warning them against profaning it by approaching it in ignorance or thoughtlessness, or in the indulgence of any known sin; and inviting them to come to it in repentance, and in faith and love towards Christ, or with an unfeigned desire to be found in Christ and to depart from iniquity.—*Larg. Catech.*, Q. 172.

THE COMMUNION PRAYER.

Then, the Congregation kneeling or devoutly bowing, the Minister offers the Prayers of Supplication, general and special Thanksgiving, Adoration, and Praise; the Prayer of Consecration, with the *Words of Institution;* and the Prayers of Self-Oblation and of general and special Intercession.

THE COMMUNION.

The People now being seated, the Minister proceeds to deliver the consecrated Elements; first the Bread, until all have received it, and afterwards the Wine. The Minister delivers the Communion to the Elders and Deacons, and they, for him, then deliver it to all the Communicants. The Minister himself receives the Communion before the Elders distribute it to the People.

While the People are receiving, or after all have communicated, the Minister solemnly repeats the sentences of sacramental instruction and admonition from the Scriptures, as appointed.

THE CLOSING PRAYER.

The Communion being ended, the People kneeling or reverently bowing, the Minister offers the Closing Prayer.

THE ANTHEM.

Then is sung by the Choir the Anthem *Te Deum laudamus*, as follows:

WE praise thee, O God;
We acknowledge thee to be the Lord.
All the earth doth worship thee,
The Father everlasting.
To thee all angels cry aloud,
The heavens and all the powers therein.

THE COMMUNION. 25

To the Cherubim and Seraphim
Continually do cry:
Holy, Holy, Holy, Lord God of Saboath;
Heaven and earth are full of the majesty of thy glory!
The glorious company of the apostles praise thee;
The goodly fellowship of the prophets praise thee;
The noble army of martyrs praise thee;
The holy church throughout all the world doth acknowledge thee,
The Father, of an infinite majesty; thine adorable, true, and only Son;
Also the Holy Ghost, the Comforter;
Thou art the King of Glory, O Christ;
Thou art the everlasting Son of the Father.
When thou tookest upon thee to deliver man,
Thou didst humble thyself to be born of a Virgin.
When thou hadst overcome the sharpness of death,
Thou didst open the kingdom of heaven to all believers.
Thou sittest at the right hand of God, in the glory of the Father.
We believe that thou shalt come to be our Judge.
We therefore pray thee, help thy servants,
Whom thou hast redeemed with thy precious blood;
Make them to be numbered with thy saints
In glory everlasting.
O Lord, save thy people, and bless thine heritage;
Govern them, and lift them up forever.
Day by day we magnify thee;
And we worship thy name ever, world without end.
Vouchsafe, O Lord, to keep us this day without sin.
O Lord, have mercy upon us, have mercy upon us.
O Lord, let thy mercy be upon us,
As our trust is in thee.
O Lord, in thee have I trusted;
Let me never be confounded.

THE BENEDICTION.

Then, the People rising and reverently bowing the head, the Minister pronounces upon them the proper *Benediction*.

THE END OF THE COMMUNION SERVICE.

THE ORDER

FOR THE

ADMINISTRATION OF BAPTISM.

Baptism is always administered in the Church, at the time of some public service, unless necessity require otherwise.

Parents intending to bring a Child to be baptized, are required to give notice thereof to the Minister before the time of Public Worship, and to give him, in writing, their own full names, and the name of the Child, and date of its birth.

The Child to be baptized is presented by one or both of the parents, immediately *after the Prayer of Confession* in either the Morning or the Evening Service.

The Introductory Sentence.

While the Parents are coming with the Child to the Font, the following Sentence is sung by the Choir:

SUFFER the little children to come unto me, and forbid them not; For of such is the kingdom of God.

The Charge to the Parents.

The Parents then standing, with the Child, before the Font, the Minister, standing by it, gives to them the Charge concerning the blessings and duties signified by holy Baptism, and demands of them a promise to be faithful thereto in behalf of their Child.

The Prayer before Baptism.

After this, the Congregation rising, the Minister offers the Prayer before the Baptism.

BAPTISM. 27

The Baptism.

The whole Congregation still standing, the Minister, taking the Child (if an infant) on his arm, or leaving it in the arms of the Parent, performs the Baptism.

The Prayer after Baptism.

Then, all still standing, the Minister, having restored the Child to the Parent, offers the Prayer after the Baptism.

The Concluding Sentence.

Then, while the Parents with the Child are departing from the Font, the Congregation sitting down, the following Sentence is sung by the Choir:

Whosoever shall not receive the kingdom of God as a little child, He shall not enter therein.

After which the regular service proceeds; the Hymn following being usually a Baptismal Hymn from among those appointed for the First Part of the service.

THE FORM

OF

'RECEIVING ADULT PERSONS

TO THE

COMMUNION.

Children, born within the pale of the visible church, and dedicated to God in baptism, are under the inspection and government of the church; and are to be taught to read, and repeat the Catechism, the Apostles' Creed, and the Lord's Prayer. They are to be taught to pray, to abhor sin, to fear God, and to obey the Lord Jesus Christ. And, when they come to years of discretion, if they be free from scandal, appear sober and steady, and have sufficient knowledge to discern the Lord's body, they ought to be informed it is their duty and their privilege to come to the Lord's Supper.

The years of discretion in young Christians cannot be precisely fixed. This must be left to the prudence of the Eldership. The officers of the church are the judges of the qualifications of those to be admitted to sealing ordinances; and of the time when it is proper to admit young Christians to them.—*Directory for Worship, Ch. IX.*

When such young persons, or adult persons who have been so baptized and instructed, are judged fit, by the proper Officers, to come to the holy Communion, they are solemnly received to the Communion in the following public form, unless necessity forbid.

Persons who have been born within the pale of the church, and instructed in Christian knowledge and duty, but for any cause have not been baptized, are also, upon giving satisfaction to the Elders in regard to their Christian desires and purposes, publicly received in the following form, being at the same time baptized in the manner shown therein.

TO THE COMMUNION. 29

The persons to be thus received to the Communion present themselves before the Minister in the Communion Service, immediately *after the Prayer of Confession.*

The Charge to the Candidates.

The Minister, standing by the Communion Table, or by the Font, as the case may require, first gives to the Candidates the Charge; demanding of such as have been baptized, that they believe and do all things which their parents then undertook for them; and of such as are to be baptized, that they be mindful of the blessings and duties signified by holy Baptism, and endeavor to walk in conformity thereto.

The Prayer before Benediction.

After this, the Congregation rising, the Minister offers the Prayer before the Benediction; and, if any of the Candidates are to be baptized, the proper Prayer before the Baptism.

The Benediction.

The whole Congregation still standing, the Minister now performs the Baptism of those who have not been baptized; each Candidate devoutly kneeling.

Upon each of these Persons, after baptizing him, the Minister solemnly pronounces the proper apostolic *Benediction;* the Person still kneeling.

Then upon each of the other Candidates he pronounces the same Benediction; each drawing near in his order, and reverently bowing to receive it.

The Charge to the Congregation.

Then the Minister gives to the Congregation, still standing, the Charge concerning their duty towards those who thus strive to walk in all faithfulness among them.

The Prayer after Benediction.

All still standing, the Minister here offers, ~~first, if occasion require, the Prayer after the Baptism, and then~~ the Prayer after the Benediction.

After which, the new Communicants withdrawing, and the People sitting down, the service proceeds according to the Order for the Communion.

THE ORDER

FOR THE

SOLEMNIZING OF MARRIAGE.

At the time appointed, the persons to be married come into the Church and stand before the Minister at the Communion Table (or, if the Marriage be in a private house, the persons take any convenient place), the Man on the Right Hand, and the Woman on the Left; witnesses also being present.

THE CHARGE TO THE WHOLE COMPANY.

The Minister first gives to all present the proper Charge; reminding them of the solemn warrant and the holy nature and duties of the estate of Marriage, and demanding of the Witnesses that, if they know any impediment to the proposed Marriage, they declare it now.

THE CHARGE TO THE PERSONS TO BE MARRIED.

The Minister, then, in like manner, solemnly charges the Man and the Woman who are come to be married, that if they know any reason why they may not be lawfully married, they confess it now.

THE COVENANT.

If no impediment appear, the Minister now requires the Persons that are to be married to join their Right Hands, and then says to the Man:

Do you (*here the Minister calls the Man by his Christian full name*) take this Woman to be your lawful and wedded Wife? and do you promise and covenant that you will be unto her a loving and faithful Husband, until you shall be separated by death?

Ans. I do.

Then the Minister says likewise to the Woman:

Do you (*here the Minister calls the Woman by her christian name*) take this Man to be your lawful and wedded Husband? and do you promise and covenant that you will be unto him a loving, faithful, and obedient Wife, until you shall be separated by death?

Ans. I do.

THE PLEDGE.

The Minister then asks of the Man:

WHAT pledge do you give to keep this holy vow?

Then the Man gives to the Woman a Ring, which the Minister then takes, and gives again to the Man, requiring him to put it upon the Finger of the Woman, and hold it there while he says with the Minister:

WITH this Ring I thee wed, and with all my worldly goods I thee endow, in the name of the Father, and of the Son, and of the Holy Ghost. Amen.

THE DECLARATION OF MARRIAGE.

The Man then leaves the Ring on the Finger of the Woman, and the Minister, joining their Right Hands, and laying his own Right Hand upon theirs, solemnly pronounces the Declaration of the Marriage.

THE PRAYER.

Then, the whole Company kneeling or reverently bowing, and (if the Marriage be in the Church) the newly married Persons and their Attendants always kneeling, the Minister offers the proper Prayer.

After which all present say with the Minister the *Lord's Prayer*, as follows:

OUR Father which art in heaven, Hallowed be thy name. Thy kingdom come. Thy will be done in earth, as it is in heaven. Give us this day our daily bread. And forgive us our debts, as we forgive our debtors. And lead us not into temptation, but deliver us from evil: for thine is the kingdom, and the power, and the glory, forever. Amen.

THE BENEDICTION.

All still kneeling or bowing, the Minister pronounces the *Benediction* upon the newly married Persons.

THE ORDER

FOR THE

BURIAL OF THE DEAD.

If the service be at the house, it is conducted by the Minister according to his discretion.

If the corpse be taken into the Church, the Minister first performs a brief service at the house, at his discretion. The proper order of the service in the Church is then as follows:

THE INTRODUCTORY SENTENCES.

When the Corpse is brought into the Church, the persons already assembled rise, and the Minister, either meeting the Corpse at the entrance and going slowly before it, or standing at the Communion Table, pronounces the Introductory Sentences from holy Scripture, as appointed.

THE ANTHEM.

Then is sung by the Choir, or read by the Minister and People responsively, the Ninetieth Psalm, as follows:

LORD, thou hast been our dwelling-place
   In all generations.
Before the mountains were brought forth,
Or ever thou hadst formed the earth and the world,
   Even from everlasting to everlasting, thou art God.
Thou turnest man to destruction;
   And sayest, Return, ye children of men.

THE BURIAL OF THE DEAD.

{ For a thousand years in thy sight
{ Are but as yesterday when it is past,
 And as a watch in the night.
Thou carriest them away as with a flood; they are as a sleep;
 In the morning they are like grass which groweth up;
In the morning it flourisheth, and groweth up;
 In the evening it is cut down, and withereth.
For we are consumed by thine anger,
 And by thy wrath are we troubled.
Thou hast set our iniquities before thee,
 Our secret sins in the light of thy countenance.
For all our days are passed away in thy wrath:
 We spend our years as a tale that is told.
The days of our years are threescore years and ten;
 And if by reason of strength they be fourscore years,
Yet is their strength labor and sorrow;
 For it is soon cut off, and we fly away.
Who knoweth the power of thine anger?
 Even according to thy fear, so is thy wrath.
So teach us to number our days,
 That we may apply our hearts unto wisdom.
Return, O Lord, how long?
 And let it repent thee concerning thy servants.
O satisfy us early with thy mercy;
 That we may rejoice and be glad all our days.
Make us glad according to the days wherein thou hast afflicted us,
 And the years wherein we have seen evil.
Let thy work appear unto thy servants,
 And thy glory unto their children.
{ And let the beauty of the Lord our God be upon us:
{ And establish thou the work of our hands upon us;
 Yea, the work of our hands establish thou it.

THE HYMN.

Then, at the discretion of the Minister, a Hymn is sung by the Choir and the Congregation standing.

THE READING OF THE SCRIPTURES.

Here the Minister reads one or more of the following or like portions of the Word of God, the People sitting: JOHN, v., 21-29; JOHN, xi., 21-27; REVELATION, xxi., 1-4; II. SAMUEL, xii., 16-23.

This is always followed by the reading of .I. CORINTHIANS, xv., 20-28, 49-58.

THE PRAYER BEFORE BURIAL.

Then, the People kneeling or reverently bowing, the Minister offers the Prayer before the Burial.

THE EXHORTATION.

After this the Minister delivers an Exhortation or Discourse, at his discretion.

THE BENEDICTION.

The Discourse being ended, the Minister pronounces a Scriptural Doxology, the Congregation rising; and then, the apostolic *Benediction*.

THE BURIAL SENTENCES.

When the Procession is come to the Graveyard, the Minister, either while going before the Corpse towards the Grave, or standing at the Grave after the coffin has been let down, says the proper Burial Sentences from holy Scripture.

THE BURIAL.

When the earth is about to be cast upon the coffin, or while a portion is cast upon it, the Minister says:

SINCE it hath pleased Almighty God, in his wise providence, to take to himself the spirit of this *our brother*, we commit *his* body to the earth as it was; earth to earth, ashes to ashes, dust to dust; looking for the resurrection of the dead, and the life of the world to come, through Jesus Christ our Lord.

THE PRAYER AFTER BURIAL, AND THE LORD'S PRAYER.

Then the Minister offers the Prayer after the Burial.

After which the People say with him the *Lord's Prayer*, as follows:

OUR Father which art in heaven, Hallowed be thy name. Thy kingdom come. Thy will be done in earth, as it is in heaven. Give us this day our daily·bread. And forgive us our debts, as we forgive our debtors. And lead us not into temptation, but deliver us from evil: For thine is the kingdom, and the power, and the glory, forever. Amen.

THE BENEDICTION.

The Minister then pronounces upon the People the apostolic *Benediction*.

THE OFFICE

FOR THE

ORDINATION AND INSTALMENT

OF

ELDERS AND DEACONS.

At any regular Morning or Evening Service of the Lord's Day, or at a special service, as may be appointed, the Elders or Deacons elect present themselves before the Minister immediately *after the General Prayer.*

If there be both Elders and Deacons elect, they present themselves together, and are ordained and installed with one service. And if any candidate have been already ordained, and require to be only installed, the Minister omits, with reference to him, those parts of the ensuing Office which belong only to Ordination. When there is only Instalment of Candidates who have been previously ordained to the same offices respectively, the Charge to the Candidates and the Charge to the Congregation, in the following Order, are used at the discretion of the Minister.

The Introductory Words to the Congregation.

After the Candidates have presented themselves, the Minister first declares to the Congregation, in the appointed Introductory Words, the occasion and object of this service.

The Charge to the Candidates.

The Minister then gives to the Candidates the Charge concerning the warrant, the nature, and the duties of the holy Offices to which they are called.

The Charge to the Congregation.

Then the Minister gives to the People the Charge concerning their duties towards the Persons about to be inducted into office among them.

The Covenant on the Part of the Candidates.

The Minister now first proposes to the Elders and Deacons who are to be ordained, the following Questions, as appointed in the *Form of Government*, ch. *XIII.*; to each of which the Candidates make the response together, but audibly and distinctly:

Do you believe the Scriptures of the Old and New Testaments to be the Word of God, the only infallible rule of faith and practice?

Ans. I do.

Do you sincerely receive and adopt the Confession of Faith of this Church, as containing the system of doctrine taught in the Holy Scriptures?

Ans. I do.

Do you approve of the government and discipline of the Presbyterian Church in these United States?

Ans. I do.

Do you promise to study the peace, unity, and purity of the Church?

Ans. I do.

Then to the Elders who are to be installed, the Minister says:

Do you, who have been called to the Eldership, accept the Office of Ruling Elder in this Congregation, and promise faithfully to perform all the duties thereof?

Ans. I do.

And afterwards to the Deacons who are to be installed:

Do you, who have been called to the Office of Deacon, accept this Office in this Congregation, and promise faithfully to perform all the duties thereof?

Ans. I do.

The Covenant on the Part of the Congregation.

In like manner the Minister then proposes to the Congregation the following Question; requesting them to signify their assent to it by raising their Right Hands:

Do you, the Members of this Church, acknowledge and receive these Brethren as Ruling Elders and Deacons; and do you promise to yield them all that honor, encouragement, and obedience, in the Lord, to which their Office, according to the Word of God and the Constitution of this Church, entitles them?

The Prayer.

Then follows the proper Prayer; the People rising, and continuing to stand through the remainder of this service.

The Ordination.

The Candidates to be ordained then draw near and devoutly kneel; and the Minister, laying his Right Hand upon the Head of each, solemnly pronounces his Ordination.

The Instalment.

The Persons ordained now rising, the Minister, addressing all the elect Officers together, solemnly declares their Instalment.

After which he pronounces upon the newly installed Persons the proper *Benediction*.

Then, the newly installed Officers withdrawing, and the People sitting down, the service proceeds according to the regular Order.

The Psalter;

or,

The Book of Psalms

Arranged as it is used in

Public Worship.

NOTE.

The lines which are set inward from the margin, and printed chiefly in Italics, are read by the People.

The words which have been supplied by the Translators, are here, in the Roman lines, printed as usual in Italics; and in the Italic lines they are printed in Roman. It therefore sometimes happens that the line read by the People begins with words in the Roman character; but it is still readily distinguished by its position.

The Superscriptions of the Psalms, and the Subscription of the LXXIInd Psalm, which are in small type, as also the technical terms *Selah*, &c., which are in parentheses, are not used in the reading.

The devout reading of the Book of Psalms as here arranged, is an excellent part of Family Worship, in addition to the reading of the other Scriptures for instruction; the head of the family and the members of it reading the alternate portions. Thus, in the Psalter and the Hymns, this book furnishes a convenient and profitable manual for Family and Private Devotion.

THE PSALTER.

LESSON 1.

Psalm I.

BLESSED *is* the man that walketh not in the counsel of the ungodly,
  Nor standeth in the way of sinners,
  Nor sitteth in the seat of the scornful.
2 But his delight *is* in the law of the Lord;
  And in his law doth he meditate day and night.
3 And he shall be like a tree planted by the rivers of water,
  That bringeth forth his fruit in his season;
His leaf also shall not wither;
  And whatsoever he doeth shall prosper.
4 The ungodly *are* not so:
  But are *like the chaff which the wind driveth away.*
5 Therefore the ungodly shall not stand in the judgment,
  Nor sinners in the congregation of the righteous.
6 For the Lord knoweth the way of the righteous:
  But the way of the ungodly shall perish.

Psalm II.

WHY do the heathen rage,
  And the people imagine a vain thing?
2 The kings of the earth set themselves,
  And the rulers take counsel together,
  Against the LORD and against his anointed, saying,
3 Let us break their bands asunder,
  And cast away their cords from us.

4 He that sitteth in the heavens shall laugh:
    The Lord shall have them in derision.
5 Then shall he speak unto them in his wrath,
    And vex them in his sore displeasure.
6 Yet have I set my king
    Upon my holy hill of Zion.
7 I will declare the decree:
    { *The LORD hath sa'd unto me, Thou art my Son ;*
    { *This day have I begotten thee.*
8 Ask of me, and I shall give *thee* the heathen *for* thine inheritance,
    And the uttermost parts of the earth for *thy possession.*
9 Thou shalt break them with a rod of iron;
    Thou shalt dash them in pieces like a potter's vessel.
10 Be wise now therefore, O ye kings:
    Be instructed, ye judges of the earth.
11 Serve the LORD with fear,
    And rejoice with trembling.
12 { Kiss the Son, lest he be angry, and ye perish *from* the way,
    { When his wrath is kindled but a little.
    Blessed are *all they that put their trust in him.*

PSALM III.

A Psalm of David, when he fled from Absalom his son.

LORD, how are they increased that trouble me!
    Many are *they that rise up against me.*
2 Many *there be* which say of my soul,
    There is *no help for him in God.* (*Selah.*)
3 But thou, O LORD, *art* a shield for me;
    My glory, and the lifter up of mine head.
3 I cried unto the LORD with my voice,
    And he heard me out of his holy hill. (*Selah.*)
5 I laid me down and slept;
    I awaked ; for the LORD sustained me.
6 I will not be afraid of ten thousands of people,
    That have set themselves *against me round about.*
7 Arise, O LORD; save me, O my God:
    { *For thou hast smitten all mine enemies* upon *the cheek bone ;*
    { *Thou hast broken the teeth of the ungodly.*

8 Salvation *belongeth* unto the LORD:
    Thy blessing is *upon thy people.* (*Selah.*)

LESSON 2.
PSALM IV.
To the chief Musician on Neginoth, A Psalm of David.

HEAR me when I call, O God of my righteousness:
    { *Thou hast enlarged me* when I was *in distress;*
    { *Have mercy upon me, and hear my prayer.*
2 O ye sons of men, how long *will ye turn* my glory into shame?
    How long *will ye love vanity,* and *seek after leasing?* (*Selah.*)
3 But know that the LORD hath set apart him that is godly for himself:
    The LORD will hear when I call unto him.
4 Stand in awe, and sin not:
    Commune with your own heart upon your bed, and be still. (*Selah*)
5 Offer the sacrifices of righteousness,
    And put your trust in the LORD.
6 *There be* many that say, Who will shew us *any* good?
    LORD, lift thou up the light of thy countenance upon us.
7 Thou hast put gladness in my heart,
    More than in the time that *their corn and their wine increased.*
8 I will both lay me down in peace, and sleep:
    For thou, LORD, only makest me dwell in safety.

PSALM V.
To the chief Musician upon Nehiloth, A Psalm of David.

GIVE ear to my words, O LORD;
    Consider my meditation.
2 Hearken unto the voice of my cry, my King, and my God:
    For unto thee will I pray.
3 My voice shalt thou hear in the morning, O LORD;
    In the morning will I direct my prayer *unto thee, and will look up.*
4 For thou *art* not a God that hath pleasure in wickedness:
    Neither shall evil dwell with thee.
5 The foolish shall not stand in thy sight:
    Thou hatest all workers of iniquity.
6 Thou shalt destroy them that speak leasing:
    The LORD will abhor the bloody and deceitful man.

7 But as for me, I will come *into* thy house in the multitude of thy mercy:
And *in thy fear will I worship toward thy holy temple.*
8 Lead me, O LORD, in thy righteousness because of mine enemies;
Make thy way straight before my face.
9 For *there is* no faithfulness in their mouth; their inward part *is* very wickedness.
Their throat is an open sepulchre; they flatter with their tongue.
10 Destroy thou them, O God; let them fall by their own counsels;
Cast them out in the multitude of their transgressions; for they have rebelled against thee.
11 But let all those that put their trust in thee rejoice: let them ever shout for joy,
Because thou defendest them: let them also that love thy name be joyful in thee.
12 For thou, LORD, wilt bless the righteous;
With favour wilt thou compass him as with a shield.

LESSON 3.

PSALM VI.

To the chief Musician on Neginoth upon Sheminith, A Psalm of David.

O LORD, rebuke me not in thine anger,
Neither chasten me in thy hot displeasure.
2 Have mercy upon me, O LORD; for I *am* weak:
O LORD, heal me; for my bones are vexed.
3 My soul is also sore vexed:
But thou, O LORD, how long?
4 Return, O LORD, deliver my soul:
Oh save me for thy mercies' sake.
5 For in death *there is* no remembrance of thee:
In the grave who shall give thee thanks?
6 { I am weary with my groaning;
All the night make I my bed to swim;
I water my couch with my tears.
7 Mine eye is consumed because of grief;
It waxeth old because of all mine enemies.
8 Depart from me, all ye workers of iniquity;
For the LORD hath heard the voice of my weeping.

9 The LORD hath heard my supplication;
   The LORD will receive my prayer.
10 Let all mine enemies be ashamed and sore vexed:
   Let them return and be ashamed suddenly.

PSALM VII.

Shiggaion of David, which he sang unto Lord, concerning the words of Cush the Benjamite.

O LORD my God, in thee do I put my trust:
   Save me from all them that persecute me, and deliver me:
2 Lest he tear my soul like a lion,
   Rending it in pieces, while there is none to deliver.
3 O LORD, my God, if I have done this;
   If there be inquity in my hands;
4 If I have rewarded evil unto him that was at peace with me;
   (Yea, I have delivered him that without cause is mine enemy;)
5 { Let the enemy persecute my soul, and take *it*;
   { Yea, let him tread down my life upon the earth,
   And lay mine honour in the dust. (Selah.)
6 { Arise, O LORD, in thine anger,
   { Lift up thyself because of the rage of mine enemies:
   And awake for me to the judgment that thou hast commanded.
7 So shall the congregation of the people compass thee about:
   For their sakes therefore return thou on high.
8 The LORD shall judge the people:
   Judge me, O LORD, according to my righteousness, and according to mine integrity that is in me.
9 Oh let the wickedness of the wicked come to an end; but establish the just:
   For the righteous God trieth the hearts and reins.
10 My defence *is* of God,
   Which saveth the upright in heart.
11 God judgeth the righteous,
   And God is angry with the wicked every day.
12 If he turn not, he will whet his sword;
   He hath bent his bow, and made it ready.
13 He hath also prepared for him the instruments of death;
   He ordaineth his arrows against the persecutors.
14 Behold, he travaileth with iniquity,
   And hath conceived mischief, and brought forth falsehood.

15 He made a pit, and digged it,
   And is fallen into the ditch which *he made.*
16 His mischief shall return upon his own head,
   And his violent dealing shall come down upon his own pate.
17 I will praise the LORD according to his righteousness :
   And will sing praise to the name of the LORD *most high.*

LESSON 4.

PSALM VIII.

To the chief Musician upon Gittith, A Psalm of David.

1 O LORD our Lord,
   How excellent *is* thy name in all the earth !
   Who hast set thy glory above the heavens.
2 Out of the mouth of babes and sucklings hast thou ordained strength
   Because of thine enemies,
   That thou mightest still the enemy and the avenger.
3 When I consider thy heavens, the work of thy fingers,
   The moon and the stars, which thou hast ordained ;
4 What is man, that thou art mindful of him ?
   And the son of man, that thou visiteth him ?
5 For thou hast made him a little lower than the angels,
   And hast crowned him with glory and honour.
6 Thou madest him to have dominion over the work of thy hands ;
   Thou hast put all things under his feet :
7 All sheep and oxen,
   Yea, and the beasts of the field ;
8 The fowl of the air, and the fish of the sea,
   And whatsoever passeth through the paths of the seas.
9 O LORD our Lord,
   How excellent is *thy name in* all *the earth !*

PSALM IX.

To the chief Musician upon Muth-labben, A Psalm of David.

1 I WILL praise *thee*, O LORD, with my whole heart ;
   I will shew forth all thy marvellous works.
2 I will be glad and rejoice in thee :
   I will sing praise to thy name, O thou Most High.

LESSON 4.

3 When mine enemies are turned back,
 They shall fall and perish at thy presence.
4 For thou hast maintained my right and my cause ;
 Thou satest in the throne judging right.
5 Thou hast rebuked the heathen, thou hast destroyed the wicked,
 Thou hast put out their name for ever and ever.
6 O thou enemy, destructions are come to a perpetual end :
 And thou hast destroyed cities; their memorial is perished with them.
7 But the LORD shall endure for ever :
 He hath prepared his throne for judgment.
8 And he shall judge the world in righteousness,
 He shall minister judgment to the people in uprightness.
9 The LORD also will be a refuge for the oppressed,
 A refuge in times of trouble.
10 And they that know thy name will put their trust in thee :
 For thou, LORD, hast not forsaken them that seek thee.
11 Sing praises to the LORD, which dwelleth in Zion :
 Declare among the people his doings.
12 When he maketh inquisition for blood, he remembereth them :
 He forgetteth not the cry of the humble.
13 Have mercy upon me, O LORD; consider my trouble *which I suffer* of them that hate me,
 Thou that liftest me up from the gates of death :   [Zion :
14 That I may shew forth all thy praise in the gates of the daughter of
 I will rejoice in thy salvation.
15 The heathen are sunk down in the pit *that* they made :
 In the net which they hid is their own foot taken.
16 The LORD is known *by* the judgment *which* he executeth :
 The wicked is snared in the work of his own hands.   (*Higgaion*.
17 The wicked shall be turned into hell,   *Selah*.)
 And all the nations that forget God.
17 For the needy shall not always be forgotten :
 The expectation of the poor shall not perish for ever.
19 Arise, O LORD ; let not man prevail :
 Let the heathen be judged in thy sight.
20 Put them in fear, O LORD :
 That *the nations may know themselves* to be but *men*. (*Selah.*)

LESSON 5.

Psalm x.

WHY standest thou afar off, O Lord?
  Why *hidest thou* thyself *in times of trouble?*
2 The wicked in *his* pride doth persecute the poor:
  Let them be taken in the devices that they have imagined.
3 For the wicked boasteth of his heart's desire,
  And blesseth the covetous, whom *the LORD abhorreth.*   [*God:*
4 The wicked, through the pride of his countenance, will not seek *after*
  God is not in all his thoughts.
5 ⸠ His ways are always grievous;
  ⸠ Thy judgments *are* far above out of his sight.
  As for *all his enemies, he puffeth at them.*
6 He hath said in his heart, I shall not be moved:
  For I shall *never* be *in adversity.*
7 His mouth is full of cursing and deceit and fraud:
  Under his tongue is *mischief and vanity.*
8 ⸠ He sitteth in the lurking places of the villages:
  ⸠ In the secret places doth he murder the innocent:
  His eyes are privily set against the poor.
9 ⸠ He lieth in wait secretly as a lion in his den:
  ⸠ He lieth in wait to catch the poor:
  He doth catch the poor, when he draweth him into his net.
10 He croucheth, *and* humbleth himself,
  That the poor may fall by his strong ones.
11 He hath said in his heart, God hath forgotten:
  He hideth his face; he will never see it.
12 Arise, O Lord; O God, lift up thine hand:
  Forget not the humble.
13 Wherefore doth the wicked contemn God?
  He hath said in his heart, Thou wilt not require it.
14 ⸠ Thou hast seen *it;* for thou beholdest mischief and spite, to requite
  ⸠ The poor committeth himself unto thee;   [*it* with thy hand:
  Thou art the helper of the fatherless.
15 Break thou the arm of the wicked,
  And the evil man:—*seek out his wickedness* till *thou find none.*
16 The Lord *is* King for ever and ever:
  The heathen are perished out of his land.

17 LORD, thou hast heard the desire of the humble:
Thou wilt prepare their heart, thou wilt cause thine ear to hear:
18 To judge the fatherless and the oppressed,
That the man of the earth may no more oppress.

PSALM XI.

To the chief Musician, *A Psalm* of David.

IN the LORD put I my trust:
{ *How say ye to my soul,*
{ *Flee as a bird to your mountain?*
2 { For, lo, the wicked bend *their* bow,
{ They make ready their arrow upon the string,
That they may privily shoot at the upright in heart.
3 If the foundations be destroyed,
What can the righteous do?
4 The LORD *is* in his holy temple,
The LORD'S throne is in heaven:
His eyes behold,
His eyelids try, the children of men.
5 The LORD trieth the righteous:
But the wicked and him that loveth violence his soul hateth.
6 Upon the wicked he shall rain snares,
Fire and brimstone, and a horrible tempest: this shall be *the portion of their cup.*
7 For the righteous LORD loveth righteousness;
His countenance doth behold the upright.

LESSON 6.

PSALM XII.

To the chief Musician upon Sheminith, A Psalm of David.

HELP, LORD; for the godly man ceaseth;
For the faithful fail from among the children of men.
2 They speak vanity every one with his neighbour:
With flattering lips and with a double heart do they speak.
3 The LORD shall cut off all flattering lips,
And the tongue that speaketh proud things:
4 Who have said, With our tongue will we prevail;
Our lips are our own: who is lord over us?

5 { For the oppression of the poor, for the sighing of the needy,
 { Now will I arise, saith the Lord;
   I will set him *in safety* from him that *puffeth at him.*
6 The words of the Lord *are* pure words:
 { As *silver tried in a furnace of earth,*
 { *Purified seven times.*
7 Thou shalt keep them, O Lord,
   Thou shalt preserve them from this generation for ever.
8 The wicked walk on every side,
   When the vilest men are exalted.

Psalm XIII.
To the chief Musician, A Psalm of David.

HOW long wilt thou forget me, O Lord? for ever?
   How long wilt thou hide thy face from me?
2 { How long shall I take counsel in my soul,
  { *Having* sorrow in my heart daily?
   How long shall mine enemy be exalted over me?
3 Consider *and* hear me, O Lord my God:
   Lighten mine eyes, lest I sleep the sleep of death;
4 Lest mine enemy say, I have prevailed against him;
   And *those that trouble me rejoice when I am moved.*
5 { But I have trusted in thy mercy;
  { My heart shall rejoice in thy salvation. [*me.*
6   *I will sing unto the LORD, because he hath dealt bountifully with*

Psalm XIV.
To the chief Musician, A Psalm of David.

THE fool hath said in his heart, *There is* no God.
 { *They are corrupt, they have done abominable works,*
 { *There is none that doeth good.*
2 The Lord looked down from heaven upon the children of men,
 { *To see if there were any that did understand,*
 { *And seek God.*
3 { They are all gone aside, they are *all* together become filthy:
  { *There is* none that doeth good,
      No, not one.

LESSON 7.

4 { Have all the workers of iniquity no knowledge?
{ Who eat up my people *as* they eat bread,
 And *call not upon the* LORD.
5 There were they in great fear:
 For God is *in the generation of the righteous;*
6 Ye have shamed the counsel of the poor,
 Because the LORD *is his refuge.*
7 { Oh that the salvation of Israel *were come* out of Zion!
{ When the LORD bringeth back the captivity of his people,
 Jacob shall rejoice, and *Israel shall be glad.*

PSALM XV.
A Psalm of David.

LORD, who shall abide in thy tabernacle?
 Who shall dwell in thy holy hill?
2 He that walketh uprightly, and worketh righteousness,
 And *speaketh the truth in his heart.*
3 { *He that* backbiteth not with his tongue,
{ Nor doeth evil to his neighbour,
 Nor taketh up a reproach against his neighbour.
4 { In whose eyes a vile person is contemned;
{ But he honoureth them that fear the LORD.
 He that *sweareth to* his own *hurt, and changeth not.*
5 { *He that* putteth not out his money to usury,
{ Nor taketh reward against the innocent.
 He that doeth these things *shall never be moved.*

LESSON 7.

PSALM XVI.
Michtam of David.

PRESERVE me, O God:
 For in thee do I put my trust.
2 *O my soul,* thou hast said unto the LORD, Thou *art* my Lord:
 My goodness extendeth *not to thee;*
3 *But* to the saints that *are* in the earth,
 And to the *excellent, in whom* is *all my delight.*
4 { Their sorrows shall be multiplied *that* hasten *after* another *god:*
{ Their drink offerings of blood will I not offer,
 Nor take up their names into my lips.

5 The Lord *is* the portion of mine inheritance and of my cup:
   Thou maintainest my lot.
6 The lines are fallen unto me in pleasant *places ;*
   Yea, I have a goodly heritage.
7 I will bless the Lord, who hath given me counsel:
   My reins also instruct me in the night seasons.
8 I have set the Lord always before me:
   Because he is at my right hand, I shall not be moved.
9 Therefore my heart is glad, and my glory rejoiceth:
   My flesh also shall rest in hope.
10 For thou wilt not leave my soul in hell;
   Neither wilt thou suffer thine Holy One to see corruption.
11 ⎰ Thou wilt show me the path of life:
   ⎱ In thy presence *is* fulness of joy;
   At thy right hand there are *pleasures for evermore.*

Psalm XVII.
A Prayer of David.

HEAR the right, O Lord, attend unto my cry;
   Give ear unto my prayer, that goeth *not out of feigned lips.*
2 Let my sentence come forth from thy presence;
   Let thine eyes behold the things that are equal.
3 ⎰ Thou hast proved mine heart; thou hast visited *me* in the night;
   ⎱ Thou hast tried me, *and* shalt find nothing:
   I am purposed that my mouth shall not transgress.
4 Concerning the works of men, [*stroyer.*
   By the word of thy lips I have kept me from *the paths of the de-*
5 Hold up my goings in thy paths,
   That *my footsteps slip not.*
6 I have called upon thee, for thou wilt hear me, O God:
   Incline thine ear unto me, and *hear my speech.*
7 Shew thy marvellous loving kindness, O thou that savest by thy right
      hand them which put their trust *in thee,*
   From those that rise up against them.
8 Keep me as the apple of the eye;
   Hide me under the shadow of thy wings,
9 From the wicked that oppress me,
   From *my deadly enemies,* who *compass me about.*

10 They are inclosed in own their fat :
   With their mouth they speak proudly.
11 They have now compassed us in our steps :
   They have set their eyes bowing down to the earth ;
12 Like as a lion *that* is greedy of his prey,
   And as it were a young lion lurking in secret places.
13 Arise, O LORD, disappoint him, cast him down :
   Deliver my soul from the wicked, which is *thy sword :*
14 { From men *which are* thy hand, O LORD, from men of the world,
   Which have their portion in *this* life, and whose belly thou fillest with thy hid *treasure :*
   They are full of children, and leave the rest of their substance *to their babes.*
15 As for me, I will behold thy face in righteousness :
   I shall be satisfied, when I awake, with thy likeness.

LESSON 8.

PSALM XVIII, FIRST PART.

To the chief Musician, *A Psalm* of David, the servant of the LORD, who spake unto the LORD the words of this song in the day *that* the LORD delivered him from the hand of all his enemies, and from the hand of Saul : And he said,

I WILL love thee, O LORD, my strength.
   2 *The LORD* is *my rock, and my fortress, and my deliverer ;*
   My God, my strength, in whom I will trust ;
   My buckler, and the horn of my salvation, and *my high tower.*
3 I will call upon the LORD, *who is worthy* to be praised :
   So shall I be saved from mine enemies.
4 The sorrows of death compassed me,
   And the floods of ungodly men made me afraid.
5 The sorrows of hell compassed me about :
   The snares of death prevented me.
6 In my distress I called upon the LORD,
   And cried unto my God :
   He heard my voice out of his temple,
   And my cry came before him, even *into his ears.*
7 Then the earth shook and trembled ;
   { *The foundations also of the hills moved*
   And were shaken, because he was wroth.

THE PSALTER.

8 { There went up a smoke out of his nostrils,
   And fire out of his mouth devoured:
      Coals were kindled *by it.*
9 He bowed the heavens also, and came down:
      And darkness was *under his feet.*
10 And he rode upon a cherub, and did fly:
      Yea, *he did fly upon the wings of the wind.*
11 He made darkness his secret place;
      His pavilion round about him were *dark waters* and *thick clouds of the skies.*
12 At the brightness *that was* before him his thick clouds passed,
      Hail stones *and coals of fire.*
13 { The LORD also thundered in the heavens,
    And the Highest gave his voice;
      Hail stones *and coals of fire.*
14 Yea, he sent out his arrows, and scattered them;
      And he shot out lightnings, *and discomfited them.*
15 Then the channels of waters were seen,
      And the foundations of the world were discovered,
   At thy rebuke, O LORD,
      At *the blast of the breath of thy nostrils.*
16 He sent from above, he took me,
      He drew me out of *many waters.*
17 He delivered me from my strong enemy,
      And from them which hated me: *for they were too strong for me.*
18 They prevented me in the day of my calamity:
      But the LORD was my *stay.*
19 He brought me forth also into a large place;
      He delivered me, *because he delighted in me.*
20 The LORD rewarded me according to my righteousness;
      According to the cleanness of my hands hath he *recompensed me.*
21 For I have kept the ways of the LORD,
      And have not wickedly *departed from my God.*
22 For all his judgments *were* before me,
      And I did not put away his *statutes from me.*
23 I was also upright before him,
      And I kept myself from mine iniquity.   [ness,
24 Therefore hath the LORD recompensed me according to my righteous-
      According to the cleanness of my hands *in his eyesight.*

LESSON 9.

Psalm XVIII, Second Part.

WITH the merciful thou wilt shew thyself merciful;
With an upright man thou wilt shew thyself upright;
26 With the pure thou wilt shew thyself pure;
And with the froward thou wilt shew thyself froward.
27 For thou wilt save the afflicted people;
But wilt bring down high looks.
28 For thou wilt light my candle:
The LORD my God will enlighten my darkness.
29 For by thee I have run through a troop;
And by my God have I leaped over a wall.
30 { *As for* God, his way *is* perfect:
{ The word of the Lord is tried:
He is a buckler to all those that trust in him.
31 For who *is* God save the Lord?
Or who is a rock save our God?
32 *It is* God that girdeth me with strength,
And maketh my way perfect.
33 He maketh my feet like hind's *feet,*
And setteth me upon my high places.
34 He teacheth my hands to war,
So that a bow of steel is broken by mine arms.
35 { Thou hast also given me the shield of thy salvation:
{ And thy right hand hath holden me up,
And thy gentleness hath made me great.
36 Thou hast enlarged my steps under me,
That my feet did not slip.
37 I have pursued mine enemies, and overtaken them:
Neither did I turn again till they were consumed.
38 I have wounded them that they were not able to rise:
They are fallen under my feet.
39 For thou hast girded me with strength unto the battle:
Thou hast subdued under me those that rose up against me.
40 Thou hast also given me the necks of mine enemies;
That I might destroy them that hate me.

41 They cried, but *there was* none to save *them:*
  Even *unto the* LORD, *but he answered them not.*
42 Then did I beat them small as the dust before the wind:
  I did cast them out as the dirt in the streets.
43 { Thou hast delivered me from the strivings of the people;
  { *And* thou hast made me the head of the heathen:
  A people whom *I have not known shall serve me.*
44 As soon as they hear of me, they shall obey me:
  The strangers shall submit themselves unto me.
45 The strangers shall fade away,
  And be afraid out of their close places.
46 The LORD liveth; and blessed *be* my rock;
  And let the God of my salvation be exalted.
47 *It is* God that avengeth me,
  And subdueth the people under me.
48 { He delivereth me from mine enemies:
  { Yea, thou liftest me up above those that rise up against me:
  Thou hast delivered me from the violent man.
49 Therefore will I give thanks unto thee, O LORD, among the heathen,
  And sing praises unto thy name.
50 Great deliverance giveth he to his king;
  { *And sheweth mercy to his anointed,*
  { *To David, and to his seed for evermore.*

LESSON 10.

PSALM XIX.

To the chief Musician, a Psalm of David.

THE heavens declare the glory of God;
  And the firmament sheweth his handywork.
2 Day unto day uttereth speech,
  And night unto night sheweth knowledge.
3 *There is* no speech nor language,
  Where *their voice is not heard.*
4 { Their line is gone out through all the earth,
  { And their words to the end of the world.
  In them hath he set a tabernacle for the sun,
5 Which *is* as a bridegroom coming out of his chamber,
  And *rejoiceth as a strong man to run a race.*

LESSON 11.

6 { His going forth *is* from the end of the heaven,
  And his circuit unto the ends of it :
  And there is nothing hid from the heat thereof.
7 The law of the LORD *is* perfect, converting the soul :
  The testimony of the LORD is sure, making wise the simple.
8 The statutes of the LORD *are* right, rejoicing the heart :
  The commandment of the LORD is pure, enlightening the eyes.
9 The fear of the LORD *is* clean, enduring for ever :
  The judgments of the LORD are true and righteous altogether.
10 More to be desired *are they* than gold, yea, than much fine gold :
  Sweeter also than honey and the honeycomb.
11 Moreover by them is thy servant warned : *and* in keeping of them
  there is great reward.
12 *Who can understand* his *errors? cleanse thou me from secret* faults.
13 Keep back thy servant also from presumptuous *sins;* let them not
  have dominion over me :
  Then shall I be upright, and I shall be innocent from the great transgression.
14 Let the words of my mouth, and the meditation of my heart, be
  acceptable in thy sight,
  O LORD, my strength, and my redeemer.

LESSON 11.

PSALM XX.

To the chief Musician, A Psalm of David.

THE LORD hear thee in the day of trouble ;
  The name of the God of Jacob defend thee ;
2 Send thee help from the sanctuary,
  And strengthen thee out of Zion ;
3 Remember all thy offerings,
  And accept thy burnt sacrifice ; (Selah.)
4 Grant thee according to thine own heart,
  And fulfil all thy counsel.
5 { We will rejoice in thy salvation,
  And in the name of our God we will set up *our* banners :
  The LORD fulfil all thy petitions.
6 { Now know I
  That the LORD saveth his anointed ;
  { *He will hear him from his holy heaven*
  { *With the saving strength of his right hand.*

7 Some *trust* in chariots, and some in horses :
    But we will remember the name of the LORD *our God.*
8 They are brought down and fallen :
    But we are risen, and stand upright.
9 Save, LORD :
    { *Let the king hear us*
      When we call.

PSALM XXI.
To the chief Musician, A Psalm of David.

THE king shall joy in thy strength, O LORD ;
    And in thy salvation how greatly shall he rejoice!
2 Thou hast given him his heart's desire,
    And hast not withholden the request of his lips. (*Selah.*)
3 For thou preventest him with the blessings of goodness :
    Thou settest a crown of pure gold on his head.
4 He asked life of thee, *and* thou gavest *it* him,
    Even *length of days for ever and ever.*
5 His glory *is* great in thy salvation :
    Honour and majesty hast thou laid upon him.
6 For thou hast made him most blessed for ever :
    Thou hast made him exceeding glad with thy countenance.
7 For the king trusteth in the LORD,
    And through the mercy of the Most High he shall not be moved.
8 Thine hand shall find out all thine enemies :
    Thy right hand shall find out those that hate thee.
9 Thou shalt make them as a fiery oven in the time of thine anger :
    The LORD shall swallow them up in his wrath, and the fire shall devour them.
10 Their fruit shalt thou destroy from the earth,
    And their seed from among the children of men.
11 For they intended evil against thee :
    They imagined a mischievous device, which *they are not able to perform.*
12 Therefore shalt thou make them turn their back,
    When *thou shalt make ready* thine arrows *upon thy strings against the face of them.*
13 Be thou exalted, Lord, in thine own strength :
    So *will we sing and praise thy power.*

LESSON 12.

PSALM XXII.

To the chief Musician upon Aijeleth Shahar, A Psalm of David.

MY God, my God, why hast thou forsaken me?
  Why art thou so *far from helping me*, and from *the words of my roaring?*
2 O my God, I cry in the daytime, but thou hearest not;
  And in the night season, and am not silent.
3 But thou *art* holy, *O thou* that inhabitest the praises of Israel.
4 Our fathers trusted in thee:
  They trusted, and thou didst deliver them.
5 They cried unto thee, and were delivered:
  They trusted in thee, and were not confounded.
6 But I *am* a worm, and no man;
  A reproach of men, and despised of the people.
7 All they that see me laugh me to scorn:
  They shoot out the lip, they shake the head, saying,
8 He trusted on the LORD *that* he would deliver him:
  Let him deliver him, seeing he delighted in him.
9 But thou *art* he that took me out of the womb:
  Thou didst make me hope when I was *upon my mother's breasts.*
10 I was cast upon thee from the womb:
  Thou art my God from my mother's belly.
11 Be not far from me; for trouble *is* near;
  For there is none to help.
12 Many bulls have compassed me:
  Strong bulls of Bashan have beset me round.
13 They gaped upon me *with* their mouths,
  As a ravening and a roaring lion.
14 I am poured out like water,
  And all my bones are out of joint:
    My heart is like wax;
    It is melted in the midst of my bowels.
15 My strength is dried up like a potsherd;
  And my tongue cleaveth to my jaws;
    And thou hast brought me into the dust of death.

16 { For dogs have compassed me :
   { The assembly of the wicked have inclosed me :
     They pierced my hands and my feet.
17 I may tell all my bones :
     They look and *stare upon me.*
18 They part my garments among them,
     And cast lots upon my vesture.
19 But be not thou far from me, O Lord :
     O my strength, haste thee to help me.
20 Deliver my soul from the sword ;
     My darling from the power of the dog.
21 Save me from the lion's mouth :
     For thou hast heard me from the horns of the unicorns.
22 I will declare thy name unto my brethren :
     In the midst of the congregation will I praise thee.
23 { Ye that fear the Lord, praise him ;
   { All ye the seed of Jacob, glorify him ;
     And fear him, all ye the seed of Israel.
24 { For he hath not despised nor abhorred the affliction of the afflicted ;
   { Neither hath he hid his face from him ;
     But when he cried unto him, he heard.
25 My praise *shall be* of thee in the great congregation :
     I will pay my vows before them that fear him.
26 { The meek shall eat and be satisfied :
   { They shall praise the Lord that seek him :
     Your heart shall live for ever.
27 All the ends of the world shall remember and turn unto the Lord :
     And all the kindreds of the nations shall worship before thee.
28 For the kingdom *is* the Lord's :
     And he is the governor among the nations.
27 All *they that be* fat upon earth shall eat and worship :
     All they that go down to the dust shall bow before him : and none can keep alive his own soul.
30 A seed shall serve him ; it shall be accounted to the Lord for a generation.
31   *They shall come, and shall declare his righteousness unto a people that shall be born, that he hath done* this.

LESSON 13.

PSALM XXIII.
A Psalm of David.

THE LORD *is* my shepherd;
   I shall not want.
2 He maketh me to lie down in green pastures:
   He leadeth me beside the still waters.
3 He restoreth my soul:
   { *He leadeth me in the paths of righteousness*
   { *For his name's sake.*
4 { Yea, though I walk through the valley of the shadow of death,
  { I will fear no evil: for thou *art* with me;
   Thy rod and thy staff they comfort me.
5 Thou preparest a table before me in the presence of mine enemies:
   { *Thou anointest my head with oil;*
   { *My cup runneth over.*
6 Surely goodness and mercy shall follow me all the days of my life:
   And I will dwell in the house of the LORD for ever.

PSALM XXIV.
A Psalm of David.

THE earth *is* the LORD's and the fulness thereof;
   The world, and they that dwell therein.
2 For he hath founded it upon the seas,
   And established it upon the floods.
3 Who shall ascend into the hill of the LORD?
   And who shall stand in his holy place?
4 He that hath clean hands, and a pure heart;
   { *Who hath not lifted up his soul unto vanity,*
   { *Nor sworn deceitfully.*
5 He shall receive the blessing from the LORD,
   And righteousness from the God of his salvation.
6 This *is* the generation of them that seek him,
   That seek thy face, O Jacob. (Selah.)
7 { Lift up your heads, O ye gates;
  { And be ye lifted up, ye everlasting doors;
   And the King of glory shall come in.

8 Who *is* this King of glory?
   { *The LORD strong and mighty,*
   { *The LORD mighty in battle.*
9 Lift up your heads, O ye gates; even lift *them* up, ye everlasting [doors;
   And the King of glory shall come in.
10 Who is this King of glory?
   { *The LORD of hosts,*
   { *He is the King of glory.* (*Selah.*)

LESSON 14.

PSALM XXV.

A Psalm of David.

{ UNTO thee, O LORD, do I lift up my soul.
  2 O my God, I trust in thee: let me not be ashamed,
   Let not mine enemies triumph over me.
3 Yea, let none that wait on thee be ashamed:
   Let them be ashamed which transgress without cause.
4 Show me thy ways, O LORD;
   Teach me thy paths.
5 { Lead me in thy truth, and teach me:
   { For thou *art* the God of my salvation;
   On thee do I wait all the day.
6 Remember, O LORD, thy tender mercies and thy loving kindnesses;
   For they have been ever of old.
7 Remember not the sins of my youth, nor my transgressions:
   { *According to thy mercy remember thou me*
   { *For thy goodness' sake, O LORD.*
8 Good and upright *is* the LORD:
   Therefore will he teach sinners in the way.
9 The meek will he guide in judgment:
   And the meek will he teach his way.
10 All the paths of the LORD *are* mercy and truth
   Unto such as keep his covenant and his testimonies.
11 For thy name's sake, O LORD, pardon mine iniquity;
   For it is great.
12 What man *is* he that feareth the LORD?
   Him shall he teach in the way that *he shall choose.*

13 His soul shall dwell at ease;
    And his seed shall inherit the earth.
14 The secret of the LORD *is* with them that fear him;
    And he will shew them his covenant.
15 Mine eyes *are* ever toward the LORD;
    For he shall pluck my feet out of the net.
16 Turn thee unto me, and have mercy upon me;
    For I am *desolate and afflicted.*
17 The troubles of my heart are enlarged:
    Oh *bring thou me out of my distresses.*
18 Look upon mine affliction and my pain;
    And forgive all my sins.
19 Consider mine enemies; for they are many;
    And they hate me with cruel hatred.
20 Oh keep my soul, and deliver me:
    Let me not be ashamed; for I put my trust in thee.
21 { Let integrity and uprightness preserve me;
   { For I wait on thee.
22   *Redeem Israel, O God, out of all his troubles.*

LESSON 15.

PSALM XXVI.

A Psalm of David.

JUDGE me O LORD; for I have walked in mine integrity:
    I have trusted also in the LORD; therefore I shall not slide.
2 Examine me, O LORD, and prove me;
    Try my reins and my heart.
3 For thy loving kindness *is* before mine eyes:
    And I have walked in thy truth.
4 I have not sat with vain persons,
    Neither will I go in with dissemblers.
5 I have hated the congregation of evil doers;
    And will not sit with the wicked.
6 I will wash mine hands in innocency:
    So will I compass thine altar, O Lord:
7 That I may publish with the voice of thanksgiving,
    And tell of all thy wondrous works.

8 Lord, I have loved the habitation of thy house,
    And the place where thine honour dwelleth.
9 Gather not my soul with sinners,
    Nor my life with bloody men :
10 In whose hands *is* mischief,
    And their right hand is full of bribes.
11 But as for me, I will walk in mine integrity :
    Redeem me, and be merciful unto me.
13 My foot standeth in an even place :
    In the congregations will I bless the LORD.

Psalm XXVII.
A Psalm of David.

THE Lord *is* my light and my salvation; whom shall I fear?
    The LORD is the strength of my life; of whom shall I be afraid?
2 When the wicked, *even* mine enemies and my foes, came upon me to [eat up my flesh,
    They stumbled and fell.
3 Though a host should encamp against me, my heart shall not fear :
    Though war should rise against me, in this will *I* be *confident.*
4 { One *thing* have I desired of the Lord, that will I seek after;
   { That I may dwell in the house of the Lord all the days of my life,
    To behold the beauty of the LORD, and to inquire in his temple.
5 { For in the time of trouble he shall hide me in his pavilion :
   { In the secret of his tabernacle shall he hide me ;
    He shall set me up upon a rock.
6 { And now shall mine head be lifted up above mine enemies round [about me :
   { Therefore will I offer in his tabernacle sacrifices of joy ;
    I will sing, yea, I will sing praises unto the LORD.
7 Hear, O Lord, *when* I cry with my voice :
    Have mercy also upon me, and answer me.
8 *When thou saidst,* Seek ye my face ;
    My heart said unto thee, Thy face, LORD, will I seek.
9 { Hide not thy face *far* from me ;
   { Put not thy servant away in anger :
    { *Thou hast been my help ;*
    { *Leave me not, neither forsake me, O God of my salvation.*
10 When my father and my mother forsake me,
    Then the LORD will take me up.

11 Teach me thy way, O LORD,
And lead me in a plain path, because of mine enemies.
12 Deliver me not over unto the will of mine enemies:
For false witnesses are risen up against me, and such as breathe out cruelty.
13 *I had fainted*, unless I had believed to see the goodness of the LORD in the land of the living.
14   *Wait on the LORD:*
Be of good courage, and he shall strengthen thine heart:
Wait, I say, on the LORD.

LESSON 16.

PSALM XXVIII.

A Psalm of David.

{ UNTO thee will I cry, O LORD my rock;
   Be not silent to me:
   Lest, if *thou be silent to me*, *I become like them that go down into the pit.*
2 Hear the voice of my supplications, when I cry unto thee,
   When I lift up my hands toward thy holy oracle.
3 { Draw me not away with the wicked,
   And with the workers of iniquity,
   { *Which speak peace to their neighbours,*
    But mischief is in their hearts.
4 Give them according to their deeds, and according to the wickedness of their endeavours:
   { *Give them after the work of their hands;*
    Render to them their desert.
5 { Because they regard not the works of the LORD,
   Nor the operation of his hands,
   He shall destroy them, and not build them up.
6 Blessed *be* the LORD, because he hath heard the voice of my supplications.
7   *The LORD is my strength and my shield;*
My heart trusted in him, and I am helped:
   Therefore my heart greatly rejoiceth; and with my song will I praise him.

8 The Lord *is* their strength,
 And he is *the saving strength of his anointed.*
9 { Save thy people,
 { And bless thine inheritance:
 Feed them also, and lift them up for ever.

Psalm XXIX.
A Psalm of David.

GIVE unto the Lord, O ye mighty,
 Give unto the LORD glory and strength.
2 Give unto the Lord the glory due unto his name;
 Worship the LORD in the beauty of holiness.
3 The voice of the Lord *is* upon the waters:
 { *The God of glory thundereth:*
 { *The LORD is upon many waters.*
4 The voice of the Lord *is* powerful;
 The voice of the LORD is *full of majesty.*
5 The voice of the Lord breaketh the cedars:
 Yea, the LORD breaketh the cedars of Lebanon.
6 He maketh them also to skip like a calf;
 Lebanon and Sirion like a young unicorn.
7 { The voice of the Lord divideth the flames of fire.
8 { The voice of the Lord shaketh the wilderness;
 The LORD shaketh the wilderness of Kadesh.
9 { The voice of the Lord maketh the hinds to calve,
 { And discovereth the forests:
 And in his temple doth every one speak of his *glory.*
10 The Lord sitteth upon the flood;
 Yea, the LORD sitteth King for ever.
11 The Lord will give strength unto his people;
 The LORD will bless his people with peace.

Psalm XXX.
A Psalm *and* Song *at* the dedication of the house of David.

I WILL extol thee, O Lord; for thou hast lifted me up,
 And hast not made my foes to rejoice over me.
2 { O Lord my God, I cried unto thee, and thou hast healed me.
3 { O Lord, thou hast brought up my soul from the grave:
 Thou hast kept me alive, that I should not go down to the pit.

4 Sing unto the LORD, O ye saints of his,
  And give thanks at the remembrance of his holiness.
5 For his anger endureth but a moment; in his favour is life:
  { Weeping may endure for a night,
  { But joy cometh in the morning.
6 And in my prosperity I said,
  I shall never be moved.
7 LORD, by thy favour thou hast made my mountain to stand strong:
  Thou didst hide thy face, and I was troubled.
8 I cried to thee, O LORD;
  And unto the LORD I made supplication.
9 What profit is there in my blood, when I go down to the pit?
  Shall the dust praise thee? shall it declare thy truth?
10 Hear, O LORD, and have mercy upon me:
  LORD, be thou my helper.
11 Thou hast turned for me my mourning into dancing:
  Thou hast put off my sackcloth, and girded me with gladness;
12 To the end that my glory may sing praise to thee, and not be silent.
  O LORD my God, I will give thanks unto thee for ever.

LESSON 17.

PSALM XXXI.

To the chief Musician, A Psalm of David.

IN thee, O LORD, do I put my trust;
  Let me never be ashamed:
  Deliver me in thy righteousness.
2   Bow down thine ear to me; deliver me speedily:
  Be thou my strong rock,
  For a house of defence to save me.
3 For thou art my rock and my fortress;
  Therefore for thy name's sake lead me, and guide me.
4 Pull me out of the net that they have laid privily for me:
  For thou art my strength.
5 Into thine hand I commit my spirit:
  Thou hast redeemed me, O LORD God of truth.
6 I have hated them that regard lying vanities:
  But I trust in the LORD.

7 { I will be glad and rejoice in thy mercy:
{ For thou hast considered my trouble;
Thou hast known my soul in adversities;
8 And hast not shut me up into the hand of the enemy:
Thou hast set my feet in a large room.
9 Have mercy upon me, O LORD, for I am in trouble:
Mine eye is consumed with grief, yea, my soul and my belly.
10 For my life is spent with grief,
And my years with sighing:
My strength faileth because of mine iniquity,
And my bones are consumed.
11 { I was a reproach among all mine enemies,
{ But especially among my neighbours, and a fear to mine acquaintance:
They that did see me without fled from me.
12 I am forgotten as a dead man out of mind:
I am like a broken vessel.
13 { For I have heard the slander of many:
{ Fear *was* on every side:
{ *While they took counsel together against me,*
{ *They devised to take away my life.*
14 But I trusted in thee, O LORD:
I said Thou art my God.
15 My times *are* in thy hand:
Deliver me from the hand of mine enemies, and from them that persecute me.
16 Make thy face to shine upon thy servant:
Save me for thy mercies' sake.
17 Let me not be ashamed, O LORD; for I have called upon thee:
Let the wicked be ashamed, and let them be silent in the grave.
18 Let the lying lips be put to silence;
Which speak grievous things proudly and contemptuously against the righteous.
19 Oh how great *is* thy goodness, which thou hast laid up for them that fear thee;
Which thou hast wrought for them that trust in thee before the sons of men!

LESSON 18.

20 Thou shalt hide them in the secret of thy presence from the pride of man:
 Thou shalt keep them secretly in a pavilion from the strife of tongues.
21 Blessed be the LORD:
 For he hath shewed me his marvellous kindness in a strong city.
22 { For I said in my haste,
 { I am cut off from before thine eyes:
 Nevertheless thou heardest the voice of my supplications when I cried unto thee.
23 O love the LORD, all ye his saints:
 { For the LORD preserveth the faithful,
 { And plentifully rewardeth the proud doer.
24 Be of good courage, and he shall strengthen your heart,
 All ye that hope in the LORD.

LESSON 18.
PSALM XXXII.
A Psalm of David, Maschil.

BLESSED is he whose transgression is forgiven, whose sin is covered.
2 { Blessed is the man unto whom the LORD imputeth not iniquity,
 { And in whose spirit there is no guile.
3 When I kept silence, my bones waxed old
 Through my roaring all the day long.
4 For day and night thy hand was heavy upon me:
 My moisture is turned into the drought of summer. (Selah.)
5 I acknowledged my sin unto thee, and mine iniquity have I not hid.
 { I said, I will confess my transgressions unto the LORD;
 { And thou forgavest the iniquity of my sin. (Selah.)
6 { For this shall every one that is godly pray unto thee
 { In a time when thou mayest be found:
 { Surely in the floods of great waters
 { They shall not come nigh unto him.
7 { Thou art my hiding place;
 { Thou shalt preserve me from trouble;
 Thou shalt compass me about with songs of deliverance. (Selah.)
8 I will instruct thee and teach thee in the way which thou shalt go:
 I will guide thee with mine eye.

9 Be ye not as the horse, *or* as the mule, *which* have no understanding:
    { *Whose mouth must be held in with bit and bridle,*
    { *Lest they come near unto thee.*
10 Many sorrows *shall be* to the wicked:
    But he that trusteth in the LORD, mercy shall compass him about.
11 Be glad in the LORD, and rejoice, ye righteous:
    And shout for joy, all ye that are upright in heart.

PSALM XXXIII.

REJOICE in the LORD, O ye righteous:
    For *praise is comely for the upright.*
2 Praise the LORD with harp:
    Sing unto him with the psaltery and *an instrument of ten strings.*
3 Sing unto him a new song;
    Play skilfully with a loud noise.
4 For the word of the LORD *is* right;
    And all his works are done in truth.
5 He loveth righteousness and judgment:
    The earth is full of the goodness of the LORD.
6 By the word of the LORD were the heavens made;
    And all the host of them by the breath of his mouth.
7 He gathereth the waters of the sea together as a heap:
    He layeth up the depth in storehouses.
8 Let all the earth fear the LORD:
    Let all the inhabitants of the world stand in awe of him.
9 For he spake, and it was *done;*
    He commanded, and it stood fast.
10 The LORD bringeth the counsel of the heathen to nought:
    He maketh the devices of the people of none effect.
11 The counsel of the LORD standeth for ever,
    The thoughts of his heart to all generations.
12 Blessed *is* the nation whose God *is* the LORD;
    And the people whom he hath chosen for his own inheritance.
13 The LORD looketh from heaven;
    He beholdeth all the sons of men.
14 From the place of his habitation he looketh
    Upon all the inhabitants of the earth.

15 He fashioneth their hearts alike;
   He considereth all their works.
16 There is no king saved by the multitude of a host:
   A mighty man is not delivered by much strength.
17 A horse *is* a vain thing for safety:
   Neither shall he deliver any *by his great strength.*
18 Behold, the eye of the Lord *is* upon them that fear him,
   Upon them that hope in his mercy;
19 To deliver their soul from death,
   And to keep them alive in famine.
20 Our soul waiteth for the Lord:
   He is *our help and our shield.*
21 For our heart shall rejoice in him,
   Because we have trusted in his holy name.
22 Let thy mercy, O Lord, be upon us,
   According as we hope in thee.

LESSON 19.

Psalm XXXIV.

A Psalm of David, when he changed his behaviour before Abimelech; who drove him away, and he departed.

I WILL bless the Lord at all times:
   His praise shall *continually* be *in my mouth.*
2 My soul shall make her boast in the Lord:
   The humble shall hear thereof, *and be glad.*
3 Oh magnify the Lord with me,
   And let us exalt his name together.
4 I sought the Lord, and he heard me,
   And delivered me from all my fears.
5 They looked unto him, and were lightened:
   And their faces were not ashamed.
6 This poor man cried, and the Lord heard *him,*
   And saved him out of all his troubles.
7 The angel of the Lord encampeth round about them that fear him,
   And delivereth them.
8 Oh taste and see that the Lord *is* good:
   Blessed is *the man* that *trusteth in him.*
9 Oh fear the Lord, ye his saints:
   For there is *no want to them that fear him.*

10 The young lions do lack, and suffer hunger:
   But they that seek the LORD shall not want any good thing.
11 Come, ye children, hearken unto me:
   I will teach you the fear of the LORD.
12 What man *is he that* desireth life,
   And *loveth many days, that he may see good?*
13 Keep thy tongue from evil,
   And thy lips from speaking guile.
14 Depart from evil, and do good;
   Seek peace, and pursue it.
15 The eyes of the LORD *are* upon the righteous,
   And his ears are open *unto their cry.*
16 The face of the LORD *is* against them that do evil,
   To cut off the remembrance of them from the earth.
17 *The righteous* cry, and the LORD heareth,
   And delivereth them out of all their troubles.
18 The LORD *is* nigh unto them that are of a broken heart;
   And saveth such as be of a contrite spirit.
19 Many *are* the afflictions of the righteous:
   But the LORD delivereth him out of them all.
20 He keepeth all his bones:
   Not one of them is broken.
21 Evil shall slay the wicked:
   And they that hate the righteous shall be desolate.
22 The LORD redeemeth the soul of his servants:
   And none of them that trust in him shall be desolate.

LESSON 20.

PSALM XXXV.

A Psalm of David.

PLEAD *my cause,* O LORD, with them that strive with me:
   Fight against them that fight against me.
2 Take hold of shield and buckler,
   And stand up for mine help.
3 Draw out also the spear, and stop *the way* against them that persecute me:
   Say unto my soul, I am *thy salvation.*

LESSON 20.

4 Let them be confounded and put to shame that seek after my soul:
Let them be turned back and brought to confusion that devise my hurt.
5 Let them be as chaff before the wind:
And let the angel of the LORD chase them.
6 Let their way be dark and slippery:
And let the angel of the LORD persecute them.
7 For without cause have they hid for me their net *in* a pit,
Which without cause they have digged for my soul.
8 { Let destruction come upon him at unawares;
{ And let his net that he hath hid catch himself:
Into that very destruction let him fall.
9 And my soul shall be joyful in the LORD:
It shall rejoice in his salvation.
10 All my bones shall say,
LORD, who is like unto thee,
Which deliverest the poor from him that is too strong for him,
Yea, the poor and the needy from him that spoileth him?
11 False witnesses did rise up;
They laid to my charge things that I knew not.
12 They rewarded me evil for good
To the spoiling of my soul.
13 But as for me, when they were sick, my clothing *was* sackcloth:
{ *I humbled my soul with fasting;*
{ *And my prayer returned into mine own bosom.*
14 I behaved myself as though *he had been* my friend *or* brother:
I bowed down heavily, as one that mourneth for his *mother.*
15 But in mine adversity they rejoiced, and gathered themselves together:
{ Yea, *the abjects gathered themselves together against me, and I knew it not;*
{ *They did tear* me, *and ceased not:*
16 With hypocritical mockers in feasts,
They gnashed upon me with their teeth.
17 Lord, how long wilt thou look on?
{ *Rescue my soul from their destructions,*
{ *My darling from the lions.*
18 I will give thee thanks in the great congregation:
I will praise thee among much people.

19 Let not them that are mine enemies wrongfully rejoice over me:
    Neither *let them wink with the eye that hate me without a cause.*
20 For they speak not peace:
    But they devise deceitful matters against them that are *quiet in the land.*
21 Yea, they opened their mouth wide against me,
    And *said, Aha, aha, our eye hath seen it.*
22 *This* thou hast seen, O Lord: keep not silence:
    O Lord, be not far from me.
23 Stir up thyself, and awake to my judgment,
    Even *unto my cause, my God and my Lord.*
24 Judge me, O Lord my God, according to thy righteousness;
    And let them not rejoice over me.
25 Let them not say in their hearts, Ah, so would we have it:
    Let them not say, We have swallowed him up.
26 { Let them be ashamed and brought to confusion together
   { That rejoice at mine hurt:
    { *Let them be clothed with shame and dishonour*
    { *That magnify themselves against me.*
27 Let them shout for joy, and be glad, that favour my righteous cause:
    { *Yea, let them say continually, Let the LORD be magnified,*
    { *Which hath pleasure in the prosperity of his servant.*
28 And my tongue shall speak of thy righteousness
    And *of thy praise all the day long.*

LESSON 21.

PSALM XXXVI.

To the chief Musician, A Psalm of David the servant of the Lord.

THE transgression of the wicked saith within my heart,
    That there is *no fear of God before his eyes.*
2 For he flattereth himself in his own eyes,
    Until his iniquity be found to be hateful.
3 The words of his mouth *are* iniquity and deceit:
    He hath left off to be wise, and to do good.
4 He deviseth mischief upon his bed;
    { *He setteth himself in a way* that is *not good;*
    { *He abhorreth not evil.*

5 Thy mercy, O Lord, *is* in the heavens;
 And thy faithfulness reacheth unto the clouds.
6 {Thy righteousness is like the great mountains:
 {Thy judgments *are* a great deep:
 O LORD, thou preservest man and beast.
7 How excellent *is* thy loving kindness, O God!
 Therefore the children of men put their trust under the shadow of thy wings.
8 They shall be abundantly satisfied with the fatness of thy house;
 And thou shalt make them drink of the river of thy pleasures.
9 For with thee *is* the fountain of life:
 In thy light shall we see light.
10 Oh continue thy loving kindness unto them that know thee;
 And thy righteousness to the upright in heart.
11 Let not the foot of pride come against me,
 And let not the hand of the wicked remove me.
12 There are the workers of iniquity fallen:
 They are cast down, and shall not be able to rise.

LESSON 22.

Psalm XXXVII, First Part.

A Psalm of David.

FRET not thyself because of evil doers,
 Neither be thou envious against the workers of iniquity.
2 For they shall soon be cut down like the grass,
 And wither as the green herb.
3 Trust in the Lord, and do good;
 So shalt thou dwell in the land, and verily thou shalt be fed.
4 Delight thyself also in the Lord;
 And he shall give the thee desires of thine heart.
5 Commit thy way unto the Lord;
 Trust also in him; and he shall bring it to pass.
6 And he shall bring forth thy righteousness as the light,
 And thy judgment as the noonday.
7 Rest in the Lord, and wait patiently for him:
 { *Fret not thyself because of him who prospereth in his way,*
 { *Because of the man who bringeth wicked devices to pass.*

8 Cease from anger, and forsake wrath:
Fret not thyself in any wise to do evil.
9 For evil doers shall be cut off:
But those that wait upon the LORD, they shall inherit the earth.
10 For yet a little while, and the wicked *shall* not *be:*
Yea, thou shalt diligently consider his place, and it shall *not* be.
11 But the meek shall inherit the earth;
And shall delight themselves in the abundance of peace.
12 The wicked plotteth against the just,
And gnasheth upon him with his teeth.
13 The LORD shall laugh at him:
For he seeth that his day is coming.
14 The wicked have drawn out the sword, and have bent their bow,
{ *To cast down the poor and needy,*
{ *And to slay such as be of upright conversation.*
15 Their sword shall enter into their own heart,
And their bows shall be broken.
16 A little that a righteous man hath *is* better
Than the riches of many wicked.
17 For the arms of the wicked shall be broken:
But the LORD upholdeth the righteous.
18 The LORD knoweth the days of the upright:
And their inheritance shall be forever.
19 They shall not be ashamed in the evil time:
And in the days of famine they shall be satisfied.
20 { But the wicked shall perish,
  { And the enemies of the LORD *shall be* as the fat of lambs:
They shall consume; into smoke shall they consume away.

LESSON 23.

PSALM XXXVII, SECOND PART.

THE wicked borroweth, and payeth not again:
But the righteous sheweth mercy, and giveth.
22 For *such as be* blessed of him shall inherit the earth;
And they that be cursed of him shall be cut off.
23 The steps of a *good* man are ordered by the LORD:
And he delighteth in his way.

24 Though he fall, he shall not be utterly cast down :
   For the LORD upholdeth him with his hand.
25 I have been young, and *now* am old ;
   { *Yet have I not seen the righteous forsaken,*
   { *Nor his seed begging bread.*
26 *He is* ever merciful, and lendeth ;
   And his seed is blessed.
27 Depart from evil, and do good ;
   And dwell for evermore.
28 For the LORD loveth judgment,
   And forsaketh not his saints ;
   They are preserved for ever :
   But the seed of the wicked shall be cut off.
29 The righteous shall inherit the land,
   And dwell therein for ever.
30 The mouth of the righteous speaketh wisdom,
   And his tongue talketh of judgment.
31 The law of his God *is* in his heart ;
   None of his steps shall slide.
32 The wicked watcheth the righteous,
   And seeketh to slay him.
33 The LORD will not leave him in his hand,
   Nor condemn him when he is judged.
34 { Wait on the LORD and keep his way,
   { And he shall exalt thee to inherit the land :
   When the wicked are cut off, thou shalt see it.
35 I have seen the wicked in great power,
   And spreading himself like a green bay tree.
36 Yet he passed away, and, lo, he *was* not :
   Yea, I sought him, but he could not be found.
37 Mark the perfect *man,* and behold the upright :
   For the end of that *man* is *peace.*
38 But the transgressors shall be destroyed together :
   The end of the wicked shall be cut off.
39 But the salvation of the righteous *is* of the LORD :
   He is *their strength in the time of trouble.*
40 And the LORD shall help them, and deliver them :
   { *He shall deliver them from the wicked,*
   { *And save them, because they trust in him.*

LESSON 24.

PSALM XXXVIII.

A Psalm of David, to bring to remembrance.

O LORD, rebuke me not in thy wrath:
 Neither chasten me in thy hot displeasure.
2 For thine arrows stick fast in me,
 And thy hand presseth me sore.
3 *There is* no soundness in my flesh because of thine anger;
 Neither is there any *rest in my bones because of my sin.*
4 For mine iniquities are gone over mine head:
 As a heavy burden they are too heavy for me.
5 My wounds stink *and* are corrupt
 Because of my foolishness.
6 I am troubled; I am bowed down greatly;
 I go mourning all the day long.
7 For my loins are filled with a loathsome *disease:*
 And there is *no soundness in my flesh.*
8 I am feeble and sore broken:
 I have roared by reason of the disquietness of my heart.
9 Lord, all my desire *is* before thee;
 And my groaning is not hid from thee.
10 My heart panteth, my strength faileth me:
 As for the light of mine eyes, it also is gone from me.
11 My lovers and my friends stand aloof from my sore;
 And my kinsmen stand afar off.
12 They also that seek after my life lay snares *for me;*
 { *And they that seek my hurt speak mischievous things,*
 { *And imagine deceits all the day long.*
13 But I, as a deaf *man,* heard not;
 And I was as a dumb man that openeth not his mouth.
14 Thus I was as a man that heareth not,
 And in whose mouth are no reproofs.
15 For in thee, O LORD, do I hope:
 Thou wilt hear, O Lord my God.
16 For I said, *Hear me,* lest *otherwise* they should rejoice over me:
 When my foot slippeth, they magnify themselves against me.
17 For I *am* ready to halt,
 And my sorrow is continually before me.

18 For I will declare mine iniquity;
 I will be sorry for my sin.
19 But mine enemies *are* lively, *and* they are strong :
 And they that hate me wrongfully are multiplied.
20 They also that render evil for good
 Are mine adversaries; because I follow the thing that *good* is.
21 Forsake me not, O LORD :
 O my God, be not far from me.
22 Make haste to help me,
 O Lord my salvation.

LESSON 26.

PSALM XXXIX.

To the chief Musician, *even* to Jeduthun, A Psalm of David.

{ I SAID, I will take heed to my ways,
 That I sin not with my tongue :
 { *I will keep my mouth with a bridle,*
 While the wicked is before me.
 { I was dumb with silence,
 I held my peace, *even* from good;
 And my sorrow was stirred.
3 { My heart was hot within me ;
 While I was musing the fire burned :
 Then *spake I with my tongue,*
4 { LORD, make me to know mine end,
 And the measure of my days what it *is;*
 That *I may know how frail I* am.
5 { Behold, thou hast made my days *as* a handbreadth ;
 And mine age *is* as nothing before thee :
 Verily every man at his best state is *altogether vanity.* (*Selah.*)
6 { Surely every man walketh in a vain shew :
 Surely they are disquieted in vain :
 He heapeth up riches, and knoweth not who shall gather them.
7 And now, Lord, what wait I for ?
 My hope is in thee.
8 Deliver me from all my transgressions :
 Make me not the reproach of the foolish.

9 I was dumb, I opened not my mouth;
   Because thou didst it.
10 Remove thy stroke away from me:
   I am consumed by the blow of thine hand.
11 { When thou with rebukes dost correct man for iniquity,
   { Thou makest his beauty to consume away like a moth:
   Surely every man is *vanity.* (*Selah.*)
12 Hear my prayer, O LORD,
   And give ear unto my cry;
  Hold not thy peace at my tears:
   { *For I* am *a stranger with thee,*
   { *And a sojourner, as all my fathers* were.
13 Oh spare me, that I may recover strength,
   Before I go hence, and be no more.

LESSON 26.

PSALM XL.

To the chief Musician, A Psalm of David.

I WAITED patiently for the LORD;
   And he inclined unto me, and heard my cry.
2 He brought me up also out of a horrible pit, out of the miry clay,
   And set my feet upon a rock, and *established my goings.*
3 And he hath put a new song in my mouth, *even* praise unto our God:
   Many shall see it, *and fear, and shall trust in the LORD.*
4 Blessed *is* that man that maketh the LORD his trust,
   And respecteth not the proud, nor such as turn aside to lies.
5 Many, O LORD my God, *are* thy wonderful works *which* thou hast done, and thy thoughts *which are* to us-ward:
   They cannot be reckoned up in order unto thee:
  If I would declare and speak *of them,*
   They are more than can be numbered.
6 { Sacrifice and offering thou didst not desire;
   { Mine ears hast thou opened:
   Burnt offering and sin offering hast thou not required.
7 Then said I, Lo, I come:
   In the volume of the book it is *written of me,*

8 I delight to do thy will, O my God:
   Yea, thy law is within my heart.
9 I have preached righteousness in the great congregation:
   { *Lo, I have not refrained my lips,*
   { *O LORD, thou knowest.*
10 { I have not hid thy righteousness within my heart;
   { I have declared thy faithfulness and thy salvation:
   I have not concealed thy lovingkindness and thy truth from the great congregation.
11 Withhold not thou thy tender mercies from me, O LORD:
   Let thy lovingkindness and thy truth continually preserve me.
12 For innumerable evils have compassed me about:
   Mine iniquities have taken hold upon me, so that I am not able to look up;
They are more than the hairs of mine head:
   Therefore my heart faileth me.
13 Be pleased, O LORD, to deliver me:
   O LORD, make haste to help me.
14 Let them be ashamed and confounded together that seek after my soul to destroy it;
   Let them be driven backward and put to shame that wish me evil.
15 Let them be desolate for a reward of their shame
   That say unto me, Aha, aha.
16 Let all those that seek thee rejoice and be glad in thee:
   Let such as love thy salvation say continually, The LORD be magnified.
17 { But I *am* poor and needy;
   { *Yet* the Lord thinketh upon me:
   { *Thou* art *my help and my deliverer;*
   { *Make no tarrying, O my God.*

PSALM XLI.

To the chief Musician, A Psalm of David.

BLESSED *is* he that considereth the poor:
   The LORD will deliver him in time of trouble.
2 { The LORD will preserve him, and keep him alive;
   { *And* he shall be blessed upon the earth:
   And thou wilt not deliver him unto the will of his enemies.

3 The LORD will strengthen him upon the bed of languishing:
Thou wilt make all his bed in his sickness.
4 I said, LORD, be merciful unto me :
Heal my soul; for I have sinned against thee.
5 Mine enemies speak evil of me,
When shall he die, and his name perish?
6 And if he come to see *me*, he speaketh vanity :
{ *His heart gathereth iniquity to itself;*
{ *When he goeth abroad, he telleth* it.
7 All that hate me whisper together against me :
Against me do they devise my hurt.
8 An evil disease, *say they*, cleaveth fast unto him :
And now that he lieth he shall rise up no more.
9 Yea, mine own familiar friend, in whom I trusted,
Which did eat of my bread, hath lifted up his *heel against me.*
10 But thou, O LORD, be merciful unto me, and raise me up,
That I may requite them.
11 By this I know that thou favourest me,
Because mine enemy doth not triumph over me.
12 And as for me, thou upholdest me in mine integrity,
And settest me before thy face for ever.
13 Blessed *be* the LORD God of Israel from everlasting, and to everlasting.
Amen and Amen.

LESSON 27.

PSALM XLII.

To the chief Musician, Maschil, for the sons of Korah.

AS the heart panteth after the water brooks,
So panteth my soul after thee, O God.
2 My soul thirsteth for God, for the living God :
When shall I come and appear before God?
3 My tears have been my meat day and night,
While they continually say unto me, Where is thy God?
4 { When I remember these *things*, I pour out my soul in me :
{ For I had gone with the multitude, I went with them to the house of God,
With the voice of joy and praise, with a multitude that kept holyday.

5 Why art thou cast down, O my soul? and *why* art thou disquieted
in me?
{ *Hope thou in God: for I shall yet praise him*
{ For *the help of his countenance.*
6 O my God, my soul is cast down within me: therefore will I
remember thee
*From the land of Jordan, and of the Hermonites, from the hill
Mizar.*
7 Deep calleth unto deep at the noise of thy waterspouts:
All thy waves and thy billows are gone over me.
8 *Yet* the LORD will command his lovingkindness in the daytime,
*And in the night his song shall be with me, and my prayer unto
the God of my life.*
9 I will say unto God my rock, Why hast thou forgotten me?
Why go I mourning because of the oppression of the enemy?
10 *As* with a sword in my bones, mine enemies reproach me;
While they say daily unto me, Where is thy God?
11 Why art thou cast down, O my soul? and why art thou disquieted
within me?
{ *Hope thou in God: for I shall yet praise him,*
{ Who is *the health of my countenance, and my God.*

PSALM XLIII.

JUDGE me, O God, and plead my cause against an ungodly nation:
Oh deliver me from the deceitful and unjust man.
2 For thou *art* the God of my strength: why dost thou cast me off?
Why go I mourning because of the oppression of the enemy?
3 Oh send out thy light and thy truth: let them lead me;
Let them bring me unto thy holy hill, and to thy tabernacles.
4 { Then will I go unto the altar of God,
{ Unto God my exceeding joy:
Yea, upon the harp will I praise thee, O God my God.
5 Why art thou cast down, O my soul? and why art thou disquieted
within me?
{ *Hope in God: for I shall yet praise him,*
{ Who is *the health of my countenance, and my God.*

LESSON 28.

PSALM XLIV.

To the chief Musician for the sons of Korah, Maschil.

WE have heard with our ears, O God,
Our fathers have told us,
   What *work thou didst in their days, in the times of old.*
2 *How* thou didst drive out the heathen with thy hand, and plantedst them;
   How *thou didst afflict the people, and cast them out.*
3 For they got not the land in possession by their own sword,
Neither did their own arm save them:
   But thy right hand, and thine arm, and the light of thy countenance,
     because thou hadst a favour unto them.
4 Thou art my King, O God:
   Command deliverances for Jacob.
5 Through thee will we push down our enemies:
   Through thy name will we tread them under that rise up against us.
6 For I will not trust in my bow,
Neither shall my sword save me.
7 But thou hast saved us from our enemies,
   And hast put them to shame that hated us.
8 In God we boast all the day long,
   And praise thy name for ever. (*Selah.*)
9 But thou hast cast off, and put us to shame;
   And goest not forth with our armies.
10 Thou makest us to turn back from the enemy:
   And they which hate us spoil for themselves.
11 Thou hast given us like sheep *appointed* for meat;
   And hast scattered us among the heathen.
12 Thou sellest thy people for nought,
   And dost not increase thy wealth by their price.
13 Thou makest us a reproach to our neighbours,
   A scorn and a derision to them that are round about us.
14 Thou makest us a byword among the heathen,
   A shaking of the head among the people.
15 My confusion *is* continually before me,
   And the shame of my face hath covered me,

LESSON 29.

16 For the voice of him that reproacheth and blasphemeth;
 By reason of the enemy and avenger.
17 All this is come upon us; yet have we not forgotten thee,
 Neither have we dealt falsely in thy covenant.
18 Our heart is not turned back,
 Neither have our steps declined from thy way;
19 Though thou hast sore broken us in the place of dragons,
 And covered us with the shadow of death.
20 If we have forgotten the name of our God,
 Or stretched out our hands to a strange god;
21 Shall not God search this out?
 For he knoweth the secrets of the heart.
22 Yea, for thy sake are we killed all the day long;
 We are counted as sheep for the slaughter.
23 Awake, why sleepest thou, O Lord?
 Arise, cast us not off for ever.
24 Wherefore hidest thou thy face,
 And forgettest our affliction and our oppression?
25 For our soul is bowed down to the dust:
 Our belly cleaveth unto the earth.
26 Arise for our help,
 And redeem us for thy mercies' sake.

LESSON 29.

PSALM XLV.

To the chief Musician upon Shoshannim, for the sons of Korah, Maschil, A Song of loves.

{ MY heart is inditing a good matter:
 I speak of the things which I have made touching the king:
 My tongue is the pen of a ready writer.
2 { Thou art fairer than the children of men:
 Grace is poured into thy lips:
 Therefore God hath blessed thee for ever.
3 Gird thy sword upon *thy* thigh, O *most* mighty,
 With thy glory and thy majesty.
4 { And in thy majesty ride prosperously,
 Because of truth and meekness *and* righteousness;
 And thy right hand shall teach thee terrible things.

5 Thine arrows *are* sharp in the heart of the king's enemies;
    Whereby the people fall under thee.
6 Thy throne, O God, *is* for ever and ever:
    The sceptre of thy kingdom is *a right sceptre.*
7 Thou lovest righteousness, and hatest wickedness:
    { *Therefore God, thy God, hath anointed thee*
    { *With the oil of gladness above thy fellows.*
8 All thy garments *smell* of myrrh, and aloes, *and* cassia,
    Out of the ivory palaces, whereby they have made thee glad.
9 Kings' daughters *were* among thy honourable women:
    { *Upon thy right hand did stand the queen*
    { *In gold of Ophir.*
10 Hearken, O daughter, and consider, and incline thine ear;
    Forget also thine own people, and thy father's house;
11 So shall the king greatly desire thy beauty:
    For he is *thy Lord; and worship thou him.*
12 And the daughter of Tyre *shall be there* with a gift;
    Even the rich among the people shall entreat thy favour.
13 The king's daughter *is* all glorious within:
    Her clothing is of wrought gold.
14 She shall be brought unto the king in raiment of needlework:
    The virgins her companions that follow her shall be brought unto thee.
15 With gladness and rejoicing shall they be brought:
    They shall enter into the king's palace.
16 Instead of thy fathers shall be thy children,
    Whom thou mayest make princes in all the earth.
17 I will make thy name to be remembered in all generations:
    Therefore shall the people praise thee for ever and ever.

Psalm XLVI.

To the chief Musician for the sons of Korah, A Song upon Alamoth.

GOD *is* our refuge and strength,
    A very present help in trouble.
2 Therefore will not we fear, though the earth be removed,
    And though the mountains be carried into the midst of the sea;
3 *Though* the waters thereof roar *and* be troubled,
    Though the mountains shake with the swelling thereof. (*Selah.*)

4 *There is* a river, the streams whereof shall make glad the city of God,
  The holy place *of the tabernacles of the Most High.*
5 God *is* in the midst of her; she shall not be moved:
  God shall help her, and that *right early.*
6 The heathen raged, the kingdoms were moved:
  He uttered his voice, the earth melted.
7 The LORD of hosts *is* with us;
  The God of Jacob is our refuge. (*Selah.*)
8 Come, behold the works of the LORD,
  What desolations he hath made in the earth.
9 He maketh wars to cease unto the end of the earth;
  { *He breaketh the bow, and cutteth the spear in sunder;*
  { *He burneth the chariot in the fire.*
10 Be still, and know that I *am* God:
  I will be exalted among the heathen, I will be exalted in the earth.
11 The LORD of hosts *is* with us;
  The God of Jacob is our refuge. (*Selah.*)

LESSON 30.

PSALM XLVII.

To the chief Musician, a Psalm for the sons of Korah.

O H clap your hands, all ye people;
  Shout unto God with the voice of triumph.
2 For the LORD most high *is* terrible;
  He is *a great King over all the earth.*
3 He shall subdue the people under us,
  And the nations under our feet.
4 He shall choose our inheritance for us,
  The excellency of Jacob whom he loved. (*Selah.*)
5 God is gone up with a shout,
  The LORD with the sound of a trumpet.
6 Sing praises to God, sing praises:
  Sing praises unto our King, sing praises.
7 For God *is* the King of all the earth:
  Sing ye praises with understanding.
8 God reigneth over the heathen:
  God sitteth upon the throne of his holiness.

9 The princes of the people are gathered together,
   Even *the people of the God of Abraham:*
   For the shields of the earth *belong* unto God:
   He is greatly exalted.

PSALM XLVIII.

A Song *and* Psalm for the sons of Korah.

GREAT *is* the LORD, and greatly to be praised
   In the city of our God, in the mountain of his holiness.
2 Beautiful for situation, the joy of the whole earth,
   { Is *mount Zion, on the sides of the north,*
   The city of the great King.
3 God is known in her palaces for a refuge.
4   *For, lo, the kings were assembled, they passed by together.*
5 They saw *it, and* so they marvelled;
   They were troubled, and hasted away.
6 Fear took hold upon them there, *and* pain, as of a woman in travail.
7   *Thou breakest the ships of Tarshish with an east wind.*
8 { As we have heard, so have we seen
   In the city of the LORD of hosts, in the city of our God:
   God will establish it for ever. (Selah.)
9 We have thought of thy lovingkindness, O God,
   In the midst of thy temple.
10 { According to thy name, O God, so *is* thy praise
   Unto the ends of the earth:
   Thy right hand is full of righteousness.
11 Let mount Zion rejoice,
   { *Let the daughters of Judah be glad,*
   Because of thy judgments.
12 Walk about Zion, and go round about her:
   Tell the towers thereof.
13 { Mark ye well her bulwarks,
   Consider her palaces;
   That ye may tell it to the generation following.
14 For this God *is* our God for ever and ever:
   He will be our guide even unto death.

LESSON 31.

Psalm XLIX.

To the chief Musician, A Psalm for the sons of Korah.

HEAR this, all *ye* people;
  Give ear, all ye *inhabitants of the world:*
2 Both low and high,
  Rich and poor, together.
3 My mouth shall speak of wisdom;
  And the meditation of my heart shall be *of understanding.*
4 I will incline mine ear to a parable:
  I will open my dark saying upon the harp.
5 Wherefore should I fear in the days of evil,
  When *the iniquity of my heels shall compass me about?*
6 They that trust in their wealth,
  And boast themselves in the multitude of their riches;
7 None *of them* can by any means redeem his brother,
  Nor give to God a ransom for him:
8 (For the redemption of their soul *is* precious,
  And it ceaseth for ever:)
9 That he should still live for ever,
  And *not see corruption.*
10 For he seeth *that* wise men die,
  { *Likewise the fool and the brutish person perish,*
  { *And leave their wealth to others.*
11 { Their inward thought *is, that* their houses *shall continue* for ever,
   { *And* their dwelling places to all generations;
  They call their *lands after their own names.*
12 Nevertheless man *being* in honor abideth not:
  He is like the beasts that *perish.*
13 This their way *is* their folly:
  Yet their posterity approve their sayings. (*Selah.*)
14 { Like sheep they are laid in the grave; death shall feed on them;
   { And the upright shall have dominion over them in the morning;
  And their beauty shall consume in the grave from their dwelling.
15 But God will redeem my soul from the power of the grave:
  For he shall receive me. (*Selah.*)

16 Be not thou afraid when one is made rich,
    When the glory of his house is increased;
17 For when he dieth he shall carry nothing away:
    His glory shall not descend after him.
18 Though while he lived he blessed his soul! :
    And men will praise thee, when thou doest well to thyself :
19 He shall go to the generation of his fathers ;
    They shall never see light.
20 Man *that is* in honour, and understandeth not,
    Is like the beasts that *perish.*

LESSON 32.

PSALM L.

A Psalm of Asaph.

THE mighty God, *even* the LORD, hath spoken,
    And called the earth from the rising of the sun unto the going down thereof.
2 Out of Zion, the perfection of beauty, God hath shined.
3   *Our God shall come, and shall not keep silence :*
A fire shall devour before him,
    And it shall be very tempestuous round about him.
4 He shall call to the heavens from above,
    And to the earth, that he may judge his people.
5 Gather my saints together unto me;
    Those that have made a covenant with me by sacrifice.
6 And the heavens shall declare his righteousness
    For God is *judge himself.* (*Selah.*)
7 { Hear, O my people, and I will speak ;
  { O Israel, and I will testify against thee :
    I am *God, even thy God.*
8 I will not reprove thee for thy sacrifices
    Or thy burnt offerings, to have been *continually before me.*
9 I will take no bullock out of thy house,
    Nor he goats out of thy folds :
10 For every beast of the forest *is* mine,
    And the cattle upon a thousand hills.

LESSON 33.

11 I know all the fowls of the mountains:
    And the wild beasts of the field are *mine.*
12 If I were hungry, I would not tell thee:
    For the world is *mine, and the fulness thereof.*
13 Will I eat the flesh of bulls,
    Or drink the blood of goats ?
14 Offer unto God thanksgiving;
    And pay thy vows unto the Most High:
15 And call upon me in the day of trouble:
    I will deliver thee, and thou shalt glorify me.
16 { But unto the wicked God saith,
    { What hast thou to do to declare my statutes,
    Or that *thou shouldest take my covenant in thy mouth ?*
17 Seeing thou hatest instruction,
    And castest my words behind thee.
18 When thou sawest a thief, then thou consentedst with him,
    And hast been partaker with adulterers.
19 Thou givest thy mouth to evil,
    And thy tongue frameth deceit.
20 Thou sittest *and* speakest against thy brother;
    Thou slanderest thine own mother's son.
21 { These *things* hast thou done, and I kept silence;
    { Thou thoughtest that I was altogether *such a one* as thyself:
    But *I will reprove thee, and set* them *in order before thine eyes.*
22 Now consider this, ye that forget God,
    Lest I tear you *in pieces, and* there be *none to deliver.*
23 Whoso offereth praise glorifieth me:
    And to him that ordereth his *conversation* aright *will I shew the salvation of God.*

LESSON 33.

PSALM LI.

To the chief Musician, A Psalm of David, when Nathan the prophet came unto him, after he had gone in to Bath-sheba.

HAVE mercy upon me, O God, according to thy lovingkindness:
    According unto the multitude of thy tender mercies blot out my transgressions.

2 Wash me thoroughly from mine iniquity,
   And cleanse me from my sin.
3 For I acknowledge my transgressions:
   And my sin is ever before me.
4 Against thee, thee only, have I sinned,
   And done this *evil in thy sight:*
   That thou mightest be justified when thou speakest,
   And *be clear when thou judgest.*
5 Behold, I was shapen in iniquity;
   And in sin did my mother conceive me.
6 Behold, thou desirest truth in the inward parts:
   And in the hidden part *thou shalt make me to know wisdom.*
7 Purge me with hyssop, and I shall be clean:
   Wash me, and I shall be whiter than snow.
8 Make me to hear joy and gladness;
   That *the bones* which *thou hast broken may rejoice.*
9 Hide thy face from my sins,
   And blot out all mine iniquities.
10 Create in me a clean heart, O God;
   And renew a right spirit within me.
11 Cast me not away from thy presence;
   And take not thy Holy Spirit from me.
12 Restore unto me the joy of thy salvation;
   And uphold me with thy *free Spirit.*
13 *Then* will I teach transgressors thy ways;
   And sinners shall be converted unto thee.
14 Deliver me from blood guiltiness, O God, thou God of my salvation
   And *my tongue shall sing aloud of thy righteousness.*
15 O Lord, open thou my lips;
   And my mouth shall shew forth thy praise.
16 For thou desirest not sacrifice; else would I give *it:*
   Thou delightest not in burnt offering.
17 The sacrifices of God *are* a broken spirit:
   A broken and a contrite heart, O God, thou wilt not despise.
18 Do good in thy good pleasure unto Zion:
   Build thou the walls of Jerusalem.
19 Then shalt thou be pleased with the sacrifices of righteousness, with burnt offering and whole burnt offering:
   Then shall they offer bullocks upon thine altar.

LESSON 34.

Psalm LII.

To the chief Musician, Maschil, A Psalm of David, when Doeg the Edomite came and told Saul, and said unto him, David is come to the house of Ahimelech.

WHY boasteth thou thyself in mischief, O mighty man?
The goodness of God endureth continually.
2 Thy tongue deviseth mischiefs;
Like a sharp razor, working deceitfully.
3 Thou lovest evil more than good;
And lying rather than to speak righteousness. (Selah.)
4 Thou lovest all devouring words, O *thou* deceitful tongue.
5 *God shall likewise destroy thee for ever.*
He shall take thee away, and pluck thee out of *thy* dwelling place,
And root thee out of the land of the living. (Selah.)
6 The righteous also shall see, and fear,
And shall laugh at him:
7 Lo, *this is* the man *that* made not God his strength;
But trusted in the abundance of his riches, and strengthened himself in his wickedness.
8 But I *am* like a green olive tree in the house of God:
I trust in the mercy of God for ever and ever.
9 I will praise thee for ever, because thou hast done *it:*
And I will wait on thy name; for it is good before thy saints.

Psalm LIII.

To the chief Musician upon Mahalath, Maschil, A Psalm of David.

THE fool hath said in his heart, *There is* no God.
{ *Corrupt are they, and have done abominable iniquity:*
{ There is *none that doeth good.*
2 God looked down from heaven upon the children of men,
{ *To see if there were* any *that did understand,*
{ *That did seek God.*
3 Every one of them is gone back: they are altogether become filthy;
{ There is *none that doeth good,*
{ *No, not one.*

4 Have the workers of iniquity no knowledge?
> Who eat up my people as *they eat bread :*
> They have not called upon God.

5 There were they in great fear, *where* no fear was:
> For God hath scattered the bones of him that encampeth against thee:
> Thou hast put them *to shame, because God hath despised them.*

6 Oh that the salvation of Israel *were* come out of Zion!
> When God bringeth back the captivity of his people,
> Jacob shall rejoice, and Israel shall be glad.

Psalm LIV.

To the chief Musician on Neginoth, Maschil, A Psalm of David, when the Ziphim came and said to Saul, Doth not David hide himself with us?

SAVE me, O God, by thy name,
  And judge me by thy strength.
2 Hear my prayer, O God;
  Give ear to the words of my mouth.
3 For strangers are risen up against me,
  And oppressors seek after my soul:
  They have not set God before them. (*Selah.*)
4 Behold, God *is* mine helper:
  The Lord is with them that uphold my soul.
5 He shall reward evil unto mine enemies:
  Cut them off in thy truth.
6 I will freely sacrifice unto thee:
  I will praise thy name, O LORD; for it is good.
7 For he hath delivered me out of all trouble:
  And mine eye hath seen his desire upon mine enemies.

LESSON 35.

Psalm LV.

To the chief Musician on Neginoth, Maschil, A Psalm of David.

GIVE ear to my prayer, O God;
  And hide not thyself from my supplication.
2 Attend unto me, and hear me:
  I mourn in my complaint, and make a noise;

LESSON 35.

3 Because of the voice of the enemy, because of the oppression of the wicked:
For they cast iniquity upon me, and in wrath they hate me.
4 My heart is sore pained within me:
And the terrors of death are fallen upon me.
5 Fearfulness and trembling are come upon me,
And horror hath overwhelmed me.
6 And I said, Oh that I had wings like a dove!
For then *would I fly away, and be at rest.*
7 Lo, *then* would I wander far off,
And *remain in the wilderness.* (*Selah.*)
8 I would hasten my escape
From the windy storm and *tempest.*
9 Destroy, O Lord, *and* divide their tongues:
For I have seen violence and strife in the city.
10 Day and night they go about it upon the walls thereof:
Mischief also and sorrow are *in the midst of it.*
11 Wickedness *is* in the midst thereof:
Deceit and guile depart not from her streets.
12 For *it was* not an enemy *that* reproached me; then could I have borne *it:*
{ *Neither* was it *he that hated me* that *did magnify* himself *against me;*
Then I would have hid myself from him:
13 But *it was* thou, a man mine equal, my guide, and mine acquaintance.
14 { *We took sweet counsel together,*
And walked unto the house of God in company.
15 { Let death seize upon them,
And let them go down quick into hell:
For wickedness is *in their dwellings,* and *among them.*
16 As for me, I will call upon God;
And the LORD shall save me.
17 Evening, and morning, and at noon, will I pray, and cry aloud:
And he shall hear my voice.
18 He hath delivered my soul in peace from the battle *that was* against me:
For there were many with me.

19 God shall hear, and afflict them,
>> Even he that abideth of old. (*Selah.*)
>> Because they have no changes,
>> *Therefore they fear not God.*
20 He hath put forth his hands against such as be at peace with him:
>> *He hath broken his covenant.*
21 *The words* of his mouth were smoother than butter, but war *was* in his heart:
>> *His words were softer than oil, yet* were *they drawn swords.*
22 { Cast thy burden upon the Lord,
{ And he shall sustain thee:
>> *He shall never suffer the righteous to be moved.*
23 { But thou, O God, shalt bring them down into the pit of destruction:
{ Bloody and deceitful men shall not live out half their days;
>> *But I will trust in thee.*

LESSON 36.

PSALM LVI.

To the chief Musician upon Jonath-elem-rechokim, Michtam of David, when the Philistines took him in Gath.

BE merciful unto me, O God: for man would swallow me up;
>> *He fighting daily oppresseth me.*
2 Mine enemies would daily swallow *me* up:
>> *For* they be *many that fight against me, O thou Most High.*
3 What time I am afraid, I will trust in thee.
4 *In God I will praise his word,*
In God I have put my trust;
>> *I will not fear what flesh can do unto me.*
5 Every day they wrest my words:
>> *All their thoughts* are *against me for evil.*
6 They gather themselves together, they hide themselves,
>> *They mark my steps, when they wait for my soul.*
7 Shall they escape by iniquity?
>> *In* thine *anger cast down the people, O God.*
8 Thou tellest my wanderings:
>> { *Put thou my tears into thy bottle:*
>> { Are they *not in thy book?*

9 When I cry *unto thee*, then shall mine enemies turn back:
 This I know; for God is for me.
10 In God will I praise *his* word :
 In the LORD will I praise his word.
11 In God have I put my trust :
 I will not be afraid what man can do unto me.
12 Thy vows *are* upon me, O God :
 I will render praises unto thee.
13 { For thou hast delivered my soul from death :
 Wilt not thou deliver my feet from falling,
  That I may walk before God in the light of the living ?

Psalm LVII.

To the chief Musician Al-taschith, Michtam of David, when he fled from Saul in the cave.

{ BE merciful unto me, O God, be merciful unto me,
 For my soul trusteth in thee :
  { *Yea, in the shadow of thy wings will I make my refuge,*
  Until these calamities be overpast.
2 I will cry unto God most high ;
 Unto God that performeth all things for me.
3 { He shall send from heaven, and save me
 From the reproach of him that would swallow me up. (*Selah.*)
 God shall send forth his mercy and his truth.
4 { My soul *is* among lions :
 And I lie even among them that are set on fire, even the sons of men,
  { *Whose teeth are spears and arrows,*
  And their tongue a sharp sword.
5 Be thou exalted, O God, above the heavens ;
 Let thy glory be above all the earth.
6 { They have prepared a net for my steps ;
 My soul is bowed down :
  { *They have digged a pit before me,*
  Into the midst whereof they are fallen themselves. (*Selah.*)
7 My heart is fixed, O God, my heart is fixed :
 I will sing and give praise.
8 { Awake up, my glory ;
 Awake, psaltery and harp :
  I myself will awake early.

9 I will praise thee, O Lord, among the people:
> *I will sing unto thee among the nations.*
10 For thy mercy *is* great unto the heavens,
> *And thy truth unto the clouds.*
11 Be thou exalted, O God, above the heavens:
> *Let thy glory be above all the earth.*

LESSON 37.

PSALM LVIII.

To the chief Musician, Al-taschith, Mitcham of David.

DO ye indeed speak righteousness, O congregation?
> *Do ye judge uprightly, O ye sons of men?*
2 Yea, in heart ye work wickedness;
> *Ye weigh the violence of your hands in the earth.*
3 The wicked are estranged from the womb:
> *They go astray as soon as they be born, speaking lies.*
4 Their poison *is* like the poison of a serpent:
> *They are like the deaf adder that stoppeth her ear;*
5 Which will not hearken to the voice of charmers,
> *Charming never so wisely.*
6 Break their teeth, O God, in their mouth:
> *Break out the great teeth of the young lions, O LORD.*
7 Let them melt away as waters *which* run continually:
> *When he bendeth his bow to shoot his arrows, let them be as cut in pieces.*
8 As a snail *which* melteth, let *every one of them* pass away:
> *Like the untimely birth of a woman, that they may not see the sun.*
9 Before your pots can feel the thorns,
> *He shall take them away as with a whirlwind, both living, and in his wrath.*
10 The righteous shall rejoice when he seeth the vengeance:
> *He shall wash his feet in the blood of the wicked.*
11 So that a man shall say, Verily *there is* a reward for the righteous:
> *Verily he is a God that judgeth in the earth.*

LESSON 37.

PSALM LIX.

To the chief Musician, Al-taschith, Mitchtam of David; when Saul sent, and they watched the house to kill him.

DELIVER me from mine enemies, O my God:
Defend me from them that rise up against me.
2 Deliver me from the workers of iniquity,
And save me from bloody men.
3 { For, lo, they lie in wait for my soul:
{ The mighty are gathered against me;
Not for *my transgression, nor* for *my sin, O LORD.*
4 They run and prepare themselves without *my* fault:
Awake to help me, and behold.
5 { Thou therefore, O LORD God of hosts, the God of Israel,
{ Awake to visit all the heathen:
Be not merciful to any wicked transgressors. (Selah.)
6 They return at evening: they make a noise like a dog,
And go round about the city.
7 Behold, they belch out with their mouth:
{ Swords are *in their lips:*
{ *For who,* say they, *doth hear?*
8 But thou, O LORD, shalt laugh at them;
Thou shalt have all the heathen in derision.
9 *Because of* his strength will I wait upon thee:
For God is *my defence.*
10 The God of mercy shall prevent me:
God shall let me see my desire *upon mine enemies.*
11 Slay them not, lest my people forget:
{ Scatter them by thy power; and bring them down,
{ O Lord our shield.
12 { *For* the sin of their mouth *and* the words of their lips
{ Let them even be taken in their pride:
And for cursing and lying which *they speak.*
13 Consume *them* in wrath, consume *them,* that they *may* not *be:*
{ And let them know that God ruleth in Jacob
{ Unto the ends of the earth. (Selah.)
14 And at evening let them return; *and* let them make a noise like a dog,
And go round about the city.

15 Let them wander up and down for meat,
    And grudge if they be not satisfied.
16 { But I will sing of thy power;
    Yea, I will sing aloud of thy mercy in the morning:
      { *For thou hast been my defence*
      And refuge in the day of my trouble.

LESSON 38.

PSALM LX.

To the chief Musician upon Shushan-eduth, Michtam of David, to teach; when he strove with Aram-naharaim and with Aram-zobah, when Joab returned, and smote of Edom in the valley of salt twelve thousand.

O GOD, thou hast cast us off, thou hast scattered us,
    Thou hast been displeased; oh turn thyself to us again.
2 Thou hast made the earth to tremble; thou hast broken it:
    Heal the breaches thereof; for it shaketh.
3 Thou has shewed thy people hard things:
    Thou hast made us to drink the wine of astonishment.
4 Thou hast given a banner to them that fear thee,
    That it may be displayed because of the truth. (*Selah.*)
5 That thy beloved may be delivered;
    Save with *thy right hand, and hear me.*
6 { God hath spoken in his holiness;
    I will rejoice: I will divide Shechem,
    And mete out the valley of Succoth.
7 Gilead *is* mine, and Manasseh *is* mine;
    { *Ephraim also is the strength of mine head;*
    Judah is *my lawgiver;*
8 { Moab *is* my washpot;
    Over Edom will I cast out my shoe:
    Philistia, triumph thou because of me.
9 Who will bring me *into* the strong city?
    Who will lead me into Edom?
10 *Wilt* not thou, O God, *which* hadst cast us off?
    And thou, O God, which didst not go out with our armies?
11 Give us help from trouble:
    For vain is *the help of man.*
12 Through God we shall do valiantly:
    For he it is that *shall tread down our enemies.*

PSALM LXI.

To the chief Musician upon Neginah, *A Psalm* of David.

HEAR my cry, O God;
  Attend unto my prayer.
2 From the end of the earth will I cry unto thee, when my heart is overwhelmed:
  Lead me to the rock that *is higher than I.*
3 For thou hast been a shelter for me,
  And *a strong tower from the enemy.*
4 I will abide in thy tabernacle for ever:
  I will trust in the covert of thy wings. (Selah.)
5 For thou, O God, hast heard my vows:
  Thou hast given me *the heritage of those that fear thy name.*
6 Thou wilt prolong the king's life:
  And *his years as many generations.*
7 He shall abide before God for ever:
  Oh prepare mercy and truth, which *may preserve him.*
8 So will I sing praise unto thy name for ever,
  That I may daily perform my vows.

LESSON 39.

PSALM LXII.

To the chief Musician, to Jeduthun, A Psalm of David.

TRULY my soul waiteth upon God:
  From him cometh *my salvation.*
2 He only *is* my rock and my salvation;
  He is *my defence; I shall not be greatly moved.*
3 How long will ye imagine mischief against a man?
  Ye shall be slain all of you; as a bowing wall shall ye be, and as *a tottering fence.*
4 They only consult to cast *him* down from his excellency:
  They delight in lies: they bless with their mouth,
  But they curse inwardly. (Selah.)
5 My soul, wait thou only upon God;
  For my expectation is *from him.*

6 He only *is* my rock and my salvation:
　He is *my defence; I shall not be moved.*
7 In God *is* my salvation and my glory:
　The rock of my strength, and *my refuge, is in God.*
8 ⎰ Trust in him at all times;
　⎱ Ye people, pour out your heart before him:
　God is a refuge for us. (*Selah.*)
9 Surely men of low degree *are* vanity, *and* men of high degree *are* a lie:
　To be laid in the balance, they are *altogether* lighter *than vanity.*
10 Trust not in oppression, and become not vain in robbery:
　If riches increase, set not your heart upon them.
11 ⎰ God hath spoken once;
　⎱ Twice have I heard this;
　That power belongeth *unto God.*
12 Also unto thee, O Lord, *belongeth* mercy:
　For thou renderest to every man according to his work.

Psalm LXIII.

A Psalm of David, when he was in the wilderness of Judah.

O GOD, thou *art* my God; early will I seek thee:
　⎰ *My soul thirsteth for thee, my flesh longeth for thee*
　⎱ *In a dry and thirsty land, where no water is;*
2 To see thy power and thy glory,
　So as I have seen thee in the sanctuary.
3 Because thy lovingkindness *is* better than life,
　My lips shall praise thee.
4 Thus will I bless thee while I live:
　I will lift up my hands in thy name.
5 My soul shall be satisfied as *with* marrow and fatness;
　And my mouth shall praise thee *with joyful lips:*
6 When I remember thee upon my bed,
　And meditate on thee in the night *watches.*
7 Because thou hast been my help,
　Therefore in the shadow of thy wings will I rejoice.
8 My soul followeth hard after thee:
　Thy right hand upholdeth me.

9 But those *that* seek my soul to destroy *it*,
   Shall go into the lower parts of the earth.
10 They shall fall by the sword:
   They shall be a portion for foxes.
11 { But the king shall rejoice in God;
   { Every one that sweareth by him shall glory:
   But the mouth of them that speak lies shall be stopped.

LESSON 40.

PSALM LXIV.

To the chief Musician, A Psalm of David.

HEAR my voice, O God, in my prayer:
   Preserve my life from fear of the enemy.
2 Hide me from the secret counsel of the wicked;
   From the insurrection of the workers of iniquity:
3 Who whet their tongue like a sword,
   And *bend* their bows to shoot *their arrows,* even *bitter words:*
4 That they may shoot in secret at the perfect:
   Suddenly do they shoot at him, and fear not.
5 { They encourage themselves *in* an evil matter:
   { They commune of laying snares privily;
   They say, Who shall see them?
6 { They search out iniquities;
   { They accomplish a diligent search;
   Both the inward thought *of every one* of them, *and the heart* is *deep.*
7 But God shall shoot at them *with* an arrow;
   Suddenly shall they be wounded.
8 So they shall make their own tongue to fall upon themselves:
   All that see them shall flee away.
9 And all men shall fear, and shall declare the work of God;
   For they shall wisely consider of his doing.
10 The righteous shall be glad in the LORD, and shall trust in him;
   And all the upright in heart shall glory.

Psalm LXV.

To the chief Musician, A Psalm and Song of David.

PRAISE waiteth for thee, O God, in Zion:
   And unto thee shall the vow be performed.
2 O thou that hearest prayer, unto thee shall all flesh come.
3 { *Iniquities prevail against me:*
   { *As for our transgressions, thou shalt purge them away.*
4 Blessed *is the man whom* thou choosest, and causest to approach
      unto thee, *that* he may dwell in thy courts:
   We shall be satisfied with the goodness of thy house, even of thy
      holy temple.
5 *By* terrible things in righteousness wilt thou answer us, O God of
      our salvation;
   Who art *the confidence of all the ends of the earth, and of them*
      that are afar off upon *the sea:*
6 Which by his strength setteth fast the mountains; *being* girded with
      power:
7 { *Which stilleth the noise of the seas, the noise of their waves,*
   { *And the tumult of the people.*
8 They also that dwell in the uttermost parts are afraid at thy tokens:
   Thou makest the outgoings of the morning and evening to rejoice.
9 Thou visitest the earth, and waterest it:
   Thou greatly enrichest it
  With the river of God, *which* is full of water:
   Thou preparest them corn, when thou hast so provided for it.
10 Thou waterest the ridges thereof abundantly; thou settlest the
      furrows thereof:
   { *Thou makest it soft with showers,*
   { *Thou blessest the springing thereof.*
11 Thou crownest the year with thy goodness;
   And thy paths drop fatness.
12 They drop *upon* the pastures of the wilderness:
   And the little hills rejoice on every side.
13 { The pastures are clothed with flocks;
    { The valleys also are covered over with corn;
     They shout for joy, they also sing.

LESSON 41.

Psalm LXVI.

To the chief Musician, A Song or Psalm.

MAKE a joyful noise unto God, all ye lands:
2 { Sing forth the honour of his name:
{ Make his praise glorious.
3 Say unto God, How terrible *art thou in* thy works!
    Through the greatness of thy power shall thine enemies submit
        themselves unto thee.
4 All the earth shall worship thee, and shall sing unto thee;
    They shall sing to thy name. (*Selah.*)
5 Come and see the works of God:
    He is *terrible* in his *doing toward the children of men.*
6 { He turned the sea into dry *land:*
  { They went through the flood on foot:
    There did we rejoice in him.
7 { He ruleth by his power for ever;
  { His eyes behold the nations:
    Let not the rebellious exalt themselves. (*Selah.*)
8 Oh bless our God, ye people,
    And make the voice of his praise to be heard:
9 Which holdeth our soul in life,
    And suffereth not our feet to be moved.
10 For thou, O God, hast proved us:
    Thou hast tried us, as silver is tried.
11 Thou broughtest us into the net;
    Thou laidst affliction upon our loins.
12 { Thou hast caused men to ride over our heads;
   { We went through fire and through water:
    But thou broughtest us out into a wealthy place.
13 I will go into thy house with burnt offerings:
    I will pay thee my vows,
14 Which my lips have uttered,
    And my mouth hath spoken, when I was in trouble.
15 { I will offer unto thee burnt sacrifices of fatlings,
   { With the incense of rams:
    I will offer bullocks with goats. (*Selah.*)

16 Come *and* hear, all ye that fear God,
    And I will declare what he hath done for my soul.
17 I cried unto him with my mouth,
    And he was extolled with my tongue.
18 If I regard iniquity in my heart,
    The Lord w ll not hear me:
19 *But* verily God hath heard *me* ;
    He hath attended to the voice of my prayer.
20 Blessed *be* God,
    { *Which hath not turned away my prayer,*
    { *Nor his mercy from me.*

PSALM LXVII.

To the chief Musician on Neginoth, A Psalm or Song.

GOD be merciful unto us, and bless us ;
    And *cause his face to shine upon us ; (Selah.)*
2 That thy way may be known upon earth,
    Thy saving health among all nations.
3 Let the people praise thee, O God ;
    Let all the people praise thee.
4 Oh let the nations be glad and sing for joy :
    { *For thou shalt judge the people righteously,*
    { *And govern the nations upon earth. (Selah.)*
5 Let the people praise thee, O God ;
    Let all the people praise thee.
6 *Then* shall the earth yield her increase ;
    And *God,* even *our own God, shall bless us.*
7 God shall bless us ;
    And all the ends of the earth shall fear him.

LESSON 42.

PSALM LXVIII.

To the chief Musician, A Psalm or Song of David.

LET God arise, let his enemies be scattered :
    Let them also that hate him flee before him.

LESSON 42.

2 As smoke is driven away, *so drive them* away:
   { *As wax melteth before the fire,*
   { So *let the wicked perish at the presence of God.*
3 But let the righteous be glad; let them rejoice before God:
   Yea, let them exceedingly rejoice.
4 { Sing unto God, sing praises to his name:
   { Extol him that rideth upon the heavens
   By his name JAH, and rejoice before him.
5 A father of the fatherless, and a judge of the widows,
   Is *God in his holy habitation.*
6 { God setteth the solitary in families:
   { He bringeth out those which are bound with chains:
   But the rebellious dwell in a dry land.
7 O God, when thou wentest forth before thy people,
   When thou didst march through the wilderness;   (*Selah:*)
8 { The earth shook,
   { The heavens also dropped at the presence of God:
   Even *Sinai itself* was moved *at the presence of God, the God of Israel.*
9 Thou, O God, didst send a plentiful rain,
   Whereby thou didst confirm thine inheritance, when it was weary.
10 Thy congregation hath dwelt therein:
    Thou, O God, hast prepared of thy goodness for the poor.
11 The Lord gave the word:
    Great was *the company of those that published* it.
12 Kings of armies did flee apace:
    And she that tarried at home divided the spoil.
13 { Though ye have lain among the pots,
    { *Yet shall ye be as* the wings of a dove covered with silver,
    And her feathers with yellow gold.
14 When the Almighty scattered kings in it,
    It was white *as snow in Salmon.*
15 The hill of God *is as* the hill of Bashan;
    A high hill as *the hill of Bashan.*
16 { Why leap ye, ye high hills?
    { *This is* the hill *which* God desireth to dwell in;
    Yea, the LORD will dwell in it *for ever.*
17 The chariots of God *are* twenty thousand, *even* thousands of angels:
    The Lord is *among them,* as in *Sinai, in the holy* place.

18 { Thou hast ascended on high, thou hast led captivity captive :
　　Thou hast received gifts for men ;
　　　　Yea, for *the rebellious also, that the* LORD *God might dwell
　　　　　　among them.*
19 { Blessed *be* the Lord,
　　Who daily loadeth us *with benefits,*
　　　　Even *the God of our salvation.* (*Selah.*)
20 *He that is* our God *is* the God of Salvation ;
　　And unto GOD *the Lord* belong *the issues from death.*
21 But God shall wound the head of his enemies,
　　And the hairy scalp of such a one as goeth on still in his trespasses.
22 The Lord said, I will bring again from Bashan, I will bring *my people
　　　　again from the depths of the sea:*
23 　{ *That thy foot may be dipped in the blood of* thine *enemies,*
　　　And the tongue of thy dogs in the same.
24 They have seen thy goings, O God ;
　　Even *the goings of my God, my King, in the sanctuary.*
25 The singers went before, the players on instruments *followed* after ;
　　Among them were *the damsels playing with timbrels.*
26 Bless ye God in the congregations,
　　Even *the Lord, from the fountain of Israel.*
27 { There *is* little Benjamin *with* their ruler,
　　 The princes of Judah *and* their council,
　　　　The princes of Zebulun, and *the princes of Naphtali.*
28 Thy God hath commanded thy strength :
　　Strengthen, O God, that which thou hast wrought for us.
29 Because of thy temple at Jerusalem
　　Shall kings bring presents unto thee.
30 { Rebuke the company of spearmen, the multitude of the bulls, with
　　　　　the calves of the people,
　　　Till every one submit himself with pieces of silver :
　　Scatter thou the people that *delight in war.*
31 Princes shall come out of Egypt ;
　　Ethiopia shall soon stretch out her hands unto God.
32 Sing unto God, ye kingdoms of the earth ;
　　Oh sing praises unto the Lord ; (*Selah :*)
33 To him that rideth upon the heavens of heavens, *which were* of old ;
　　Lo, he doth send out his voice, and that *a mighty voice.*

LESSON 43.

34 Ascribe ye strength unto God :
  { *His excellency* is *over Israel,*
  { *And his strength* is *in the clouds.*
35 { O God, *thou art* terrible out of thy holy places :
  { The God of Israel *is* he that giveth strength and power unto *his*
  {   people.
  Blessed be *God.*

LESSON 43.

PSALM LXIX.

To the chief Musician upon Shoshannim, *A Psalm* of David.

{ SAVE me, O God ; for the waters are come in unto *my* soul.
{ 2 I sink in deep mire, where *there is* no standing :
  I *am come into deep waters, where the floods overflow me.*
3 I am weary of my crying : my throat is dried :
  Mine eyes fa'l while I wait for my God.
4 { They that hate me without a cause are more than the hairs of mine
  {   head :
  { They that would destroy me, *being* mine enemies wrongfully, are
  {   mighty :
5 O God, thou knowest my foolishness ;
  And my sins are not hid from thee.
6 Let not them that wait on thee, O Lord GOD of hosts, be ashamed
      for my sake :
  Let not those that seek thee be confounded for my sake, O God of
      Israel.
7 Because for thy sake I have borne reproach ;
  Shame hath covered my face.
8 I am become a stranger unto my brethren,
  And an alien unto my mother's children.
9 For the zeal of thine house hath eaten me up ;
  And the reproaches of them that reproached thee are fallen upon me.
10 When I wept, *and chastened* my soul with fasting,
  That was to my reproach.
11 I made sackcloth also my garment ;
  And I became a proverb to them.

12 They that sit in the gate speak against me;
  And I was *the song of the drunkards.*
13 But as for me, my prayer *is* unto thee, O Lord, *in* an acceptable time:
  O God, in the multitude of thy mercy hear me, in the truth of thy salvation.
14 Deliver me out of the mire, and let me not sink:
  Let me be delivered from them that hate me, and out of the deep waters.
15 ⎰ Let not the waterflood overflow me,
 ⎱ Neither let the deep swallow me up,
  And let not the pit shut her mouth upon me.
16 Hear me, O Lord; for thy lovingkindness *is* good:
  Turn unto me according to the multitude of thy tender mercies.
17 And hide not thy face from thy servant;
  For I am in trouble: hear me speedily.
18 Draw nigh unto my soul, *and* redeem it:
  Deliver me because of mine enemies.
19 Thou hast known my reproach, and my shame, and my dishonour:
  Mine adversaries are all before thee.
20 Reproach hath broken my heart; and I am full of heaviness:
 ⎰ *And I looked* for some *to take pity, but* there was *none;*
 ⎱ *And for comforters, but I found none.*
21 They gave me also gall for my meat;
  And in my thirst they gave me vinegar to drink.
22 Let their table become a snare before them:
  And that which should have been *for* their *welfare,* let it become *a trap.*
23 Let their eyes be darkened, that they see not;
  And make their loins continually to shake.
24 Pour out thine indignation upon them,
  And let thy wrathful anger take hold of them.
25 Let their habitation be desolate;
  And let none dwell in their tents.
26 For they persecute *him* whom thou hast smitten;
  And they talk to the grief of those whom thou hast wounded.
27 Add iniquity unto their iniquity:
  And let them not come into thy righteousness.

28 Let them be blotted out of the book of the living,
And not be written with the righteous.
29 But I *am* poor and sorrowful:
Let thy salvation, O God, set me up on high.
30 I will praise the name of God with a song,
And will magnify him with thanksgiving.
31 *This* also shall please the LORD better than an ox *or* bullock
That hath horns and hoofs.
32 The humble shall see *this, and* be glad:
And your heart shall live that seek God.
33 For the LORD heareth the poor,
And despiseth not his prisoners.
34 Let the heaven and earth praise him,
The seas, and every thing that moveth therein.
35 For God will save Zion, and will build the cities of Judah,
That they may dwell there, and have it in possession.
36 The seed also of his servants shall inherit it:
And they that love his name shall dwell therein.

LESSON 44.

PSALM LXX.

To the chief Musician, *A Psalm* of David, to bring to remembrance.

*M*AKE *haste*, O God, to deliver me;
Make haste to help me, O LORD.
2 Let them be ashamed and confounded that seek after my soul:
Let them be turned backward, and put to confusion, that desire my hurt.
3 Let them be turned back for a reward of their shame
That say, Aha, aha.
4 Let all those that seek thee rejoice and be glad in thee:
And let such as love thy salvation say continually, Let God be magnified.
5 But I *am* poor and needy;
Make haste unto me, O God:
Thou *art* my help and my deliverer;
O LORD, make no tarrying.

PSALM LXXI.

IN thee, O Lord, do I put my trust;
 Let me never be put to confusion.
2 Deliver me in thy righteousness, and cause me to escape:
 Incline thine ear unto me, and save me.
3 {Be thou my strong habitation, whereunto I may continually resort:
 Thou hast given commandment to save me;
 For thou art *my rock and my fortress.*
4 Deliver me, O my God, out of the hand of the wicked,
 Out of the hand of the unrighteous and cruel man.
5 For thou *art* my hope, O Lord God:
 Thou art *my trust from my youth.*
6 {By thee have I been holden up from the womb:
 Thou art he that took me out of my mother's bowels:
 My praise shall be continually of thee.
7 I am as a wonder unto many;
 But thou art my strong refuge.
8 Let my mouth be filled *with* thy praise
 And with *thy honour all the day.*
9 Cast me not off in the time of old age;
 Forsake me not when my strength faileth.
10 For mine enemies speak against me;
 And they that lay wait for my soul take counsel together,
11 Saying, God hath forsaken him:
 Persecute and take him; for there is *none to deliver* him.
12 O God, be not far from me:
 O my God, make haste for my help.
13 Let them be confounded *and* consumed that are adversaries to my soul;
 Let them be covered with *reproach and dishonour that seek my hurt.*
14 But I will hope continually,
 And will yet praise thee more and more.
15 My mouth shall shew forth thy righteousness
 And *thy salvation all the day; for I know not the numbers* thereof.
16 I will go in the strength of the Lord God:
 I will make mention of thy righteousness, even of thine only.

17 O God, thou hast taught me from my youth:
 And hitherto have I declared thy wondrous works.
18 Now also when I am old and grayheaded, O God, forsake me not;
 Until I have shewed thy strength unto this *generation, and thy power to every one* that *is to come.*
19 Thy righteousness also, O God, *is* very high,
 Who hast done great things: O God, who is like unto thee!
20 { Thou, which hast shewed me great and sore troubles,
 Shalt quicken me again,
 And shalt bring me up again from the depths of the earth.
21 { Thou shalt increase my greatness, and comfort me on every side.
22 { I will also praise thee with the psaltery, *even* thy truth, O my God.
 Unto thee will I sing with the harp, O thou Holy One of Israel.
23 My lips shall greatly rejoice when I sing unto thee;
 And my soul, which thou hast redeemed.
24 My tongue also shall talk of thy righteousness all the day long:
 For they are confounded, for they are brought unto shame, that seek my hurt.

LESSON 45.

PSALM LXXII.

A Psalm for Solomon.

GIVE the king thy judgments, O God,
 And thy righteousness unto the king's son.
2 He shall judge thy people with righteousness,
 And thy poor with judgment.
3 The mountains shall bring peace to the people,
 And the little hills, by righteousness.
4 He shall judge the poor of the people,
 He shall save the children of the needy, and shall break in pieces the oppressor.
5 They shall fear thee as long as the sun and moon endure,
 Throughout all generations.
6 He shall come down like rain upon the mown grass:
 As showers that water the earth.
7 In his days shall the righteous flourish;
 And abundance of peace so long as the moon endureth.
8

8 He shall have dominion also from sea to sea,
   And from the river unto the ends of the earth.
9 They that dwell in the wilderness shall bow before him;
   And his enemies shall lick the dust.
10 The kings of Tarshish and of the isles shall bring presents:
   The kings of Sheba and Seba shall offer gifts.
11 Yea, all kings shall fall down before him:
   All nations shall serve him.
12 For he shall deliver the needy when he crieth;
   The poor also, and him *that hath no helper.*
13 He shall spare the poor and needy,
   And shall save the souls of the needy.
14 He shall redeem their soul from deceit and violence:
   And precious shall their blood be in his sight.
15 And he shall live, and to him shall be given of the gold of Sheba:
   Prayer also shall be made for him continually; and *daily shall he be praised.*
16 { There shall be a handful of corn in the earth upon the top of the mountains:
   The fruit thereof shall shake like Lebanon:
   And they of the city shall flourish like grass of the earth.
17 { His name shall endure for ever:
   His name shall be continued as long as the sun:
   And men shall be blessed in him: all nations shall call him blessed.
18 Blessed *be* the LORD God, the God of Israel,
   Who only doeth wondrous things.
19 { And blessed *be* his glorious name for ever:
   And let the whole earth be filled *with* his glory.
   Amen, and Amen.
20 The prayers of David the son of Jesse are ended.

LESSON 46.

Psalm LXXIII.

A Psalm of Asaph.

TRULY God *is* good to Israel,
   Even *to such as are of a clean heart.*
2 But as for me, my feet were almost gone;
   My steps had well nigh slipped.

LESSON 46.

3 For I was envious at the foolish,
  When I saw the prosperity of the wicked.
4 For *there are* no bands in their death :
  But their strength is firm.
5 They *are* not in trouble *as other* men ;
  Neither are they plagued like other men.
6 Therefore pride compasseth them about as a chain ;
  Violence covereth them as a garment.
7 Their eyes stand out with fatness :
  They have more than heart could wish.
8 They are corrupt, and speak wickedly *concerning* oppression :
  They speak loftily.
9 They set their mouth against the heavens,
  And their tongue walketh through the earth.
10 Therefore his people return hither :
  And waters of a full cup are wrung out to them.
11 And they say, How doth God know ?
  And is there knowledge in the Most High?
12 Behold these *are* the ungodly,
  Who prosper in the world ; they increase in *riches.*
13 Verily I have cleansed my heart *in* vain,
  And washed my hands in innocency.
14 For all the day long have I been plagued,
  And chastened every morning.
15 If I say, I will speak thus ;
  Behold, I should offend against *the generation of thy children.*
16 When I thought to know this,
  It was *too painful for me ;*
17 Until I went into the sanctuary of God ;
  Then *understood I their end.*
18 Surely thou didst set them in slippery places :
  Thou castedst them down into destruction.
19 How are they *brought* into desolation, as in a moment !
  They are utterly consumed with terrors.
20 As a dream when *one* awaketh ;
  So, *O Lord, when thou awakest, thou shalt despise their image.*
21 Thus my heart was grieved,
  And I was pricked in my reins.

22 So foolish *was* I, and ignorant:
   I was as *a beast before thee.*
23 Nevertheless I *am* continually with thee:
   Thou hast holden me *by my right hand.*
24 Thou shalt guide me with thy counsel,
   And afterward receive me to *glory.*
25 Whom have I in heaven *but thee?*
   And there is *none upon earth* that *I desire besides thee.*
26 My flesh and my heart faileth:
   But *God* is *the strength of my heart, and my portion for ever.*
27 For, lo, they that are far from thee shall perish:
   . *Thou hast destroyed all them that go a whoring from thee.*
28 But *it is* good for me to draw near to God:
   { *I have put my trust in the Lord GOD,*
   { *That I may declare all thy works.*

LESSON 47.

PSALM LXXIV.

Maschil of Asaph.

O GOD, why hast thou cast *us* off for ever?
   Why *doth thine anger smoke against the sheep of thy pasture?*
2 { Remember thy congregation, *which* thou hast purchased of old;
   { The rod of thine inheritance, *which* thou hast redeemed;
   This mount Zion, wherein thou hast dwelt.
3 Lift up thy feet unto the perpetual desolations;
   Even *all* that *the enemy hath done wickedly in the sanctuary.*
4 Thine enemies roar in the midst of thy congregations;
   They set up their ensigns for signs.
5 { *A man* was famous according as he had lifted up
   { Axes upon the thick trees.
6 { *But now they break down the carved work thereof at once*
   { *With axes and hammers.*
7 They have cast fire into thy sanctuary,
   They have defiled by casting down *the dwellingplace of thy name to the ground.*
8 They said in their hearts, Let us destroy them together:
   They have burned up all the synagogues of God in the land.

LESSON 47.

9 { We see not our signs:
{ There is no more any prophet:
    Neither is there *among us any that knoweth how long.*
10 O God, how long shall the adversary reproach?
    Shall the enemy blaspheme thy name for ever?
11 Why withdrawest thou thy hand, even thy right hand?
    Pluck it *out of thy bosom.*
12 For God *is* my King of old,
    Working salvation in the midst of the earth.
13 Thou didst divide the sea by thy strength:
    Thou brakest the heads of the dragons in the waters.
14 Thou brakest the heads of leviathan in pieces,
    And *gavest him* to be *meat to the people inhabiting the wilderness.*
15 Thou didst cleave the fountain and the flood:
    Thou driedst up mighty rivers.
16 The day *is* thine, the night also *is* thine:
    Thou hast prepared the light and the sun.
17 Thou hast set all the borders of the earth:
    Thou hast made summer and winter.
18 Remember this, *that* the enemy hath reproached, O LORD,
    And that *the foolish people have blasphemed thy name.*
19 Oh deliver not the soul of thy turtledove unto the multitude *of the wicked:*
    Forget not the congregation of thy poor for ever.
20 Have respect unto the covenant:
    For the dark places of the earth are full of the habitations of cruelty.
21 Oh let not the oppressed return ashamed:
    Let the poor and needy praise thy name.
22 Arise, O God, plead thine own cause:
    Remember how the foolish man reproacheth thee daily.
23 Forget not the voice of thine enemies:
    The tumult of those that rise up against thee increaseth continually.

LESSON 48.

PSALM LXXV.

To the chief Musician, Al-taschith, A Psalm or Song of Asaph.

UNTO thee, O God, do we give thanks, *unto thee* do we give thanks:
  For that thy name is near
  Thy wondrous works declare.
2 When I shall receive the congregation
  I will judge uprightly.
3 The earth and all the inhabitants thereof are dissolved:
  I bear up the pillars of it. (Selah.)
4 I said unto the fools, Deal not foolishly:
  And to the wicked, Lift not up the horn:
5 Lift not up your horn on high:
  Speak not with a stiff neck.
6 For promotion *cometh* neither from the east,
  Nor from the west, nor from the south.
7 But God *is* the judge:
  He putteth down one, and setteth up another.
8 For in the hand of the LORD *there is* a cup,
  And the wine is red; it is full of mixture;
And he poureth out of the same: but the dregs thereof,
  All the wicked of the earth shall wring them *out,* and *drink* them.
9 But I will declare for ever;
  I will sing praises to the God of Jacob.
10 All the horns of the wicked also will I cut off;
  But the horns of the righteous shall be exalted.

PSALM LXXVI.

To the chief Musician on Neginoth, A Psalm or Song of Asaph,

IN Judah *is* God known:
  His name is great in Israel.
2 In Salem also is his tabernacle,
  And his dwellingplace in Zion.
3 There brake he the arrows of the bow,
  The shield, and the sword, and the battle. (Selah.)

4 { Thou *art* more glorious *and* excellent than the mountains of prey.
5 { The stouthearted are spoiled,
  { *They have slept their sleep:*
  { *And none of the men of might have found their hands.*
6 At thy rebuke, O God of Jacob,
  Both the chariot and horse are cast into a dead sleep.
7 Thou, *even* thou, *art* to be feared:
  And who may stand in thy sight when once thou art angry?
8 Thou didst cause judgment to be heard from heaven;
  The earth feared, and was still,
9 When God arose to judgment,
  To save all the meek of the earth. (*Selah.*)
10 Surely the wrath of man shall praise thee:
  The remainder of wrath shalt thou restrain.
11 Vow, and pay unto the LORD your God:
  Let all that be round about him bring presents unto him that ought to be feared.
12 He shall cut off the spirit of princes:
  He is *terrible to the kings of the earth.*

LESSON 49.

PSALM LXXVII.

To the chief Musician, to Jeduthun, A Psalm of Asaph.

I CRIED unto God with my voice,
  Even *unto God with my voice; and he gave ear unto me.*
2 { In the day of my trouble I sought the Lord:
  { My sore ran in the night, and ceased not:
    My soul refused to be comforted.
3 I remembered God, and was troubled:
  I complained, and my spirit was overwhelmed. (*Selah.*)
4 Thou holdest mine eyes waking:
  I am so troubled that I cannot speak.
5 I have considered the days of old,
  The years of ancient times.
6 I call to remembrance my song in the night:
  I commune with mine own heart: and my spirit made diligent search.

7 Will the Lord cast off for ever?
   And will he be favourable no more?
8 Is his mercy clean gone for ever?
   Doth his *promise fail for evermore?*
9 Hath God forgotten to be gracious?
   Hath he in anger shut up his tender mercies?   (*Selah.*)
10 And I said, This *is* my infirmity:
   But I will remember *the years of the right hand of the Most High.*
11 I will remember the works of the LORD:
   Surely I will remember thy wonders of old.
12 I will meditate also of all thy work,
   And talk of thy doings.
13 Thy way, O God, *is* in the sanctuary:
   Who is so *great a God as* our *God!*
14 Thou *art* the God that doest wonders:
   Thou hast declared thy strength among the people.
15 Thou hast with *thine* arm redeemed thy people,
   The sons of Jacob and Joseph.   (*Selah.*)
16 { The waters saw thee, O God,
   { The waters saw thee; they were afraid:
   The depths also were troubled.
17 { The clouds poured out water:
   { The skies sent out a sound:
   Thine arrows also went abroad.
18 { The voice of thy thunder *was* in the heaven:
   { The lightnings lightened the world:
   The earth trembled and shook.
19 { Thy way *is* in the sea,
   { And thy path in the great waters,
   And thy footsteps are not known.
20 Thou leddest thy people like a flock,
   By the hand of Moses and Aaron.

LESSON 50.

PSALM LXXVIII, FIRST PART.

Maschil of Asaph.

GIVE ear, O my people, *to* my law :
 Incline your ears to the words of my mouth.
2 I will open my mouth in a parable :
 I will utter dark sayings of old :
3 Which we have heard and known,
 And our fathers have told us.
4 { We will not hide *them* from their children,
 { Shewing to the generation to come the praises of the LORD,
 And his strength and his wonderful works that he hath done.
5 { For he established a testimony in Jacob,
 { And appointed a law in Israel,
 { *Which he commanded our fathers,*
 { *That they should make them known to their children :*
6 That the generation to come might know *them, even* the children
 which should be born ;
 Who *should arise and declare* them *to their children* :
7 That they might set their hope in God,
 { *And not forget the works of God,*
 { *But keep his commandments :*
8 And might not be as their fathers, a stubborn and rebellious generation ;
 { *A generation* that *set not their hearts aright,*
 { *And whose spirit was not steadfast with God.*
9 The children of Ephraim, *being* armed, *and* carrying bows,
 Turned back in the day of battle.
10 They kept not the covenant of God,
 And refused to walk in his law ;
11 And forgat his works,
 And his wonders that he had shewed them.
12 Marvellous things did he in the sight of their fathers,
 In the land of Egypt, in *the field of Zoan.*
13 He divided the sea, and caused them to pass through ;
 And he made the waters to stand as a heap.

14 In the daytime also he led them with a cloud,
   And all the night with a light of fire.
15 He clave the rocks in the wilderness,
   And gave them drink as out of the great depths.
16 He brought streams also out of the rock,
   And caused water to run down like rivers.
17 And they sinned yet more against him
   By provoking the Most High in the wilderness.
18 And they tempted God in their heart
   By asking meat for their lust.
19 Yea, they spake against God;
   They said, Can God furnish a table in the wilderness?
20 { Behold, he smote the rock, that the waters gushed out,
   And the streams overflowed;
     { Can he give bread also?
     { Can he provide flesh for his people?
21 Therefore the LORD heard this, and was wroth:
     { So a fire was kindled against Jacob,
     { And anger also came up against Israel;
22 Because they believed not in God,
   And trusted not in his salvation:
23 Though he had commanded the clouds from above,
   And opened the doors of heaven,
24 And had rained down manna upon them to eat,
   And had given them of the corn of heaven.
25 Man did eat angels' food:
   He sent them meat to the full.
26 He caused an east wind to blow in the heaven:
   And by his power he brought in the south wind.
27 He rained flesh also upon them as dust,
   And feathered fowls like as the sands of the sea:
28 And he let it fall in the midst of their camp,
   Round about their habitations.
29 So they did eat, and were well filled:
   For he gave them their own desire;
30 They were not estranged from their lust:
   But while their meat was yet in their mouths,

31 { The wrath of God came upon them,
  And slew the fattest of them,
   And smote down the chosen men *of Israel.*
32 For all this they sinned still,
   And believed not for his wondrous works.
33 Therefore their days did he consume in vanity,
   And their years in trouble.
34 When he slew them, then they sought him:
   And they returned and inquired early after God.

LESSON 51.

Psalm lxxviii, Second Part.

35 And they remembered that God *was* their rock,
   And the high God their redeemer.
36 Nevertheless they did flatter him with their mouth,
   And they lied unto him with their tongues.
37 For their heart was not right with him,
   Neither were they steadfast in his covenant.
38 { But he, *being* full of compassion,
   Forgave *their* iniquity, and destroyed *them* not:
   { *Yea, many a time turned he his anger away,*
    And did not stir up all his wrath.
39 For he remembered that they *were but* flesh;
   A wind that passeth away, and cometh not again.
40 How oft did they provoke him in the wilderness,
   And *grieve him in the desert!*
41 Yea, they turned back and tempted God,
   And limited the Holy One of Israel.
42 They remembered not his hand,
   Nor *the day when he delivered them from the enemy:*
43 How he had wrought his signs in Egypt,
   And his wonders in the field of Zoan:
44 And had turned their rivers into blood;
   And their floods, that they could not drink.
45 He sent divers sorts of flies among them, which devoured them;
   And frogs, which destroyed them.

46 He gave also their increase unto the caterpillar,
 And their labour unto the locust.
47 He destroyed their vines with hail,
 And their sycamore trees with frost.
48 He gave up their cattle also to the hail,
 And their flocks to hot thunderbolts.
49 He cast upon them the fierceness of his anger,
 { *Wrath, and indignation, and trouble,*
 { *By sending evil angels* among them.
50 He made a way to his anger;
 { *He spared not their soul from death,*
 { *But gave their life over to the pestilence;*
51 And smote all the firstborn in Egypt;
 The chief of their *strength in the tabernacles of Ham:*
52 But made his own people to go forth like sheep,
 And guided them in the wilderness like a flock.
53 And he led them on safely, so that they feared not:
 But the sea overwhelmed their enemies.
54 And he brought them to the border of his sanctuary,
 Even to *this mountain,* which *his right hand had purchased.*
55 { He cast out the heathen also before them,
 { And divided them an inheritance by line,
 And made the tribes of Israel to dwell in their tents.
56 Yet they tempted and provoked the most high God,
 And kept not his testimonies:
57 But turned back, and dealt unfaithfully like their fathers:
 They were turned aside like a deceitful bow.
58 For they provoked him to anger with their high places,
 And moved him to jealousy with their graven images.
59 When God heard *this,* he was wroth,
 And greatly abhorred Israel:
60 So that he forsook the tabernacle of Shiloh,
 The tent which *he placed among men;*
61 And delivered his strength into captivity,
 And his glory into the enemy's hands.
62 He gave his people over also unto the sword;
 And was wroth with his inheritance.

63 The fire consumed their young men;
  And their maidens were not given to marriage.
64 Their priests fell by the sword;
  And their widows made no lamentation.
65 Then the Lord awaked as one out of sleep,
  And *like a mighty man that shouteth by reason of wine.*
66 And he smote his enemies in the hinder parts:
  He put them to a perpetual reproach.
67 Moreover he refused the tabernacle of Joseph,
  And chose not the tribe of Ephraim:
68 But chose the tribe of Judah,
  The mount Zion which he loved.
69 And he built his sanctuary like high *palaces,*
  Like the earth which he hath established forever.
70 He chose David also his servant,
  And took him from the sheepfolds:
71 From following the ewes great with young
  { *He brought him to feed Jacob his people,*
  { *And Israel his inheritance.*
72 So he fed them according to the integrity of his heart;
  And guided them by the skilfulness of his hands.

LESSON 52.

PSALM LXXIX.

A Psalm of Asaph.

{ O GOD, the heathen are come into thine inheritance;
  Thy holy temple have they defiled;
  They have laid Jerusalem on heaps.
2 The dead bodies of thy servants have they given *to be* meat unto the fowls of the heaven,
  The flesh of thy saints unto the beasts of the earth.
3 Their blood have they shed like water
  Round about Jerusalem; and there was *none to bury* them.
4 We are become a reproach to our neighbours,
  A scorn and derision to them that are round about us.
5 How long, LORD? wilt thou be angry for ever?
  Shall thy jealousy burn like fire?

6 Pour out thy wrath upon the heathen that have not known thee,
　　And upon the kingdoms that have not called upon thy name.
7 For they have devoured Jacob,
　　And laid waste his dwellingplace.
8 { Oh remember not against us former iniquities:
　　Let thy tender mercies speedily prevent us;
　　　For we are brought very low.
9 Help us, O God of our salvation, for the glory of thy name:
　　And deliver us, and purge away our sins, for thy name's sake.
10 Wherefore should the heathen say, Where is their God?
　　{ Let him be known among the heathen in our sight
　　By the revenging of the blood of thy servants which is shed.
11 Let the sighing of the prisoner come before thee;
　　According to the greatness of thy power preserve thou those that are appointed to die;
12 And render unto our neighbours sevenfold into their bosom
　　Their reproach, wherewith they have reproached thee, O Lord.
13 { So we thy people and sheep of thy pasture
　　Will give thee thanks for ever:
　　　We will shew forth thy praise to all generations.

Psalm LXXX.

To the chief Musician upon Shoshannim-Eduth, A Psalm of Asaph.

{ GIVE ear, O Shepherd of Israel,
　Thou that leadest Joseph like a flock;
　　Thou that dwellest between *the cherubim, shine forth.*
2 { Before Ephraim and Benjamin and Manasseh
　Stir up thy strength,
　　And come and *save us.*
3 Turn us again, O God,
　　And cause thy face to shine; and we shall be saved.
4 O Lord God of hosts,
　　How long wilt thou be angry against the prayer of thy people?
5 Thou feedest them with the bread of tears;
　　And givest them tears to drink in great measure.
6 Thou makest us a strife unto our neighbours:
　　And our enemies laugh among themselves.

7 Turn us again, O God of hosts,
   And cause thy face to shine ; and we shall be saved.
8 Thou hast brought a vine out of Egypt :
   Thou hast cast out the heathen, and planted it.
9 Thou preparedst *room* before it,
   And didst cause it to take deep root, and it filled the land.
10 The hills were covered with the shadow of it,
   And the boughs thereof were like *the goodly cedars.*
11 She sent out her boughs unto the sea,
   And her branches unto the river.
12 Why hast thou *then* broken down her hedges,
   So that all they which pass by the way do pluck her ?
13 The boar out of the wood doth waste it,
   And the wild beast of the field doth devour it.
14 Return, we beseech thee, O God of hosts :
   Look down from heaven, and behold, and visit this vine ;
15 And the vineyard which thy right hand hath planted,
   And the branch that *thou madest strong for thyself.*
16 *It is* burned with fire, *it is* cut down :
   They perish at the rebuke of thy countenance.
17 Let thy hand be upon the man of thy right hand,
   Upon the son of man whom *thou madest strong for thyself.*
18 So will not we go back from thee :
   Quicken us, and we will call upon thy name.
19 Turn us again, O LORD God of hosts,
   Cause thy face to shine ; and we shall be saved.

LESSON 53.

PSALM LXXXI.

To the chief Musician upon Gittith, A *Psalm* of Asaph.

SING aloud unto God our strength :
   Make a joyful noise unto the God of Jacob.
2 Take a psalm, and bring hither the timbrel,
   The pleasant harp with the psaltery.
3 Blow up the trumpet in the new moon,
   In the time appointed, on our solemn feast day.
4 For this *was* a statute for Israel,
   And a law of the God of Jacob.

5 { This he ordained in Joseph *for* a testimony,
{ When he went out through the land of Egypt:
    Where *I heard a language that I understood not.*
6 I removed his shoulder from the burden:
    His hands were delivered from the pots.
7 { Thou calledst in trouble, and I delivered thee;
{ I answered thee in the secret place of thunder:
    I proved thee at the waters of Meribah. (*Selah.*)
8 Hear, O my people, and I will testify unto thee:
    O Israel, if thou wilt hearken unto me;
9 There shall no strange god be in thee;
    Neither shalt thou worship any strange god.
10 { I *am* the LORD thy God,
{ Which brought thee out of the land of Egypt:
    Open thy mouth wide, and I will fill it.
11 But my people would not hearken to my voice;
    And Israel would none of me.
12 So I gave them up unto their own hearts' lust:
    And *they walked in their own counsels.*
13 Oh that my people had hearkened unto me,
    And *Israel had walked in my ways!*
14 I should soon have subdued their enemies,
    And turned my hand against their adversaries.
15 The haters of the LORD should have submitted themselves unto him:
    But their time should have endured for ever.
16 He should have fed them also with the finest of the wheat:
    And with honey out of the rock should I have satisfied thee.

LESSON 54.

PSALM LXXXII.

A Psalm of Asaph.

GOD standeth in the congregation of the mighty;
    He judgeth among the gods.
2 How long will ye judge unjustly,
    And *accept the persons of the wicked?* (*Selah.*)
3 Defend the poor and fatherless:
    Do justice to the afflicted and needy.

4 Deliver the poor and needy:
  Rid them *out of the hand of the wicked.*
5 { They know not, neither will they understand;
  { They walk on in darkness:
  All the foundations of the earth are out of course.
6 I have said, Ye *are* gods;
  And all of you are *children of the Most High.*
7 But ye shall die like men,
  And fall like one of the princes.
8 Arise, O God, judge the earth:
  For thou shalt inherit all nations.

PSALM LXXXIII.

A Song or Psalm of Asaph.

KEEP not thou silence, O God:
  Hold not thy peace, and be not still, O God.
2 For, lo, thine enemies make a tumult:
  And they that hate thee have lifted up the head.
3 They have taken crafty counsel against thy people,
  And consulted against thy hidden ones.
4 They have said, Come, and let us cut them off from *being* a nation;
  That the name of Israel may be no more in remembrance.
5 For they have consulted together with one consent:
  They are confederate against thee.
6 The tabernacles of Edom, and the Ishmaelites;
  Of Moab, and the Hagarenes;
7 Gebal, and Ammon, and Amalek;
  The Philistines with the inhabitants of Tyre;
8 Assur also is joined with them:
  They have holpen the children of Lot. (*Selah.*)
9 Do unto them as *unto* the Midianites;
  As to *Sisera, as* to *Jabin, at the brook of Kishon:*
10 *Which* perished at En-dor:
  They became as dung for the earth.
11 Make their nobles like Oreb, and like Zeeb:
  Yea, all their princes as Zebah, and as Zalmunna:
12 Who said,
  Let us take to ourselves the houses of God in possession.

13 O my God, make them like a wheel;
   As the stubble before the wind.
14 As the fire burneth a wood,
   And as the flame setteth the mountains on fire;
15 So persecute them with thy tempest,
   And make them afraid with thy storm.
16 Fill their faces with shame;
   That they may seek thy name, O LORD.
17 Let them be confounded and troubled for ever;
   Yea, let them be put to shame, and perish:
18 That *men* may know that thou, whose name alone *is* JEHOVAH,
   Art *the most high over all the earth.*

LESSON 55.

PSALM LXXXIV.

To the chief Musician upon Gittith, A Psalm for the sons of Korah.

HOW amiable *are* thy tabernacles,
   O LORD *of hosts!*
2 { My soul longeth, yea, even fainteth
   { For the courts of the LORD:
   My heart and my flesh crieth out for the living God.
3 { Yea, the sparrow hath found a house,
   { And the swallow a nest for herself, where she may lay her young,
     { Even *thine altars, O LORD of hosts,*
     { *My King and my God.*
4 Blessed *are* they that dwell in thy house:
   They will be still praising thee. (Selah.)
5 Blessed *is* the man whose strength *is* in thee;
   In whose heart are the ways of them.
6 { *Who* passing through the valley of Baca
   { Make it a well;
   The rain also filleth the pools.
7 They go from strength to strength,
   Every one of them in Zion appeareth before God.
8 { O LORD God of hosts,
   { Hear my prayer:
     Give ear, O God of Jacob. (Selah.)

9 Behold, O God our shield,
 And look upon the face of thine anointed.
10 For a day in thy courts *is* better than a thousand.
 { *I had rather be a doorkeeper in the house of my God,*
 Than to dwell in the tents of wickedness.
11 { For the LORD God *is* a sun and shield:
 { The LORD will give grace and glory:
 No good thing will he withhold from them that walk uprightly.
12 O LORD of hosts,
 Blessed is *the man that trusteth in thee.*

PSALM LXXXV.
To the chief Musician, A Psalm for the sons of Korah.

LORD, thou hast been favourable unto thy land:
 Thou hast brought back the captivity of Jacob.
2 Thou hast forgiven the iniquity of thy people;
 Thou hast covered all their sin. (Selah.)
3 Thou hast taken away all thy wrath:
 Thou hast turned thyself *from the fierceness of thine anger.*
4 Turn us, O God of our salvation,
 And cause thine anger toward us to cease.
5 Wilt thou be angry with us for ever?
 Wilt thou draw out thine anger to all generations?
6 Wilt thou not revive us again:
 That thy people may rejoice in thee?
7 Shew us thy mercy, O LORD,
 And grant us thy salvation.
8 { I will hear what God the LORD will speak:
 { For he will speak peace unto his people, and to his saints:
 But let them not turn again to folly.
9 Surely his salvation *is* nigh them that fear him;
 That glory may dwell in our land.
10 Mercy and truth are met together;
 Righteousness and peace have kissed each other.
11 Truth shall spring out of the earth;
 And righteousness shall look down from heaven.
12 Yea, the LORD shall give *that which is* good;
 And our land shall yield her increase.

13 Righteousness shall go before him;
  And shall set us *in the way of his steps.*

LESSON 56.

PSALM LXXXVI.

A Prayer of David.

BOW down thine ear, O LORD, hear me:
  For I am *poor and needy.*
2 Preserve my soul; for I *am* holy:
  { *O thou my God, save thy servant*
  { *That trusteth in thee.*
3 Be merciful unto me, O Lord:
  For I cry unto thee daily.
4 Rejoice the soul of thy servant:
  For unto thee, O Lord, do I lift up my soul.
5 For thou, Lord, *art* good, and ready to forgive;
  And plenteous in mercy unto all them that call upon thee.
6 Give ear, O LORD, unto my prayer;
  And attend to the voice of my supplications.
7 In the day of my trouble I will call upon thee:
  For thou wilt answer me.
8 Among the Gods *there is* none like unto thee, O Lord;
  Neither are there any works *like unto thy works.*
9 All nations whom thou hast made shall come and worship before thee, O Lord;
  And shall glorify thy name.
10 For thou *art* great, and doest wondrous things:
  Thou art *God alone.*
11 { Teach me thy way, O LORD;
   { I will walk in thy truth:
  Unite my heart to fear thy name.
12 I will praise thee, O Lord my God, with all my heart:
  And I will glorify thy name for evermore.
13 For great *is* thy mercy toward me:
  And thou hast delivered my soul from the lowest hell.
14 { O God, the proud are risen against me,
   { And the assemblies of violent *men* have sought after my soul;
  And have not set thee before them.

15 But thou, O Lord, *art* a God full of compassion, and gracious,
    Longsuffering, and plenteous in mercy and truth.
16 Oh turn unto me, and have mercy upon me;
    { *Give thy strength unto thy servant,*
    { *And save the son of thine handmaid.*
17 { Shew me a token for good;
    { That they which hate me may see *it*, and be ashamed:
    Because thou, LORD, hast holpen me, and comforted me.

Psalm LXXXVII.

A Psalm or Song for the sons of Korah.

{ HIS foundation *is* in the holy mountains.
{   2 The LORD loveth the gates of Zion
    More than all the dwellings of Jacob.
3 Glorious things are spoken of thee,
    O city of God. (Selah.)
4 I will make mention of Rahab and Babylon to them that know me:
    { *Behold Philistia, and Tyre, with Ethiopia;*
    { *This man was born there.*
5 { And of Zion it shall be said,
    { This and that man was born in her:
    And the Highest himself shall establish her.
6 The LORD shall count, when he writeth up the people,
    That *this* man *was born there. (Selah.)*
7 As well the singers as the players on instruments *shall be there:*
    All my springs are in thee.

LESSON 57.

Psalm LXXXVIII.

A Song or Psalm for the sons of Korah, to the chief Musician upon Mahalath Leannoth, Maschil of Heman the Ezrahite.

O LORD God of my salvation,
    I have cried day and night before thee:
2 Let my prayer come before thee:
    Incline thine ear unto my cry;
3 For my soul is full of troubles:
    And my life draweth nigh unto the grave.

4 I am counted with them that go down into the pit:
    I am as a man that hath no strength:
5 { Free among the dead,
   { Like the slain that lie in the grave,
    { *Whom thou rememberest no more:*
    { *And they are cut off from thy hand.*
6 Thou hast laid me in the lowest pit,
    In darkness, in the deeps.
7 Thy wrath lieth hard upon me,
    And thou hast afflicted me *with all thy waves.* (*Selah.*)
8 { Thou hast put away mine acquaintance far from me;
   { Thou hast made me an abomination unto them:
    I am *shut up, and I cannot come forth.*
9 Mine eye mourneth by reason of affliction:
    { *LORD, I have called daily upon thee,*
    { *I have stretched out my hands unto thee.*
10 Wilt thou shew wonders to the dead?
    Shall the dead arise and *praise thee?* (*Selah.*)
11 Shall thy lovingkindness be declared in the grave?
    Or *thy faithfulness in destruction?*
12 Shall thy wonders be known in the dark?
    And thy righteousness in the land of forgetfulness?
13 But unto thee have I cried, O Lord;
    And in the morning shall my prayer prevent thee.
14 Lord, why castest thou off my soul?
    Why hidest thou thy face from me?
15 I *am* afflicted and ready to die from *my* youth up:
    While *I suffer thy terrors I am distracted.*
16 Thy fierce wrath goeth over me;
    Thy terrors have cut me off.
17 They came round about me daily like water;
    They compassed me about together.
18 Lover and friend hast thou put far from me,
    And *mine acquaintance into darkness.*

LESSON 58.

PSALM LXXXIX, FIRST PART.

Maschil of Ethan the Ezrahite.

I WILL sing of the mercies of the LORD for ever:
With my mouth will I make known thy faithfulness to all generations.
2 For I have said, Mercy shall be built up for ever:
Thy faithfulness shalt thou establish in the very heavens.
3 I have made a covenant with my chosen,
I have sworn unto David my servant,
4 Thy seed will I establish for ever,
And build up thy throne to all generations. (Selah.)
5 And the heavens shall praise thy wonders, O LORD:
Thy faithfulness also in the congregation of the saints.
6 For who in the heaven can be compared unto the LORD?
Who among the sons of the mighty can be likened unto the LORD?
7 God is greatly to be feared in the assembly of the saints,
And to be had in reverence of all them that are about him.
8 O LORD God of hosts, who *is* a strong LORD like unto thee?
Or to thy faithfulness round about thee?
9 Thou rulest the raging of the sea:
When the waves thereof arise, thou stillest them.
10 Thou hast broken Rahab in pieces, as one that is slain;
Thou hast scattered thine enemies with thy strong arm.
11 The heavens *are* thine, the earth also *is* thine:
As for the world and the fulness thereof, thou hast founded them.
12 The north and the south thou hast created them:
Tabor and Hermon shall rejoice in thy name.
13 Thou hast a mighty arm:
Strong is thy hand, and *high is thy right hand.*
14 Justice and judgment *are* the habitation of thy throne:
Mercy and truth shall go before thy face.
15 Blessed *is* the people that know the joyful sound:
They shall walk, O LORD, in the light of thy countenance.
16 In thy name shall they rejoice all the day:
And in thy righteousness shall they be exalted.
17 For thou *art* the glory of their strength:
And in thy favour our horn shall be exalted.

18 For the Lord *is* our defence;
    And the Holy One of Israel is our king.
19 ⎰ Then thou spakest in vision to thy holy one, and saidst,
   ⎱ I have laid help upon one *that is* mighty;
    I have exalted one *chosen out of the people.*
20 I have found David my servant;
    With my holy oil have I anointed him:
21 With whom my hand shall be established:
    Mine arm also shall strengthen him.
22 The enemy shall not exact upon him:
    Nor the son of wickedness afflict him.
23 And I will beat down his foes before his face,
    And plague them that hate him.
24 But my faithfulness and my mercy *shall be* with him:
    And in my name shall his horn be exalted.
25 I will set his hand also in the sea,
    And his right hand in the rivers.
26 He shall cry unto me, Thou *art* my father,
    My God, and the rock of my salvation.
27 Also I will make him *my* firstborn,
    Higher than the kings of the earth.
28 My mercy will I keep for him for evermore,
    And my covenant shall stand fast with him.
29 His seed also will I make *to endure* for ever,
    And his throne as the days of heaven.
30 If his children forsake my law,
    And walk not in my judgments;
31 If they break my statutes,
    And keep not my commandments;
32 Then will I visit their transgression with the rod,
    And their iniquity with stripes.
33 Nevertheless my lovingkindness will I not utterly take from him,
    Nor suffer my faithfulness to fail.

LESSON 59.

Psalm lxxxix, Second Part.

MY covenant will I not break,
    Nor alter the thing that is *gone out of my lips.*

35 Once have I sworn by my holiness
   That I will not lie unto David.
36 His seed shall endure for ever,
   And his throne as the sun before me.
37 It shall be established for ever as the moon,
   And as a faithful witness in heaven. (*Selah.*)
38 But thou hast cast off and abhorred,
   Thou hast been wroth with thine anointed.
39 Thou hast made void the covenant of thy servant:
   Thou hast profaned his crown by casting it to the ground.
40 Thou hast broken down all his hedges;
   Thou hast brought his strong holds to ruin.
41 All that pass by the way spoil him:
   He is a reproach to his neighbours.
42 Thou hast set up the right hand of his adversaries;
   Thou hast made all his enemies to rejoice.
43 Thou hast also turned the edge of his sword,
   And hast not made him to stand in the battle.
44 Thou hast made his glory to cease,
   And cast his throne down to the ground.
45 The days of his youth hast thou shortened:
   Thou hast covered him with shame. (*Selah.*)
46 How long, LORD? wilt thou hide thyself for ever?
   Shall thy wrath burn like fire?
47 Remember how short my time is:
   Wherefore hast thou made all men in vain?
48 What man *is he that* liveth, and shall not see death?
   Shall he deliver his soul from the hand of the grave. (*Selah.*)
49 Lord, where *are* thy former lovingkindnesses,
   Which thou swarest unto David in thy truth?
50 Remember, Lord, the reproach of thy servants;
   How I do bear in my bosom the reproach of *all the mighty people;*
51 Wherewith thine enemies have reproached, O LORD;
   Wherewith they have reproached the footsteps of thine anointed.
52 Blessed *be* the LORD for evermore.
   Amen, and Amen.

LESSON 60.

PSALM XC.

A Prayer of Moses the man of God.

LORD, thou hast been our dwellingplace
   In all generations.
2 { Before the mountains were brought forth,
   { Or ever thou hadst formed the earth and the world,
   Even from everlasting to everlasting, thou art God.
3 Thou turnest man to destruction;
   And sayest, Return, ye children of men.
4 { For a thousand years in thy sight
   { *Are but* as yesterday when it is past,
   And as a watch in the night.
5 Thou carriest them away as with a flood; they are *as a* sleep;
   In the morning they are like grass which groweth up;
6 In the morning it flourisheth, and groweth up;
   In the evening it is cut down, and withereth.
7 For we are consumed by thine anger,
   And by thy wrath are we troubled.
8 Thou hast set our iniquities before thee,
   Our secret sins *in the light of thy countenance.*
9 For all our days are passed away in thy wrath :
   We spend our years as a tale that is told.
10 The days of our years *are* threescore years and ten;
   And if by reason of strength they be *fourscore years,*
   Yet *is* their strength labour and sorrow;
   For it is soon cut off, and we fly away.
11 Who knoweth the power of thine anger?
   Even according to thy fear, so is *thy wrath.*
12 So teach *us* to number our days,
   That we may apply our *hearts unto wisdom.*
13 Return, O LORD, how long?
   And let it repent thee concerning thy servants.
14 O satisfy us early with thy mercy;
   That we may rejoice and be glad all our days.
15 Make us glad according to the days *wherein* thou hast afflicted us,
   And *the years* wherein *we have seen evil.*

16 Let thy work appear unto thy servants,
   And thy glory unto their children.
17 ⎰ And let the beauty of the LORD our God be upon us:
   ⎱ And establish thou the work of our hands upon us;
   Yea, the work of our hands establish thou it.

LESSON 61.

PSALM XCI.

H E that dwelleth in the secret place of the Most High
   Shall abide under the shadow of the Almighty.
2 I will say of the LORD, *He is* my refuge and my fortress:
   My God; in him will I trust.
3 Surely he shall deliver thee from the snare of the fowler,
   And from the noisome pestilence.
4 ⎰ He shall cover thee with his feathers,
   ⎱ And under his wings shalt thou trust:
   His truth shall be thy shield and buckler.
5 Thou shalt not be afraid for the terror by night;
   Nor for the arrow that flieth by day;
6 *Nor* for the pestilence *that* walketh in darkness;
   Nor for the destruction that wasteth at noonday.
7 A thousand shall fall at thy side, and ten thousand at thy right hand;
   But it shall not come nigh thee.
8 Only with thine eyes shalt thou behold
   And see the reward of the wicked.
9 Because thou hast made the LORD, *which is* my refuge,
   Even the Most High, thy habitation;
10 There shall no evil befall thee,
   Neither shall any plague come nigh thy dwelling.
11 For he shall give his angels charge over thee,
   To keep thee in all thy ways.
12 They shall bear thee up in *their* hands,
   Lest thou dash thy foot against a stone.
13 Thou shalt tread upon the lion and adder:
   The young lion and the dragon shalt thou trample under feet.

14 Because he hath set his love upon me, therefore will I deliver him :
    I will set him on high, because he hath known my name.
15 { He shall call upon me, and I will answer him :
   { *I will be* with him in trouble;
    I will deliver him, and honour him.
16 With long life will I satisfy him,
    And shew him my salvation.

LESSON 62.

Psalm XCII.

A Psalm or Song for the sabbath day.

*I*T *is a good thing* to give thanks unto the LORD,
    And to sing praises unto thy name, O Most High.
2 To shew forth thy lovingkindness in the morning,
    And thy faithfulness every night.
3 Upon an instrument of ten strings, and upon the psaltery;
    Upon the harp with a solemn sound.
4 For thou, LORD, hast made me glad through thy work :
    I will triumph in the works of thy hands.
5 O LORD, how great are thy works!
    And thy thoughts are very deep.
6 A brutish man knoweth not;
    Neither doth a fool understand this.
7 { When the wicked spring as the grass,
   { And when all the workers of iniquity do flourish ;
    It is *that they shall be destroyed for ever :*
8 { But thou, LORD, *art most* high for evermore.
9 { For, lo, thine enemies, O LORD,
   { *For, lo, thine enemies shall perish ;*
   { *All the workers of iniquity shall be scattered.*
10 But my horn shalt thou exalt like *the horn of* a unicorn :
    I shall be anointed with fresh oil.
11 Mine eye also shall see *my desire* on mine enemies,
    And *mine ears shall hear* my desire *of the wicked that rise up against me.*

12 The righteous shall flourish like the palm tree :
  He shall grow like a cedar in Lebanon.
13 Those that be planted in the house of the LORD
  Shall flourish in the courts of our God.
14 They shall still bring forth fruit in old age ;
  They shall be fat and flourishing ;
15 To show that the LORD *is* upright :
  He is *my rock, and* there is *no unrighteousness in him.*

PSALM XCIII.

THE LORD reigneth, he is clothed with majesty ;
The LORD is clothed with strength, *wherewith* he hath girded himself :
  The world also is stablished, that it cannot be moved.
2 Thy throne *is* established of old :
  Thou art from everlasting.
3 The floods have lifted up, O LORD,
  The floods have lifted up their voice.
  The floods lift up their waves.
4 The LORD on high *is* mightier than the noise of many waters,
  Yea, than *the mighty waves of the sea.*
5 Thy testimonies are very sure :
  Holiness becometh thine house,
  O LORD, for ever.

LESSON 63.

PSALM XCIV.

O LORD God, to whom vengeance belongeth ;
  O God, to whom vengeance belongeth, shew thyself.
2 Lift up thyself, thou judge of the earth :
  Render a reward to the proud.
3 LORD, how long shall the wicked,
  How long shall the wicked triumph ?
4 *How long* shall they utter *and* speak hard things ?
  And *all the workers of iniquity boast themselves.*
5 They break in pieces thy people, O LORD,
  And afflict thine heritage.

6 They slay the widow and the stranger,
   And murder the fatherless.
7 Yet they say, The LORD shall not see,
   Neither shall the God of Jacob regard it.
8 Understand, ye brutish among the people:
   And ye fools, when will ye be wise?
9 He that planted the ear, shall he not hear?
   He that formed the eye, shall he not see?
10 He that chastiseth the heathen, shall not he correct?
   He that teacheth man knowledge, shall not he know?
11 The LORD knoweth the thoughts of man,
   That they are vanity.
12 Blessed *is* the man whom thou chastenest, O LORD,
   And teachest him out of thy law;
13 That thou mayest give him rest from the days of adversity,
   Until the pit be digged for the wicked.
14 For the Lord will not cast off his people,
   Neither will he forsake his inheritance.
15 But judgment shall return unto righteousness:
   And all the upright in heart shall follow it.
16 Who will rise up for me against the evil doers?
   Or who will stand up for me against the workers of iniquity?
17 Unless the LORD *had been* my help,
   My soul had almost dwelt in silence.
18 When I said, My foot slippeth;
   Thy mercy, O LORD, held me up.
19 In the multitude of my thoughts within me
   Thy comforts delight my soul.
20 Shall the throne of iniquity have fellowship with thee,
   Which frameth mischief by a law?
21 They gather themselves together against the soul of the righteous,
   And condemn the innocent blood.
22 But the LORD is my defence;
   And my God is the rock of my refuge.
23 { And he shall bring upon them their own iniquity,
   { And shall cut them off in their own wickedness:
   Yea, the LORD our God shall cut them off.

LESSON 64.

Psalm XCV.

OH come, let us sing unto the Lord:
Let us make a joyful noise to the rock of our salvation.
2 Let us come before his presence with thanksgiving,
And make a joyful noise unto him with psalms.
3 For the Lord *is* a great God,
And a great king above all gods.
4 In his hand *are* the deep places of the earth:
The strength of the hills is *his also.*
5 The sea *is* his and he made it:
And his hands formed the dry land.
6 Oh come let us worship and bow down:
Let us kneel before the LORD our maker.
7 For he *is* our God;
And we are *the people of his pasture, and the sheep of his hand.*
8 ｛ To day if ye will hear his voice,
　 Harden not your heart, as in the provocation,
And as in the day of temptation in the wilderness:
9 When your fathers tempted me,
Proved me, and saw my work.
10 ｛ Forty years long was I grieved with *this* generation,
　 And said, It *is* a people that do err in their heart,
And they have not known my ways:
11 Unto whom I sware in my wrath
That they should not enter into my rest.

Psalm XCVI.

OH sing unto the Lord a new song:
Sing unto the LORD, all the earth.
2 Sing unto the Lord, bless his name;
Shew forth his salvation from day to day.
3 Declare his glory among the heathen,
His wonders among all people.
4 For the Lord *is* great, and greatly to be praised:
He is *to be feared above all gods.*

5 For all the gods of the nations *are* idols :
   But the *LORD* made the heavens.
6 Honor and majesty *are* before him :
   Strength and beauty are in his sanctuary.
7 Give unto the Lord, O ye kindreds of the people,
   Give unto the *LORD* glory and strength.
8 Give unto the Lord the glory *due unto* his name :
   Bring an offering and come into his courts.
9 Oh worship the Lord in the beauty of holiness :
   Fear before him, all the earth.
10 { Say among the heathen *that* the Lord reigneth :
   { The world also shall be established that it shall not be moved :
   He shall judge the people righteously.
11 { Let the heavens rejoice,
   { And let the earth be glad ;
   Let the sea roar, and the fulness thereof.
12 Let the field be joyful, and all that *is* therein :
   Then shall all the trees of the wood rejoice
13 Before the Lord : for he cometh,
   For he cometh to judge the earth :
   He shall judge the world with righteousness,
   And the people with his truth.

LESSON 65.

Psalm xcvii.

THE Lord reigneth ; let the earth rejoice ;
   Let the multitude of isles be glad thereof.
2 Clouds and darkness *are* round about him :
   Righteousness and judgment are the habitation of his throne.
3 A fire goeth before him,
   And burneth up his enemies round about.
4 His lightnings enlightened the world :
   The earth saw, and trembled.
5 The hills melted like wax at the presence of the Lord,
   At the presence of the Lord of the whole earth.
6 The heavens declare his righteousness,
   And all the people see his glory.

7 { Confounded be all they that serve graven images,
That boast themselves of idols :
Worship him, all ye gods.
8 { Zion heard, and was glad ;
And the daughters of Judah rejoiced
Because of thy judgments, O LORD.
9 For thou, LORD, *art* high above all the earth :
Thou art exalted far above all gods.
10 { Ye that love the LORD, hate evil :
He preserveth the souls of his saints ;
He delivereth them out of the hand of the wicked.
11 Light is sown for the righteous,
And gladness for the upright in heart.
12 Rejoice in the LORD, ye righteous ;
And give thanks at the remembrance of his holiness.

PSALM XCVIII.
A Psalm.

{ OH sing unto the LORD a new song ;
For he hath done marvellous things :
His right hand, and his holy arm, hath gotten him the victory.
2 The LORD hath made known his salvation :
His righteousness hath he openly shewed in the sight of the heathen.
3 He hath remembered his mercy and his truth toward the house of Israel :
All the ends of the earth have seen the salvation of our God.
4 Make a joyful noise unto the LORD, all the earth :
Make a loud noise, and rejoice, and sing praise.
5 Sing unto the LORD with the harp ;
With the harp, and the voice of a psalm.
6 With trumpets and sound of cornet
Make a joyful noise before the LORD, the King.
7 Let the sea roar, and the fulness thereof;
The world, and they that dwell therein.
8 Let the floods clap *their* hands :
Let the hills be joyful together
9 Before the LORD ; for he cometh to judge the earth :
{ *With righteousness shall he judge the world,*
And the people with equity.
10

LESSON 66.

Psalm xcix.

THE Lord reigneth; let the people tremble:
  He sitteth between *the cherubim; let the earth be moved.*
2 The Lord *is* great in Zion;
  And he is high above all the people.
3 Let them praise thy great and terrible name;
  For *it* is *holy.*
4 { The king's strength also loveth judgment;
  { Thou dost establish equity,
    Thou executest judgment and righteousness in Jacob.
5 { Exalt ye the Lord our God,
  { And worship at his footstool;
    For *he* is *holy.*
6 { Moses and Aaron among his priests,
  { And Samuel among them that call upon his name;
    They called upon the LORD, and he answered them.
7 He spake unto them in the cloudy pillar:
  { *They kept his testimonies,*
  { *And the ordinance* that *he gave them.*
8 Thou answeredst them, O Lord our God:
  { *Thou wast a God that forgavest them,*
  { *Though thou tookest vengeance of their inventions.*
9 { Exalt the Lord our God,
  { And worship at his holy hill;
    For the LORD our God is holy.

Psalm c.

A Psalm of praise.

MAKE a joyful noise unto the Lord, all ye lands.
2 { *Serve the LORD with gladness:*
  { *Come before his presence with singing.*
3 { Know ye that the Lord he *is* God:
  { *It is* he *that* hath made us, and not we ourselves;
    We are *his people, and the sheep of his pasture.*

4 { Enter into his gates with thanksgiving,
   { *And* into his courts with praise :
       Be thankful unto him, and *bless his name.*
5 { For the LORD *is* good ;
   { His mercy *is* everlasting ;
       And his truth endureth *to all generations.*

PSALM CI.

A Psalm of David.

I WILL sing of mercy and judgment :
    Unto thee O LORD, will I sing.
2 I will behave myself wisely in a perfect way. Oh when wilt thou come unto me ?
    I will walk within my house with a perfect heart.
3 I will set no wicked thing before mine eyes :
    I hate the work of them that turn aside ; it *shall not cleave to me.*
4 A froward heart shall depart from me :
    I will not know a wicked person.
5 Whoso privily slandereth his neighbour, him will I cut off:
    Him that hath a high look and a proud heart will not I suffer.
6 Mine eyes *shall be* upon the faithful of the land, that they may dwell with me :
    He that walketh in a perfect way, he shall serve me.
7 He that worketh deceit shall not dwell within my house :
    He that telleth lies shall not tarry in my sight.
8 I will early destroy all the wicked of the land ;
    That I may cut off all wicked doers from the city of the LORD.

LESSON 67.

PSALM CII.

A Prayer of the afflicted, when he is overwhelmed, and poureth out his complaint before the LORD.

HEAR my prayer, O LORD,
    And let my cry come unto thee.
2 { Hide not thy face from me
   { In the day *when* I am in trouble ; incline thine ear unto me :
       In the day when *I call answer me speedily.*

3 For my days are consumed like smoke,
  And my bones are burned as a hearth.
4 My heart is smitten, and withered like grass;
  So that I forget to eat my bread.
5 { By reason of the voice of my groaning my bones cleave to my skin.
6 { I am like a pelican of the wilderness:
  I am like an owl of the desert.
7 { I watch, and am as a sparrow alone upon the housetop.
8 { Mine enemies reproach me all the day;
  And *they that are mad against me are sworn against me.*
9 For I have eaten ashes like bread,
  And mingled my drink with weeping,
10 Because of thine indignation and thy wrath:
  For thou hast lifted me up, and cast me down.
11 My days *are* like a shadow that declineth;
  And I am withered like grass.
12 But thou, O LORD, shalt endure for ever;
  And thy remembrance unto all generations.
13 Thou shalt arise, *and* have mercy upon Zion:
  For the time to favour her, yea, the set time, is come.
14 For thy servants take pleasure in her stones,
  And favour the dust thereof.
15 So the heathen shall fear the name of the LORD,
  And all the kings of the earth thy glory.
16 When the LORD shall build up Zion,
  He shall appear in his glory.
17 He will regard the prayer of the destitute,
  And not despise their prayer.
18 This shall be written for the generation to come:
  And the people which shall be created shall praise the LORD.
19 For he hath looked down from the height of his sanctuary;
  From heaven did the LORD behold the earth;
20 To hear the groaning of the prisoner;
  To loose those that are appointed to death;
21 To declare the name of the LORD in Zion,
  And his praise in Jerusalem;
22 When the people are gathered together,
  And the kingdoms, to serve the LORD.

23 { He weakened my strength in the way; he shortened my days.
24 { I said, O my God, take me not away in the midst of my days:
   Thy years are throughout all generations.
25 Of old hast thou laid the foundation of the earth:
   And the heavens are the work of thy hands.
26 They shall perish, but thou shalt endure:
   Yea, all of them shall wax old like a garment;
   As a vesture shalt thou change them, and they shall be changed:
27 But thou art *the same, and thy years shall have no end.*
28 The children of thy servants shall continue,
   And their seed shall be established before thee.

LESSON 68.

PSALM CIII.

A Psalm of David.

BLESS the LORD, O my soul:
  And all that is within me, bless his holy name.
2 Bless the LORD, O my soul,
  And forget not all his benefits:
3 Who forgiveth all thine iniquities;
  Who healeth all thy diseases;
4 Who redeemeth thy life from destruction;
  Who crowneth thee with lovingkindness and tender mercies;
5 Who satisfieth thy mouth with good *things;*
  So that *thy youth is renewed like the eagle's.*
6 The LORD executeth righteousness
  And judgment for all that are oppressed.
7 He made known his ways unto Moses,
  His acts unto the children of Israel.
8 The LORD *is* merciful and gracious,
  Slow to anger and plenteous in mercy.
9 He will not always chide:
  Neither will he keep his anger *for ever.*
10 He hath not dealt with us after our sins;
  Nor rewarded us according to our iniquities.
11 For as the heaven is high above the earth,
  So great is his mercy toward them that fear him.
12 As far as the east is from the west,
  So far hath he removed our transgressions from us.

13 Like as a father pitieth *his* children,
   So *the LORD pitieth them that fear him.*
14 For he knoweth our frame;
   He remembreth that we are dust.
15 *As for* man, his days *are* as grass:
   As a flower of the field, so he flourisheth.
16 For the wind passeth over it, and it is gone;
   And the place thereof shall know it no more.
17 But the mercy of the Lord *is* from everlasting to everlasting upon them that fear him,
   And his righteousness unto children's children ;
18 To such as keep his covenant,
   And to those that remember his commandments to do them.
19 The Lord hath prepared his throne in the heavens;
   And his kingdom ruleth over all.
20 { Bless the Lord, ye his angels,
   { That excel in strength, that do his commandments,
   Hearkening unto the voice of his word.
21 Bless ye the Lord, all *ye* his hosts;
   Ye *ministers of his, that do his pleasure.*
22 { Bless the Lord, all his works
   { In all places of his dominion:
   Bless the LORD, O my soul.

LESSON 69.

Psalm civ.

{ BLESS the Lord, O my soul.
{ O Lord my God, thou art very great;
   Thou art clothed with honour and majesty.
2 Who coverest *thyself* with light as *with* a garment:
   Who stretchest out the heavens like a curtain:
3 { Who layeth the beams of his chambers in the waters:
   { Who maketh the clouds his chariot:
   Who walketh upon the wings of the wind:
4 Who maketh his angels spirits;
   His ministers a flaming fire :
5 *Who* laid the foundations of the earth,
   That *it should not be removed for ever.*

6 Thou coveredst it with the deep as *with* a garment:
  The waters stood above the mountains.
7 At thy rebuke they fled;
  At the voice of thy thunder they hasted away.
8 They go up by the mountains; they go down by the valleys
  Unto the place which thou hast founded for them.
9 Thou hast set a bound that they may not pass over;
  That they turn not again to cover the earth.
10 He sendeth the springs into the valleys,
  Which run among the hills.
11 They give drink to every beast of the field:
  The wild asses quench their thirst.
12 By them shall the fowls of the heaven have their habitation,
  Which sing among the branches.
13 He watereth the hills from his chambers:
  The earth is satisfied with the fruit of thy works.
14 He causeth the grass to grow for the cattle,
  And herb for the service of man:
  That he may bring forth food out of the earth;
15   *And wine that maketh glad the heart of man,*
  And oil to make *his* face to shine,
  And bread which strengtheneth man's heart.
16 The trees of the LORD are full *of sap;*
  The cedars of Lebanon, which he hath planted;
17 Where the birds make their nests:
  As for *the stork, the fir trees* are *her house.*
18 The high hills *are* a refuge for the wild goats;
  And *the rocks for the conies.*
19 He appointed the moon for seasons:
  The sun knoweth his going down.
20 Thou makest darkness, and it is night:
  Wherein all the beasts of the forest do creep forth.
21 The young lions roar after their prey,
  And seek their meat from God.
22 The sun ariseth, they gather themselves together,
  And lay them down in their dens.
23 Man goeth forth unto his work
  And to his labour until the evening.

24 { O Lord, how manifold are thy works!
{ In wisdom hast thou made them all:
   The earth is full of thy riches.
25 { *So is* this great and wide sea,
{ Wherein *are* things creeping innumerable,
   Both small and great beasts.
26 There go the ships:
   There is *that leviathan,* whom *thou hast made to play therein.*
27 These wait all upon thee;
   That thou mayest give them *their meat in due season.*
28 *That* thou givest them they gather:
   Thou openest thine hand, they are filled with good.
29 Thou hidest thy face, they are troubled:
   { *Thou takest away their breath, they die,*
   { *And return to their dust.*
30 Thou sendest forth thy spirit, they are created:
   And thou renewest the face of the earth.
31 The glory of the Lord shall endure for ever:
   The LORD shall rejoice in his works.
32 He looketh on the earth, and it trembleth:
   He toucheth the hills, and they smoke.
33 I will sing unto the Lord as long as I live:
   I will sing praise to my God while I have my being
34 My meditation of him shall be sweet:
   I will be glad in the LORD.
35 Let the sinners be consumed out of the earth,
   And let the wicked be no more.
  Bless thou the Lord, O my soul.
   Praise ye the LORD.

LESSON 70.

Psalm cv, First Part.

1 O give thanks unto the Lord; call upon his name:
   Make known his deeds among the people.
2 Sing unto him, sing psalms unto him:
   Talk ye of all his wondrous works.

LESSON 70.

3 Glory ye in his holy name:
    Let the heart of them rejoice that seek the LORD.
4 Seek the LORD, and his strength:
    Seek his face evermore.
5 Remember his marvellous works that he hath done;
    His wonders, and the judgments of his mouth;
6 O ye seed of Abraham his servant,
    Ye children of Jacob his chosen.
7 He *is* the LORD our God:
    His judgments are in all the earth.
8 He hath remembered his covenant for ever,
    The word which he commanded to a thousand generations.
9 Which *covenant* he made with Abraham,
    And his oath unto Isaac;
10 And confirmed the same unto Jacob for a law,
    And *to Israel* for *an everlasting covenant:*
11 Saying, Unto thee will I give the land of Canaan,
    The lot of your inheritance:
12 When they were *but* a few men in number;
    Yea, very few, and strangers in it.
13 When they went from one nation to another,
    From one *kingdom to another people;*
14 He suffered no man to do them wrong:
    Yea, he reproved kings for their sakes;
15 *Saying,* Touch not mine anointed,
    And do my prophets no harm.
16 Moreover he called for a famine upon the land:
    He brake the whole staff of bread.
17 He sent a man before them,
    Even *Joseph, who was sold for a servant:*
18 Whose feet they hurt with fetters:
    He was laid in iron:
19 Until the time that his word came:
    The word of the LORD tried him.
20 The king sent and loosed him:
    Even *the ruler of the people, and let him go free.*
21 He made him lord of his house,
    And ruler of all his substance:

22 To bind his princes at his pleasure;
　　And teach his senators wisdom.

LESSON 71.

Psalm cv, Second Part.

ISRAEL also came into Egypt;
　　And Jacob sojourned in the land of Ham.
24 And he increased his people greatly;
　　And made them stronger than their enemies.
25 He turned their heart to hate his people,
　　To deal subtilely with his servants.
26 He sent Moses his servant;
　　And *Aaron whom he had chosen.*
27 They shewed his signs among them,
　　And wonders in the land of Ham.
28 He sent darkness, and made it dark;
　　And they rebelled not against his word.
29 He turned their waters into blood,
　　And slew their fish.
30 Their land brought forth frogs in abundance,
　　In the chambers of their kings.
31 He spake, and there came divers sorts of flies,
　　And *lice in all their coasts.*
32 He gave them hail for rain,
　　And *flaming fire in their land.*
33 He smote their vines also and their fig trees;
　　And brake the trees of their coasts.
34 He spake, and the locusts came,
　　And caterpillars, and that without number,
35 And did eat up all the herbs in their land,
　　And devoured the fruit of their ground.
36 He smote also all the firstborn in their land,
　　The chief of all their strength.
37 He brought them forth also with silver and gold:
　　And there was *not one feeble* person *among their tribes.*
38 Egypt was glad when they departed:
　　For the fear of them fell upon them.

39 He spread a cloud for a covering;
   And fire to give light in the night.
40 The people asked, and he brought quails,
   And satisfied them with the bread of heaven.
41 He opened the rock, and the water gushed out;
   They ran in the dry places like a river.
42 For he remembered his holy promise,
   And Abraham his servant.
43 And he brought forth his people with joy,
   And his chosen with gladness:
44 And gave them the lands of the heathen:
   And they inherited the labour of the people;
45 That they might observe his statutes,
   And keep his laws. Praise ye the LORD.

LESSON 72.

PSALM CVI, FIRST PART.

{ PRAISE ye the LORD.
{ Oh give thanks unto the LORD; for *he is* good:
   For his mercy endureth *for ever*.
2 Who can utter the mighty acts of the LORD?
   Who *can shew forth all his praise?*
3 Blessed *are* they that keep judgment,
   And *he that doeth righteousness at all times.*
4 Remember me, O LORD, with the favour *that thou bearest unto* thy people:
   Oh visit me with thy salvation;
5 { That I may see the good of thy chosen,
  { That I may rejoice in the gladness of thy nation,
   That I may glory with thine inheritance.
6 We have sinned with our fathers,
   We have committed iniquity, we have done wickedly.
7 { Our fathers understood not thy wonders in Egypt;
  { They remembered not the multitude of thy mercies;
   But provoked him at the sea, even at the Red sea.
8 Nevertheless he saved them for his name's sake,
   That he might make his mighty power to be known.

9 He rebuked the Red sea also, and it was dried up:
   So he led them through the depths, as through the wilderness.
10 And he saved them from the hand of him that hated *them,*
   And redeemed them from the hand of the enemy.
11 And the waters covered their enemies:
   There was not one of them left.
12 Then believed they his words:
   They sang his praise.
13 They soon forgat his works;
   They waited not for his counsel:
14 But lusted exceedingly in the wilderness,
   And tempted God in the desert.
15 And he gave them their request;
   But sent leanness into their soul.
16 They envied Moses also in the camp,
   And Aaron the saint of the LORD.
17 The earth opened and swallowed up Dathan,
   And covered the company of Abiram.
18 And a fire was kindled in their company;
   The flame burned up the wicked.
19 They made a calf in Horeb,
   And worshipped the molten image.
20 Thus they changed their glory
   Into the similitude of an ox that eateth grass.
21 They forgat God their saviour,
   Which had done great things in Egypt;
22 Wondrous works in the land of Ham,
   And terrible things by the Red sea.
23 { Therefore he said that he would destroy them,
    { Had not Moses his chosen stood before him in the breach,
   { *To turn away his wrath,*
   { *Lest he should destroy them.*

LESSON 73.

PSALM CVI, SECOND PART.

YEA, they despised the pleasant land,
   They believed not his word:

LESSON 73.

25 But murmured in their tents,
   And *hearkened not unto the voice of the* LORD.
26 Therefore he lifted up his hand against them,
   To overthrow them in the wilderness:
27 To overthrow their seed also among the nations,
   And to scatter them in the lands.
28 They joined themselves also unto Baal-peor,
   And ate the sacrifices of the dead.
29 Thus they provoked *him* to anger with their inventions:
   And the plague brake in upon them.
30 Then stood up Phinehas, and executed judgment:
   And so the plague was stayed.
31 And that was counted unto him for righteousness
   Unto all generations for evermore.
32 They angered *him* also at the waters of strife,
   So that it went ill with Moses for their sakes:
33 Because they provoked his spirit,
   So that he spake unadvisedly with his lips.
34 They did not destroy the nations,
   Concerning whom the LORD commanded them:
35 But were mingled among the heathen,
   And learned their works.
36 And they served their idols:
   Which were a snare unto them.
37 Yea, they sacrificed their sons
   And their daughters unto devils,
38 { And shed innocent blood,
   Even the blood of their sons and of their daughters,
   { *Whom they sacrificed unto the idols of Canaan:*
   { *And the land was polluted with blood.*
39 Thus were they defiled with their own works,
   And went a whoring with their own inventions.
40 Therefore was the wrath of the LORD kindled against his people,
   Insomuch that he abhorred his own inheritance.
41 And he gave them into the hand of the heathen;
   And they that hated them ruled over them.
42 Their enemies also oppressed them,
   And they were brought into subjection under their hand.

43 Many times did he deliver them;
   { But they provoked him *with their counsel,*
   { *And were brought low for their iniquity.*
44 Nevertheless he regarded their affliction,
   When he heard their cry:
45 And he remembered for them his covenant,
   And repented according to the multitude of his mercies.
46 He made them also to be pitied
   Of all those that carried them captives.
47 Save us, O LORD our God,
   And gather us from among the heathen,
   To give thanks unto thy holy name,
   And to triumph in thy praise.
48 Blessed *be* the LORD God of Israel from everlasting to everlasting:
   { *And let all the people say, Amen.*
   { *Praise ye the LORD.*

LESSON 74.

PSALM CVII, FIRST PART.

OH give thanks unto the LORD, for *he is* good:
   For his mercy endureth for ever.
2 Let the redeemed of the LORD say *so,*
   Whom he hath redeemed from the hand of the enemy;
3 And gathered them out of the lands,
   From the east, and from the west, from the north, and from the south.
4 They wandered in the wilderness in a solitary way;
   They found no city to dwell in.
5 Hungry and thirsty,
   Their soul fainted in them.
6 Then they cried unto the LORD in their trouble,
   And he delivered them out of their distresses.
7 And he led them forth by the right way,
   That they might go to a city of habitation.
8 Oh that *men* would praise the LORD *for* his goodness,
   And for his wonderful works to the children of men!

9 For he satisfieth the longing soul,
And filleth the hungry soul with goodness.
10 Such as sit in darkness and the shadow of death,
Being *bound in affliction and iron;*
11 Because they rebelled against the words of God,
And contemned the counsel of the Most High:
12 Therefore he brought down their heart with labour;
They fell down, and there was *none to help.*
13 Then they cried unto the LORD in their trouble,
And *he saved them out of their distresses.*
14 He brought them out of darkness and the shadow of death,
And brake their bands in sunder.
15 Oh that *men* would praise the LORD *for* his goodness,
And for *his wonderful works to the children of men!*
16 For he hath broken the gates of brass,
And cut the bars of iron in sunder.
17 Fools, because of their transgression,
And because of their iniquities, are afflicted.
18 Their soul abhorreth all manner of meat;
And they draw near unto the gates of death.
19 Then they cry unto the LORD in their trouble,
And *he saveth them out of their distresses.*
20 He sent his word, and healed them,
And delivered them from their destructions.
21 Oh that *men* would praise the LORD *for* his goodness,
And for *his wonderful works to the children of men!*
22 And let them sacrifice the sacrifices of thanksgiving,
And declare his works with rejoicing.

LESSON 75.

PSALM CVII, SECOND PART.

THEY that go down to the sea in ships,
That do business in great waters;
24 These see the works of the LORD,
And his wonders in the deep.
25 For he commandeth, and raiseth the stormy wind,
Which lifteth up the waves thereof.

26 They mount up to the heaven, they go down again to the depths:
    Their soul is melted because of trouble.
27 They reel to and fro, and stagger like a drunken man,
    And are at their wit's end.
28 Then they cry unto the LORD in their trouble,
    And he bringeth them out of their distresses.
29 He maketh the storm a calm,
    So that the waves thereof are still.
30 Then are they glad because they be quiet;
    So he bringeth them unto their desired haven.
31 Oh that *men* would praise the LORD *for* his goodness,
    And for his wonderful works to the children of men!
32 Let them exalt him also in the congregation of the people,
    And praise him in the assembly of the elders.
33 He turneth rivers into a wilderness,
    And the watersprings into dry ground;
34 A fruitful land into barrenness,
    For the wickedness of them that dwell therein.
35 He turneth the wilderness into a standing water,
    And dry ground into watersprings.
36 And there he maketh the hungry to dwell,
    That they may prepare a city for habitation;
37 And sow the fields, and plant vineyards,
    Which may yield fruits of increase.
38 He blesseth them also, so that they are multiplied greatly;
    And suffereth not their cattle to decrease.
39 Again, they are minished and brought low
    Through oppression, affliction, and sorrow.
40 He poureth contempt upon princes,
    And causeth them to wander in the wilderness, where there is *no way.*
41 Yet setteth he the poor on high from affliction,
    And maketh him *families like a flock.*
42 The righteous shall see *it,* and rejoice:
    And all iniquity shall stop her mouth.
43 Whoso *is* wise, and will observe these *things,*
    Even they shall understand the lovingkindness of the LORD.

LESSON 76.

PSALM CVIII.

A Song or Psalm of David.

O GOD, my heart is fixed ;
 I will sing and give praise,
 Even with my glory.
2 Awake, psaltery and harp :
 I myself will awake early.
3 I will praise thee, O LORD, among the people :
 And I will sing praises unto thee among the nations.
4 For thy mercy *is* great above the heavens :
 And thy truth reacheth unto the clouds.
5 Be thou exalted, O God, above the heavens :
 And thy glory above all the earth ;
6 That thy beloved may be delivered :
 Save with thy right hand, and answer me.
7 God hath spoken in his holiness ;
 I will rejoice, I will divide Shechem,
 And mete out the valley of Succoth.
8 Gilead *is* mine ; Manasseh *is* mine ;
 Ephraim also *is* the strength of mine head ;
 Judah is *my lawgiver ;*
9 Moab *is* my washpot ;
 Over Edom will I cast out my shoe ;
 Over Philistia will I triumph.
10 Who will bring me into the strong city ?
 Who will lead me into Edom ?
11 *Wilt* not *thou*, O God, *who* hast cast us off ?
 And wilt not thou, O God, go forth with our hosts ?
12 Give us help from trouble :
 For vain is *the help of man.*
13 Through God we shall do valiantly :
 For he it is that shall tread out our enemies.

LESSON 77.

PSALM CIX.

To the chief Musician, A Psalm of David.

{ HOLD not thy peace, O God of my praise;
2 For the mouth of the wicked and the mouth of the deceitful are opened against me:
They have spoken against me with a lying tongue.
3 They compassed me about also with words of hatred;
And fought against me without a cause.
4 For my love they are my adversaries:
But I give myself unto prayer.
5 And they have rewarded me evil for good,
And hatred for my love.
6 Set thou a wicked man over him;
And let Satan stand at his right hand.
7 When he shall be judged, let him be condemned:
And let his prayer become sin.
8 Let his days be few;
And *let another take his office.*
9 Let his children be fatherless,
And his wife a widow.
10 Let his children be continually vagabonds, and beg:
Let them seek their bread also out of their desolate places.
11 Let the extortioner catch all that he hath;
And let the strangers spoil his labour.
12 Let there be none to extend mercy unto him:
Neither let there be any to favour his fatherless children.
13 Let his posterity be cut off;
And *in the generation following let their name be blotted out.*
14 Let the iniquity of his fathers be remembered with the LORD;
And let not the sin of his mother be blotted out.
15 Let them be before the LORD continually,
That he may cut off the memory of them from the earth.
16 { Because that he remembered not to shew mercy,
But persecuted the poor and needy man,
That he might even slay the broken in heart.

17 As he loved cursing, so let it come unto him:
As he delighted not in blessing, so let it be far from him.
18 As he clothed himself with cursing like as with his garment,
{ *So let it come into his bowels like water,*
{ *And like oil into his bones.*
19 Let it be unto him as the garment *which* covereth him,
And for a girdle wherewith he is girded continually.
20 *Let* this *be* the reward of mine adversaries from the Lord,
And of them that speak evil against my soul.
21 But do thou for me, O God the Lord, for thy name's sake:
Because thy mercy is good, deliver thou me.
22 For I *am* poor and needy,
And my heart is wounded within me.
23 I am gone like the shadow when it declineth:
I am tossed up and down as the locust.
24 My knees are weak through fasting;
And my flesh faileth of fatness.
25 I became also a reproach unto them:
When *they looked upon me they shaked their heads.*
26 Help me, O Lord my God:
Oh save me according to thy mercy:
27 That they may know that this *is* thy hand;
That *thou, LORD, hast done it.*
28 Let them curse, but bless thou:
When they arise, let them be ashamed; but let thy servant rejoice.
29 Let mine adversaries be clothed with shame;
And let them cover themselves with their own confusion, as with a mantle.
30 I will greatly praise the Lord with my mouth;
Yea, I will praise him among the multitude.
31 For he shall stand at the right hand of the poor,
To save him from those that condemn his soul.

LESSON 78.
PSALM CX.
A Psalm of David.

{ THE Lord said unto my Lord,
{ Sit thou at my right hand,
Until I make thine enemies thy foot

2 The LORD shall send the rod of thy strength out of Zion:
 Rule thou in the midst of thine enemies.
3 {Thy people *shall be* willing in the day of thy power,
 {In the beauties of holiness from the womb of the morning:
 Thou hast the dew of thy youth.
4 The LORD hath sworn, and will not repent,
 { *Thou art a priest for ever*
 { *After the order of Melchizedek.*
5 The Lord at thy right hand
 Shall strike through kings in the day of his wrath.
6 {He shall judge among the heathen,
 {He shall fill *the places* with the dead bodies;
 He shall wound the heads over many countries.
7 He shall drink of the brook in the way:
 Therefore shall he lift up the head.

PSALM CXI.

{PRAISE ye the LORD.
{I will praise the LORD with *my* whole heart,
 In the assembly of the upright, and in the congregation.
2 The works of the LORD *are* great,
 Sought out of all them that have pleasure therein.
3 His work *is* honourable and glorious:
 And his righteousness endureth for ever.
4 He hath made his wonderful works to be remembered:
 The LORD is gracious and full of compassion.
5 He hath given meat unto them that fear him:
 He will ever be mindful of his covenant.
6 He hath shewed his people the power of his works,
 That he may give them the heritage of the heathen.
7 The works of his hands *are* verity and judgment;
 All his commandments are sure.
8 They stand fast for ever and ever,
 And are done in truth and uprightness.
9 { He sent redemption unto his people:
 { He hath commanded his covenant for ever:
 Holy and reverend is his name.

LESSON 79.

10 The fear of the LORD *is* the beginning of wisdom:
  { *A good understanding have all they that do* his commandments:
  { *His praise endureth for ever.*

LESSON 79.

PSALM CXII.

{ PRAISE ye the LORD.
{ Blessed *is* the man *that* feareth the LORD,
  That *delighteth greatly in his commandments.*
2 His seed shall be mighty upon earth:
  The generation of the upright shall be blessed.
3 Wealth and riches *shall be* in his house:
  And his righteousness endureth for ever.
4 Unto the upright there ariseth light in the darkness:
  He is *gracious, and full of compassion, and righteous.*
5 A good man sheweth favour, and lendeth:
  He will guide his affairs with discretion.
6 Surely he shall not be moved for ever:
  The righteous shall be in everlasting remembrance.
7 He shall not be afraid of evil tidings:
  His heart is fixed, trusting in the LORD.
8 His heart *is* established, he shall not be afraid,
  Until he see his desire *upon his enemies.*
9 { He hath dispersed, he hath given to the poor;
  { His righteousness endureth for ever;
  His horn shall be exalted with honour.
10 { The wicked shall see *it,* and be grieved;
  { He shall gnash with his teeth, and melt away:
  The desire of the wicked shall perish.

PSALM CXIII.

{ PRAISE ye the LORD.
{ Praise, O ye servants of the LORD,
  Praise the name of the LORD.
2 Blessed be the name of the LORD
  From this time forth and for evermore.

3 From the rising of the sun unto the going down of the same
   The *LORD'S* name is *to be praised.*
4 The LORD *is* high above all nations,
   And *his glory above the heavens.*
5 Who *is* like unto the LORD our God,
   Who dwelleth on high,
6 Who humbleth *himself* to behold
   The things that are *in heaven, and in the earth!*
7 He raiseth up the poor out of the dust,
   And *lifteth the needy out of the dunghill;*
8 That he may set *him* with princes,
   Even *with the princes of his people.*
9 { He maketh the barren woman to keep house,
   { *And to be* a joyful mother of children.
   Praise ye the LORD.

LESSON 80.

PSALM CXIV.

WHEN Israel went out of Egypt,
   The house of Jacob from a people of strange language;
2 Judah was his sanctuary,
   And *Israel his dominion.*
3 The sea saw *it,* and fled:
   Jordan was driven back.
4 The mountains skipped like rams,
   And *the little hills like lambs.*
5 What *ailed* thee, O thou sea, that thou fleddest?
   Thou Jordan, that thou wast driven back?
6 Ye mountains, *that* ye skipped like rams;
   And *ye little hills, like lambs?*
7 Tremble, thou earth, at the presence of the Lord,
   At the presence of the God of Jacob;
8 Which turned the rock *into* a standing water,
   The flint into a fountain of waters.

LESSON 80.

PSALM CXV.

NOT unto us, O LORD, not unto us,
But unto thy name give glory,
For thy mercy, and *for thy truth's sake.*
2 Wherefore should the heathen say,
Where is now their God?
3 But our God *is* in the heavens:
He hath done whatsoever he hath pleased.
4 Their idols *are* silver and gold,
The work of men's hands.
5 They have mouths, but they speak not:
Eyes have they, but they see not:
6 They have ears, but they hear not:
Noses have they, but they smell not:
7 They have hands, but they handle not:
{ *Feet have they, but they walk not:*
{ *Neither speak they through their throat.*
8 They that make them are like unto them;
So is *every one that trusteth in them.*
9 O Israel, trust thou in the LORD :
He is their help and their shield.
10 O house of Aaron, trust in the LORD :
He is their help and their shield.
11 Ye that fear the LORD, trust in the LORD :
He is their help and their shield.
12 { The LORD hath been mindful of us: he will bless *us;*
 { He will bless the house of Israel;
He will bless the house of Aaron.
13 He will bless them that fear the LORD,
Both *small and great.*
14 The LORD shall increase you more and more,
You and your children.
15 Ye *are* blessed of the Lord
Which made heaven and earth.
16 The heaven, *even* the heavens, *are* the LORD'S :
But the earth hath he given to the children of men.
17 The dead praise not the LORD,
Neither any that go down into silence.

18 { But we will bless the LORD
From this time forth and for evermore.
Praise the LORD.

LESSON 81.

PSALM CXVI.

I LOVE the LORD, because he hath heard
My voice and *my supplications.*
2 Because he hath inclined his ear unto me,
Therefore will I call upon him *as long as I live.*
3 { The sorrows of death compassed me,
And the pains of hell gat hold upon me:
I found trouble and sorrow.
4 Then called I upon the name of the LORD;
O LORD, I beseech thee, deliver my soul.
5 Gracious *is* the LORD, and righteous;
Yea, our God is *merciful.*
6 The LORD preserveth the simple:
I was brought low, and he helped me.
7 Return unto thy rest, O my soul;
For the LORD hath dealt bountifully with thee.
8 For thou hast delivered my soul from death,
{ *Mine eyes from tears,*
And my feet from falling.
9 I will walk before the LORD
In the land of the living.
10 I believed, therefore have I spoken:
I was greatly afflicted:
11 I said in my haste,
All men are *liars.*
12 What shall I render unto the LORD
For *all his benefits toward me?*
13 I will take the cup of salvation,
And call upon the name of the LORD.
14 I will pay my vows unto the LORD
Now in the presence of all his people.
15 Precious in the sight of the LORD
Is *the death of his saints.*

16 { O Lord, truly I *am* thy servant;
  { I *am* thy servant, *and* the son of thine handmaid:
  Thou hast loosed my bonds. .
17 I will offer to thee the sacrifice of thanksgiving,
  And will call upon the name of the LORD.
18 I will pay my vows unto the Lord
  Now in the presence of all his people,
19 { In the courts of the Lord's house,
  { In the midst of thee, O Jerusalem.
  Praise ye the LORD.

Psalm cxvii.

OH praise the Lord, all ye nations:
  Praise him, all ye people.
2 { For his merciful kindness is great toward us:
  { And the truth of the Lord *endureth* for ever.
  Praise ye the LORD.

LESSON 82.

Psalm cxviii.

OH give thanks unto the Lord; for *he is* good:
  Because his mercy endureth *for ever.*
2 Let Israel now say,
  That his mercy endureth *for ever.*
3 Let the house of Aaron now say,
  That his mercy endureth *for ever.*
4 Let them now that fear the Lord say,
  That his mercy endureth *for ever.*
5 I called upon the Lord in distress:
  The LORD answered me, and set me *in a large place.*
6 The Lord *is* on my side; I will not fear:
  What can man do unto me?
7 The Lord taketh my part with them that help me:
  Therefore shall I see my desire *upon them that hate me.*
8 { *It is* better to trust in the Lord
  Than to put confidence in man.

9 *It is* better to trust in the LORD
   Than to put confidence in princes.
10 All nations compassed me about: .
   But in the name of the LORD will I destroy them.
11 They compassed me about; yea, they compassed me about:
   But in the name of the LORD I will destroy them.
12 ⎰ They compassed me about like bees;
   ⎱ They are quenched as the fire of thorns:
   For in the name of the LORD I will destroy them.
13 Thou hast thrust sore at me that I might fall:
   But the LORD helped me.
14 The LORD *is* my strength and song,
   And is become my salvation.
15 The voice of rejoicing and salvation *is* in the tabernacles of the righteous:
   The right hand of the LORD doeth valiantly.
16 The right hand of the LORD is exalted:
   The right hand of the LORD doeth valiantly.
17 I shall not die but live,
   And declare the works of the LORD.
18 The LORD hath chastened me sore:
   But he hath not given me over unto death.
19 Open to me the gates of righteousness:
   I will go into them, and I will praise the LORD.
20 This gate of the LORD,
   Into which the righteous shall enter.
21 I will praise thee: for thou hast heard me,
   And art become my salvation.
22 The stone *which* the builders refused
   Is become the head stone of the corner.
23 This is the LORD's doing;
   It is marvellous in our eyes.
24 This *is* the day *which* the LORD hath made;
   We will rejoice and be glad in it.
25 Save now, I beseech thee, O LORD:
   O LORD, I beseech thee, send now prosperity.
26 Blessed *be* he that cometh in the name of the LORD:
   We have blessed you out of the house of the LORD.

27 God *is* the LORD which hath shewed us light:
{ *Bind the sacrifice with cords*,
{ Even *unto the horns of the altar.*
28 Thou *art* my God, and I will praise thee:
Thou art *my God, I will exalt thee.*
29 Oh give thanks unto the LORD; for *he is* good:
For his mercy endureth *for ever.*

LESSON 83.

PSALM CXIX, FIRST PART.

ALEPH.

BLESSED *are* the undefiled in the way,
Who walk in the law of the LORD.
2 Blessed *are* they that keep his testimonies,
And that *seek him with the whole heart.*
3 They also do no iniquity:
They walk in his ways.
4 Thou hast commanded *us*
To keep thy precepts diligently.
5 Oh that my ways were directed
To keep thy statutes!
6 Then shall I not be ashamed,
When I have respect unto all thy commandments.
7 I will praise thee with uprightness of heart,
When I shall have learned thy righteous judgments.
8 I will keep thy statutes:
Oh forsake me not utterly.

BETH.

9 Wherewithal shall a young man cleanse his way?
By taking heed thereto *according to thy word.*
10 With my whole heart have I sought thee:
Oh let me not wander from thy commandments.
11 Thy word have I hid in mine heart,
That I might not sin against thee.
12 Blessed *art* thou, O LORD:
Teach me thy statutes.

13 With my lips have I declared
   All the judgments of thy mouth.
14 I have rejoiced in the way of thy testimonies,
   As much as *in all riches*.
15 I will meditate in thy precepts,
   And have respect unto thy ways.
16 I will delight myself in thy statutes:
   I will not forget thy word.

GIMEL.

17 Deal bountifully with thy servant, *that* I may live,
   And keep thy word.
18 Open thou mine eyes, that I may behold
   Wondrous things out of thy law.
19 I *am* a stranger in the earth:
   Hide not thy commandments from me.
20 My soul breaketh for the longing
   That it hath *unto thy judgments at all times.*
21 Thou hast rebuked the proud *that are* cursed,
   Which do err *from thy commandments.*
22 Remove from me reproach and contempt;
   For I have kept thy testimonies.
23 Princes also did sit *and* speak against me:
   But *thy servant did meditate in thy statutes.*
24 Thy testimonies also *are* my delight,
   And *my counsellors.*

LESSON 84.

PSALM CXIX, SECOND PART.

DALETH.

MY soul cleaveth unto the dust:
   Quicken thou me according to thy word.
26 I have declared my ways, and thou heardest me:
   Teach me thy statutes.
27 Make me to understand the way of thy precepts:
   So shall I talk of thy wondrous works.
28 My soul melteth for heaviness:
   Strengthen thou me according unto thy word.

29 Remove from me the way of lying:
 And grant me thy law graciously.
30 I have chosen the way of truth:
 Thy judgments have I laid before me.
31 I have stuck unto thy testimonies:
 O LORD, put me not to shame.
32 I will run the way of thy commandments,
 When thou shalt enlarge my heart.

HE.

33 Teach me, O Lord, the way of thy statutes;
 And I shall keep it unto the end.
34 Give me understanding, and I shall keep thy law;
 Yea, I shall observe it with my whole heart.
35 Make me to go in the path of thy commandments;
 For therein do I delight.
36 Incline my heart unto thy testimonies,
 And not to covetousness.
37 Turn away mine eyes from beholding vanity;
 And quicken thou me in thy way.
38 Stablish thy word unto thy servant,
 Who is devoted to thy fear.
39 Turn away my reproach which I fear:
 For thy judgments are good.
40 Behold, I have longed after thy precepts:
 Quicken me in thy righteousness.

VAU.

41 Let thy mercies come also unto me, O Lord,
 Even thy salvation, according to thy word.
42 So shall I have wherewith to answer him that reproacheth me:
 For I trust in thy word.
43 And take not the word of truth utterly out of my mouth;
 For I have hoped in thy judgments.
44 So shall I keep thy law continually
 For ever and ever.
45 And I will walk at liberty:
 For I seek thy precepts.
46 I will speak of thy testimonies also before kings,
 And will not be ashamed.

47 And I will delight myself in thy commandments,
   Which I have loved.
48 My hands also will I lift up unto thy commandments, which I have loved;
   And I will meditate in thy statutes.

LESSON 85.

Psalm cxix, Third Part.

ZAIN.

REMEMBER the word unto thy servant,
   Upon which thou hast caused me to hope.
50 This *is* my comfort in my affliction:
   For thy word hath quickened me.
51 The proud have had me greatly in derision:
   Yet *have I not declined from thy law.*
52 I remembered thy judgments of old, O Lord;
   And have comforted myself.
53 Horror hath taken hold upon me because of the wicked
   That forsake thy law.
54 Thy statutes have been my songs
   In the house of my pilgrimage.
55 I have remembered thy name, O Lord, in the night,
   And have kept thy law.
56 This I had,
   Because I kept thy precepts.

CHETH.

57 *Thou art* my portion, O Lord:
   I have said that I would keep thy words.
58 I entreated thy favour with *my* whole heart:
   Be merciful unto me according to thy word.
59 I thought on my ways,
   And turned my feet unto thy testimonies.
60 I made haste, and delayed not
   To keep thy commandments.
61 The bands of the wicked have robbed me:
   But *I have not forgotten thy law.*

62 At midnight I will rise to give thanks unto thee
Because of thy righteous judgments.
63 I *am* a companion of all *them* that fear thee,
And of them that keep thy precepts.
64 The earth, O LORD, is full of thy mercy:
Teach me thy statutes.

TETH.

65 Thou hast dealt well with thy servant,
O LORD, according unto thy word.
66 Teach me good judgment and knowledge:
For I have believed thy commandments.
67 Before I was afflicted I went astray:
But now have I kept thy word.
68 Thou *art* good, and doest good:
Teach me thy statutes.
69 The proud have forged a lie against me:
But I will keep thy precepts with my whole heart.
70 Their heart is as fat as grease:
But I delight in thy law.
71 *It is* good for me that I have been afflicted;
That I might learn thy statutes.
72 The law of thy mouth *is* better unto me
Than thousands of gold and silver.

LESSON 86.

PSALM CXIX, FOURTH PART.

JOD.

THY hands have made me and fashioned me:
Give me understanding, that I may learn thy commandments.
74 They that fear thee will be glad when they see me;
Because I have hoped in thy word.
75 I know, O LORD, that thy judgments *are* right,
And that thou in faithfulness hast afflicted me.
76 Let, I pray thee, thy merciful kindness be for my comfort,
According to thy word unto thy servant.

77 Let thy tender mercies come unto me, that I may live:
    For thy law is my delight.
78 Let the proud be ashamed; for they dealt perversely with me without a cause:
    But I will meditate in thy precepts.
79 Let those that fear thee turn unto me,
    And those that have known thy testimonies.
80 Let my heart be sound in thy statutes;
    That I be not ashamed.

CAPH.

81 My soul fainteth for thy salvation:
    But I hope in thy word.
82 Mine eyes fail for thy word,
    Saying, When wilt thou comfort me?
83 For I am become like a bottle in the smoke;
    Yet do I not forget thy statutes.
84 How many are the days of thy servant?
    When wilt thou execute judgment on them that persecute me?
85 The proud have digged pits for me,
    Which are not after thy law.
86 All thy commandments are faithful:
    They persecute me wrongfully; help thou me.
87 They had almost consumed me upon earth;
    But I forsook not thy precepts.
88 Quicken me after thy lovingkindness;
    So shall I keep the testimony of thy mouth.

LAMED.

89 For ever, O LORD,
    Thy word is settled in heaven.
90 Thy faithfulness is unto all generations:
    Thou hast established the earth, and it abideth.
91 They continue this day according to thine ordinances:
    For all are thy servants.
92 Unless thy law had been my delights,
    I should then have perished in mine affliction.
93 I will never forget thy precepts:
    For with them thou hast quickened me.
94 I am thine, save me;
    For I have sought thy precepts.

95 The wicked have waited for me to destroy me:
   But *I will consider thy testimonies.*
96 I have seen an end of all perfection:
   But *thy commandment is exceeding broad.*

LESSON 87.

Psalm cxix, Fifth Part.
MEM.

OH how love I thy law!
   It is my meditation all the day.
98 Thou through thy commandments hast made me wiser than mine enemies:.
   For they are ever with me.
99 I have more understanding than all my teachers:
   For thy testimonies are my meditation.
100 I understand more than the ancients,
   Because I keep thy precepts.
101 I have refrained my feet from every evil way,
   That I might keep thy word.
102 I have not departed from thy judgments:
   For thou hast taught me.
103 How sweet are thy words unto my taste!
   Yea, sweeter *than honey to my mouth.*
104 Through thy precepts I get understanding:
   Therefore I hate every false way.

NUN.

105 Thy word *is* a lamp unto my feet,
   And a light unto my path.
106 I have sworn, and I will perform *it,*
   That I will keep thy righteous judgments.
107 I am afflicted very much:
   Quicken me, O LORD, according unto thy word.
108 Accept, I beseech thee, the freewill offerings of my mouth, O Lord,
   And teach me thy judgments.
109 My soul *is* continually in my hand:
   Yet do I not forget thy law.

110 The wicked have laid a snare for me:
   Yet I erred not from thy precepts.
111 Thy testimonies have I taken as a heritage for ever:
   For they are *the rejoicing of my heart.*
112 I have inclined mine heart to perform thy statutes
   Always, even unto *the end.*

SAMECH.

113 I hate *vain* thoughts :
   But thy law do I love.
114 Thou *art* my hiding place and my shield:
   I hope in thy word.
115 Depart from me, ye evil doers:
   For I will keep the commandments of my God.
116 Uphold me according unto thy word, that I may live:
   And let me not be ashamed of my hope.
117 Hold thou me up, and I shall be safe:
   And I will have respect unto thy statutes continually.
118 Thou hast trodden down all them that err from thy statutes:
   For their deceit is *falsehood.*
119 Thou puttest away all the wicked of the earth *like* dross:
   Therefore I love thy testimonies.
120 My flesh trembleth for fear of thee;
   And I am afraid of thy judgments.

LESSON 88.

Psalm cxix, Sixth Part.

AIN.

I HAVE done judgment and justice:
   Leave me not to mine oppressors.
122 Be surety for thy servant for good:
   Let not the proud oppress me.
123 Mine eyes fail for thy salvation,
   And for the word of thy righteousness.
124 Deal with thy servant according unto thy mercy,
   And teach me thy statutes.
125 I *am* thy servant; give me understanding,
   That I may know thy testimonies.

126 *It is* time for *thee,* LORD, to work:
   For *they have made void thy law.*
127 Therefore I love thy commandments
   Above gold; yea, above fine gold.
128 Therefore I esteem all *thy* precepts *concerning* all *things to be* right;
   And *I* hate *every false way.*

PE.

129 Thy testimonies *are* wonderful:
   Therefore doth my soul keep them.
130 The entrance of thy words giveth light;
   It giveth understanding unto the simple.
131 I opened my mouth, and panted:
   For I longed for thy commandments.
132 Look thou upon me, and be merciful unto me,
   As thou usest to do unto those that love thy name.
133 Order my steps in thy word:
   And let not any iniquity have dominion over me.
134 Deliver me from the oppression of man:
   So will I keep thy precepts.
135 Make thy face to shine upon thy servant;
   And teach me thy statutes.
136 Rivers of waters run down mine eyes,
   Because they keep not thy law.

LESSON 89.

PSALM CXIX, SEVENTH PART.

TZADDI.

137 Righteous *art* thou O LORD,
   And upright are *thy judgments.*
138 Thy testimonies *that* thou hast commanded *are* righteous
   And very faithful.
139 My zeal hath consumed me,
   Because mine enemies have forgotten thy words.
140 Thy word *is* very pure:
   Therefore thy servant loveth it.
141 I *am* small and despised:
   Yet *do not I forget thy precepts.*

142 Thy righteousness *is* an everlasting righteousness,
   And thy law is *the truth*.
143 Trouble and anguish have taken hold on me:
   Yet *thy commandments* are *my delights*.
144 The righteousness of thy testimonies *is* everlasting:
   Give *me understanding, and I shall live*.

KOPH.

145 I cried with *my* whole heart; hear me, O Lord:
   I will keep thy statutes.
146 I cried unto thee; save me,
   And I shall keep thy testimonies.
147 I prevented the dawning of the morning, and cried:
   I hoped in thy word.
148 Mine eyes prevent the *night* watches,
   That I might meditate in thy word.
149 Hear my voice according unto thy lovingkindness:
   O LORD, quicken me according to thy judgment.
150 They draw nigh that follow after mischief:
   They are far from thy law.
151 Thou *art* near, O Lord;
   And all thy commandments are *truth*.
152 Concerning thy testimonies, I have known of old
   That thou hast founded them for ever.

RESH.

153 Consider mine affliction, and deliver me:
   For I do not forget thy law.
154 Plead my cause, and deliver me:
   Quicken me according to thy word.
155 Salvation *is* far from the wicked:
   For they seek not thy statutes.
156 Great *are* thy tender mercies, O Lord:
   Quicken me according to thy judgments.
157 Many *are* my persecutors and mine enemies;
   Yet *do I not decline from thy testimonies*.
158 I beheld the transgressors, and was grieved;
   Because they kept not thy word.
159 Consider how I love thy precepts:
   Quicken me, O LORD, according to thy lovingkindness.

160 Thy word *is* true *from* the beginning:
And every one of thy righteous judgments endureth *for ever.*

LESSON 90.

PSALM CXIX, EIGHTH PART.

SCHIN.

161 Princes have persecuted me without a cause:
But my heart standeth in awe of thy word.
162 I rejoice at thy word,
As one that findeth great spoil.
163 I hate and abhor lying:
But *thy law do I love.*
164 Seven times a day do I praise thee,
Because of thy righteous judgments.
165 Great peace have they which love thy law:
And nothing shall offend them.
166 LORD, I have hoped for thy salvation,
And done thy commandments.
167 My soul hath kept thy testimonies;
And I love them exceedingly.
168 I have kept thy precepts and thy testimonies:
For all my ways are before thee.

TAU.

169 Let my cry come near before thee, O LORD:
Give me understanding according to thy word.
170 Let my supplication come before thee:
Deliver me according to thy word.
171 My lips shall utter praise,
When thou hast taught me thy statutes.
172 My tongue shall speak of thy word:
For all thy commandments are *righteousness.*
173 Let thine hand help me;
For I have chosen thy precepts.
174 I have longed for thy salvation, O LORD;
And thy law is my delight.
175 Let my soul live, and it shall praise thee;
And let thy judgments help me.
176 I have gone astray like a lost sheep: seek thy servant;
For I do not forget thy commandments.

LESSON 91.

PSALM CXX.

A Song of degrees.

IN my distress I cried unto the LORD,
   And he heard me.
2 Deliver my soul, O LORD, from lying lips,
   And *from a deceitful tongue.*
3 What shall be given unto thee? or what shall be done unto thee,
   Thou false tongue?
4 Sharp arrows of the mighty,
   With coals of juniper.
5 Woe is me, that I sojourn in Mesech,
   That *I dwell in the tents of Kedar!*
6 My soul hath long dwelt
   With him that hateth peace.
7 I *am for* peace: but when I speak,
   They are *for war.*

PSALM CXXI.

A Song of degrees.

I WILL lift up mine eyes unto the hills,
   From whence cometh my help.
2 My help *cometh* from the LORD,
   Which made heaven and earth.
3 He will not suffer thy foot to be moved:
   He that keepeth thee will not slumber.
4 Behold, he that keepeth Israel
   Shall neither slumber nor sleep.
5 The LORD *is* thy keeper:
   The LORD is thy shade upon thy right hand.
6 The sun shall not smite thee by day,
   Nor the moon by night.
7 The LORD shall preserve thee from all evil:
   He shall preserve thy soul.
8 The LORD shall preserve thy going out and thy coming in
   From this time forth, and even for evermore.

LESSON 92.

PSALM CXXII.
A Song of degrees of David.

I WAS glad when they said unto me,
   Let us go into the house of the LORD.
2 Our feet shall stand
   Within thy gates, O Jerusalem.
3 Jerusalem is builded
   As a city that is compact together:
4 { Whither the tribes go up,
    Tthe tribes of the LORD,
   { *Unto the testimony of Israel,*
     To give thanks unto the name of the LORD.
5 For there are set thrones of judgment,
   The thrones of the house of David.
6 Pray for the peace of Jerusalem:
   They shall prosper that love thee.
7 Peace be within thy walls,
   And prosperity within thy palaces.
8 For my brethren and companions' sakes,
   I will now say, Peace be within thee.
9 Because of the house of the LORD our God
   I will seek thy good.

LESSON 92.

PSALM CXXIII.
A Song of degrees.

UNTO thee lift I up mine eyes,
   O thou that dwellest in the heavens.
2 { Behold, as the eyes of servants *look* unto the hand of their masters,
    And as the eyes of a maiden unto the hand of her mistress;
      So our eyes wait *upon the LORD our God, until that he have*
      mercy upon us.
3 Have mercy upon us, O LORD, have mercy upon us:
   For we are exceedingly filled with contempt.
4 { Our soul is exceedingly filled
    With the scorning of those that are at ease,
      And with the contempt of the proud.

Psalm CXXIV.

A Song of degrees of David.

IF *it had* not *been* the LORD who was on our side,
 Now may Israel say;
2 If *it had* not *been* the LORD who was on our side,
 When men rose up against us:
3 Then they had swallowed us up quick,
 When their wrath was kindled against us:
4 Then the waters had overwhelmed us,
 The stream had gone over our soul:
5 Then the proud waters
 Had gone over our soul.
6 Blessed *be* the LORD, who hath not given us
 As *a prey to their teeth.*
7 { Our soul is escaped as a bird
 Out of the snare of the fowlers:
 { *The snare is broken,*
 { *And we are escaped.*
8 Our help *is* in the name of the LORD,
 Who made heaven and earth.

Psalm CXXV.

A Song of degrees.

THEY that trust in the LORD *shall be* as mount Zion,
 Which *cannot be removed,* but *abideth for ever.*
2 *As* the mountains *are* round about Jerusalem,
 { *So the LORD is round about his people*
 { *From henceforth even for ever.*
3 { For the rod of the wicked shall not rest
 { Upon the lot of the righteous;
 { *Lest the righteous put forth*
 { *Their hands unto iniquity.*
4 Do good, O LORD, unto *those that be* good,
 And *to* them that are *upright in their hearts.*
5 { As for such as turn aside unto their crooked ways,
 { The LORD shall lead them forth with the workers of iniquity:
 But *peace* shall be *upon Israel.*

LESSON 93.

PSALM CXXVI.

A Song of degrees.

WHEN the LORD turned again the captivity of Zion,
We were like them that dream.
2 Then was our mouth filled with laughter,
And our tongue with singing:
Then said they among the heathen,
The LORD hath done great things for them.
3 The LORD hath done great things for us;
Whereof we are glad.
4 Turn again our captivity, O LORD,
As the streams in the south.
5 They that sow in tears
Shall reap in joy.
6 He that goeth forth and weepeth,
Bearing precious seed,
Shall doubtless come again with rejoicing,
Bringing his sheaves with him.

LESSON 93.

PSALM CXXVII.

A Song of degrees for Solomon.

EXCEPT the LORD build the house,
They labour in vain that build it:
Except the LORD keep the city,
The watchman waketh but in vain.
2 *It is* vain for you to rise up early,
To sit up late,
To eat the bread of sorrows:
For so he giveth his beloved sleep.
3 Lo, children *are* a heritage of the LORD:
And the fruit of the womb is his reward.
4 As arrows *are* in the hand of a mighty man;
So are *children of the youth.*

5 { Happy *is* the man
{ That hath his quiver full of them :
   { *They shall not be ashamed,*
   { *But they shall speak with the enemies in the gate.*

PSALM CXXVIII.

A Song of degrees.

BLESSED *is* every one that feareth the LORD ;
That walketh in his ways.
2 For thou shalt eat the labour of thine hands :
Happy shalt *thou* be, *and* it shall be *well with thee.*
3 { Thy wife *shall be* as a fruitful vine
{ By the side of thine house :
   { *Thy children like olive plants*
   { *Round about thy table.*
4 Behold, that thus shall the man be blessed
That feareth the LORD.
5 The LORD shall bless thee out of Zion :
   { *And thou shalt see the good of Jerusalem*
   { *All the days of thy life.*
6 Yea, thou shalt see thy children's children,
And *peace upon Israel.*

PSALM CXXIX.

A Song of degrees.

MANY a time have they afflicted me from my youth,
May Israel now say :
2 Many a time have they afflicted me from my youth :
Yet they have not prevailed against me.
3 The ploughers ploughed upon my back :
They make long their furrows.
4 The LORD *is* righteous :
He hath cut asunder the cords of the wicked.
5 Let them all be confounded and turned back
That hate Zion.
6 Let them be as the grass *upon* the housetops,
Which withereth afore it groweth up:
7 Wherewith the mower filleth not his hand ;
Nor he that bindeth sheaves his bosom.

LESSON 93.

8 { Neither do they which go by say,
  { The blessing of the LORD *be* upon you :
   { *We bless you*
   { *In the name of the LORD.*

PSALM CXXX.
A Song of degrees.

OUT of the depths have I cried unto thee, O LORD.
2 *Lord, hear my voice :*
  Let thine ears be attentive
   To the voice of my supplications.
3 If thou, LORD, shouldest mark iniquities,
   O Lord, who shall stand ?
4 But *there is* forgiveness with thee,
   That thou mayest be feared.
5 I wait for the LORD, my soul doth wait,
   And in his word do I hope.
6 { My soul *waiteth* for the Lord
  { More than they that watch for the morning :
   I say, more than *they that watch for the morning.*
7 { Let Israel hope in the LORD :
  { For with the LORD *there is* mercy,
   And with him is *plenteous redemption.*
8 And he shall redeem Israel
   From all his iniquities.

PSALM CXXXI.
A Song of degrees of David.

LORD, my heart is not haughty, nor mine eyes lofty :
   { *Neither do I exercise myself in great matters,*
   { *Or in things too high for me.*
2 { Surely I have behaved and quieted myself,
  { As a child that is weaned of his mother :
   My soul is *even as a weaned child.*
3 Let Israel hope in the LORD
   From henceforth and for ever.

LESSON 94.

Psalm CXXXII.
A Song of degrees.

LORD, remember David,
  And *all his afflictions:*
2 How he sware unto the LORD,
  And *vowed unto the mighty* God *of Jacob;*
3 Surely I will not come into the tabernacle of my house,
  Nor go up into my bed;
4 I will not give sleep to mine eyes,
  Or *slumber to mine eyelids,*
5 Until I find out a place for the LORD,
  A habitation for the mighty God of Jacob.
6 Lo, we heard of it at Ephratah:
  We found it in the fields of the wood.
7 We will go into his tabernacles:
  We will worship at his footstool.
8 Arise, O LORD, into thy rest;
  Thou, and the ark of thy strength.
9 Let thy priests be clothed with righteousness;
  And let thy saints shout for joy.
10 For thy servant David's sake
  Turn not away the face of thine anointed.
11 { The LORD hath sworn *in* truth unto David;
  { He will not turn from it;
    { *Of the fruit of thy body*
    { *Will I set upon thy throne.*
12 { If thy children will keep my covenant
    { And my testimony that I shall teach them,
  Their children shall also sit upon thy throne for evermore.
13 For the LORD hath chosen Zion;
  He hath desired it for his habitation.
14 This *is* my rest for ever:
  Here will I dwell; for I have desired it.
15 I will abundantly bless her provision:
  I will satisfy her poor with bread.

16 I will also clothe her priests with salvation :
And her saints shall shout aloud for joy.
17 There will I make the horn of David to bud :
I have ordained a lamp for mine anointed.
18 His enemies will I clothe with shame :
But upon himself shall his crown flourish.

PSALM CXXXIII.

A Song of degrees of David.

BEHOLD, how good and how pleasant *it is*
For brethren to dwell together in unity.
2 { *It is* like the precious ointment upon the head,
{ That ran down upon the beard, *even* Aaron's beard :
That went down to the skirts of his garments;
3 As the dew of Hermon, *and as the dew* that descended upon the mountains of Zion :
{ *For there the LORD commanded the blessing,*
{ *Even life for evermore.*

PSALM CXXXIV.

A Song of degrees.

BEHOLD, bless ye the LORD, all *ye* servants of the LORD,
Which by night stand in the house of the LORD.
2 Lift up your hands *in* the sanctuary,
And bless the LORD.
3 The LORD that made heaven and earth
Bless thee out of Zion.

LESSON 95.

PSALM CXXXV.

{ PRAISE ye the LORD.
{ Praise ye the name of the LORD;
Praise him, O ye servants of the LORD.
2 Ye that stand in the house of the LORD,
In the courts of the house of our God,
3 Praise the LORD ; for the LORD *is* good :
Sing praises unto his name; for it is *pleasant.*

4 For the Lord hath chosen Jacob unto himself,
 And *Israel for his peculiar treasure.*
5 For I know that the Lord *is* great,
 And that *our Lord* is *above all gods.*
6 { Whatsoever the Lord pleased, *that* did he
 { In heaven, and in earth,
 In the seas, and all deep places.
7 { He causeth the vapours to ascend from the ends of the earth;
 { He maketh lightnings for the rain;
 He bringeth the wind out of his treasuries.
8 Who smote the firstborn of Egypt,
 Both of man and beast.
9 { *Who* sent tokens and wonders
 { Into the midst of thee, O Egypt,
 Upon Pharaoh, and upon all his servants.
10 Who smote great nations,
 And slew mighty kings;
11 { Sihon king of the Amorites,
 { And Og king of Bashan,
 And all the kingdoms of Canaan:
12 And gave their land *for* a heritage,
 A heritage unto Israel his people.
13 Thy name, O Lord, *endureth* for ever;
 And *thy memorial, O LORD, throughout all generations.*
14 For the Lord will judge his people,
 And he will repent himself concerning his servants.
15 The idols of the heathen *are* silver and gold,
 The work of men's hands.
16 They have mouths, but they speak not;
 Eyes have they, but they see not;
17 They have ears, but they hear not;
 Neither is there any breath in their mouths.
18 They that make them are like unto them:
 So is *every one that trusteth in them.*
19 Bless the Lord, O house of Israel:
 Bless the LORD, O house of Aaron:
20 Bless the Lord, O house of Levi;
 Ye that fear the LORD, bless the LORD.

21 Blessed be the LORD out of Zion,
Which dwelleth at Jerusalem. *Praise ye the LORD.*

LESSON 96.

PSALM CXXXVI.

OH give thanks unto the LORD; for *he is* good:
For his mercy endureth for ever.
2 Oh give thanks unto the God of gods:
For his mercy endureth for ever.
3 Oh give thanks to the Lord of lords:
For his mercy endureth for ever.
4 To him who alone doeth great wonders:
For his mercy endureth for ever.
5 To him that by wisdom made the heavens:
For his mercy endureth for ever.
6 To him that stretched out the earth above the waters:
For his mercy endureth for ever.
7 To him that made great lights:
For his mercy endureth for ever:
8 The sun to rule by day:
For his mercy endureth for ever:
9 The moon and stars to rule by night:
For his mercy endureth for ever.
10 To him that smote Egypt in their firstborn:
For his mercy endureth for ever:
11 And brought out Israel from among them:
For his mercy endureth for ever:
12 With a strong hand, and with a stretched out arm:
For his mercy endureth for ever.
13 To him which divided the Red sea into parts:
For his mercy endureth for ever:
14 And made Israel to pass through the midst of it:
For his mercy endureth for ever:
15 But overthrew Pharaoh and his host in the Red sea:
For his mercy endureth for ever.

16 To him which led his people through the wilderness :
For his mercy endureth for ever.
17 To him which smote great kings :
For his mercy endureth for ever.
18 And slew famous kings :
For his mercy endureth for ever :
19 Sihon king of the Amorites :
For his mercy endureth for ever :
20 And Og the king of Bashan :
For his mercy endureth for ever :
21 And gave their land for a heritage :
For his mercy endureth for ever :
22 *Even* a heritage unto Israel his servant :
For his mercy endureth for ever.
23 Who remembered us in our low estate :
For his mercy endureth for ever :
24 And hath redeemed us from our enemies :
For his mercy endureth for ever.
25 Who giveth food to all flesh :
For his mercy endureth for ever.
26 Oh give thanks unto the God of heaven :
For his mercy endureth for ever.

LESSON 97.

PSALM CXXXVII.

BY the rivers of Babylon, there we sat down, yea, we wept,
When we remembered Zion.
2 We hanged our harps upon the willows
In the midst thereof,
3 For there they that carried us away captive required of us a song ;
And they that wasted us required of us *mirth,* saying, *Sing us* one
of the songs of Zion.
4 How shall we sing the LORD's song
In a strange land ?
5 If I forget thee, O Jerusalem,
Let my right hand forget her cunning.

6 If I do not remember thee,
  Let my tongue cleave to the roof of my mouth ;
  If I prefer not Jerusalem
  Above my chief joy.
7 Remember, O LORD, the children of Edom
  In the day of Jerusalem ;
  Who said, Rase *it*, rase *it*,
  Even *to the foundation thereof.*
8 O daughter of Babylon, who art to be destroyed; happy *shall he be,*
  that rewardeth thee
  As thou hast served us.
9 Happy *shall he be*, that taketh and dasheth thy little ones
  Against the stones.

PSALM CXXXVIII.

A Psalm of David.

I WILL praise thee with my whole heart:
  Before the gods will I sing praise unto thee.
2 I will worship toward thy holy temple,
  And praise thy name
  For thy lovingkindness and for thy truth:
  For thou hast magnified thy word above all thy name.
3 In the day when I cried thou answeredst me,
  And *strengthenedst me* with *strength in my soul.*
4 All the kings of the earth shall praise thee, O LORD,
  When they hear the words of thy mouth.
5 Yea, they shall sing in the ways of the LORD:
  For great is the glory of the LORD.
6 Though the LORD *be* high, yet hath he respect unto the lowly:
  But the proud he knoweth afar off.
7 Though I walk in the midst of trouble, thou wilt revive me:
  { *Thou shalt stretch forth thine hand against the wrath of mine*
  enemies,
  And thy right hand shall save me.
8 { The LORD will perfect *that which* concerneth me:
  { Thy mercy, O LORD, *endureth* for ever:
  Forsake not the works of thine own hands.

LESSON 98.

Psalm CXXXIX.

To the chief Musician, A Psalm of David.

{O LORD, thou hast searched me, and know *me*.
2 Thou knowest my downsitting and mine uprising;
Thou understandest my thought afar off.
3 Thou compassest my path and my lying down,
And art acquainted with *all my ways.*
4 For *there is* not a word in my tongue,
But, *lo, O LORD, thou knowest it altogether.*
5 Thou hast beset me behind and before,
And laid thine hand upon me.
6 *Such* knowledge *is* too wonderful for me;
It is high, I cannot attain *unto it.*
7 Whither shall I go from thy spirit?
Or whither shall I flee from thy presence?
8 If I ascend up into heaven, thou *art* there:
If I make my bed in hell, behold, thou art there.
9 *If* I take the wings of the morning,
And *dwell in the uttermost parts of the sea;*
10 Even there shall thy hand lead me,
And thy right hand shall hold me.
11 If I say, Surely the darkness shall cover me;
Even the night shall be light about me.
12 { Yea, the darkness hideth not from thee;
{ But the night shineth as the day:
The darkness and the light are *both alike* to thee.
13 For thou hast possessed my reins:
Thou hast covered me in my mother's womb.
14 { I will praise thee; for I am fearfully *and* wonderfully made:
{ Marvellous *are* thy works;
And that *my soul knoweth right well.*
15 { My substance was not hid from thee,
{ When I was made in secret,
And *curiously wrought in the lowest parts of the earth.*

16 { Thine eyes did see my substance, yet being unperfect;
    And in thy book all *my members* were written,
    Which *in continuance were fashioned, when* as yet there was *none of them.*
17 How precious also are thy thoughts unto me, O God!
    How great is the sum of them!
18 *If* I should count them, they are more in number than the sand:
    When I awake, I am still with thee.
19 Surely thou wilt slay the wicked, O God:
    Depart from me therefore, ye bloody men.
20 For they speak against thee wickedly,
    And *thine enemies take* thy name *in vain.*
21 Do not I hate them, O LORD, that hate thee?
    And am not I grieved with those that rise up against thee?
22 I hate them with perfect hatred:
    I count them mine enemies.
23 Search me, O God, and know my heart:
    Try me, and know my thoughts:
24 And see if *there be any* wicked way in me,
    And lead me in the way everlasting.

LESSON 99.

PSALM CXL.

To the chief Musician, A Psalm of David.

DELIVER me, O LORD, from the evil man:
    Preserve me from the violent man;
2 Which imagine mischiefs in *their* heart;
    Continually are they gathered together for *war.*
3 They have sharpened their tongues like a serpent;
    Adders' poison is under their lips. (*Selah.*)
4 { Keep me, O LORD, from the hands of the wicked;
    Preserve me from the violent man;
    Who have purposed to overthrow my goings.
5 The proud have hid a snare for me, and cords;
    { *They have spread a net by the way side;*
    They have set gins for me. (*Selah.*)

6 I said unto the Lord, Thou *art* my God:
   Hear the voice of my supplications, O LORD.
7 O God the Lord, the strength of my salvation,
   Thou hast covered my head in the day of battle.
8 Grant not, O Lord, the desires of the wicked:
   Further not his wicked device; lest they exalt themselves. (*Selah.*)
9 *As for* the head of those that compass me about,
   Let the mischief of their own lips cover them.
10 Let burning coals fall upon them: let them be cast into the fire;
    Into deep pits, that they rise not up again.
11 Let not an evil speaker be established in the earth:
    Evil shall hunt the violent man to overthrow him.
12 I know that the Lord will maintain the cause of the afflicted,
    And *the right of the poor.*
13 Surely the righteous shall give thanks unto thy name:
    The upright shall dwell in thy presence.

Psalm CXLI.

A Psalm of David.

LORD, I cry unto thee: make haste unto me;
   Give ear unto my voice, when I cry unto thee.
2 Let my prayer be set forth before thee *as* incense;
   And the lifting up of my hands as the evening sacrifice.
3 Set a watch, O Lord, before my mouth;
   Keep the door of my lips.
4 { Incline not my heart to *any* evil thing,
    To practice wicked works
    With men that work iniquity:
   And let me not eat of their dainties.
5 { Let the righteous smite me; *it shall be* a kindness: and let him re-
       prove me;
    It shall be an excellent oil, *which* shall not break my head:
   For yet my prayer also shall be in their calamities.
6 When their judges are overthrown in stony places,
   They shall hear my words; for they are sweet.
7 Our bones are scattered at the grave's mouth,
   As when one cutteth and cleaveth wood *upon the earth.*
8 But mine eyes *are* unto thee, O God the Lord:
   In thee is my trust; leave not my soul destitute.

9 Keep me from the snare *which* they have laid for me,
    And the gins of the workers of iniquity.
10 Let the wicked fall into their own nets,
    Whilst that I withal escape.

LESSON 100.

Psalm CXLII.
Maschil of David; A Prayer when he was in the cave.

I CRIED unto the Lord with my voice;
    With my voice unto the LORD did I make my supplication.
2 I poured out my complaint before him;
    I shewed before him my trouble.
3 When my spirit was overwhelmed within me,
    Then thou knewest my path.
  In the way wherein I walked
    Have they privily laid a snare for me.
4 I looked on *my* right hand, and beheld, but *there was* no man that
    would know me:
    Refuge failed me; no man cared for my soul.
5 { I cried unto thee, O Lord:
  { I said, Thou *art* my refuge
    And *my portion in the land of the living.*
6 Attend unto my cry; for I am brought very low:
    Deliver me from my persecutors; for they are stronger than I.
7 Bring my soul out of prison, that I may praise thy name:
    The righteous shall compass me about; for thou shalt deal bountifully with me.

Psalm CXLIII.
A Psalm of David.

HEAR my prayer, O Lord, give ear to my supplications:
    In thy faithfulness answer me, and in thy righteousness.
2 And enter not into judgment with thy servant:
    For in thy sight shall no man living be justified.
3 { For the enemy hath persecuted my soul;
  { He hath smitten my life down to the ground;
    He hath made me to dwell in darkness, as those that have been long dead.

4 Therefore is my spirit overwhelmed within me;
  My heart within me is desolate.
5 {I remember the days of old;
   I meditate on all thy works;
  I muse on the work of thy hands.
6 I stretch forth my hands unto thee:
  My soul thirsteth after thee, as a thirsty land. (*Selah.*)
7 {Hear me speedily, O LORD; my spirit faileth:
   Hide not thy face from me,
  Lest I be like unto them that go down into the pit.
8 Cause me to hear thy lovingkindness in the morning;
  For in thee do I trust.
  Cause me to know the way wherein I should walk;
  For I lift up my soul unto thee.
9 Deliver me, O LORD, from mine enemies;
  I flee unto thee to hide me.
10 {Teach me to do thy will;
    For thou *art* my God:
  Thy spirit is *good; lead me into the land of uprightness.*
11 Quicken me, O LORD, for thy name's sake:
  For thy righteousness' sake bring my soul out of trouble.
12 {And of thy mercy cut off mine enemies,
    And destroy all them that afflict my soul:
  For I am *thy servant.*

LESSON 101.

PSALM CXLIV.

A Psalm of David.

BLESSED *be* the LORD my strength,
   { *Which teacheth my hands to war,*
     And my fingers to fight.
2 My goodness, and my fortress;
  My high tower, and my deliverer;
  My shield, and *he* in whom I trust;
  Who subdueth my people under me.
3 LORD, what *is* man, that thou takest knowledge of him!
  Or *the son of man, that thou makest account of him!*

4 Man is like to vanity:
  His days are *as a shadow that passeth away.*
5 Bow thy heavens, O LORD, and come down:
  Touch the mountains, and they shall smoke.
6 Cast forth lightning, and scatter them:
  Shoot out thine arrows and destroy them.
7 { Send thine hand from above;
  { Rid me, and deliver me out of great waters,
  From the hand of strange children;
8 Whose mouth speaketh vanity,
  And their right hand is *a right hand of falsehood.*
9 I will sing a new song unto thee, O God:
  Upon a psaltery and an instrument of ten strings will I sing praises unto thee.
10 *It is he* that giveth salvation unto kings:
  Who delivereth David his servant from the hurtful sword.
11 { Rid me, and deliver me from the hand of strange children,
   { Whose mouth speaketh vanity,
  And their right hand is *a right hand of falsehood:*
12 That our sons *may be* as plants grown up in their youth;
  That *our daughters* may be *as corner stones, polished* after *the similitude of a palace;*
13 *That* our garners *may be* full, affording all manner of store;
  That *our sheep may bring forth thousands and ten thousands in our streets:*
14 *That* our oxen *may be* strong to labour; *that there be* no breaking in, nor going out;
  That there be *no complaining in our streets.*
15 Happy *is that* people, that is in such a case:
  Yea, *happy* is that *people, whose God* is *the LORD.*

LESSON 102.

PSALM CXLV.

David's *Psalm* of praise.

I WILL extol thee, my God, O king;
  And I will bless thy name for ever and ever.
2 Every day will I bless thee;
  And I will praise thy name for ever and ever.

3 Great *is* the LORD, and greatly to be praised;
And his greatness is unsearchable.
4 One generation shall praise thy works to another,
And shall declare thy mighty acts.
5 I will speak of the glorious honour of thy majesty,
And of thy wondrous works.
6 And *men* shall speak of the might of thy terrible acts:
And I will declare thy greatness.
7 They shall abundantly utter the memory of thy great goodness,
And shall sing of thy righteousness.
8 The LORD *is* gracious, and full of compassion;
Slow to anger, and of great mercy.
9 The LORD *is* good to all:
And his tender mercies are over all his works.
10 All thy works shall praise thee, O LORD;
And thy saints shall bless thee.
11 They shall speak of the glory of thy kingdom,
And talk of thy power;
12 To make known to the sons of men his mighty acts,
And the glorious majesty of his kingdom.
13 Thy kingdom *is* an everlasting kingdom,
And thy dominion endureth throughout all generations.
14 The LORD upholdeth all that fall,
And raiseth up all those that be bowed down.
15 The eyes of all wait upon thee;
And thou givest them their meat in due season.
16 Thou openest thine hand,
And satisfiest the desire of every living thing.
17 The LORD *is* righteous in all his ways,
And holy in all his works.
18 The LORD *is* nigh unto all them that call upon him,
To all that call upon him in truth.
19 He will fulfil the desire of them that fear him:
He also will hear their cry, and will save them.
20 The LORD preserveth all them that love him:
But all the wicked will he destroy.
21 My mouth shall speak the praise of the LORD:
And let all flesh bless his holy name for ever and ever.

LESSON 103.

PSALM CXLVI.

PRAISE ye the LORD.
   Praise the LORD, O my soul.
2 While I live will I praise the LORD:
   I will sing praises unto my God while I have any being.
3 Put not your trust in princes,
   Nor *in the son of man, in whom* there is *no help.*
4 His breath goeth forth, he returneth to his earth;
   In that very day his thoughts perish.
5 Happy *is he* that *hath* the God of Jacob for his help,
   Whose hope is *in the LORD his God.*
6 Which made heaven, and earth, the sea, and all that therein *is:*
   Which keepeth truth for ever:
7 Which executeth judgment for the oppressed:
   Which giveth food to the hungry.
   The LORD looseth the prisoners:
8   *The LORD openeth* the eyes of *the blind:*
   The LORD raiseth them that are bowed down:
   The LORD loveth the righteous:
9 {The LORD preserveth the strangers:
   He relieveth the fatherless and the widow:
   But the way of the wicked he turneth upside down.
10 {The LORD shall reign for ever,
   Even thy God, O Zion, unto all generations.
   Praise ye the LORD.

PSALM CXLVII.

{PRAISE ye the LORD:
   For *it is* good to sing praises unto our God;
   For it is *pleasant; and praise is comely.*
2 The LORD doth build up Jerusalem:
   He gathereth together the outcasts of Israel.
3 He healeth the broken in heart,
   And bindeth up their wounds.
4 He telleth the number of the stars;
   He calleth them all by their names.

5 Great *is* our Lord, and of great power :
   His understanding is *infinite.*
6 The LORD lifteth up the meek :
   He casteth the wicked down to the ground.
7 Sing unto the LORD with thanksgiving ;
   Sing praise upon the harp unto our God :
8 {Who covereth the heaven with clouds,
   {Who prepareth rain for the earth,
   Who maketh grass to grow upon the mountains.
9 He giveth to the beast his food,
   And *to the young ravens which cry.*
10 He delighteth not in the strength of the horse :
   He taketh not pleasure in the legs of a man.
11 The LORD taketh pleasure in them that fear him,
   In those that hope in his mercy.
12 Praise the LORD, O Jerusalem ;
   Praise thy God, O Zion.
13 For he hath strengthened the bars of thy gates ;
   He hath blessed thy children within thee.
14 He maketh peace *in* thy borders,
   And *filleth thee with the finest of the wheat.*
15 He sendeth forth his commandment *upon* earth :
   His word runneth very swiftly.
16 He giveth snow like wool :
   He scattereth the hoar frost like ashes.
17 He casteth forth his ice like morsels :
   Who can stand before his cold?
18 He sendeth out his word, and melteth them :
   He causeth his wind to blow, and *the waters flow.*
19 He sheweth his word unto Jacob,
   His statutes and his judgments unto Israel.
20 {He hath not dealt so with any nation :
   {And *as for his* judgments, they have not known them.
   Praise ye the LORD.

LESSON 104.

PSALM CLXVIII.

{ PRAISE ye the LORD.
Praise ye the LORD from the heavens:
Praise him in the heights.
2 Praise ye him, all his angels:
Praise ye him, all his hosts.
3 Praise ye him, sun and moon:
Praise him, all ye stars of light.
4 Praise him, ye heavens of heavens,
And ye waters that be above the heavens.
5 Let them praise the name of the LORD:
For he commanded, and they were created.
6 He hath also stablished them for ever and ever:
He hath made a decree which shall not pass.
7 Praise the LORD from the earth,
Ye dragons, and all deeps:
8 Fire, and hail; snow, and vapour;
Stormy wind fulfilling his word:
9 Mountains, and all hills;
Fruitful trees, and all cedars:
10 Beasts, and all cattle;
Creeping things, and flying fowl:
11 Kings of the earth, and all people;
Princes, and all judges of the earth:
12 Both young men, and maidens:
Old men, and children:
13 { Let them praise the name of the LORD:
For his name alone is excellent;
His glory is above the earth and heaven.
14 He also exalteth the horn of his people,
The praise of all his saints;
Even of the children of Israel, a people near unto him.
Praise ye the LORD.

Psalm CXLIX.

PRAISE ye the LORD.
Sing unto the LORD a new song,
  And *his praise in the congregation of saints.*
2 Let Israel rejoice in him that made him:
  Let the children of Zion be joyful in their King.
3 Let them praise him in the dance:
  Let them sing praises unto him with the timbrel and harp.
4 For the LORD taketh pleasure in his people:
  He will beautify the meek with salvation.
5 Let the saints be joyful in glory:
  Let them sing aloud upon their beds.
6 *Let* the high *praises* of God *be* in their mouth,
  And a two-edged sword in their hand;
7 To execute vengeance upon the heathen,
  And punishments upon the people;
8 To bind their kings with chains,
  And their nobles with fetters of iron;
9 To execute upon them the judgment written:
  This honour have all his saints.
  Praise ye the LORD.

Psalm CL.

PRAISE ye the LORD.
Praise God in his sanctuary:
  Praise him in the firmament of his power.
2 Praise him for his mighty acts:
  Praise him according to his excellent greatness.
3 Praise him with the sound of the trumpet:
  Praise him with the psaltery and harp.
4 Praise him with the timbrel and dance:
  Praise him with stringed instruments and organs.
5 Praise him upon the loud cymbals:
  Praise him upon the high sounding cymbals.
6 Let everything that hath breath praise the LORD.
  Praise ye the LORD.

Hymns

for the Several Parts of

Public Worship;

With others for

Social, Family, and Private Devotion,

And for

Children.

NOTE.

The Hymns marked "I" and "II," at each opening, are appointed for Public Worship in the Church; and respectively for the First Part of the service, after the Prayer of Confession, and for the Second Part, after the Reading of the Psalter; according to the Classification at the end of the book. They are also used in social, Sunday-school, and private worship, at discretion.

The remaining Hymns at each opening, under the title "FOR SOCIAL AND PRIVATE WORSHIP," are *not used* in the regular public service. They comprise three classes, which, so far as they occur on any one page, are generally placed in the following order, but without marked divisions:—(1.) Hymns most suitable for the chapel services of Lecture and Prayer-meeting; (2.) Those more especially suited to the devotions of the Family and the Sunday-school; (3.) Those strictly adapted to private devotion.

A few set devotional Songs for Children are placed together at the end of the book; but not as the only ones to be used by them. It is an excellent practice to make children familiar, in the family and the Sunday-school, with the standard Hymns of the Church, as well as with the Creed and Catechism.

HYMNS.

HYMNS 1, 2, 3.

ALFRETON. L. M.

1

I.

WITH all my powers of heart and tongue
I'll praise my Maker in my song:
Angels shall hear the notes I raise,
Approve the song, and join the praise.

2 I'll sing thy truth and mercy, Lord;
I'll sing the wonders of thy word;
Not all the works and names below,
So much thy power and glory show.

3 Amidst a thousand snares I stand,
Upheld and guarded by thy hand;
Thy words my fainting soul revive,
And keep my dying faith alive.

4 Grace will complete what grace begins,
To save from sorrows and from sins;
The work that wisdom undertakes,
Eternal mercy ne'er forsakes.

2

II.

PRAISE ye the Lord, exalt his name,
While in his earthly courts ye wait,
Ye saints that to his house belong,
Or stand attending at his gate.

2 Praise ye the Lord, the Lord is good;
To praise his name is sweet employ;
Israel he chose of old, and still
His church is his peculiar joy.

3 Bless ye the Lord who taste his love,
People and priests exalt his name;
Among his saints he ever dwells;
His church is his Jerusalem.

3

II.

GIVE to our God immortal praise;
Mercy and truth are all his ways;
Wonders of grace to God belong,
Repeat his mercies in your song.

2 Give to the Lord of lords renown!
The King of kings with glory crown:
His mercies ever shall endure,
When lords and kings are known no more.

3 He built the earth, he spread the sky,
And fixed the starry lights on high:
Wonders of grace to God belong,
Repeat his mercies in your song.

4 He saw the Gentiles dead in sin,
And felt his pity move within:
His mercies ever shall endure,
When death and sin shall reign no more.

5 He sent his Son with power to save
From guilt, and darkness, and the grave:
Wonders of grace to God belong,
Repeat his mercies in your song.

6 Thro' this vain world he guides our feet,
And leads us to his heavenly seat:
His mercies ever shall endure,
When this vain world shall be no more.

4 II.

THINE earthly Sabbaths, Lord, we love,
But there's a nobler rest above;
To that our longing souls aspire,
With ardent love and strong desire.

2 In thy blest kingdom we shall be
From every mortal trouble free;
No groans shall mingle with the songs
Which warble from immortal tongues.

3 No rude alarms of raging foes,
No cares to break the long repose,
No midnight shade, no clouded sun,
But sacred, high, eternal noon.

4 O, long-expected day, begin;
Dawn on this world of woe and sin:
Fain would we leave this weary road,
And sleep in death, and rest in God.

5 II.

GREAT God, we sing thy mighty hand,
By which supported still we stand:
The opening year thy mercy shows;
Let mercy crown it till its close.

2 By day, by night, at home, abroad,
Still we are guarded by our God;
By his incessant bounty fed,
By his unerring counsels led.

3 With grateful hearts the past we own;
The future, all to us unknown,
We to thy guardian care commit,
And peaceful leave before thy feet.

4 In scenes exalted or depressed,
Be thou our joy and thou our rest;
Thy goodness all our hopes shall raise,
Adored through all our changing days.

5 When death shall interrupt our songs,
And seal in silence mortal tongues,
Our helper, God, in whom we trust,
In better worlds our souls shall boast.

FOR SOCIAL AND PRIVATE WORSHIP.

6

REJOICE, ye saints, rejoice and praise
The blessings of redeeming grace!
Jesus, your everlasting tower, [power.
Stands firm against the tempest's

2 He is a refuge ever nigh;
His love endures as mountains high;
His name's a rock, which winds above,
And waves below, can never move.

3 While all things change, he changes
He ne'er forgets, though oft forgot; [not;
His love will ever be the same;
His word enduring as his name.

4 Rejoice, ye saints, rejoice and praise
The blessings of his wondrous grace!
Jesus, your everlasting tower, [power.
Can bear, unmoved, the tempest's

7

DESCEND from heaven, immortal Dove,
Stoop down, and take us on thy wings,
And mount and bear us far above
The reach of these inferior things:

2 Beyond, beyond this lower sky,
Up where eternal ages roll,
Where solid pleasures never die,
And fruits immortal feast the soul.

3 O for a sight, a pleasing sight
Of our almighty Father's throne!
There sits our Saviour, crowned with light,
Clothed in a body like our own.

4 Adoring saints around him stand,
And thrones and powers before him fall;
The God shines gracious through the man,
And sheds sweet glories on them all.

5 O what amazing joys they feel,
While to their golden harps they sing,
And sit on every heavenly hill,
And spread the triumphs of their king.

6 When shall the day, dear Lord, appear,
That I shall mount to dwell above,
And stand and bow amongst them there,
And view thy face, and sing and love?

8

SWEET peace of conscience, heavenly guest,
Come fix thy mansion in my breast,
Dispel my doubts, my fears control,
And heal the anguish of my soul.

2 Come, smiling hope, and joy sincere,
Come, make your constant dwelling here;
Still let your presence cheer my heart,
Nor sin compel you to depart.

3 Thou God of hope, and peace divine,
O! make these sacred pleasures mine;
Forgive my sins, my fears remove,
And send the tokens of thy love.

4 Then, should mine eyes, without a tear,
See death, with all his terrors near;
My heart should then in death rejoice,
And raptures tune my faltering voice.

HYMNS 9, 10, 11.

BAVA. L. M.

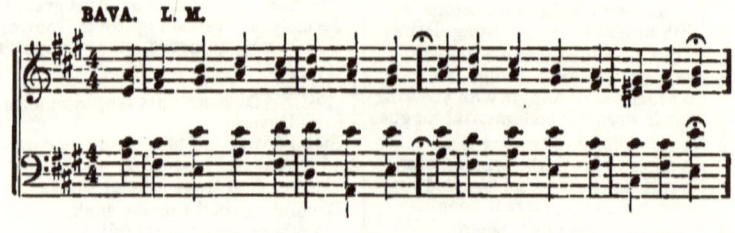

9 I.

BLESSED be the Lord, who heard my prayer,
The Lord my shield, my help, my song,
Who saved my soul from sin and fear,
And tuned with praise my thankful tongue.

2 In the dark hour of deep distress,
By foes beset, of death afraid,
My spirit trusted in his grace,
And sought, and found his heavenly aid.

3 O blest Redeemer of mankind!
Thy shield, thy saving strength, shall be
The shield, the strength, of every mind,
That loves his name, and trusts in thee.

4 Remember, Lord, thy chosen seed;
Israel defend from guilt and woe;
Thy flock in richest pastures feed,
And guard their steps from every foe.

5 Zion exalt, her cause maintain,
With peace and joy her courts surround:
In showers let endless blessings rain,
And saints eternal praise resound.

10 I.

COME, O Creator Spirit blest!
And in our souls take up thy rest;
Come with thy grace and heavenly aid,
To fill the hearts which thou hast made.

2 Great Comforter! to thee we cry;
O highest gift of God most high!
O fount of life! O fire of love!
And sweet anointing from above!

3 Kindle our senses from above, [love;
And make our hearts o'erflow with
With patience firm, and virtue high,
The weakness of our flesh supply.

4 Far from us drive the foe we dread,
And grant us thy true peace instead;
So shall we not, with thee for guide,
Turn from the path of life aside.

11 I.

GREAT Shepherd of thine Israel,
Who didst between the cherubs dwell,
And lead the tribes, thy chosen sheep,
Safe through the desert and the deep:

2 Thy church is in the desert now:
Shine from on high, and guide us thro';
Turn us to thee, thy love restore,
We shall be saved, and sigh no more.

3 Great God, whom heavenly hosts obey,
How long shall we lament and pray,
And wait in vain thy kind return?
How long shall thy fierce anger burn?

4 Instead of wine and cheerful bread,
Thy saints with their own tears are fed;
Turn us to thee, thy love restore,
We shall be saved, and sigh no more.

12 II.

HAPPY the church, thou sacred place,
The seat of thy Creator's grace;
Thy holy courts are his abode,
Thou earthly palace of our God.

2 Thy walls are strength, and at thy gates
A guard of heavenly warriors waits;
Nor shall thy deep foundations move,
Fixed on his counsels and his love.

3 Thy foes in vain designs engage;
Against his throne in vain they rage;
Like rising waves, with angry roar,
That dash and die upon the shore.

4 Then let our souls in Zion dwell,
Nor fear the wrath of earth and hell;
His arms embrace this happy ground,
Like brazen bulwarks built around.

5 God is our shield, and God our sun;
Swift as the fleeting moments run,
On us he sheds new beams of grace,
And we reflect his brightest praise.

13 II.

HE that hath made his refuge God,
Shall find a most secure abode;
Shall walk all day beneath his shade,
And there at night shall rest his head.

2 Thrice happy man! thy Maker's care
Shall keep thee from the fowler's snare;
From Satan's wiles, who still betrays
Unguarded souls, a thousand ways.

3 What though a thousand at thy side,
Around thy path ten thousand died,
Thy God his chosen people saves
Amongst the dead, amidst the graves.

4 The sword, the pestilence, or fire
Shall but fulfil their best desire;
From sins and sorrows set them free,
And bring thy children, Lord, to thee.

14 II.

NOW be my heart inspired to sing
The glories of my Saviour King,
Jesus the Lord; how heavenly fair
His form! how bright his beauties are!

2 O'er all the sons of human race
He shines with far superior grace;
Love from his lips divinely flows,
And blessings all his state compose.

3 Thy throne, O God, forever stands,
Grace is the sceptre in thy hands;
Thy laws and works are just and right,
But grace and justice thy delight.

4 God, thine own God, has richly shed
His oil of gladness on thy head;
And with his sacred Spirit blessed
His first-born Son above the rest.

For Social and Private Worship.

15

COME, dearest Lord, who reign'st above,
And draw with me the cords of love,
And while the gospel does abound,
O may I know the joyful sound!

2 Sweet are the tidings, free the grace,
It brings to our apostate race:
It spreads a heavenly light around;
O may I know the joyful sound!

3 The gospel bids the sin-sick soul
Look up to Jesus and be whole;
In him are peace and pardon found;
O may I know the joyful sound!

4 It stems the tide of swelling grief,
Affords the needy sure relief;
Releases those by Satan bound:
O may I know the joyful sound!

16

'TIS by the faith of joys to come,
We walk through deserts dark as night;
Till we arrive at heaven our home,
Faith is our guide, and faith our light.

2 The want of sight she well supplies;
She makes the pearly gates appear;
Far into distant worlds she pries,
And brings eternal glories near.

3 Cheerful we tread the desert through,
While faith inspires a heavenly ray,
Though lions roar, and tempests blow,
And rocks and dangers fill the way.

17

LET me but hear my Saviour say,
"Strength shall be equal to thy day;"
Then I rejoice in deep distress,
Leaning on all-sufficient grace.

2 I glory in infirmity, [me;
That Christ's own power may rest on
When I am weak, then am I strong,
Grace is my shield, and Christ my song.

DUKE STREET. L. M.

18   I.

THEE will I love, O Lord, my strength,
  My rock, my tower, my high defence;
Thy mighty arm shall be my trust,
  For I have found salvation thence.

2 Death, and the terrors of the grave,
  Stood round me with their dismal shade;
While floods of high temptations rose,
  And made my sinking soul afraid.

3 Temptations fled at his rebuke,—
  The blast of his almighty breath:
He sent salvation from on high,
  And drew me from the deeps of death.

4 My song forever shall record
  That terrible, that joyful hour;
And give the glory to the Lord,
  Due to his mercy and his power.

19   II.

NOW to the Lord that makes us know
  The wonders of his dying love,
Be humble honors paid below,
  And strains of nobler praise above.

2 'Twas he that cleansed our foulest sins,
  And washed us in his richest blood;
'Tis he that makes us priests and kings,
  And brings us rebels near to God.

3 To Jesus our atoning Priest,
  To Jesus our exalted King,
Be everlasting power confessed,
  And every tongue his glory sing.

4 Behold, on flying clouds he comes,
  And every eye shall see him move;
Tho' with our sins we pierced him once,
  Still he displays his pardoning love.

20   II.

JUST are thy ways, and true thy word,
  Great Rock of my secure abode;
Who is a God beside the Lord?
  Or where's a refuge like our God?

2 'Tis he that girds me with his might,
  Gives me his holy sword to wield;
And, while with sin and hell I fight,
  Spreads his salvation for my shield.

3 He lives, and blessings crown his reign,
  The God of my salvation lives:
The dark designs of hell are vain,
  While heavenly peace my Father gives.

4 Before the scoffers of the age,
  I will exalt my Father's name;
Nor tremble at their mighty rage,
  But meet reproach, and bear the shame.

5 To David and his royal seed
  Thy grace forever shall extend:
Thy love to saints, in Christ their head
  Knows not a limit, nor an end.

21
II.

LORD, when thou didst ascend on high
Ten thousand angels filled the sky;
Those heavenly guards around thee wait,
Like chariots that attend thy state.

2 Not Sinai's mountain could appear,
More glorious when the Lord was there;
While he pronounced his holy law,
And struck the chosen tribes with awe.

3 How bright the triumph none can tell,
When the rebellious powers of hell,
That thousand souls had captive made,
Were all in chains, like captives, led.

4 Raised by his Father to the throne,
He sent his promised Spirit down,
With gifts and grace for rebel men,
That God might dwell on earth again.

FOR SOCIAL AND PRIVATE WORSHIP.

22

JOIN, all who love the Saviour's name,
To sing his everlasting fame;
Great God, prepare each heart and voice,
In him for ever to rejoice.

2 With him I daily love to walk;
Of him my soul delights to talk;
On him I cast my every care;
Like him, one day, I shall appear.

3 Bless him, my soul, from day to day,
Trust him to lead thee on thy way;
Give him thy poor, weak, sinful heart;
With him, O never, never part.

4 Take him for strength and righteousness,
Make him thy refuge in distress;
Love him, above all earthly joy,
And him in every thing employ.

5 Praise him in cheerful, grateful songs;
To him your highest praise belongs;
Bless him who does your heaven prepare,
And makes you meet his joy to share.

23

GREAT God! to thee my evening song
With humble gratitude I raise;
O let thy mercy tune my tongue,
And fill my heart with lively praise.

2 My days unclouded as they pass,
And every gentle, rolling hour,
Are monuments of wondrous grace,
And witness to thy love and power.

3 And yet this thoughtless, wretched heart,
Too oft regardless of thy love,
Ungrateful, can from thee depart,
And, fond of trifles, vainly rove.

4 Seal my forgiveness in the blood
Of Jesus; his dear name alone
I plead for pardon, gracious God!
And kind acceptance at thy throne.

5 Let this blest hope mine eyelids close,
With sleep refresh my feeble frame;
Safe in thy care may I repose,
And wake with praises to thy name.

24
For Children Only.

WE are but young—yet we may sing
The praises of our heavenly King;
He made the earth, the sea, the sky,
And all the starry worlds on high.

2 We are but young—we need a guide;
Jesus, in thee we would confide;
O lead us in the path of truth,
Protect and bless our helpless youth.

3 We are but young—yet God has shed
Unnumbered blessings on our head;
Then let our youth and riper days
Be all devoted to his praise.

25

HOW blest the righteous when he dies;
When sinks a weary soul to rest,
How mildly beam the closing eyes,
How gently heaves the expiring breast;

2 So fades a summer cloud away,
So sinks the gale when storms are o'er;
So gently shuts the eye of day,
So dies a wave along the shore.

3 A holy quiet reigns around,
A calm which life nor death destroys;
Nothing disturbs that peace profound,
Which his unfettered soul enjoys.

4 Farewell, conflicting hopes and fears,
Where lights and shades alternate dwell;
How bright the unchanging morn appears,
Farewell, inconstant world, farewell!

5 Life's duty done, as sinks the clay,
Light from its load the spirit flies;
While heaven and earth combine to say,
"How blest the righteous when he dies!"

EVENING HYMN. L. M.

26 I.

ERE the blue heavens were stretched abroad,
From everlasting was the Word;
With God he was; the Word was God,
And must divinely be adored.

2 By his own power were all things made;
By him supported all things stand;
He is the whole creation's head,
And angels fly at his command.

3 But lo! he leaves those heavenly forms,
The Word descends and dwells in clay,
That he may converse hold with worms,
Dressed in such feeble flesh as they.

4 Mortals with joy beheld his face,
The eternal Father's only Son:
How full of truth, how full of grace,
The brightness of the Godhead shone!

5 The angels leave their high abode,
To learn new mysteries here, and tell
The love of our descending God,
The glories of Immanuel.

27 I.

PRAISE, everlasting praise, be paid
To him that earth's foundation laid;
Praise to the God, whose strong decrees
Sway the creation as he please.

2 Praise to the goodness of the Lord,
Who rules his people by his word;
And there, as strong as his decrees,
He sets his kindest promises.

3 Firm are the words his prophets give,
Sweet words, on which his children live;
Each of them is the voice of God,
Who spoke, and spread the skies abroad.

4 Each of them powerful as that sound,
That bid the new-made world go round,
And stronger than the solid poles,
On which the wheel of nature rolls.

28 I.

LORD, what is man that he should prove
The object of thy boundless love!
Say, why should he so largely share
Thy favor, and thy tender care?

2 While these my lips draw vital breath,
Or till I close my eyes in death,
I'll ne'er forget thy wondrous love,
Nor thoughtless of thy kindness prove.

3 Beneath thy shadowing wings' defence,
I'll place my only confidence:
In every danger and distress,
To thee will I my prayer address.

4 Should all my hopes on earth be lost,
In thee I'll make my constant boast:
I'll spread the glories of thy name,
And thy unbounded love proclaim.

29
II.

LET Zion in her king rejoice,
Tho' tyrants rage, and kingdoms rise;
He utters his almighty voice,
The nations melt, the tumult dies.
2 The Lord of old for Jacob fought,
And Jacob's God is still our aid;
Behold the works his hand has wrought,
What desolations he has made!
3 Be still, and learn that he is God,
He reigns exalted o'er the lands;
He will be known and feared abroad,
But still his throne in Zion stands.
4 O Lord of hosts, almighty King,
While we so near thy presence dwell,
Our faith shall sit secure and sing,
Nor fear the raging powers of hell.

FOR SOCIAL AND PRIVATE WORSHIP.

30

BENEATH a numerous train of ills,
Our feeble flesh and heart may fail;
Yet shall our hope in thee, our God,
O'er every gloomy fear prevail.
2 Parent and Husband, Guard and Guide,
Thou art each tender name in one;
On thee we cast our heavy cares,
And comfort seek from thee alone.
3 Our Father, God, to thee we look;
Our Rock, our Portion, and our Friend;
And on thy covenant love and truth,
Our sinking souls shall still depend.

31

I SEND the joys of earth away;
Away, ye tempters of the mind,
False as the smooth, deceitful sea,
And empty as the whistling wind.
2 Your streams were floating me along,
Down to the gulf of black despair,
And whilst I listened to your song,
Your streams had e'en conveyed me there.
3 Lord, I adore thy matchless grace,
That warned me of that dark abyss,
That drew me from those treach'rous seas
And bade me seek superior bliss.
4 Now to the shining realms above,
I stretch my hands, and glance my eyes:
O for the pinions of a dove,
To bear me to the upper skies.

5 There from the bosom of my God,
Oceans of endless pleasure roll;
There would I fix my last abode,
And drown the sorrows of my soul.

32

AWAKE, my soul, and with the sun,
Thy daily stage of duty run:
Shake off dull sloth and joyful rise,
To pay thy morning sacrifice.
2 Lord, I my vows to thee renew,
Scatter my sins as morning dew;
Guard my first springs of thought and will,
And with thyself my spirit fill.
3 Direct, control, suggest this day,
All I design, or do, or say;
That all my powers with all my might,
In thy sole glory may unite.
4 All praise to thee who safe hast kept,
And hast refreshed me while I slept:
Grant, Lord, when I from death shall wake,
I may of endless life partake.

33

GLORY to thee, my God, this night,
For all the blessings of the light;
Keep me, O keep me, King of kings,
Beneath thine own almighty wings.
2 Forgive me, Lord, for thy dear Son,
The ill that I this day have done;
That with the world, myself and thee,
I, ere I sleep, at peace may be.
3 Teach me to live, that I may dread
The grave as little as my bed:
Teach me to die, that so I may
Rise glorious, at the awful day.
4 O let my soul on thee repose,
And may sweet sleep my eyelids close:
Sleep that shall me more vigorous make,
To serve my God, when I awake.
5 If in the night I sleepless lie,
My soul with heavenly thoughts supply;
Let no ill dreams disturb my rest,
No powers of darkness me molest.
6 O when shall I, in endless day,
For ever chase dark sleep away;
And hymns divine with angels sing,
Glory to thee, eternal King?
7 Praise God, from whom all blessings flow;
Praise him all creatures below;
Praise him above, ye heavenly host,
Praise Father, Son, and Holy Ghost.

FEDERAL STREET. L. M.

34 I.

ALL praise to thee, eternal Lord!
Clothed in a garb of flesh and blood;
Choosing a manger for thy throne,
While worlds on worlds are thine alone.

2 Once did the skies before thee bow;
A virgin's arms contain thee now:
Angels, who did in thee rejoice,
Now listen for thine infant voice.

3 A little child, thou art our guest,
That weary ones in thee may rest;
Forlorn and lowly is thy birth,
That we may rise to heaven from earth.

4 Thou comest in the darksome night
To make us children of the light,—
To make us, in the realms divine,
Like thine own angels round thee shine.

5 All this for us thy love hath done;
By this to thee our love is won:
For this we tune our cheerful lays,
And shout our thanks in ceaseless praise.

35 I.

JESUS, the spring of joys divine,
Whence all our hopes and comforts flow;
Jesus, no other name but thine,
Can save us from eternal wo.

2 In vain would boasting reason find
The way to happiness and God;
Her weak directions leave the mind
Bewildered in a dubious road.

3 No other name will heaven approve;
Thou art the true, the living way,
Ordained by everlasting love,
To the bright realms of endless day.

4 Safe lead us through this world of night,
And bring us to the blissful plains,
The regions of unclouded light,
Where perfect joy for ever reigns.

36 I.

FATHER of mercies, God of love,
Send down thy Spirit from above;
Let me his sacred influence feel,
To quicken, purify, and heal.

2 May he these stubborn lusts subdue,
And form my nature all anew;
To thee my grovelling spirit raise,
Excite to humble prayer and praise.

3 He is the source of every grace,
Of light, and life, and holiness;
By him alone may I be taught,
And all my works in him be wrought.

4 O! let thy Holy Spirit come,
And make my heart his constant home.
There his abundant grace display,
And lead me in a perfect way.

37   I.

WHY droops my soul with grief oppressed?
Why these wild tumults in my breast?
Is there no balm to heal my wound,
No kind physician to be found?

2 Raise to the cross thy weeping eyes;
Behold the Prince of glory dies:
He dies, extended on the tree;
Thence sheds a sovereign balm for me.

3 Expand, my soul, with holy joy,
Hosannas be thy best employ,
Salvation thy eternal theme;
And swell the song with Jesus' name.

38   II.

MY God, in whom are all the springs
Of boundless love and grace unknown,
Hide me beneath thy spreading wings,
Till the dark cloud is overblown.

2 Up to the heavens I send my cry,
The Lord will my desires perform;
He sends his angels from the sky, [storm.
And saves me from the threatening

3 Be thou exalted, O my God,
Above the heavens where angels dwell;
Thy power on earth be known abroad,
And land to land thy wonders tell.

4 My heart is fixed; my song shall raise
Immortal honors to thy name;
Awake, my tongue, to sound his praise,
My tongue, the glory of my frame.

5 High o'er the earth his mercy reigns,
And reaches to the utmost sky;
His truth to endless years remains,
When lower worlds dissolve and die.

6 Be thou exalted, O my God,
Above the heavens where angels dwell;
Thy power on earth be known abroad,
And land to land thy wonders tell.

39   II.

THOUGH now the nations sit beneath
The darkness of o'erspreading death,
God will arise with light divine,
On Zion's holy towers shine.

2 That light shall glance on distant lands,
And heathen tribes, in joyful bands,
Come with exulting haste to prove
The power and greatness of his love.

3 Lord, may the triumphs of thy grace
Abound, while righteousness and peace,
In mild and lovely forms, display
The glories of the latter day.

FOR SOCIAL AND PRIVATE WORSHIP.

40

AWAY from every mortal care,
Away from earth our souls retreat;
We leave this worthless world afar,
And wait and worship near thy seat.

2 Lord, in the temple of thy grace,
We see thy feet, and we adore;
We gaze upon thy lovely face,
And learn the wonders of thy power.

3 Father, my soul would still abide
Within thy temple, near thy side;
But if my feet must hence depart,
Still keep thy dwelling in my heart.

41

MY God, permit me not to be
A stranger to myself and thee;
Amidst a thousand thoughts I rove,
Forgetful of my highest love.

2 Why should my passions mix with earth,
And thus debase my heavenly birth?
Why should I cleave to things below,
And let my God, my Saviour, go?

3 Call me away from flesh and sense;
One sovereign word can draw me
I would obey the voice divine, [thence;
And all inferior joys resign.

42

UNVEIL thy bosom, faithful tomb,
Take this new treasure to thy trust;
And give these sacred relics room,
To slumber in the silent dust.

2 Nor pain, nor grief, nor anxious fear
Invade thy bounds: no mortal woes
Can reach the peaceful sleeper here,
While angels watch the soft repose.

3 So Jesus slept;—God's dying Son
Passed through the grave, and blessed the bed;
Rest here, blest saint, till from his throne
The morning break, and pierce the shade.

4 Break from his throne, illustrious morn;
Attend, O earth! his sovereign word;
Restore thy trust—a glorious form
Shall then arise to meet the Lord.

HAMBURG. L. M.

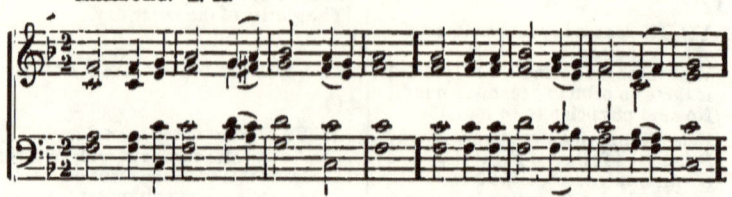

43 I.

WHO shall ascend thy heavenly place,
Great God, and dwell before thy face?
The man that minds religion now,
And humbly walks with God below:

2 Whose hands are pure, whose heart is clean, [mean;
Whose lips still speak the thing they
No slanders dwell upon his tongue;
He hates to do his neighbor wrong.

3 Yet, when his holiest works are done,
His soul depends on grace alone:
This is the man thy face shall see,
And dwell for ever, Lord, with thee.

44 I.

BLEST is the man, for ever blest,
Whose guilt is pardoned by his God;
Whose sins with sorrow are confessed,
And covered with his Saviour's blood.

2 Before his judgment seat the Lord
No more permits his crimes to rise;
He pleads no merit of reward,
And not on works, but grace, relies.

3 From guilt his heart and lips are free,
His humble joy, his holy fear,
With deep repentance well agree,
And join to prove his faith sincere.

4 How glorious is that righteousness
That hides and cancels all his sins!
While a bright evidence of grace
Through all his life appears and shines.

For Social and Private Worship.

45

SHEW pity, Lord, O Lord forgive,
Let a repenting rebel live;
Are not thy mercies large and free?
May not a sinner trust in thee?

2 O! wash my soul from every sin,
And make my guilty conscience clean;
Here on my heart the burden lies,
And past offences pain my eyes.

3 My lips with shame my sins confess,
Against thy law, against thy grace;
Lord, should thy judgments grow severe,
I am condemned, but thou art clear.

4 Yet save a trembling sinner, Lord,
Whose hope, still hovering round thy word, [there,
Would light on some sweet promise
Some sure support against despair.

46

JUST as I am—without one plea,
But that thy blood was shed for me,
And that thou bidd'st me come to thee,
I come, O Lamb of God, I come.

2 Just as I am—and waiting not,
  To rid my soul of one dark blot, [spot,
  To thee, whose blood can cleanse each
  I come, O Lamb of God, I come.
3 Just as I am, though tossed about
  With many a conflict, many a doubt,
  Fightings and fears within, without—
  I come, O Lamb of God, I come.
4 Just as I am—poor, wretched, blind:
  Sight, riches, healing of the mind,
  Yea, all I need, in thee to find,
  I come, O Lamb of God, I come.
5 Just as I am—thou wilt receive,
  Wilt welcome, pardon, cleanse, relieve,
  Because thy promise I believe—
  I come, O Lamb of God, I come.
6 Just as I am—thy love unknown
  Has broken every barrier down;
  Now to be thine, yea, thine alone,
  I come, O Lamb of God, I come.

47

NO more, my God, I boast no more
  Of all the duties I have done;
I quit the hopes I held before,
To trust the merits of thy Son.

2 Now for the love I bear his name,
  What was my gain I count my loss;
  My former pride I call my shame,
  And nail my glory to his cross.
3 Yes, and I must and will esteem
  All things but loss for Jesus's sake;
  O may my soul be found in him,
  And of his righteousness partake.
4 The best obedience of my hands
  Dares not appear before thy throne;
  But faith can answer thy demands,
  By pleading what my Lord has done.

48

O THOU, to whose all-searching sight,
  The darkness shineth as the light;
Search, prove my heart, it pants for thee;
O burst these bonds, and set it free.

2 If in this darksome wild I stray,
  Be thou my Light, be thou my Way;
  No foes, nor violence I fear,   [near.
  Nor fraud, while thou, my God, art
3 When rising floods my soul o'erflow,
  When sinks my heart in waves of wo;
  Jesus, thy timely aid impart,
  And raise my head, and cheer my heart.

4 Saviour, where'er thy steps I see,
  Dauntless, untired, I follow thee:
  O let thy hand support me still,
  And lead me to thy holy hill.

49

COME, gracious Lord, descend and dwell
  By faith and love in every breast:
Then shall we know, and taste, and feel
The joys that cannot be expressed.

2 Come, fill our hearts with inward strength,
  Make our enlarged souls possess,
  And learn the height, and breadth, and
  Of thine immeasurable grace. [length
3 Now to the God whose power can do
  More than our thoughts or wishes
  Be everlasting honors done,   [know,
  By all the church, through Christ his Son.

50

MY God, my King, thy various praise
  Shall fill the remnant of my days;
Thy grace employ my humble tongue,
Till death and glory raise the song.

2 The wings of every hour shall bear
  Some thankful tribute to thine ear;
  And every setting sun shall see
  New works of duty done for thee.
3 Thy works with sovereign glory shine,
  And speak thy majesty divine;
  Let every realm with joy proclaim
  The sound and honor of thy name.
4 Let distant times and nations raise
  The long succession of thy praise;
  And unborn ages make my song
  The joy and triumph of their tongue.
5 But who can speak thy wondrous deeds?
  Thy greatness all our thoughts exceeds;
  Vast and unsearchable thy ways;
  Vast and immortal be thy praise!

51

O THOU, true life of all that live,
  Who dost unmoved all motion sway,
Who dost the morn and evening give,
And thro' its changes guide the day;

2 Thy light upon our evening pour:
  So may our souls no sunset see;
  But death to us an open door
  To an eternal morning be.

HEBRON. L. M.

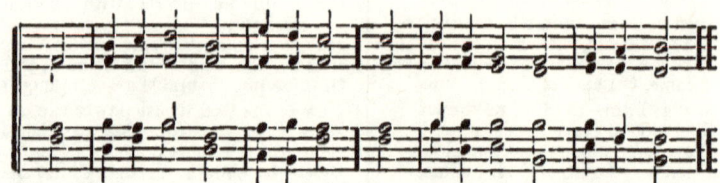

52 I.

GOD, in the gospel of his Son,
Makes his eternal counsels known:
Where love in all its glory shines,
And truth is drawn in fairest lines.

2 Here sinners, of an humble frame,
May taste his grace, and learn his name;
May read, in characters of blood,
The wisdom, power and grace of God.

3 The prisoner here may break his chains;
The weary rest from all his pains;
The captive feel his bondage cease;
The mourner find the way of peace.

4 Here faith reveals to mortal eyes
A brighter world beyond the skies:
Here shines the light which guides our way,
From earth to realms of endless day.

5 O! grant us grace, almighty Lord,
To read and mark thy holy word;
Its truths with meekness to receive,
And by its holy precepts live.

53 I.

SWEET is thy work, my God, my King, [sing,
To praise thy name, give thanks and
To show thy love by morning light,
And talk of all thy truth at night.

2 Sweet is the day of sacred rest;
No mortal care shall seize my breast;
O! may my heart in tune be found,
Like David's harp of solemn sound!

3 My heart shall triumph in my Lord,
And bless his works, and bless his word; [shine!
Thy works of grace how bright they
How deep thy counsels! how divine!

4 But I shall share a glorious part,
When grace hath well refined my heart
And fresh supplies of joy are shed,
Like holy oil to cheer my head.

5 Then shall I see, and hear, and know
All I desired or wished below;
And every power find sweet employ
In that eternal world of joy.

54 I.

BURIED in shadows of the night,
We lie, till Christ restores the light;
Wisdom descends to heal the blind,
And chase the darkness of the mind.

2 Our guilty souls are drowned in tears,
Till his atoning blood appears;
Then we awake from deep distress,
And sing "The Lord our righteousness."

3 Jesus beholds where Satan reigns,
Binding his slaves in heavy chains:
He sets the prisoners free, and breaks
The iron bondage from our necks.

4 Poor helpless worms in thee possess
  Grace, wisdom, power, and righteousness;
  Thou art our mighty all, and we
  Give our whole selves, O Lord, to thee.

55 II.

UP to the hills I lift mine eyes,
  Th' eternal hills beyond the skies;
  Thence all her help my soul derives;
  There my almighty Refuge lives.

2 He lives; the everlasting God,
  That built the world, that spread the flood; [made,
  The heavens, with all their hosts, he
  And the dark regions of the dead.

3 He guides our feet, he guards our way;
  His morning smiles adorn the day:
  He spreads the evening veil, and keeps
  The silent hours while Israel sleeps.

4 Israel, a name divinely blest,
  May rise secure, securely rest;
  Thy holy Guardian's wakeful eyes
  Admit no slumber nor surprise.

56 II.

WHAT sinners value, I resign;
  Lord, 'tis enough that thou art
  I shall behold thy blissful face, [mine:
  And stand complete in righteousness.

2 This life's a dream, an empty show;
  But the bright world to which I go,
  Hath joys substantial and sincere;
  When shall I wake and find me there?

3 O glorious hour! O blest abode!
  I shall be near, and like my God;
  And flesh and sin no more control
  The sacred pleasures of the soul.

4 My flesh shall slumber in the ground,
  Till the last trumpet's joyful sound;
  Then burst the chains with sweet surprise,
  And in my Saviour's image rise.

FOR SOCIAL AND PRIVATE WORSHIP.

57

FATHER of all, whose love profound
  A ransom for our souls hath found,
  Before thy throne we sinners bend;
  To us thy pardoning love extend.

2 Almighty Son, incarnate Word,
  Our Prophet, Priest, Redeemer, Lord,
  Before thy throne we sinners bend;
  To us thy saving grace extend.

3 Eternal Spirit, by whose breath
  The soul is raised from sin and death,
  Before thy throne we sinners bend;
  To us thy quickening power extend.

4 Jehovah! Father, Spirit, Son,
  Mysterious Godhead, Three in One!
  Before thy throne we sinners bend;
  Grace, pardon, life, to us extend.

58

O SUN of righteousness arise,
  With gentle beams on Zion shine;
  Dispel the darkness from our eyes,
  And souls awake to life divine.

2 On all around let grace descend,
  Like heavenly dew, or copious showers;
  That we may call our God our friend;
  That we may hail salvation ours.

59

MY God, how endless is thy love!
  Thy gifts are every evening new;
  And morning mercies from above
  Gently distill, like early dew.

2 Thou spread'st the curtain of the night,
  Great Guardian of my sleeping hours;
  Thy sovereign word restores the light,
  And quickens all my drowsy powers.

3 I yield my powers to thy command,
  To thee I consecrate my days:
  Perpetual blessings from thy hand
  Demand perpetual songs of praise.

60

THUS far the Lord has led me on,
  Thus far his power prolongs my days,
  And every evening shall make known
  Some fresh memorial of his grace.

2 Much of my time has run to waste,
  And I, perhaps, am near my home;
  But he forgives my follies past;
  He gives me strength for days to come.

3 I lay my body down to sleep,
  Peace is the pillow for my head;
  While well appointed angels keep
  Their watchful stations round my bed.

4 Thus when the night of death shall come,
  My flesh shall rest beneath the ground,
  And wait thy voice to rouse the tomb,
  With sweet salvation in the sound.

INVOCATION. L. M.

61 I.

FROM deep distress and troubled thoughts,
To thee, my God, I raised my cries:
If thou severely mark our faults,
No flesh can stand before thine eyes.

2 But thou hast built thy throne of grace,
Free to dispense thy pardons there.
That sinners may approach thy face,
And hope, and love, as well as fear.

3 My trust is fixed upon thy word,
Nor shall I trust thy word in vain;
Let mourning souls address the Lord,
And find relief from all their pain.

4 Great is his love, and large his grace,
Through the redemption of his Son:
He turns our feet from sinful ways,
And pardons what our hands have done.

62 I.

LET everlasting glories crown
Thy head, my Saviour, and my Lord;
Thy hands have brought salvation down,
And writ the blessings in thy word.

2 In vain the trembling conscience seeks
Some solid ground to rest upon:
With long despair the spirit breaks,
Till we apply to Christ alone.

3 How well thy blessed truths agree!
How wise and holy thy commands!
Thy promises, how firm they be!
How firm our hope and comfort stands!

4 Should all the forms that men devise
Assault my faith with treacherous art,
I'll call them vanity and lies,
And bind the gospel to my heart.

63 II.

MY soul, thy great Creator praise;
When clothed in his celestial rays,
He in full majesty appears,
And like a robe his glory wears.

2 The world's foundations by his hand
Were laid, and shall for ever stand;
The swelling billows know their bound,
And in their channels take their round;

3 Vast are thy works, almighty Lord!
All nature rests upon thy word;
And the whole race of creatures stand
Waiting their portion from thy hand.

4 The earth stands trembling at thy stroke,
And at thy touch the mountains smoke,
Great is the Lord! what tongue can frame
An honor equal to his name!

5 In thee my hopes and wishes meet,
And make my meditations sweet;
Thy praises shall my breath employ,
Till it expire in endless joy.

64
II.

THOU whom my soul admires above
All earthly joy, and earthly love,
Tell me, dear Shepherd, let me know,
Where doth thy sweetest pasture grow?

2 Where is the shadow of that rock
That from the sun defends thy flock?
Fain would I feed among thy sheep,
Among them rest, among them sleep.

3 Why should thy bride appear like one,
That turns aside to paths unknown?
My constant feet would never rove,
Would never seek another love.

4 The footsteps of thy flock I see;
Thy sweetest pastures here they be;
A wondrous feast thy love prepares,
Bought with thy wounds, and groans, and tears.

5 His dearest flesh he makes my food,
And bids me drink his richest blood:
Here to these hills my soul will come,
Till my Beloved leads me home.

FOR SOCIAL AND PRIVATE WORSHIP.

65

THROUGH every age, eternal God,
Thou art our rest, our safe abode;
High was thy throne ere heaven was made,
Or earth, thy humble footstool laid.

2 Long hadst thou reigned ere time began,
Or dust was fashioned into man;
And long thy kingdom shall endure,
When earth and time shall be no more.

3 Death, like an overflowing stream,
Sweeps us away; our life's a dream,
An empty tale, a morning flower,
Cut down and withered in an hour.

4 Teach us, O Lord, how frail is man;
And kindly lengthen out the span,
Till thine own grace, so rich, so free,
Fit us to die and dwell with thee.

66

COME, weary souls, with sins distressed,
Come and accept the promised rest;
The Saviour's gracious call obey,
And cast your gloomy fears away.

2 Oppressed with guilt, a painful load,
O! come and spread your woes abroad;
Divine compassion, mighty love,
Will all the painful loads remove.

3 Here mercy's boundless ocean flows,
To cleanse your guilt and heal your woes;
Pardon, and life and endless peace;
How rich the gift! how free the grace!

4 Lord, we accept with thankful heart,
The hope thy gracious words impart;
We come, believing we rejoice,
And bless the kind inviting voice.

67
For Children only.

LORD, look upon a little child,
By nature sinful, rude, and wild;
Oh! put thy gracious hand on me,
And make me all I ought to be.

68

THE hour of my departure's come,
I hear the voice that calls me home;
Now, O my God, let trouble cease,
And let thy servant die in peace.

2 The race appointed I have run,
The combat's o'er, the prize is won,
And now my witness is on high,
And now my record's in the sky.

3 Not in mine innocence I trust;
I bow before thee in the dust,
And through my Saviour's blood alone,
I look for mercy at thy throne.

4 I come, I come, at thy command,
I give my spirit to thy hand:
Stretch forth thine everlasting arms,
And shield me in the last alarms.

69

WHY should we start and fear to die?
What timorous worms we mortals are!
Death is the gate of endless joy,
And yet we dread to enter there.

2 The pains, the groans and dying strife,
Fright our approaching souls away;
Still we shrink back again to life,
Fond of our prison and our clay.

3 O! if my Lord would come and meet,
My soul would stretch her wings in haste,
Fly fearless through death's iron gate,
Nor feel the terrors as she passed.

4 Jesus can make a dying bed
Feel soft as downy pillows are,
While on his breast I lean my head,
And breathe my life out sweetly there.

IOSCO. L. M.

70 I.

LORD, I will bless thee all my days,
  Thy praise shall dwell upon my
      tongue;
My soul shall glory in thy grace,
  While saints rejoice to hear the song.

2 Come magnify the Lord with me,
  Let every heart exalt his name;
I sought th' eternal God, and he
  Has not exposed my hope to shame.

3 I told him all my secret grief,
  My secret groaning reached his ears:
He gave my inward pains relief,
  And calmed the tumult of my fears.

4 His holy angels pitch their tents
  Around the men that serve the Lord;
O! fear and love him, all his saints,
  Taste of his grace and trust his word.

71 I.

THE Lord, how wondrous are his ways!
  How firm his truth! how large his
      grace!
He takes his mercy for his throne,
  And thence he makes his glories
      known.

2 Not half so high his power hath spread
  The starry heavens above our head,
  As his rich love exceeds our praise,
  Exceeds the highest hopes we raise.

3 Not half so far hath nature placed
  The rising morning from the west,
  As his forgiving grace removes
  The daily guilt of those he loves.

4 How slow his awful wrath to rise!
  On swifter wings salvation flies;
  And if he lets his anger burn,
  How soon his frowns to pity turn!

5 But his eternal love is sure
  To all the saints, and shall endure:
From age to age his truth shall reign,
  Nor children's children hope in vain.

72 I.

BLESS, O my soul, the living God,
  Call home thy thoughts that rove
      abroad,
Let all the powers within me join
  In work and worship so divine.

2 Bless, O my soul, the God of grace;
  His favours claim the highest praise;
  Why should the wonders he hath
      wrought
Be lost in silence and forgot?

3 'Tis he, my soul, that sent his Son
  To die for crimes which thou hast done;
  He owns the ransom, and forgives
  The hourly follies of our lives.

4 His power he showed by Moses' hands
  And gave to Israel his commands;
  But sent his truth and mercy down
  To all the nations by his Son.

5 Let the whole earth his power confess,
   Let the whole earth adore his grace;
   The Gentile with the Jew shall join
   In work and worship so divine.

73   I.

THOU loving Maker of mankind,
   Before thy throne we pray and weep:
Oh strengthen us with grace divine,
   Duly this sacred fast to keep.
2 Searcher of hearts! thou dost our ills
   Discern, and all our weakness know:
Again to thee with tears we turn;
   Again to us thy mercy show.
3 Much have we sinn'd; but we confess
   Our guilt, and all our faults deplore;
Oh, for the praise of thy great name,
   Our fainting souls to health restore!
4 And grant us, while by fasts we strive
   This mortal body to control,
To fast from all the food of sin,
   And so to purify the soul.
5 Hear us, O Trinity thrice blest!
   Sole Unity! to thee we cry:
Vouchsafe us from these fasts below
   To reap immortal fruit on high.

For Social and Private Worship.

74

JESUS, where'er thy people meet,
   There they behold thy mercy seat;
Where'er they seek thee, thou art found,
   And every place is hallowed ground.
2 For thou, within no walls confined,
   Inhabitest the humble mind;
Such ever bring thee where they come,
   And going, take thee to their home.
3 Dear Shepherd of thy chosen few,
   Thy former mercies here renew;
Here, to our waiting hearts proclaim
   The sweetness of thy saving name.
4 Here may we prove the power of prayer
To strengthen faith, and sweeten care;
   To teach our faint desires to rise,
And bring all heaven before our eyes.

75

JESUS, engrave it on my heart, [art;
   That thou the one thing needful
I could from all things parted be,
   But never, never, Lord, from thee.

2 Needful art thou to make me live;
   Needful art thou all grace to give;
Needful to guide me, lest I stray;
   Needful to help me every day.
3 Needful is thy most precious blood;
   Needful is thy correcting rod;
Needful is thy indulgent care;
   Needful thy all-prevailing prayer.
4 Needful thy presence, dearest Lord;
   True peace and comfort to afford;
Needful thy promise, to impart
   Fresh life and vigor to my heart.
5 Needful art thou to be my stay
   Through all life's dark and thorny way;
Nor less in death thou'lt needful be,
   When I yield up my soul to thee.
6 Needful art thou to raise my dust,
   In shining glory with the just;
Needful when I in heaven appear,
   To crown and to present me there.

76

O GOD, thou art my God alone;
   Early to thee my soul shall cry,
A pilgrim in a land unknown,
   A thirsty land whose springs are dry.
2 Yet thro' this rough and thorny maze,
   I follow hard on thee, my God;
Thine hand unseen upholds my ways,
   I safely tread where thou hast trod.
3 When in the watches of the night,
   Thee I remember on my bed,
Thy presence makes the darkness light,
   Thy guardian wings are round my head.
4 Better than life itself thy love,
   Dearer than all beside to me;
For whom have I in heaven above,
   Or what on earth, compared with thee?
5 Praise with my heart, my mind, my
   For all thy mercy I will give; [voice,
My soul shall still in God rejoice,
   My tongue shall bless thee while I live.

77

MY God, accept my early vows,
   Like morning incense, in thine house,
And let my nightly worship rise
   Sweet as the evening sacrifice.
2 Watch o'er my lips, and guard them, Lord,
From every rash and heedless word;
   Nor let my feet incline to tread
The guilty path where sinners lead.

HYMNS 78, 79, 80, 81.

MENDON. L. M.

78 I.

FAREWELL, ye transitory things,
The wealth of kingdoms and of kings;
A nobler object far than you,
Appears to my enraptured view:

2 Jesus! in whom all glories meet,
Holy and just, and good and great,
Ever compassionate and kind,
My Saviour, Advocate, and Friend.

3 His blood redeemed my guilty soul,
On him I all my burdens roll;
From him I seek, in him possess, [ness.
Wisdom and strength and righteous-

4 His praise shall all my powers employ,
My present hope, my future joy;
For him I count my gain but loss,
And glory only in his cross.

79 I.

WHEN I survey the wondrous cross,
On which the Prince of glory died,
My richest gain I count but loss,
And pour contempt on all my pride.

2 Forbid it, Lord, that I should boast
Save in the death of Christ, my God;
All the vain things that charm me most,
I sacrifice them to his blood.

3 See, from his head, his hands, his feet,
Sorrow and love flow mingled down:
Did e'er such love and sorrow meet,
Or thorns compose so rich a crown?

4 Were the whole realm of nature mine,
That were a present far too small;
Love so amazing, so divine,
Demands my soul, my life, my all.

80 I.

HERE at thy cross, incarnate God,
I lay my soul beneath thy love,
Beneath the droppings of thy blood,
Jesus, nor shall it e'er remove.

2 Not all that tyrants think or say,
With rage and lightning in their eyes,
Nor hell shall fright my heart away,
Should hell with all its legions rise.

3 Yes, I'm secure beneath thy blood,
And all my foes shall lose their aim;
Hosanna to my Saviour God,
And my best honors to his name.

81 I.

NATURE with open volume stands,
To spread her Maker's praise abroad;
And every labor of his hands
Shows something worthy of a God.

2 But in the grace that rescued man,
His brightest form of glory shines;
Here, on the cross, 'tis fairest drawn,
In precious blood and crimson lines.
3 O the sweet wonders of that cross,
Where God the Saviour loved and died;
Her noblest life my spirit draws [side.
From his dear wounds and bleeding
4 I would for ever speak his name,
In sounds to mortal ears unknown;
With angels join to praise the Lamb,
And worship at his father's throne.

82   II.

TH' Almighty reigns, exalted high,
O'er all the earth, o'er all the sky;
Tho' clouds and darkness veil his feet,
His dwelling is the mercy-seat.
2 O! ye that love his holy name,
Hate every work of sin and shame;
He guards the souls of all his friends,
And from the snares of hell defends.
3 Immortal light, and joys unknown,
Are for the saints in darkness sown;
Those glorious seeds shall spring and rise,
And the bright harvest bless our eyes.
4 Rejoice, ye righteous, and record
The sacred honors of the Lord;
None but the soul that feels his grace
Can triumph in his holiness.

83   II.

LET Zion praise the mighty God,
And make his honors known abroad;
For sweet the joy our songs to raise,
And glorious is the work of praise.
2 Our children live secure and blest;
Our shores have peace, our cities rest;
He feeds our sons with finest wheat,
And adds his blessings to their meat.
3 The changing seasons he ordains,
The early and the latter rains;
His flakes of snow like wool he sends,
And thus the springing corn defends.
4 He bids the warmer breezes blow,
The ice dissolves, the waters flow;
But he hath nobler works and ways
To call his people to his praise.
5 Through all our land his laws are shown;
His gospel through our borders known;
He hath not thus revealed his word
To every land—Praise ye the Lord.

84   II.

GIVE thanks to God, he reigns above;
Kind are his tho'ts, his name is love;
His mercy ages past have known,
And ages long to come shall own.
2 Let the redeemed of the Lord
The wonders of his grace record;
Israel, the nation whom he chose,
And rescued from their mighty foes.
3 He feeds and clothes us all the way,
He guides our footsteps lest we stray;
He guards us with a powerful hand,
And brings us to the heavenly land.
4 O let the saints with joy record
The truth and goodness of the Lord!
How great his works! how kind his ways!
Let every tongue pronounce his praise.

FOR SOCIAL AND PRIVATE WORSHIP.

85

ETERNAL Spirit, we confess
And sing the wonders of thy grace! [down,
Thy power conveys our blessings
From God the Father, and the Son.
2 Enlightened by thy heavenly ray,
Our shades and darkness turn to day;
Thine inward teachings make us know
Our danger, and our refuge too.
3 Thy power and glory work within,
And break the chains of reigning sin;
Do our imperious lusts subdue,
And form our wretched hearts anew.
4 The troubled conscience knows thy voice,
Thy cheering words awake our joys;
Thy words allay the stormy wind,
And calm the surges of the mind.

86

PURE light of light! eternal Day,
Who dost the Father's brightness share,
Our chant the midnight silence breaks;
Be nigh, and hearken to our prayer.
2 Scatter the darkness of our minds,
And turn the hosts of hell to flight;
Let not our souls in sloth repose,
And sleeping sink in endless night.
3 Oh! Christ, for thy dear mercy's sake,
Spare us who put our trust in thee;
Nor let our hymn ascend in vain
To thy immortal majesty.

NAZARETH. L. M.

87 I.

MY spirit looks to God alone;
My rock and refuge is his throne;
In all my fears, in all my straits,
My soul on his salvation waits.

2 Trust him, ye saints, in all your ways,
Pour out your hearts before his face;
When helpers fail, and foes invade,
God is our all-sufficient aid.

3 Once has his awful voice declared,
Once and again my ears have heard,
"All power is his eternal due;
He must be feared and trusted too."

4 For sovereign power reigns not alone,
Grace is a partner of the throne;
Thy grace and justice, mighty Lord,
Shall well divide our last reward.

88 I.

SALVATION is for ever nigh
The souls that fear and trust the Lord:
And grace descending from on high
Fresh hopes of glory shall afford.

2 Mercy and truth on earth are met,
Since Christ the Lord came down from heaven;
By his obedience, so complete,
Justice is pleased, and peace is given.

3 Now truth and honor shall abound,
Religion dwell on earth again,
And heavenly influence bless the ground,
In our Redeemer's gentle reign.

4 His righteousness is gone before,
To give us free access to God;
Our wandering feet shall stray no more,
But mark his steps, and keep the road.

89 I.

THE praise of Zion waits for thee,
My God, and praise becomes thy house;
There shall thy saints thy glory see,
And there perform their public vows.

2 O thou, whose mercy bends the skies,
To save when humble sinners pray;
All lands to thee shall lift their eyes,
And every yielding heart obey.

3 Against my will my sins prevail,
But grace shall purge away the stain:
The blood of Christ will never fail
To wash my garments white again.

4 Blest is the man whom thou shalt choose,
And give him kind access to thee;
Give him a place within thy house,
To taste thy love divinely free.

5 Then shall the flocking nations run
To Zion's hill, and own their Lord;
The rising and the setting sun
Shall see the Saviour's name adored.

90 II.

How pleasant, and how divinely fair
    O Lord of hosts, thy dwellings are;
With long desire my spirit faints,
To meet th' assemblies of thy saints.

2 Blest are the saints who sit on high,
    Around thy throne above the sky;
Thy brightest glories shine above,
And all their work is praise and love.

3 Blest are the saints who find a place,
    Within the temple of thy grace;
There they behold thy gentler rays,
And seek thy face, and learn thy praise.

4 Blest are the men whose hearts are set
    To find the way to Zion's gate; [road
God is their strength; and through the
They lean upon their Helper, God.

5 Cheerful they walk with growing strength,
Till all shall meet in heaven at length.
Till all before thy face appear,
And join in nobler worship there.

91 II.

Great God, whose universal sway,
    The known and unknown worlds obey;
Now give the kingdom to thy Son,
Extend his power, exalt his throne.

2 Thy sceptre well becomes his hands,
All heaven submits to his commands;
His justice shall avenge the poor,
And pride and rage prevail no more.

3 As rain on meadows newly mown,
So shall he send his influence down;
His grace on fainting souls distils,
Like heavenly dew on thirsty hills.

4 The heathen lands that lie beneath
The shades of overspreading death,
Revive at his first dawning light,
And deserts blossom at the sight.

5 The saints shall flourish in his days,
Drest in the robes of joy and praise;
Peace, like a river from his throne,
Shall flow to nations yet unknown.

92 II.

Jesus shall reign where'er the sun
    Does his successive journeys run;
His kingdom stretch from shore to shore, [more.
Till moons shall wax and wane no

2 For him shall endless prayer be made,
And endless praises crown his head;

His name, like sweet perfume, shall rise
With every morning sacrifice.

3 People and realms of every tongue,
Dwell on his love with sweetest song;
And infant voices shall proclaim
Their early blessings on his name.

4 Blessings abound where'er he reigns,
The joyful prisoner bursts his chains;
The weary find eternal rest,
And all the sons of want are blest.

5 Where he displays his healing power,
Death and the curse are known no more,
In him the tribes of Adam boast
More blessings than their father lost.

6 Let every creature rise and bring
Peculiar honors to our King;
Angels descend with songs again,
And earth repeat the loud amen.

For Social and Private Worship.

93

The God of my salvation lives,
    My nobler life he will sustain;
His word immortal vigor gives,
Nor shall my glorious hopes be vain.

2 Thy presence, Lord, can cheer my heart,
    Though every earthly comfort die;
Thy smile can bid my pains depart,
And raise my sacred pleasures high.

3 O let me hear thy blissful voice,
    Inspiring life and joy divine;
The barren desert shall rejoice;
'Tis paradise, if thou art mine.

94

My dear Redeemer, and my Lord,
    I read my duty in thy word;
But in thy life the law appears,
Drawn out in living characters.

2 Such was thy truth, and such thy zeal,
Such deference to thy Father's will,
Such love, and meekness so divine,
I would transcribe and make them mine.

3 Cold mountains and the midnight air,
Witnessed the fervor of thy prayer;
The desert thy temptations knew,
Thy conflict and thy victory too.

4 Be thou my pattern; make me bear
More of thy gracious image here;
Then God the Judge shall own my name
Among the followers of the Lamb.

OLD HUNDRED. L. M.

DOXOLOGY.

TO God the Father, God the Son,
 And God the Spirit, Three in One,
Be honor, praise, and glory given,
By all on earth, and all in heaven.

95   I.

MY Shepherd is the living Lord;
 Now shall my wants be well supplied;
His providence and holy word
 Become my safety and my guide.

2 In pastures where salvation grows,
 He makes me feed, he makes me rest;
There living water gently flows,
 And all the food's divinely blest.

3 My wandering feet his ways mistake;
 But he restores my soul to peace,
And leads me, for his mercy's sake,
 In the fair paths of righteousness.

4 Though I walk through the gloomy vale,
 Where death and all its terrors are,—
My heart and hope shall never fail,
 For God my Shepherd's with me there.

5 Amid the darkness and the deeps,
 Thou art my comfort, thou my stay:
Thy staff supports my feeble steps,
 Thy rod directs my doubtful way.

6 Surely the mercies of the Lord,
 Attend his household all their days:
There will I dwell to hear his word,
 To seek his face and sing his praise.

96   II.

FROM all that dwell below the skies,
 Let the Creator's praise arise;
Let the Redeemer's name be sung
 Through every land, by every tongue.

2 Eternal are thy mercies, Lord;
 Eternal truth attends thy word;
Thy praise shall sound from shore to shore,
 Till suns shall set and rise no more.

97   II.

BEFORE Jehovah's awful throne,
 Ye nations, bow with sacred joy:
Know that the Lord is God alone;
 He can create, and he destroy.

2 His sovereign power, without our aid,
 Made us of clay, and formed us men;
And when like wandering sheep we strayed,
 He brought us to his fold again.

3 We are his people, we his care,
 Our souls, and all our mortal frame:
What lasting honors shall we rear,
 Almighty Maker, to thy name!

4 We'll crowd thy gates with thankful
   songs,
   High as the heavens our voices raise,
   And earth, with her ten thousand tongues,
   Shall fill thy courts with sounding
      praise.
5 Wide as the world is thy command,
   Vast as eternity thy love;
   Firm as a rock thy truth must stand,
   When rolling years shall cease to move.

98
II.

NOW, at the Lamb's high royal feast,
   In robes of saintly white we sing,
Through the Red Sea in safety brought
   By Jesus, our immortal King.
2 O depth of love! for us he drinks
   The chalice of his agony:
   For us, a victim on the cross,
   He meekly lays him down to die.
3 Hail, purest Victim Heaven could find,
   The powers of hell to overthrow!
   Who didst the chains of death destroy;
   Who dost the prize of life bestow.
4 Hail, victor Christ! hail, risen King!
   To thee alone belongs the crown;
   Who hast the heavenly gates unbarr'd,
   And dragg'd the prince of darkness
      down.
5 O Jesus! from the death of sin
   Keep us, we pray; so shalt thou be
   The everlasting Paschal joy
   Of all the souls new born in thee.

FOR SOCIAL AND PRIVATE WORSHIP.

99

COME, Holy Spirit, calm my mind,
   And fit me to approach my God;
Remove each vain, each worldly tho't,
   And lead me to thy blest abode.
2 Hast thou imparted to my soul
   A living spark of holy fire?
   O! kindle now the sacred flame,
   Make me to burn with pure desire.
3 A brighter faith and hope impart,
   And let me now my Saviour see:
   O! soothe and cheer my burdened heart,
   And bid my spirit rest in thee.

100

O SUN of Righteousness divine,
   On us with beams of mercy shine
Chase the dark clouds of guilt away,
And turn our darkness into day.

2 While mourning o'er our guilt and
      shame,
   And asking mercy in thy name,
   Dear Saviour, cleanse us with thy blood,
   And be our advocate with God.
3 Sustain, when sinking in distress,
   And guide us through this wilderness;
   Teach our low thoughts form earth to
   And lead us onward to the skies. [rise,

101

DISMISS us with thy blessing, Lord;
   Help us to feed upon thy word;
   All that has been amiss forgive,
   And let thy truth within us live.
2 Though we are guilty, thou art good;
   Wash all our works in Jesus' blood;
   Give every burdened soul release,
   And bid us all depart in peace.

102

O CHRIST! with each returning morn
   Thine image to our heart be borne;
   And may we ever clearly see
   Our God and Saviour, Lord, in thee!
2 All hallowed be our walk this day; *
   May meekness form our early ray,
   And faithful love our noontide light,
   And hope our sunset, calm and bright.
3 May grace each idle thought control,
   And sanctify our wayward soul;
   May guile depart, and malice cease,
   And all within be joy and peace.
4 Our daily course, O Jesus, bless;
   Make plain the way of holiness:
   From sudden falls our feet defend,
   And cheer at last our journey's end.

103

THE day of wrath, that dreadful day,
   When heaven and earth shall pass
      away!
   What power shall be the sinner's stay?
   How shall he meet that dreadful day?
2 When, shriveling like a parched scroll,
   The flaming heavens together roll;
   When louder yet, and yet more dread,
   Swells the high trump that wakes the
      dead.
3 O on that day, that wrathful day, [clay,
   When man to judgment wakes from
   Be thou the trembling sinner's stay,
   Though heaven and earth shall pass
      away.

ROTHWELL. L. M.

104 I.

TO God the great, the ever blest,
Let songs of honor be addressed;
His mercy firm for ever stands;
Give him the thanks his love demands.

2 Who knows the wonders of thy ways?
Who shall fulfil thy boundless praise?
Blest are the souls that fear thee still,
And pay their duty to thy will.

3 Remember what thy mercy did
For Jacob's race, thy chosen seed;
And with the same salvation bless
The meanest suppliant of thy grace.

4 O! may I see thy tribes rejoice,
And aid their triumphs with my voice!
This is my glory, Lord, to be
Joined to thy saints, and near to thee.

105 II.

GREAT God, attend while Zion sings
The joy that from thy presence springs;
To spend one day with thee on earth,
Exceeds a thousand days of mirth.

2 God is our sun, he makes our day;
God is our shield, he guards our way
From all th' assaults of hell and sin,
From foes without and foes within.

3 All needful grace will God bestow,
And crown that grace with glory too :
He gives us all things, and withholds
No real good from upright souls.

4 O God, our King, whose sovereign sway
The glorious hosts of heaven obey,
And devils at thy presence flee :
Blest is the man that trusts in thee.

106 II.

O THOU, whose hand the kingdom sways, [obeys,
Whom earth, and hell, and heaven
To help thy chosen sons appear,
And show thy power and glory here.

2 O haste, with every gift inspired,
With glory, truth, and grace attired.
Thou Star of heaven's eternal morn;
Thou Sun, whose beams divine adorn!

3 Assert the honor of thy name; [shame;
O'erwhelm thy foes with fear and
Bid them beneath thy footstool lie,
Nor let their souls forever die.

4 Saints shall be glad before thy face,
And grow in love, and truth, and grace ;
Thy church shall blossom in thy sight,
And yield her fruits of pure delight.

5 O hither, then, thy footsteps bend ;
Swift as a roe, from hills descend ;
Mild as the sabbath's cheerful ray,
Till life unfolds eternal day !

107

JEHOVAH reigns; he dwells in light,
 Girded with majesty and might:
The world, created by his hands,
Still on its first foundation stands.

2 But ere this spacious world was made,
 Or had its first foundation laid,
Thy throne eternal ages stood,
Thyself the ever-living God.

3 Like floods the angry nations rise,
 And aim their rage against the skies;
Vain floods that aim their rage so high
 At thy rebuke the billows die.

4 For ever shall thy throne endure;
 Thy promise stands for ever sure;
And everlasting holiness,
 Becomes the dwellings of thy grace.

108

JEHOVAH reigns, his throne is high,
 His robes are light and majesty;
His glory shines with beams so bright,
 No mortal can sustain the sight.

2 His terrors keep the world in awe;
 His justice guards his holy law;
His love reveals a smiling face,
 His truth and promise seal the grace.

3 Thro' all his works his wisdom shines,
 And baffles Satan's deep designs;
His power is sovereign to fulfil
 The noblest counsels of his will.

4 And will this glorious Lord descend
 To be my Father and my friend?
Then let my songs with angels join;
 Heaven is secure, if God is mine.

109

TRIUMPHANT Zion! lift thy head
 From dust and darkness and the dead;
Though humbled long,awake at length,
And gird thee with thy Saviour's strength.

2 Put all thy beauteous garments on,
 And let thy various charms be known:
Then, decked in robes of righteousness,
 The world thy glories shall confess.

3 No more shall foes unclean invade,
 And fill thy hallowed walls with dread;
No more shall hell's insulting host
 Their vict'ry and thy sorrows boast.

4 God, from on high, has heard thy
 His hand thy ruin shall repair; [pray'r;

Nor will thy watchful monarch cease
 To guard thee in eternal peace.

FOR SOCIAL AND PRIVATE WORSHIP.

110

THOU only Sovereign of my heart,
 My Refuge, my almighty Friend—
And can my soul from thee depart,
 On whom alone my hopes depend?

2 Whither, ah! whither shall I go,
 A wretched wanderer from my Lord?
Can this dark world of sin and woe
 One glimpse of happiness afford?

3 Eternal life thy words impart:
 On these my fainting spirit lives;
Here sweeter comforts cheer my heart,
 Than all the round of nature gives.

4 Let earth's alluring joys combine;
 While thou art near, in vain they call;
One smile, one blissful smile of thine,
 My dearest Lord, outweighs them all.

5 Low at thy feet my soul would lie;
 Here safety dwells, and peace divine;
Still let me live beneath thine eye,
 For life, eternal life, is thine.

111

JESUS, and shall it ever be,
 A mortal man ashamed of thee?
Ashamed of thee, whom angels praise,
 Whose glories shine thro' endless days.

2 Ashamed of Jesus! sooner far
 Let evening blush to own a star;
He sheds the beams of light divine
 O'er this benighted soul of mine.

3 Ashamed of Jesus! just as soon
 Let midnight be ashamed of noon;
'Tis midnight with my soul, till he,
 Bright Morning Star, bid darkness flee.

4 Ashamed of Jesus! that dear friend
 On whom my hopes of heaven depend,
No, when I blush, be this my shame,
 That I no more revere his name.

5 Ashamed of Jesus! yes, I may,
 When I've no guilt to wash away,
No tear to wipe, no good to crave,
 No fears to quell, no soul to save.

6 Till then—nor is my boasting vain—
 Till then, I boast a Saviour slain:
And O may this my glory be,
 That Christ is not ashamed of me.

HYMNS 112, 113, 114.

STONEFIELD. L. M.

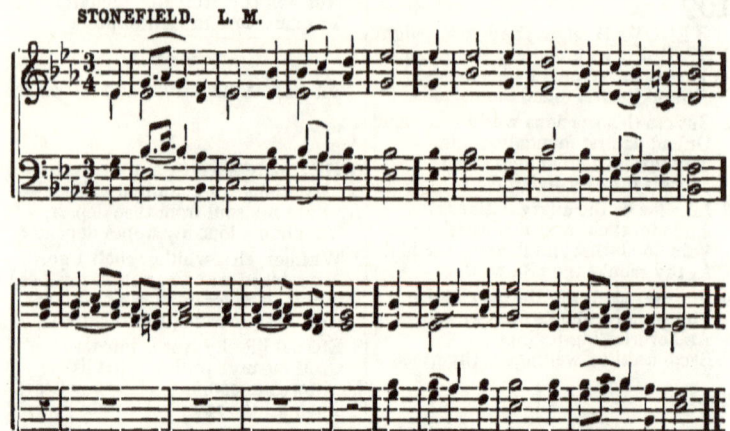

112 I.

BEHOLD the sin-atoning Lamb,
With wonder, gratitude, and love;
To take away our guilt and shame,
See him descending from above!

2 Our sins and griefs on him were laid;
He meekly bore the mighty load;
Our ransom-price he fully paid,
In groans and tears, in sweat and [blood.

3 Pardon and peace through him abound;
He can the richest blessings give;
Salvation in his name is found,
He bids the dying sinner live.

4 Jesus, our Lord, we look to thee;
Where else can helpless sinners go?
Thy boundless love shall set us free
From all our wretchedness and woe.

113 I.

O CHRIST! our King, Creator, Lord!
Saviour of all who trust thy word!
To them who seek thee ever near,
Now to our praises bend an ear.

2 In thy dear cross a grace is found—
It flows from every streaming wound—
Whose power our inbred sin controls,
Breaks the firm bond, and frees our
  souls.

3 Thou didst create the stars of night;
Yet thou hast veiled in flesh thy light—
Hast deigned a mortal form to wear,
A mortal's painful lot to bear.

4 When thou didst hang upon the tree,
The quaking earth acknowledged thee;
When thou didst there yield up thy
  breath, [death.
The world grew dark as shades of

5 Now in the Father's glory high,
Great Conqu'ror, never more to die,
Us by thy mighty power defend,
And reign through ages without end!

114 I.

GREAT God, indulge my humble claim;
Thou art my hope, my joy, my rest;
The glories that compose thy name
Stand all engaged to make me blest.

2 Thou great and good, thou just and
  wise,
Thou art my Father, and my God;
And I am thine, by sacred ties, [blood.
Thy son, thy servant, bought with

3 With early feet I love t'appear
Among thy saints, and seek thy face;
Oft have I seen thy glory there,
And felt the power of sovereign grace.

4 I'll lift my hands, I'll raise my voice,
While I have breath to pray or praise;
This work shall make my heart rejoice,
And bless the remnant of my days.

115 II.

THEE we adore, eternal Lord!
We praise thy name with one accord;
Thy saints, who here thy goodness see,
Through all the world do worship thee.

2 To thee aloud all angels cry, [high
The heavens and all the powers on
Thee, holy, holy, holy King,
Lord God of hosts, they ever sing.

3 Th' apostles join the glorious throng;
The prophets swell th' immortal song;
The martyrs' noble army raise
Eternal anthems to thy praise.

4 From day to day, O Lord, do we
Highly exalt and honor thee!
Thy name we worship and adore,
World without end, for evermore!

116 II.

NOW to the Lord a noble song;
Awake, my soul, awake, my tongue;
Hosanna to th' eternal Name,
And all his boundless love proclaim.

2 See where it shines in Jesus' face,
The brightest image of his grace;
God, in the person of his Son,
Has all his mightiest works outdone.

3 The spacious earth, and spreading flood,
Proclaim the wise and powerful God;
And thy rich glories from afar
Sparkle in every rolling star.

4 But in his looks a glory stands,
The noblest labor of thine hands;
The pleasing lustre of his eyes
Outshines the wonders of the skies.

5 O! may I live to reach the place
Where he unveils his lovely face!
Where all his beauties you behold,
And sing his name to harps of gold.

117 II.

ETERNAL source of every joy,
Well may thy praise our lips employ,
While in thy temple we appear, [ploy,
To hail thee, Sovereign of the year.

2 Wide as the wheels of nature roll,
Thy hand supports and guides the whole;
The sun is taught by thee to rise,
And darkness when to veil the skies.

3 The flowery spring at thy command,
Perfumes the air, adorns the land;
The summer rays with vigor shine,
To raise the corn, and cheer the vine.

4 Thy hand, in autumn, richly pours,
Thro' all our coasts, redundant stores:
And winters, softened by thy care,
No more the face of horror wear.

5 Seasons and months and weeks and days,
Demand successive songs of praise;
And be the grateful homage paid,
With morning light and evening shade.

6 Here in thy house let incense rise,
And circling Sabbaths bless our eyes,
Till to those lofty heights we soar,
Where days and years revolve no more.

FOR SOCIAL AND PRIVATE WORSHIP.

118

SWIFT as declining shadows pass,
Our days in quick succession fly;
And, transient as the withering grass,
Amid our youthful hopes we die.

2 But thou, our Saviour, shalt endure,
Thy years unchanged, eternal Lord!
Thy grace through every age is sure,
And firm the promise of thy word.

119

WHEN marshalled on the nightly plain,
The glittering hosts bestud the sky,
One star alone of all the train,
Can fix the sinner's wandering eye.

2 Hark! hark! to God the chorus breaks,
From every host, from every gem;
But one alone the Saviour speaks:
It is the Star of Bethlehem.

3 Once on the raging seas I rode: [dark;
The storm was loud, the night was
The ocean yawned, and rudely blowed
The wind that tossed my foundering bark.

4 Deep horror then my vitals froze;
Death-struck, I ceased the tide to stem;
When suddenly a star arose!
It was the Star of Bethlehem.

5 It was my guide, my light, my all;
It bade my dark forebodings cease;
And through the storm, and danger's [thrall,
It led me to the port of peace.

6 Now safely moored, my perils o'er,
I'll sing, first in night's diadem,
For ever and for evermore,
The Star—the Star of Bethlehem!

UXBRIDGE. L. M.

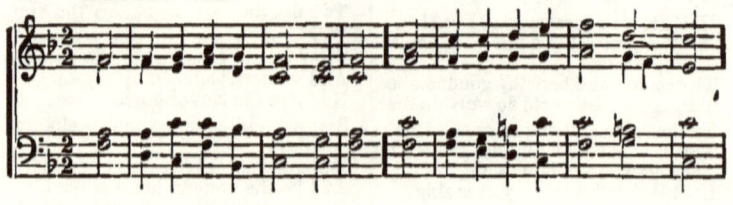
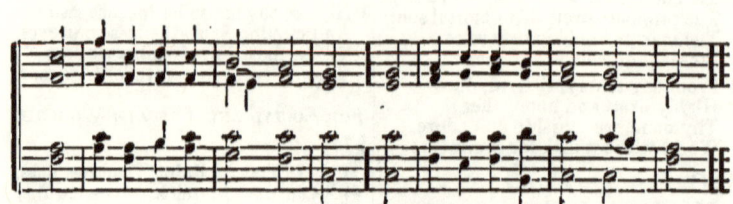

120   I.

FORGIVENESS! 'tis a joyful sound
To guilty rebels doomed to die:
Publish the bliss the world around;
Ye seraphs, shout it from the sky.

2 'Tis the rich gift of love divine,
'Tis full, effacing every crime:
Unbounded shall its glories shine,
And feel no change by changing time.

3 For this stupendous love of heaven,
What grateful honors shall we show?
Where much transgression is forgiven,
Let love with equal ardor glow.

4 By this inspired, let all our days
With every heavenly grace be crown'd;
Let truth and goodness, prayer and praise,
In all abide, in all abound.

121   I.

THE heavens declare thy glory, Lord;
In every star thy wisdom shines;
But when our eyes behold thy word,
We read thy name in fairer lines.

2 The rolling sun, the changing light,
And nights and days thy power confess,
But the blest volume thou hast writ,
Reveals thy justice and thy grace.

3 Sun, moon, and stars convey thy praise
Round the whole earth, and never stand,
So when thy truth began its race,
It touched and glanced on every land.

4 Nor shall thy spreading gospel rest,
Till thro' the world thy truth has run;
Till Christ has all the nations blest,
That see the light or feel the sun.

5 Great Sun of Righteousness, arise,
Bless the dark world with heavenly light;
Thy gospel makes the simple wise,
Thy laws are pure, thy judgments right.

6 Thy noblest wonders here we view,
In souls renewed and sins forgiven;
Lord, cleanse my sins, my soul renew,
And make thy word my guide to heav'n.

122   II.

HIGH in the heavens, eternal God,
Thy goodness in full glory shines:
Thy truth shall break thro' every cloud
That veils and darkens thy designs.

2 For ever firm thy justice stands,
As mountains their foundations keep;
Wise are the wonders of thy hands,
Thy judgments are a mighty deep.

3 My God, how excellent thy grace!
Whence all our hope and comfort springs;
The sons of Adam in distress
Fly to the shadow of thy wings.

HYMNS 123, 124, 125, 126, 127.   237

4 From the provisions of thy house
  We shall be fed with sweet repast,
  There mercy like a river flows,
  And brings salvation to our taste.
5 Life, like a fountain rich and free,
  Springs from the presence of my Lord,
  And in thy light our souls shall see
  The glories promised in thy word.

123   II.

GOD in his earthly temple lays
  Foundations for his heavenly praise;
He likes the tents of Jacob well,
But still in Zion loves to dwell.

2 His mercy visits every house [vows:
  That pay their night and morning
  But makes a more delightful stay [pray.
  Where churches meet to praise and

3 What glories were described of old!
  What wonders are of Zion told!
  Thou city of our God below,
  Thy fame shall tyre and Egypt know

4 Egypt and Tyre, and Greek and Jew,
  Shall there begin their lives anew:
  Angels and men shall join to sing
  The hill where living waters spring.

124   II.

AT thy command, our dearest Lord,
  Here we attend thy dying feast;
Thy love has spread the sacred board,
To feed the faith of every guest.

2 Our faith adores thy bleeding love,
  And trusts for life in One that died;
  We hope for heavenly crowns above,
  From a Redeemer crucified.

3 Let the vain world pronounce it shame,
  And cast contempt upon thy cause:
  We glory in our Saviour's name,
  And make our triumphs in his cross.

4 With joy we tell the scoffing age,
  He that was dead has left his tomb;
  He lives above their utmost rage,
  And we are waiting till he come.

For Social and Private Worship.

125

LORD, in thy great, thy glorious name,
  I place my hope, my only trust:
Save me from sorrow, guilt, and shame,
  Thou ever gracious, ever just.

2 Thou art my rock—thy name alone
  The fortress where my hopes retreat;
  O, make thy power and mercy known;
  To safety guide my wandering feet.

3 Blessed be the Lord—forever blessed,
  Whose mercy bids my fears remove;
  The sacred walls which guard my rest,
  Are his almighty power and love.

4 Ye humble souls, who seek his face,
  Let sacred courage fill your heart!
  Hope in the Lord, and trust his grace,
  And he shall heavenly strength impart.

126

GREAT One in Three, great Three in One!
Thy wondrous name we sound abroad;
Prostrate we fall before thy throne,
  O holy, holy, holy Lord!

2 Thee, Holy Father, we confess;
  Thee, Holy Saviour, we adore;
  And thee, O Holy Ghost, we bless
  And praise and worship evermore.

127

AWAKE, my soul, in joyful lays,
  And sing thy great Redeemer's praise;
He justly claims a song from thee;
His loving-kindness, O how free!

2 He saw me ruined in the fall,
  Yet loved me notwithstanding all;
  He saved me from my lost estate;
  His loving-kindness, O! how great!

3 Tho' numerous hosts of mighty foes,
  Tho' earth and hell my way oppose,
  He safely leads my soul along;
  His loving-kindness, O! how strong!

4 When trouble, like a gloomy cloud,
  Has gathered thick and thundered loud,
  He near my soul has always stood;
  His loving-kindness, O! how good!

5 Often I feel my sinful heart,
  Prone from my Saviour to depart;
  But though I oft have him forgot,
  His loving-kindness changes not.

6 Soon shall I pass the gloomy vale,
  Soon all my mortal powers must fail;
  O may my last expiring breath,
  His loving-kindness sing in death.

7 Then let me mount and soar away,
  To the bright world of endless day;
  And sing with rapture and surprise,
  His loving-kindness in the skies.

WARD. L. M.

128 I.

GOD is the refuge of his saints,
When storms of sharp distress invade;
Ere we can offer our complaints,
Behold him present with his aid.

2 There is a stream, whose gentle flow
Supplies the city of our God!
Life, love, and joy still gliding through,
And watering our divine abode.

3 That sacred stream, thine holy word,
Supports our faith, our fear controls;
Sweet peace thy promises afford,[souls.
And give new strength to fainting

4 Zion enjoys her Monarch's love,
Secure against a threatening hour;
Nor can her firm foundation move,
Built on his truth, and armed with power.

129 I.

COME, gracious Spirit, heavenly Dove,
With light and comfort from above:
Be thou our guardian, thou our guide;
O'er every thought and step preside.

2 The light of truth to us display, [way;
And make us know and choose thy
Plant holy fear in every heart,
That we from God may not depart.

3 Lead us to holiness—the road
That we must take to dwell with God;
Lead us to Christ, the living way,
Nor let us from his precepts stray.

4 Lead us to God, our final rest,
In his enjoyment to be blest;
Lead us to heaven, the seat of bliss,
Where pleasure in perfection is.

130 I.

O THOU that hear'st when sinners cry,
Though all my crimes before thee lie,
Behold them not with angry look,
But blot their memory from my book.

2 Create my nature pure within,
And form my soul averse to sin:
Let thy good spirit ne'er depart,
Nor hide thy presence from my heart.

3 I cannot live without thy light,
Cast out and banished from thy sight;
Thine holy joys, my God, restore,
And guard me, that I fall no more.

4 Though I have grieved thy Spirit, Lord,
Thy help and comfort still afford,
And let a wretch come near thy throne,
To plead the merits of thy Son.

5 A broken heart, my God, my King,
Is all the sacrifice I bring;
The God of grace will ne'er despise
A broken heart for sacrifice.

6 My soul lies humbled in the dust,
  And owns thy dreadful sentence just;
  Look down, O Lord, with pitying eye,
  And save the soul condemned to die.
7 Then will I teach the world thy ways;
  Sinners shall learn thy sovereign grace;
  I'll lead them to my Saviour's blood,
  And they shall praise a pardoning God.
8 O! may thy love inspire my tongue!
  Salvation shall be all my song;
  And all my powers shall join to bless
  The Lord, my Strength and Righteousness.

For Social and Private Worship.

131

FROM every stormy wind that blows,
  From every swelling tide of woes,
There is a calm, a sure retreat,
'Tis found beneath the mercy seat.

2 There is a place, where Jesus sheds
  The oil of gladness on our heads;
  A place than all besides more sweet,
  It is the blood-bought mercy seat.

3 There is a scene, where spirits blend,
  Where friend holds fellowship with friend; [meet,
  Though sundered far, by faith they
  Around one common mercy seat.

4 Ah! whither could we flee for aid,
  When tempted, desolate, dismayed?
  Or how the hosts of hell defeat,
  Had suffering saints no mercy seat?

5 There, there on eagles' wings we soar,
  And sin and sense seem all no more;
  And heaven comes down our souls to greet,
  And glory crowns the mercy seat.

6 O let my hand forget her skill,
  My tongue be silent, cold and still,
  This bounding heart forget to beat,
  If I forget thy mercy seat.

132

WHEN sins and fears prevailing rise,
  And fainting hope almost expires;
Jesus, to thee I lift mine eyes,
  To thee I breathe my soul's desires.

2 Art thou not mine, my living Lord?
  And can my hope, my comfort die,
  Fixed on thy everlasting word, [sky?
  That word which built the earth and

3 If my immortal Saviour lives,
  Then my immortal life is sure;
  His word a firm foundation gives,
  Here let me build and rest secure.

4 Here let my faith unshaken dwell,
  Immovable the promise stands;
  Nor all the powers of earth, or hell,
  Can e'er dissolve the sacred bands.

133

LORD, how mysterious are thy ways?
  How blind are we, how mean our praise!
Thy steps no mortal eyes explore;
  'Tis ours to wonder and adore.

2 Thy purposes from creature sight
  Are hid in shades of awful night;
  Amid the lines, with curious eye,
  Not angel minds presume to pry.

3 Great God! I do not ask to see
  What in futurity shall be;
  Let light and bliss attend my days,
  And then my future hours be praise.

4 Are darkness and distress my share?
  Give me to trust thy guardian care;
  Enough for me, if love divine [shine.
  At length through every cloud shall

5 Yet this my soul desires to know,
  Be this my only wish below; [quest
  That Christ is mine!—this great re-
  Grant, bounteous God, and I am blest.

134

SURE the blest Comforter is nigh,
  'Tis he sustains my fainting heart;
Else would my hope for ever die,
  And every cheering ray depart.

2 When some kind promise cheers my
  Do I not find his healing voice, [soul,
  The tempest of my fears control,
  And bid my drooping powers rejoice?

3 Whene'er to call the Saviour mine,
  With ardent wish my heart aspires,
  Can it be less than power divine,
  Which animates these strong desires.

4 What less than thine almighty word,
  Can raise my heart from earth and dust,
  And bid me cleave to thee, my Lord,
  My life, my treasure, and my trust?

5 And when my cheerful hope can say,
  I love my God, and taste his grace,
  Lord, is it not thy blissful ray, [peace?
  Which brings this dawn of sacred

6 Let thy kind Spirit in my heart,
  For ever dwell, O God of love;
  And light, and heavenly peace impart,
  Sweet earnest of the joys above.

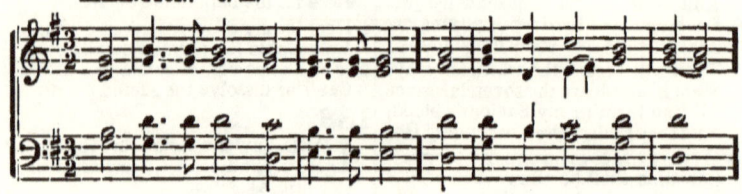

ARLINGTON. C. M.

135 I.

WE bless the Prophet of the Lord,
 Who comes with truth and grace;
Jesus, thy Spirit and thy word,
 Shall lead us in thy ways.

2 We reverence our High Priest above,
 Who offered up his blood,
And lives to carry on his love,
 By pleading with our God.

3 We honor our exalted King;
 How sweet are his commands!
He guards our souls from hell and sin,
 By his almighty hands.

4 Hosanna to his glorious name,
 Who saves by different ways;
His mercies lay a sovereign claim
 To our immortal praise.

136 I.

LORD, I have made thy word my
 My lasting heritage;   [choice
There shall my noblest powers rejoice,
 My warmest thoughts engage.

2 I'll read the histories of thy love,
 And keep thy laws in sight,
While through the promises I rove,
 With ever fresh delight.

3 'Tis a broad land of wealth unknown,
 Where springs of life arise;
Seeds of immortal bliss are sown,
 And hidden glory lies.

4 The best relief that mourners have,
 It makes our sorrows blest;
Our fairest hope beyond the grave,
 And our eternal rest.

137 I.

HOW large the promise, how divine,
 To Abraham and his seed!
"I'll be a God to thee and thine,
 Supplying all their need."

2 The words of his extensive love,
 From age to age endure;
The Angel of the covenant proves
 And seals the blessings sure.

3 Jesus the ancient faith confirms
 To our great father given;
He takes young children to his arms,
 And calls them heirs of heaven.

4 Our God! how faithful are his ways!
 His love endures the same;
Nor from the promise of his grace,
 Blots out the children's name.

138 II.

ARISE, my soul, my joyful powers,
 And triumph in thy God;

Awake, my voice, and loud proclaim
  His glorious grace abroad.
2 The arms of everlasting love
  Beneath my soul he placed,
  And on the Rock of ages set
  My slippery footsteps fast.
3 The city of my blest abode
  Is walled around with grace;
  Salvation for a bulwark stands
  To shield the sacred place.
4 Arise, my soul, awake my voice,
  And tunes of pleasure sing;
  Loud hallelujahs shall address
  My Saviour and my King.

139 II.

THIS is the day the Lord hath made,
  He calls the hours his own;
  Let heaven rejoice, let earth be glad,
  And praise surround the throne.
2 To-day he rose and left the dead,
  And Satan's empire fell;
  To-day the saints his triumph spread,
  And all his wonders tell.
3 Hosanna to th' anointed King,
  To David's holy Son;
  Help us, O Lord, descend and bring
  Salvation from thy throne.
4 Blest is the Lord who comes to men
  With messages of grace;
  Who comes in God his Father's name,
  To save our sinful race.
5 Hosanna in the highest strains
  The church on earth can raise;
  The highest heavens, in which he reigns,
  Shall give him nobler praise.

For Social and Private Worship.

140

NOW let our cheerful eyes survey
  Our great High Priest above;
  And celebrate his constant care,
  And sympathetic love.
2 The names of all his saints he bears,
  Deep graven on his heart;
  Nor shall the meanest Christian say,
  That he hath lost his part.
3 Those characters shall fair abide,
  Our everlasting trust, [crowns,
  When gems, and monuments, and
  Are mouldered down to dust.

16

4 So, gracious Saviour, on my breast
  May thy dear name be worn:
  A sacred ornament and guard,
  To endless ages borne.

141

ALAS! and did my Saviour bleed,
  And did my Sovereign die?
  Would he devote that sacred head
  For such a worm as I?
2 Thy body slain, dear Jesus, thine,
  And bathed in its own blood,
  While all exposed to wrath divine,
  The glorious sufferer stood!
3 Was it for crimes that I had done,
  He groaned upon the tree?
  Amazing pity! grace unknown!
  And love beyond degree!
4 Well might the sun in darkness hide,
  And shut his glories in,
  When God, the mighty Maker, died,
  For man, the creature's sin.
5 Thus might I hide my blushing face,
  While his dear cross appears,
  Dissolve my heart in thankfulness,
  And melt my eyes to tears.
6 But drops of grief can ne'er repay
  The debt of love I owe:
  Here, Lord, I give myself away;
  'Tis all that I can do.

142

I LOVE to steal awhile away
  From every cumbering care;
  And spend the hours of setting day
  In humble, grateful prayer.
2 I love in solitude to shed
  The penitential tear,
  And all his promises to plead,
  Where none but God can hear.
3 I love to think on mercies past,
  And future good implore,
  And all my cares and sorrows cast
  On him whom I adore.
4 I love by faith to take a view
  Of brighter scenes in heaven;
  The prospect does my strength renew,
  While here by tempests driven.
5 Thus, when life's toilsome day is o'er,
  May its departing ray
  Be calm as this impressive hour,
  And lead to endless day.

HYMNS 143, 144, 145.

BALERMA. C. M.

143 I.

THE Lord of glory is my light,
And my salvation too;
God is my strength; nor will I fear
What all my foes can do.

2 One privilege my heart desires;
O! grant me mine abode
Among the churches of thy saints,
The temples of my God.

3 There shall I offer my requests,
And see thy beauty still,
Shall hear thy messages of love,
And there inquire thy will.

4 When troubles rise and storms appear,
There may his children hide;
God is a strong pavilion, where
He makes my soul abide.

5 Now shall my head be lifted high
Above my foes around,
And songs of joy and victory
Within thy temple sound.

144 I.

WHAT shall I render to my God
For all his kindness shown?
My feet shall visit thine abode,
My songs address thy throne.

2 How happy all thy servants are!
How great thy grace to me!
My life which thou hast made thy care,
Lord, I devote to thee.

3 Now I am thine, for ever thine,
Nor shall my purpose move;
Thy hand has loosed my bonds of pain,
And bound me with thy love.

4 Here in thy courts I leave my vow,
And thy rich grace record;
Witness, ye saints who hear me now,
If I forsake the Lord.

145 II.

MY never-ceasing song shall show
The mercies of the Lord;
And make succeeding ages know
How faithful is his word.

2 The sacred truths his lips pronounce
Shall firm as heaven endure;
And if he speaks a promise once,
The eternal grace is sure.

3 How long the race of David held
The promised Jewish throne!
But there's a nobler covenant sealed
To David's greater Son.

4 His seed for ever shall possess
A throne above the skies;
The meanest subject of his grace
Shall to that glory rise.

·5 Lord God of hosts, thy wondrous ways
   Are sung by saints above:
   And saints on earth their honors raise
   To thy unchanging love.

For Social and Private Worship.

146

WHOM have we, Lord, in heaven but
   And whom on earth beside? [thee,
Where else for succor can we flee,
Or in whose strength confide?

2 Thou art our portion here below,
   Our promised bliss above;
Ne'er may our souls an object know
   So precious as thy love,

3 When heart and flesh, O Lord, shall
   Thou wilt our spirits cheer, [fail,
Support us through life's thorny vale,
   And calm each anxious fear.

4 Yes—thou shalt be our guide thro' life,
   And help and strength supply;
Sustain us in death's fearful strife,
   And welcome us on high.

147

DEAREST of all the names above,
   My Jesus and my God,
Who can resist thy heavenly love,
   Or trifle with thy blood?

2 Till God in human flesh I see,
   My thoughts no comfort find;
The holy, just and sacred Three
   Are terrors to my mind.

3 But if Immanuel's face appear,
   My hope, my joy begins,
His name forbids my slavish fear,
   His grace removes my sins.

4 While Jews on their own law rely,
   And Greeks of wisdom boast,
I love the incarnate mystery,
   And there I fix my trust.

148

O FOR a closer walk with God,
   A calm and heavenly frame:
A light to shine upon the road
   That leads me to the Lamb.

2 Where is the blessedness I knew
   When first I saw the Lord?
Where is the soul-refreshing view
   Of Jesus and his word?

3 What peaceful hours I once enjoyed,
   How sweet their memory still!
But they have left an aching void
   The world can never fill.

4 Return, O holy Dove, return
   Sweet messenger of rest;
I hate the sins that made thee mourn,
   And drove thee from my breast.

5 The dearest idol I have known,
   Whate'er that idol be,
Help me to tear it from thy throne,
   And worship only thee.

6 So shall my walk be close with God,
   Calm and serene my frame;
So purer light shall mark the road
   That leads me to the Lamb.

149

WHEN I can read my title clear,
   To mansions in the skies,
I'll bid farewell to every fear,
   And wipe my weeping eyes.

2 Should earth against my soul engage,
   And hellish darts be hurled,
Then I can smile at Satan's rage,
   And face a frowning world.

3 Let cares like a wild deluge come,
   And storms of sorrow fall;
May I but safely reach my home,
   My God, my heaven, my all.

4 There shall I bathe my weary soul
   In seas of heavenly rest,
And not a wave of trouble roll
   Across my peaceful breast.

150

LORD, thou wilt hear me when I pray,
   I am for ever thine:
I fear before thee all the day,
   Nor would I dare to sin.

2 And while I rest my weary head
   From cares and business free,
'Tis sweet conversing on my bed
   With my own heart and thee.

3 I pay this evening sacrifice;
   And when my work is done,
Great God, my faith and hope relies
   Upon thy grace alone.

4 Thus with my thoughts composed to
   I'll give mine eyes to sleep; [peace
Thy hand in safety keeps my days,
   And will my slumbers keep.

BEDFORD. C. M.

151   I.

WHEN God revealed his gracious name,
   And changed my mournful state,
My rapture seemed a pleasing dream,
   The grace appeared so great.

2 The world beheld the glorious change,
   And did thy hand confess; [strains
My tongue broke out in unknown
   And sung surprising grace.

3 The Lord can clear the darkest skies,
   Can give us day for night;
Make drops of sacred sorrow rise
   To rivers of delight.

4 Let those that sow in sadness, wait
   Till the fair harvest come; [great,
They shall confess their sheaves are
   And shout the blessings home.

152   I.

THY mercies fill the earth, O Lord,
   How good thy works appear!
Open my eyes to read thy word,
   And see thy wonders there.

2 My heart was fashioned by thy hand,
   My service is thy due;
O! make thy servant understand
   The duties he must do.

3 Since I'm a stranger here below,
   Thy path O! do not hide,
But mark the road my feet should go,
   And be my constant guide.

4 When I confessed my wandering ways,
   Thou heardst my soul complain;
Grant me the teachings of thy grace
   Or I shall stray again.

5 If God to me his statutes show,
   And heavenly truth impart,
His work for ever I'll pursue,
   His law shall rule my heart.

153   II.

THE Lord descended from above,
   And bowed the heavens most high;
And underneath his feet he cast
   The darkness of the sky.

2 On cherub and on cherubim,
   Full royally, he rode;
And on the wings of mighty winds
   Came flying all abroad.

3 He sat serene upon the floods,
   Their fury to restrain;
And he, as sovereign Lord and King,
   For evermore shall reign.

4 The Lord will give his people strength,
   Whereby they shall increase;
And he will bless his chosen flock
   With everlasting peace.

154 II.

'TIS by thy strength the mountains
 God of eternal power; [stand,
The sea grows calm at thy command,
And tempests cease to roar.
2 Thy morning light and evening shade
Successive comforts bring;
Thy plenteous fruits make harvest glad,
Thy flowers adorn the spring.
3 Seasons and times, and moons and hours,
Heaven, earth, and air are thine;
When clouds distil in fruitful showers,
The author is divine.
4 The thirsty ridges drink their fill,
And ranks of corn appear;
Thy ways abound with blessings still,
Thy goodness crowns the year.

155 II.

THROUGH endless years thou art the
 O thou eternal God! [same,
Ages to come shall know thy name,
And tell thy works abroad.
2 The strong foundations of the earth,
Of old by thee were laid;
By thee the beauteous arch of heaven,
With matchless skill was made.
3 Soon shall this goodly frame of things,
Formed by thy powerful hand,
Be, like a vesture, laid aside,
And changed at thy command.
4 But thy perfections all divine,
Eternal as thy days,
Through everlasting ages shine,
With undiminished rays.
5 Thy children's children, still thy care,
Shall own their father's God;
To latest times thy favor share,
And spread thy praise abroad.

FOR SOCIAL AND PRIVATE WORSHIP.

156

HOW precious is the book divine,
 By inspiration given!
Bright as a lamp its doctrines shine,
To guide our souls to heaven.
2 It sweetly cheers our drooping hearts
In this dark vale of tears;
Life, light, and joy it still imparts,
And quells our rising fears.

3 This lamp, through all the tedious
Of life, shall guide our way, [night
Till we behold the clearer light
Of an eternal day.

157

O LORD, I would delight in thee,
 And on thy care depend;
To thee in every trouble flee,
My best, my only Friend.
2 When all created streams are dried,
Thy fulness is the same;
May I with this be satisfied,
And glory in thy name.
3 Why should the soul a drop bemoan,
Who has a fountain near,
A fountain which shall ever run,
With waters sweet and clear?
4 No good in creatures can be found,
But may be found in thee:
I must have all things and abound,
While God is God to me.
5 He who has made my heaven secure,
Will here all good provide:
Whilst Christ is rich, can I be poor?
What can I want beside?
6 O Lord, I cast my care on thee,
I triumph and adore;
Henceforth my great concern shall be,
To love and praise thee more.

158

THY way, O God, is in the sea,
 Thy paths I cannot trace;
Nor comprehend the mystery
Of thy unbounded grace.
2 Here the dark veils of flesh and sense
My captive soul surround;
Mysterious deeps of providence
My wondering thoughts confound.
3 As through a glass, I dimly see
The wonders of thy love;
How little do I know of thee,
Or of the joys above!
4 'Tis but in part I know thy will;
I bless thee for the sight;
When will thy love the rest reveal,
In glory's clearer light?
5 With rapture shall I then survey
Thy providence and grace;
And spend an everlasting day
In wonder, love, and praise.

BURFORD. C. M.

159 I.

1 OUT of the deeps of long distress,
  The borders of despair,
I sent my cries to seek thy grace,
  My groans to reach thine ear.

2 Great God, should thy severer eye,
  And thine impartial hand,
Mark and revenge iniquity,
  No mortal flesh could stand.

3 But there are pardons with my God,
  For crimes of high degree; [blood,
Thy Son hath bought them with his
  To draw us near to thee.

4 Then in the Lord let Israel trust,
  Let Israel seek his face;
The Lord is good, as well as just,
  And plenteous is his grace.

5 There's full redemption at his throne
  For sinners long enslaved;
The great Redeemer is his Son,
  And Israel shall be saved.

160 I.

1 PLUNGED in a gulf of dark despair,
  We wretched sinners lay,
Without one cheerful beam of hope,
  Or spark of glimmering day.

2 With pitying eyes the Prince of grace
  Beheld our helpless grief;
He saw, and, O amazing love!
  He ran to our relief.

3 Down from the shining seats above,
  With joyful haste he fled,
Entered the grave in mortal flesh,
  And dwelt among the dead.

4 He spoiled the powers of darkness thus,
  And brake our iron chains:
Jesus has freed our captive souls
  From everlasting pains.

5 O! for this love, let rocks and hills
  Their lasting silence break;
And all harmonious human tongues
  The Saviour's praises speak.

FOR SOCIAL AND PRIVATE WORSHIP.

161

1 O GOD of mercy, hear my call,
  My load of guilt remove;
Break down this separating wall,
  That bars me from thy love.

2 Give me the presence of thy grace;
  Then my rejoicing tongue
Shall speak aloud thy righteousness,
  And make thy praise my song.

3 No blood of goats nor heifers slain,
  For sin could e'er atone;
The death of Christ shall still remain
  Sufficient and alone.

4 A soul oppressed with sin's desert
　My God will ne'er despise;
　An humble groan, a broken heart,
　Is our best sacrifice.

162

O! THAT I knew the secret place
　Where I might find my God!
I'd spread my wants before his face,
　And pour my woes abroad.

2 I'd tell him how my sins arise,
　What sorrows I sustain;
How grace decays, and comfort dies,
　And leaves my heart in pain.

3 He knows what arguments I'd take
　To wrestle with my God;
I'd plead for his own mercy's sake,
　And for my Saviour's blood.

4 My God will pity my complaints,
　And heal my broken bones;
He takes the meaning of his saints,
　The language of their groans.

5 Arise, my soul, from deep distress,
　And banish every fear;
He calls thee to his throne of grace,
　To spread thy sorrows there.

163

DEAR Refuge of my weary soul,
　On thee, when sorrows rise,
On thee, when waves of trouble roll,
　My fainting hope relies.

2 To thee I tell each rising grief,
　For thou alone canst heal;
Thy word can bring a sweet relief,
　For every pain I feel.

3 But O when gloomy doubts prevail,
　I fear to call thee mine;
The springs of comfort seem to fail,
　And all my hopes decline.

4 Yet, gracious God, where shall I flee?
　Thou art my only trust;
And still my soul would cleave to thee,
　Though prostrate in the dust.

5 Hast thou not bid me seek thy face?
　And shall I seek in vain?
And can the ear of sovereign grace
　Be deaf when I complain?

6 No, still the ear of sovereign grace
　Attends the mourner's prayer:
O may I ever find access,
　To breathe my sorrows there.

164

JESUS, my Saviour, bind me fast,
　In cords of heavenly love;
Then sweetly draw me to thy breast,
　Nor let me thence remove.

2 Draw me from all created good,
　From self, the world, and sin;
To the dear fountain of thy blood,
　And make me pure within.

3 O lead me to thy mercy-seat,
　Attract me nearer still;
Draw me, like Mary, to thy feet,
　To sit and learn thy will.

165

MY times of sorrow and of joy,
　Great God, are in thy hand;
All my enjoyments come from thee,
　And go at thy command.

2 O Lord, shouldst thou withhold them all,
　Yet would I not repine;
Before they were by me possessed,
　They were entirely thine.

3 Nor would I drop a murmuring word
　If all the world were gone,
But seek substantial happiness,
　In thee, and thee alone.

166

WHY do we mourn departing friends,
　Or shake at death's alarms?
'Tis but the voice that Jesus sends
　To call them to his arms.

2 Are we not tending upward too,
　As fast as time can move?
Nor should we wish our hours more slow,
　To keep us from our love.

3 Why should we tremble to convey
　Their bodies to the tomb?
There the dear flesh of Jesus lay,
　And left a long perfume.

4 The graves of all the saints he blest,
　And softened every bed;
Where should the dying members rest,
　But with their dying Head?

5 Thence he arose, ascending high,
　And showed our feet the way;
Up to the Lord our flesh shall fly
　At the great rising day.

HYMNS 167, 168, 169, 170.

CAMBRIDGE. C. M.

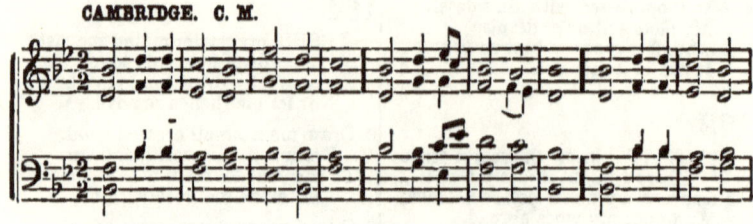

167   I.

LORD, thou hast heard thy servant cry,
And rescued from the grave;
Now shall he live, and none can die,
If God resolve to save.

2 Thy praise, more constant than before,
Shall fill his daily breath;
Thy hand, that hath chastised him sore,
Defends him still from death.

3 Open the gates of Zion now,
For we shall worship there,
The house where all the righteous go,
Thy mercy to declare.

4 Among the assemblies of thy saints
Our thankful voice we raise;
There we have told thee our complaints,
And there we speak thy praise.

168   I.

BLEST are the souls who hear and know
The gospel's joyful sound:
Peace shall attend the path they go,
And light their steps surround.

2 Their joy shall bear their spirits up
Through their Redeemer's name;
His righteousness exalts their hope,
And fills their foes with shame.

3 The Lord, our glory and defence,
Strength and salvation gives;
Israel, thy King for ever reigns,
Thy God for ever lives.

169   II.

JOY to the world, the Lord is come,
Let earth receive her King;
Let every heart prepare him room,
And heaven and nature sing.

2 Joy to the earth, the Saviour reigns,
Let men their songs employ;
While fields and floods, rocks, hills, and
Repeat the sounding joy.   [plains

3 No more let sins and sorrows grow,
Nor thorns infest the ground:
He comes to make his blessings flow
Far as the curse is found.

4 He rules the world with truth and
And makes the nations prove [grace,
The glories of his righteousness,
And wonders of his love.

170   II.

OH, praise the Lord! for he is good;
In him we rest obtain:
His mercy has through ages stood,
And ever shall remain.

2 Let all the people of the Lord
   His praises spread around;
   Let them his grace and love record,
   Who have salvation found.
3 Now let the east in him rejoice,
   The west its tribute bring,
   The north and south lift up their voice
   In honor of their King.
4 Oh, praise the Lord! for he is good;
   In him we rest obtain:
   His mercy has through ages stood,
   And ever shall remain.

171   II.

COME, ye that love the Saviour's
   And joy to make it known; [name,
   The sovereign of your heart proclaim,
   And bow before his throne.
2 Behold your King, your Saviour
   With glories all divine; [crowned
   And tell the wondering nations round
   How bright these glories shine.
3 Infinite power and boundless grace
   In him unite their rays;
   Ye that have e'er beheld his face,
   Can ye forbear his praise?
4 When in his earthly courts we view
   The glories of our King,
   We long to love as angels do,
   And wish like them to sing.
5 And shall we long and wish in vain?
   Lord, teach our songs to rise;
   Thy love can animate the strain,
   And bid it reach the skies.
6 O happy period! glorious day!
   When heaven and earth shall raise,
   With all their powers, the raptured lay,
   To celebrate thy praise.

172   II.

SHINE, mighty God, on Zion shine,
   With beams of heavenly grace;
   Reveal thy power through all our
   And show thy smiling face. [coasts,
2 When shall thy name from shore to
   Sound all the earth abroad; [shore
   And distant nations know and 'love
   Their Saviour and their God?
3 Sing to the Lord, ye distant lands,
   Sing loud with solemn voice;
   Let every tongue exalt his praise
   And every heart rejoice.

4 He, the great Lord, the sovereign
   That sits enthroned above, [Judge,
   In wisdom rules the worlds he made,
   And bids them taste his love.
5 Earth shall obey his high command,
   And yield a full increase;
   Our God shall crown his chosen land
   With fruitfulness and peace.
6 God the Redeemer scatters round
   His choicest favors here,
   While the creations utmost bound
   Shall see, adore, and fear.

173   II.

O ALL ye nations, praise the Lord,
   Each with a different tongue;
   In every language learn his word,
   And let his name be sung.
2 His mercy reigns through every land,
   Proclaim his grace abroad;—
   Forever firm his truth shall stand,—
   Praise ye the faithful God.

174   II.

JERUSALEM, my happy home,
   Name ever dear to me!
   When shall my labors have an end,
   In joy, and peace, and thee?
2 When shall these eyes thy heaven-built
   And pearly gates behold? [walls
   Thy bulwarks with salvation strong,
   And streets of shining gold?
3 O when, thou city of my God,
   Shall I thy courts ascend,
   Where congregations ne'er break up,
   And Sabbaths have no end.
4 There happier bowers than Eden's
   Nor sin nor sorrow know: [bloom,
   Blest seats, through rude and stormy
   I onward press to you. [scenes,
5 Why should I shrink at pain and woe,
   Or feel at death dismay?
   I've Canaan's goodly land in view,
   And realms of endless day.
6 Apostles, martyrs, prophets there
   Around my Saviour stand;
   And soon my friends in Christ below
   Will join the glorious band.
7 Jerusalem, my happy home,
   My soul still pants for thee;
   Then shall my labors have an end,
   When I thy joys shall see.

HYMNS 175, 176, 177.

CHRISTMAS. C. M.

175   I.

GLORY to God the Father's name,
Who from our sinful race,
Chose us his people, to proclaim
The honours of his grace.

2 Glory to God the Son be paid,
Who dwelt in humble clay,
And to redeem us from the dead,
Gave his own life away.

3 Glory to God the Spirit give,
From whose almighty power,
Our souls their heavenly birth derive,
And bless the happy hour.

4 Glory to God who reigns above,
The eternal Three in One;
Who, by the wonders of his love,
Has made his nature known.

176   I.

NOW O my soul, for ever praise,
For ever love his name;
Who turns thy feet from dangerous ways
Of folly, sin and shame.

2 'Tis not by works of righteousness
Which our own hands have done;
But we are saved by sovereign grace,
Abounding through the Son.

3 'Tis from the mercy of our God
That all our hopes begin;
'Tis by the water and the blood,
Our souls are washed from sin.

4 Raised from the dead, we live anew;
And justified by grace,
We shall appear in glory too,
And see our Father's face.

177   II.

SING to the Lord, ye distant lands,
Ye tribes of every tongue;
His new discovered grace demands
A new and nobler song.

2 Say to the nations, Jesus reigns,
God's own almighty Son;
His power the sinking world sustains,
And grace surrounds his throne.

3 Let heaven proclaim the joyful day,
Joy through the earth be seen;
Let cities shine in bright array,
And fields in cheerful green.

4 The joyous earth, the bending skies,
His glorious train display;
Ye mountains sink, ye valleys rise,
Prepare the Lord his way.

5 Behold he comes, he comes to bless
The nations as their God;
To show the world his righteousness,
And send his truth abroad.

178 L. M.

From thee, my God, my joys shall rise,
And run eternal rounds
Beyond the limits of the skies,
And all created bounds.

2 The holy triumphs of my soul
Shall death itself outbrave,
Leave dull mortality behind,
And fly beyond the grave.

3 There, where my blessed Jesus reigns,
In heaven's unmeasured space,
I'll spend a long eternity
In pleasure and in praise.

4 Haste, my Beloved, fetch my soul
Up to thy blest abode;
Fly, for my spirit longs to see
My Saviour and my God.

179 L. M.

Daughter of Zion, from the dust,
Exalt thy fallen head;
Again in thy Redeemer trust,
He calls thee from the dead.

2 Awake, awake, put on thy strength,
Thy beautiful array;
The day of freedom dawns at length,
The Lord's appointed day.

3 They come, they come—thine exiled bands,
Where'er they rest or roam,
Have heard thy voice in distant lands,
And hasten to their home.

4 Thus, though the universe shall burn,
And God his works destroy,
With songs thy ransomed shall return,
And everlasting joy.

For Social and Private Worship.

180

My God, the spring of all my joys,
The life of my delights,
The glory of my brightest days,
And comfort of my nights.

2 In darkest shades if he appear,
My dawning is begun;
He is my soul's bright morning star,
And he my rising sun.

3 The opening heavens around me shine
With beams of sacred bliss,
While Jesus shows his heart is mine,
And whispers I am his.

4 My soul would leave this heavy clay,
At that transporting word;
Run up with joy the shining way,
To embrace my dearest Lord.

5 Fearless of hell and ghastly death,
I'd break through every foe:
The wings of love and arms of faith
Should bear me conqueror through.

181

Awake, my soul, stretch every nerve,
And press with vigour on:
A heavenly race demands thy zeal,
A bright, immortal crown.

2 A cloud of witnesses around
Hold thee in full survey:
Forget the steps already trod,
And onward urge thy way.

3 'Tis God's all animating voice,
That calls thee from on high;
'Tis his own hand presents the prize
To thine aspiring eye.

4 Blest Saviour, introduced by thee,
Have I my race begun;
And crowned with victory at thy feet
I'll lay my honours down.

182

There is a land of pure delight,
Where saints immortal reign;
Infinite day excludes the night,
And pleasures banish pain.

2 There everlasting spring abides,
And never withering flowers;
Death, like a narrow sea, divides
This heavenly land from ours.

3 Sweet fields beyond the swelling flood,
Stand dressed in living green;
So to the Jews old Canaan stood,
While Jordan rolled between.

4 But timorous mortals start and shrink,
To cross this narrow sea;
And linger, shivering on the brink,
And fear to launch away.

5 O could we make our doubts remove,
Those gloomy doubts that rise,
And see the Canaan that we love
With unbeclouded eyes:

6 Could we but climb where Moses stood,
And view the landscape o'er,
Not Jordan's stream, nor death's cold flood
Should fright us from the shore.

HYMNS 183, 184, 185, 186.

CORONATION. C. M.

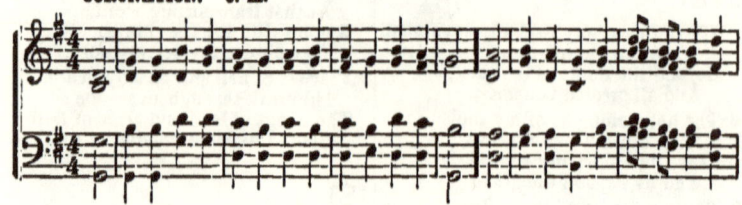

183 I.

THE God of mercy be adored,
Who calls our souls from death:
Who saves by his redeeming Word,
And new creating Breath.

2 To praise the Father, and the Son,
And spirit, all divine,
The One in Three. and Three in One,
Let saints and angels join.

184 I.

HARK the glad sound, the Saviour comes,
The Saviour promised long;
Let every heart prepare a throne,
And every voice a song.

2 On him the Spirit, largely poured,
Exerts his sacred fire;
Wisdom and might, and zeal and love
His holy breast inspire.

3 He comes the prisoners to release,
In Satan's bondage held;
The gates of brass before him burst,
The iron fetters yield.

4 He comes the broken heart to bind,
The bleeding soul to cure;
And with the treasures of his grace
To enrich the humble poor.

5 Our glad Hosannas, Prince of Peace,
Thy welcome shall proclaim;
And heaven's eternal arches ring
With thy beloved name.

185 I.

TO us a Child of hope is born,
To us a Son is given;
Him shall the tribes of earth obey,
Him all the hosts of heaven.

2 His name shall be the Prince of Peace,
For evermore adored;
The Wonderful, the Counselor,
The great and mighty Lord!

3 His power, increasing, still shall spread;
His reign no end shall know:
Justice shall guard his throne above,
And peace abound below.

4 To us a Child of hope is born,
To us a Son is given;
The Wonderful, the Counselor,
The mighty Lord of heaven.

186 I.

A GLORY gilds the sacred page,
Majestic, like the sun;
It gives a light to every age,
It gives, but borrows none.

2 The hand that gave it still supplies
   ~~Those~~ gracious light and heat;
   His truths upon the nations rise;
   They rise but never set.
3 Let everlasting thanks be thine
   For such a bright display,
   As makes a world of darkness shine
   With beams of heavenly day.
4 My soul rejoices to pursue
   The steps of him I love,
   Till glory breaks upon my view
   In brighter worlds above.

187   II.

ALL hail the power of Jesus' name!
   Let angels prostrate fall;
Bring forth the royal diadem
And crown him Lord of all.
2 Ye chosen seed of Israel's race,
   Ye ransomed from the fall;
Hail him who saves you by his grace,
   And crown him Lord of all.
3 Sinners, whose love can ne'er forget
   The wormwood and the gall;
Go spread your trophies at his feet,
   And crown him Lord of all.
4 Let every kindred, every tribe,
   On this terrestrial ball,
To him all majesty ascribe,
   And crown him Lord of all.
5 O that with yonder sacred throng,
   We at his feet may fall;
We'll join the everlasting song,
   And crown him Lord of all.

188   II.

O FOR a shout of sacred joy
   To God, the sovereign King!
Let every land their tongues employ,
   And hymns of triumph sing.
2 Jesus, our God, ascends on high;
   His heavenly guards around
Attend him rising through the sky,
   With trumpet's joyful sound.
3 While angels shout and praise their King,
   Let mortals learn their strains;
Let all the earth his honors sing;
   O'er all the earth he reigns.
4 In Israel stood his ancient throne;
   He loved that chosen race;
But now he calls the world his own,
   And heathens taste his grace.

5 The Gentile nations are the Lord's
   There Abraham's God is known;
While powers and princes, shields and
   Submit before his throne.   [swords

189   II.

LO! what a glorious sight appears
   To our believing eyes!
The earth and seas are passed away,
   And the old rolling skies.
2 From the third heaven, where God re-
   That holy, happy place,   [sides,
The new Jerusalem comes down,
   Adorned with shining grace.
3 Attending angels shout for joy,
   And the bright armies sing;
" Mortals, behold the sacred seat
   Of your descending King.
4 " The God of glory down to men
   Removes his blest abode;
Men, the dear objects of his grace,
   And he the loving God.
5 " His own soft hand shall wipe the tears
   From every weeping eye;
And pains and groans, and griefs and
   And death itself shall die."   [fears,
6 How long, dear Saviour, O how long
   Shall this bright hour delay?
Fly swifter round, ye wheels of time,
   And bring the welcome day.

FOR SOCIAL AND PRIVATE WORSHIP.

190

ON Jordan's stormy banks I stand,
   And cast a wishful eye
To Canaan's fair and happy land,
   Where my possessions lie.
2 O the transporting, rapturous scene,
   That rises to my sight;
Sweet fields arrayed in living green,
   And rivers of delight.
3 There generous fruits, that never fail,
   On trees immortal grow;
There rocks and hills, and brooks and
   With milk and honey flow.   [vales,
4 On all these wide extended plains
   Shines one eternal day;
There God the Son forever reigns,
   And scatters night away.
5 No chilling winds nor poisonous breath
   Can reach that healthful shore;
Sickness and sorrow, pain and death,
   Are felt and feared no more.

DENFIELD. C. M.

191   I.

WE praise and bless thee, gracious
  Our Saviour kind and true, [Lord,
For all the old things passed away,
  For all thou hast made new.

2 Thou, only thou, must carry on
  The work thou hast begun:
Of thine own strength thou must im-
  In thine own ways to run.   [part,

3 When the flesh sinks, then strengthen
  The spirit from above;   [thou
Make us to feel thy service sweet,
  And light thy yoke of love.

4 So shall we faultless stand at last
  Before the Father's throne,
The blessedness for ever ours,
  The glory all thine own.

192   I.

HOW sweet the name of Jesus sounds
  In a believer's ear!   [wounds,
It soothes his sorrows, heals his
  And drives away his fear.

2 It makes the wounded spirit whole,
  And calms the troubled breast;
'Tis manna to the hungry soul,
  And to the weary rest.

3 Dear Name, the Rock on which I build,
  My shield and hiding-place;

My never-failing treasury, filled
  With boundless stores of grace.

4 Jesus, my Shepherd, Husband, Friend,
  My Prophet, Priest, and King;
My Lord, my Life, my Way, my End,
  Accept the praise I bring.

5 Weak is the effort of my heart,
  And cold my warmest thought;
But when I see thee as thou art,
  I'll praise thee as I ought.

6 Till then I would thy love proclaim
  With every fleeting breath;
And may the music of thy name
  Refresh my soul in death.

193   II.

NOT to the terrors of the Lord,
  The tempest, fire and smoke;
Not to the thunder of that word,
  Which God on Sinai spoke;

2 But we are come to Zion's hill,
  The city of our God,
Where milder words declare his will,
  And spread his love abroad.

3 Behold the innumerable host
  Of angels clothed in light;
Behold the spirits of the just,
  Whose faith is turned to sight.

4 Behold the blest assembly there,
   Whose names are writ in heaven;
   And God, the judge of all declares
   Their vilest sins forgiven.
5 The saints on earth, and all the dead,
   But one communion make;
   All join in Christ, their living head,
   And of his grace partake.

194 II.

COME, let us lift our joyful eyes,
   Up to the courts above,
And smile to see our Father there,
   Upon a throne of love.
2 Now we may bow before his feet,
   And venture near the Lord:
No fiery cherub guards his seat,
   Nor double flaming sword.
3 The peaceful gates of heavenly bliss,
   Are opened by the Son;
High let us raise our notes of praise,
   And reach the eternal throne.
4 To thee ten thousand thanks we bring,
   Great Advocate on high;
And glory to the almighty King,
   That lays his fury by.

FOR SOCIAL AND PRIVATE WORSHIP.

195

MY God! my Father! blissful name!
   Oh! may I call thee mine!
May I with sweet assurance claim
   A portion so divine?
2 This only can my fears control,
   And bid my sorrows fly:
What harm can ever reach my soul
   Beneath my Father's eye?
3 Whate'er thy providence denies,
   I calmly would resign;
For thou art good, and just, and wise;
   Oh! bend my will to thine.
4 Whate'er thy sacred will ordains,
   Oh! give me strength to bear;
Let me but know my father reigns,
   And trust his tender care.

196

THERE is a fountain filled with blood,
   Drawn from Immanuel's veins,
And sinners plunged beneath that flood,
   Lose all their guilty stains.
2 The dying thief rejoiced to see
   That fountain in his day;
And there may I, though vile as he,
   Wash all my sins away.
3 Dear dying Lamb, thy precious blood
   Shall never lose its power,
Till all the ransomed church of God
   Be saved to sin no more.
4 E'er since by faith I saw the stream,
   Thy flowing wounds supply,
Redeeming love has been my theme,
   And shall be till I die.
5 Then, in a nobler, sweeter song,
   I'll sing thy power to save;
When this poor lisping, stammering
   Lies silent in the grave. [tongue

197

BLEST morning, whose first dawning
   Beheld our rising God; [light
That saw him triumph o'er the dust,
   And leave his last abode.
2 To thy great name, almighty Lord,
   These sacred hours we pay,
And loud hosannas shall proclaim
   The triumph of the day.
3 In the cold prison of the tomb,
   The dear Redeemer lay,
Till the revolving skies had brought
   The third, the appointed day.
4 Hell and the grave unite their force,
   To hold our God, in vain;
The sleeping Conqueror arose,
   And burst their feeble chain.
5 Salvation and immortal praise
   To our victorious King;
Let heaven and earth, and rocks and
   With glad hosannas ring. [seas,

198 *For Children Only.*

I THANK the goodness and the grace
   That on my birth have smiled,
And made me, in these latter days,
   A happy, Christian child.
2 I was not born as thousands are,
   Where God is never known,
And taught to say a useless prayer
   To gods of wood and stone.
3 My God, I thank thee, who hast planned
   A better lot for me,
And placed me in this favored land,
   Where I may hear of thee.

DEVIZES. C. M.

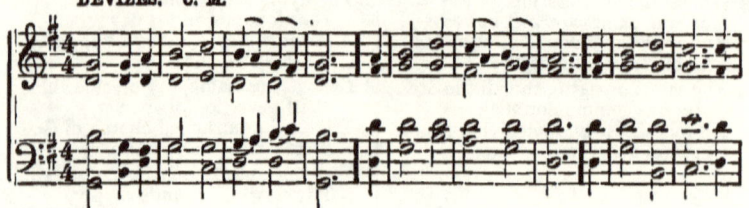

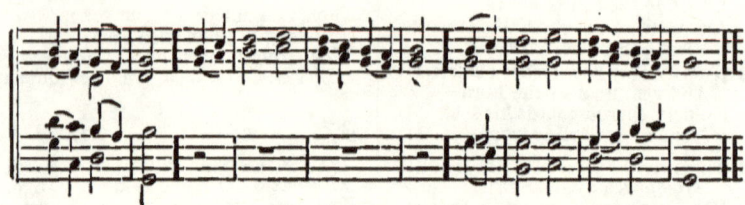

199 I.

PRAISE waits in Zion, Lord, for thee,
There shall our vows be paid;
Thou hast an ear when sinners pray,
All flesh shall seek thine aid.

2 Lord, our iniquities prevail,
But pardoning grace is thine,
And thou wilt grant us power and skill
To conquer every sin.

3 Blest are the men whom thou wilt
To bring them near thy face, [choose
Give them a dwelling in thy house,
To feast upon thy grace.

4 In answering what thy church requests,
Thy truth and terror shine,
Thy works of dreadful righteousness
Fulfil thy kind design.

5 Thus shall the wondering nations see
The Lord is good and just;
And distant islands fly to thee,
And make thy name their trust.

200 I.

EARLY, my God, without delay,
I haste to seek thy face;
My thirsty spirit faints away,
Without thy cheering grace.

2 I've seen thy glory and thy power
Through all thy temple shine;
My God, repeat that heavenly hour,
That vision so divine.

3 Not all the blessings of a feast
Can please my soul so well,
As when thy richer grace I taste,
And in thy presence dwell.

4 Not life itself, with all its joys,
Can my best passions move,
Or raise so high my cheerful voice,
As thy forgiving love.

5 Thus till my last expiring day,
I'll bless my God and King;
Thus will I lift my hands to pray,
And tune my lips to sing.

201 I.

LET them neglect thy glory, Lord,
Who never knew thy grace;
But our loud songs shall still record
The wonders of thy praise.

2 We raise our shouts, O God, to thee,
And send them to thy throne;
All glory to the United Three,
The Undivided One.

3 'Twas he, and we'll adore his name,
That formed us by a word;
'Tis he restores our ruined frame;
Salvation to the Lord!

4 Hosanna! let the earth and skies
   Repeat the joyful sound;
 Rocks, hills and vales, reflect the voice
   In one eternal round.

202   II.

COME, let us join our cheerful songs,
   With angels round the throne;
 Ten thousand thousand are their
   But all their joys are one.   [tongues,
2 "Worthy the Lamb that died, they cry,
   "To be exalted thus."
 "Worthy the Lamb," our lips reply,
   "For he was slain for us."
3 Let all that dwell above the sky,
   And air, and earth, and seas,
 Conspire to lift thy glories high,
   And speak thine endless praise.
4 The whole creation join in one,
   To bless the sacred name
 Of him who sits upon the throne,
   And to adore the Lamb.

203   II.

HOW glorious is the sacred place
   Where we adoring stand;
 Zion, the joy of all the earth,
   The beauty of the land.
2 Bulwarks of mighty grace defend
   The city where we dwell;
 The walls, of strong salvation made,
   Defy the assaults of hell.
3 Lift up the everlasting gates,
   The doors wide open fling;
 Enter ye nations that obey
   The statutes of your King.
4 Trust in the Lord, forever trust,
   And banish all your fears;
 Strength in the Lord Jehovah dwells,
   Eternal as his years.

204   II.

PRAISE to the Lord for all the host
   Who have gone safe above,
 Have passed the sea by tempests toss'd,
   And reached the land of love.
2 Mourners they were—they weep not
     now;
 Sick—now they know not pain:
 And glory shines on every brow
   Of that once feeble train.
3 O blest, and beautiful, and bright,
   How fair their white robes gleam!

O to behold the glorious sight,
   Without a veil between!
4 Yet once, like us, with trembling fear,
   Their unknown paths they viewed:
 Now, God has wiped away each tear,
   From all that multitude.
5 Shout! they have gained their rest at
   The port where they would be; [last,
 Thro' adverse gales and tempest's blast,
   Their followers still are we.

For SOCIAL AND PRIVATE WORSHIP.

205

FIRM as the earth thy gospel stands,
   My Lord, my hope, my trust:
 If I am found in Jesus' hands,
   My soul can ne'er be lost.
2 His honor is engaged to save
   The meanest of his sheep;
 All that his heavenly Father gave,
   His hands securely keep.
3 Nor death nor hell shall e'er remove
   His favorites from his breast;
 In the dear bosom of his love,
   They must forever rest.

206

WHILST thee I seek, protecting pow-
   Be my vain wishes stilled;   [er,
 And may this consecrated hour
   With better hopes be filled.
2 Thy love the power of thought bestow-
   To thee my thoughts would soar; [ed,
 Thy mercy o'er my life has flowed;
   That mercy I adore.
3 In each event of life, how clear
   Thy ruling hand I see;
 Each blessing to my soul most dear,
   Because conferred by thee.
4 In every joy that crowns my days,
   In every pain I bear,
 My heart shall find delight in praise,
   Or seek relief in prayer.
5 When gladness wings the favored hour,
   Thy love my thoughts shall fill;
 Resigned, when storms of sorrow lour,
   My soul shall meet thy will.
6 My lifted eye, without a tear,
   The gathering storm shall see,
 My steadfast heart shall know no fear;
   That heart will rest on thee.

17

HYMNS 207, 208, 209.

DUNDEE. C. M.

207 I.

I WAITED patient for the Lord,
   He bowed to hear my cry;
He saw me resting on his word,
   And brought salvation nigh.

2 Firm on a rock he made me stand,
   And taught my cheerful tongue
To praise the wonders of his hand,
   In a new thankful song.

3 I'll spread his works of grace abroad,
   The saints with joy shall hear,
And sinners learn to make my God,
   Their only hope and fear.

208 I.

O! that the Lord would guide my
   To keep his statutes still! [ways
O! that my God would grant me grace
   To know and do his will!

2 O! send thy Spirit down to write
   Thy law upon my heart;
Nor let my tongue indulge deceit,
   Nor act the liar's part.

3 From vanity turn off my eyes;
   Let no corrupt design,
Nor covetous desires arise
   Within this soul of mine.

4 Order my footsteps by thy word,
   And make my heart sincere:
Let sin have no dominion, Lord,
   But keep my conscience clear.

209 II.

OUR God, our help in ages past,
   Our hope for years to come,
Our shelter from the stormy blast,
   And our eternal home.

2 Before the hills in order stood,
   Or earth received her frame,
From everlasting thou art God,
   To endless years the same.

3 Thy word commands our flesh to dust,
   "Return, ye sons of men;"
All nations rose from earth at first,
   And turn to earth again.

4 A thousand ages in thy sight
   Are like an evening gone;
Short as the watch that ends the night
   Before the rising dawn.

5 Time, like an ever-rolling stream,
   Bears all its sons away;
They fly, forgotten, as a dream
   Dies at the opening day.

6 Our God, our help in ages past,
   Our hope for years to come,
Be thou our guard while troubles last,
   And our eternal home.

210
II.

BEHOLD, the mountain of the Lord,
In latter days, shall rise
Above the mountains and the hills,
And draw the wondering eyes.
2 To this the joyful nations round,
All tribes and tongues shall flow;
"Up to the hill of God," they say,
"And to his courts we'll go."
3 The beams that shine on Zion's hill
Shall lighten every land;
The King who reigns in Zion's towers,
Shall all the world command.
4 Come then—O! come from every land,
To worship at his shrine:
And walking in the light of God,
With holy beauties shine.

FOR SOCIAL AND PRIVATE WORSHIP.

211

DEAR Shepherd of thy people, hear;
Thy presence now display;
As thou hast given a place for prayer,
So give us hearts to pray.
2 Within these walls let holy peace,
And love and concord dwell;
Here give the troubled conscience ease,
The wounded spirit heal.

212

DIDST thou, dear Jesus, suffer shame,
And bear the cross for me?
And shall I fear to own thy name,
Or thy disciple be?
2 Forbid it, Lord, that I should dread
To suffer shame or loss;
O! let me in thy footsteps tread,
And glory in thy cross.
3 Inspire my soul with life divine,
And holy courage bold: [shine,
Let knowledge, faith, and meekness
Nor love nor zeal grow cold.
4 Say to my soul, "Why dost thou fear
The face of feeble clay?
Behold thy Saviour ever near,
Will guard thee in the way."
5 O! how my soul would rise and run,
At this reviving word;
Nor any painful sufferings shun,
To follow thee, my Lord.

213

MY Saviour, let me hear thy voice
Pronounce the word of peace,
And all my warmest powers shall join
To celebrate thy grace.
2 Cheerful, where'er thy hand shall lead,
The darkest path I'll tread;
Cheerful I'll quit these mortal shores,
And mingle with the dead.
3 When dreadful guilt is done away,
No other fears we know:
That hand which scatters pardon
Shall crowns of life bestow. [down,

214

IN all my vast concerns with thee,
In vain my soul would try
To shun thy presence, Lord, or flee
The notice of thine eye.
2 Thy all-surrounding sight surveys
My rising and my rest,
My public walks, my private ways,
And secrets of my breast.
3 O wondrous knowledge, deep and high,
Where can a creature hide?
Within thy circling arms I lie,
Enclosed on every side.
4 So let thy grace surround me still,
And like a bulwark prove,
To guard my soul from every ill,
Secured by sovereign love.

215

GREAT God, before thy mercy seat,
Abased in dust I fall;
My crimes of complicated guilt,
Aloud for judgment call.
2 I own my ways to be corrupt,
My duties stained with sin:
Make thou my broken spirit whole,
My burdened conscience clean.
3 Lord, send thy Spirit from above,
Implant a holy fear;
And through thine all abounding grace,
Bring thy salvation near.
4 On my distressed, benighted soul,
O! cause thy face to shine;
Make me to hear thy pardoning voice,
And tell me I am thine.

HYMNS 216, 217, 218.

HOWARD. C. M.

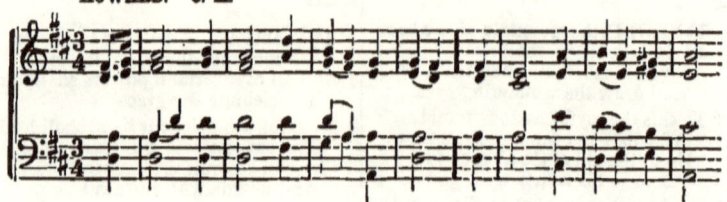

216 I.

FATHER of peace, and God of love,
  We own thy power to save;
That power by which our Shepherd
  Victorious o'er the grave. [rose,

2 We triumph in that Shepherd's name,
  Still watchful for our good,
Who brought the eternal covenant
  And sealed it with his blood. [down,

3 So may thy Spirit seal my soul,
  And mould it to thy will;
That my fond heart no more may stray,
  But keep thy covenant still.

4 Still may we gain superior strength,
  And press with vigor on,
Till full perfection crown our hopes,
  And fix us near thy throne.

217 I.

FATHER, I sing thy wondrous grace,
  I bless my Saviour's name,
He bought salvation for the poor,
  And bore the sinner's shame.

2 His deep distress has raised us high,
  His duty and his zeal
Fulfilled the law which mortals broke,
  And finished all thy will.

3 His dying groans, his living songs,
  Shall better please my God,
Than harp or trumpet's solemn sound,
  Than goat's or bullock's blood.

4 This shall his humble followers see,
  And set their hearts at rest;
They by his death draw near to thee,
  And live for ever blest.

5 Let heaven and all that dwell on high,
  To God their voices raise,
While lands and seas assist the sky,
  And join t' advance his praise.

6 Zion is thine, most holy God,
  Thy Son shall bless her gates;
And glory purchased by his blood,
  For thine own Israel waits.

218 I.

JESUS, the very thought of thee
  With gladness fills my breast;
But dearer far thy face to see,
  And in thy presence rest.

2 Nor voice can sing, nor heart can frame,
  Nor can the memory find
A sweeter sound than thy blest name,
  O Saviour of mankind!

3 O Hope of every contrite heart,
  O Joy of all the meek!
To those who fall, how kind thou art,
  How good to those who seek!

4 And those who find thee, find a bliss
  Nor tongue nor pen can show:
  The love of Jesus—what it is,
  None but his loved ones know.
5 Jesus, our only joy be thou!
  As thou our prize wilt be;
  Jesus, be thou our glory now,
  And through eternity!

219   II.

1 LONG as I live I'll bless thy name,
  My King, my God of love;
  My work and joy shall be the same,
  In the bright world above.
2 Great is the Lord, his power unknown,
  And let his praise be great:
  I'll sing the honors of thy throne,
  Thy works of grace repeat.
3 Thy grace shall dwell upon my tongue;
  And while my lips rejoice,
  The men that hear my sacred song
  Shall join their cheerful voice.
4 Fathers to sons shall teach thy name,
  And children learn thy ways;
  Ages to come thy truth proclaim,
  And nations sound thy praise.

220   II.

1 WHEN all thy mercies, O my God,
  My rising soul surveys,
  Transported with the view I'm lost
  In wonder, love and praise.
2 Unnumbered comforts to my soul
  Thy tender care bestowed,
  Before my infant heart conceived
  From whom those comforts flowed.
3 When in the slippery paths of youth,
  With heedless steps I ran,
  Thine arm, unseen, conveyed me safe,
  And led me up to man.
4 When worn by sickness, oft hast thou
  With health renewed my face;
  And when in sin and sorrow sunk,
  Revived my soul with grace.
5 Ten thousand thousand precious gifts
  My daily thanks employ;
  Nor is the least a cheerful heart,
  That tastes those gifts with joy.
6 Through every period of my life
  Thy goodness I'll pursue;
  And after death, in distant worlds,
  The glorious theme renew.

7 Through all eternity to thee
  A joyful song I'll raise;
  But O! eternity's too short
  To utter all thy praise.

For Social and Private Worship.

221

1 COME, let our hearts and voices join,
  To praise the Saviour's name;
  Whose truth and kindness are divine,
  Whose love's a constant flame.
2 When most we need his gracious hand,
  This Friend is always near;
  With heaven and earth at his command,
  He waits to answer prayer.
3 His love no end nor measure knows,
  No change can turn his course:
  Immutably the same it flows,
  From one eternal source.
4 When frowns appear to veil his face,
  And clouds surround his throne;
  He hides the purpose of his grace,
  To make it better known.
5 And when our dearest comforts fall,
  Before his sovereign will,
  He never takes away our all;
  Himself he gives us still.

222

1 O THOU who driest the mourner's tear,
  How dark this world would be,
  If, pierced by sins and sorrows here,
  We could not fly to thee!
2 The friends, who in our sunshine live,
  When winter comes, are flown;
  And he who has but tears to give,
  Must weep those tears alone.
3 But thou wilt heal that broken heart,
  Which, like the plants that throw
  Their fragrance from the wounded part,
  Breathes sweetness out of wo.
4 When joy no longer soothes or cheers,
  And e'en the hope that threw
  A moment's sparkle o'er our tears,
  Is dimmed and vanished too;
5 O who can bear life's stormy doom,
  Did not thy wing of love [gloom
  Come brightly wafting through the
  Our peace-branch from above?
6 Then sorrow, touched by thee, grows
  With more than rapture's ray; [bright
  As darkness shows us worlds of light,
  We never saw by day.

MEAR. C. M.

223   I.

FOR ever blessed be the Lord,
 My Saviour and my Shield;
He sends his Spirit with his word,
 To arm me for the field.

2 When sin and hell their force unite,
 He makes my soul his care;
Instructs me in the heavenly fight,
 And guards me through the war.

3 A Friend and Helper so divine
 My fainting hope shall raise;
He makes the glorious victory mine,
 And his shall be the praise.

224   I.

O! HOW I love thy holy law!
 'Tis daily my delight:
And thence my meditations draw
 Divine advice by night.

2 My waking eyes prevent the day,
 To meditate thy word:
My soul with longing melts away,
 To hear thy gospel, Lord.

3 Thy heavenly words my heart engage,
 And well employ my tongue,
And in my tiresome pilgrimage
 Yield me a heavenly song.

4 Am I a stranger, or at home,
 'Tis my perpetual feast;
Not honey dropping from the comb
 So much allures the taste.

5 No treasures so enrich the mind;
 Nor shall thy word be sold
For loads of silver well refined,
 Nor heaps of choicest gold.

6 When nature sinks, and spirits droop,
 Thy promises of grace
Are pillars to support my hope;
 And there I write thy praise.

225   II.

BEHOLD the glories of the Lamb,
 Amidst his Father's throne:
Prepare new honors for his name,
 And songs before unknown.

2 Now to the Lamb that once was slain,
 Be endless blessings paid;
Salvation, glory, joy remain
 For ever on thy head.

3 Thou hast redeemed our souls with
 Hast set the prisoners free, [blood,
Hast made us kings and priests to God,
 And we shall reign with thee.

4 The worlds of nature and of grace
 Are put beneath thy power;
Then shorten these delaying days,
 And bring the promised hour.

226

II.

1 HOW did my heart rejoice to hear
   My friends devoutly say,
 In Zion let us all appear,
   And keep the solemn day.

2 I love her gates, I love the road;
   The church, adorned with grace,
 Stands like a palace built for God,
   To show his milder face.

3 Up to her courts, with joy unknown,
   The holy tribes repair;
 The Son of David holds his throne,
   And sits in judgment there.

4 Peace be within this sacred place,
   And joy a constant guest;
 With holy gifts and heavenly grace
   Be her attendants blest.

5 My soul shall pray for Zion still,
   While life or breath remains; [dwell,
 There my best friends, my kindred
   There God, my Saviour, reigns.

227

II.

1 OUR land, O Lord, with songs of praise,
 Shall in thy strength rejoice;
 And, blest with thy salvation raise
   To heaven a cheerful voice.

2 Thy sure defence, thro' nations round,
   Hath spread our country's name;
 And all her humble efforts crowned
   With freedom and with fame.

3 In deep distress a patriot band
   Implored thy power to save;
 For liberty they prayed; thy hand
   The timely blessing gave.

4 On thee, in want, in wo or pain,
   Our hearts alone rely;
 Our rights thy mercy will maintain,
   And all our wants supply.

5 Thus, Lord, thy wondrous power de-
   And still exalt thy fame; [clare,
 While we glad songs of praise prepare,
   For thine almighty name.

228

II.

1 LO, what a cloud of witnesses
   Encompass us around;
 Men once like us with suffering tried,
   But now with glory crowned.

2 Let us with zeal like theirs inspired,
   Strive in the Christian race;
 And freed from every weight of sin,
   Their holy footsteps trace.

3 Behold a Witness nobler still,
   Who trod affliction's path;
 Jesus, the author, finisher,
   Rewarder of our faith.

4 He for the joy before him set,
   And moved by pitying love,
 Endured the cross, despised the shame,
   And now he reigns above.

5 Thither, forgetting things behind,
   Press we to God's right hand;
 There, with the Saviour and his saints,
   Triumphantly to stand.

FOR SOCIAL AND PRIVATE WORSHIP.

229

1 COME, Lord, and warm each languid heart,
 Inspire each lifeless tongue;
 And let the joys of heaven impart
   Their influence to our song.

2 Come, Lord, thy love alone can raise
   In us the heavenly flame;
 Then shall our lips resound thy praise,
   Our hearts adore thy name.

3 Dear Saviour, let thy glory shine,
   And fill thy dwellings here,
 Till life, and love, and joy divine,
   A heaven on earth appear.

230

1 COME, Holy Spirit, heavenly Dove,
   With all thy quickening powers,
 Kindle a flame of sacred love
   In these cold hearts of ours.

2 Look how we grovel here below,
   Fond of these trifling toys:
 Our souls can neither fly nor go,
   To reach eternal joys.

3 In vain we tune our formal songs,
   In vain we strive to rise;
 Hosannas languish on our tongues,
   And our devotion dies.

4 Dear Lord, and shall we ever live
   At this poor, dying rate;
 Our love so faint, so cold to thee,
   And thine to us so great?

5 Come, Holy Spirit, heavenly Dove,
   With all thy quickening powers,
 Come, shed abroad a Saviour's love,
   And that shall kindle ours.

NAOMI. C. M.

231 I.

ENTHRONED on high, Almighty Lord,
The Holy Ghost send down;
Fulfil in us thy faithful word,
And all thy mercies crown.

2 Spirit of life, and light, and love,
Thy heavenly influence give;
Quicken our souls, our guilt remove,
That we in Christ may live.

3 To our benighted minds reveal
The glories of his grace,
And bring us where no clouds conceal
The brightness of his face.

4 His love within us shed abroad,
Life's ever-springing well;
Till God in us, and we in God,
In love eternal dwell.

232 I.

THE promise of my Father's love
Shall stand forever good;
He said, and gave his soul to death,
And sealed the grace with blood.

2 To this dear covenant of thy word
I set my worthless name;
I seal the engagement to my Lord,
And make my humble claim.

3 Thy light, and strength, and pardoning
And glory shall be mine; [grace,
My life and soul, my heart and flesh,
And all my powers are thine.

233 II.

GOD of our life, thy various praise
Let mortal voices sound;
Thy hand revolves our fleeting days,
And brings the seasons round.

2 In every scene of life, thy care,
In every age, we see;
And constant as thy favors are,
So let our praises be.

3 Still may thy love, in every scene,
To every age appear;
And let the same compassion deign
To bless the opening year.

4 If mercy smile, let mercy bring
My wandering soul to God;
And in affliction I shall sing,
If thou wilt bless the rod.

FOR SOCIAL AND PRIVATE WORSHIP.

234

FATHER of mercies, in thy word,
What endless glory shines!
For ever be thy name adored,
For these celestial lines.

2 Here the Redeemer's welcome voice,
  Spreads heavenly peace around;
  And life and everlasting joys
  Attend the blissful sound.
3 O! may these heavenly pages be
  My ever dear delight;
  And still new beauties may I see,
  And still increasing light.
4 Divine Instructor, gracious Lord,
  Be thou for ever near!
  Teach me to love thy sacred word,
  And view my Saviour there.

285

FATHER, whate'er of earthly bliss
  Thy sovereign will denies,
Accepted at thy throne of grace,
Let this petition rise:—
2 Give me a calm, a thankful heart,
  From every murmur free;
  The blessings of thy grace impart,
  And make me live to thee.
3 Let the sweet hope that thou art mine
  My life and death attend;
  Thy presence thro' my journey shine,
  And crown my journey's end.

236

GOD, my supporter and my hope,
  My help for ever near,
Thine arm of mercy held me up,
  When sinking in despair.
2 Thy counsels, Lord, shall guide my feet
  Through life's dark wilderness;
  Thine hand conduct me near thy seat,
  To dwell before thy face.
3 Were I in heaven without my God,
  'Twould be no joy to me;
  And whilst this earth is my abode,
  I long for none but thee.
4 But to draw near to thee, my God,
  Shall be my sweet employ;
  My tongue shall sound thy works
  And tell the world my joy. [abroad,

237

O GOD of Bethel, by whose hand
  Thy people still are fed;
Who through this weary pilgrimage
  Hast all our fathers led;

2 Our vows, our prayers, we now present
  Before thy throne of grace;
  God of our fathers, be the God
  Of their succeeding race.
3 Through each perplexing path of life
  Our wandering footsteps guide;
  Give us each day our daily bread,
  And raiment fit provide.
4 O spread thy covering wings around,
  Till all our wanderings cease,
  And at our Father's loved abode
  Our souls arrive in peace.

238

HOSANNA with a cheerful sound,
  To God's upholding hand;
Ten thousand snares attend us round,
  And yet secure we stand.
2 That was a most amazing power,
  That raised us with a word;
  And every day and every hour,
  We lean upon the Lord.
3 The evening rests our weary head,
  And angels guard the room;
  We wake, and we admire the bed,
  That was not made our tomb.
4 God is our Sun, whose daily light
  Our joy and safety brings;
  Our feeble flesh lies safe at night,
  Beneath his spreading wings.

239

TO thee, my God, whose presence fills
  The earth and seas and skies,
To thee, whose name, whose heart is
  With all my powers I rise. [Love.
2 Troubles in long succession roll;
  Wave rushes upon wave:
  Pity, O pity my distress;
  Thy child, thy suppliant save.
3 O bid the roaring tempest cease,
  Or give me strength to bear
  Whate'er thy holy will appoints,
  And save me from despair.
4 To thee, my God, alone I look;
  On thee alone confide:
  Thou never hast deceived the soul
  That on thy grace relied.
5 Though oft thy ways are wrapt in
  Mysterious and unknown, [clouds,
  Truth, Righteousness, and Mercy
  The pillars of thy throne. [stand,

ORTONVILLE. C. M.

240   I.

O! FOR a thousand tongues to sing
   My dear Redeemer's praise;
The glories of my God and King,
   The triumphs of his grace.

2 My gracious Master, and my God,
   Assist me to proclaim,
To spread through all the earth abroad
   The honors of thy name.

3 Jesus, the name that calms our fears,
   That bids our sorrows cease;
'Tis music in the sinner's ears:
   'Tis life, and health, and peace.

4 He breaks the power of reigning sin;
   He sets the prisoner free;
His blood can make the foulest clean,
   His blood availed for me.

5 Let us obey, we then shall know,
   Shall feel our sins forgiven;
Anticipate our heaven below,
   And own that love is heaven.

241   I.

THE Saviour! O what endless charms
   Dwell in the blissful sound!
Its influence every fear disarms,
   And spreads sweet comfort round.

2 Here pardon, life and joys divine,
   In rich effusion flow,
For guilty rebels lost in sin,
   And doomed to endless woe.

3 The almighty Former of the skies
   Stooped to our vile abode;
While angels viewed with wondering eyes,
   And hailed the incarnate God.

4 O! the rich depths of love divine!
   Of bliss a boundless store!
Dear Saviour, let me call thee mine;
   I cannot wish for more.

5 On thee alone my hope relies,
   Beneath thy cross I fall;
My Lord, my Life, my Sacrifice,
   My Saviour, and my All!

242   II.

GOD is our refuge, tried and proved,
   Amid a stormy world;
We will not fear though earth be moved,
   And hills in ocean hurled.

2 The waves may roar, the mountains shake,
   Our comforts shall not cease;
The Lord his saints will not forsake,
   The Lord will give us peace.

3 A gentle stream of hope and love
   To us shall ever flow;
It issues from his throne above,—
   It cheers his church below.

4 When earth and hell against us came,
    He spake and quelled their powers:
    The Lord of hosts is still the same;
    The God of grace is ours.

243   II.

COME, let us join our friends above,
    That have obtained the prize;
And on the eagle wings of love,
    To joy celestial rise.
2 Let saints below his praises sing,
    With those to glory gone;
  For all the servants of our King,
    In heaven and earth, are one.
3 One family, we dwell in him,
    One church above, beneath:
  Though now divided by the stream,
    The narrow stream of death.
4 One army of the living God,
    To his commands we bow;
  Part of the host have crossed the flood,
    And part are crossing now.
5 Dear Saviour, be our constant guide;
    Then when the word is given,
  Bid the cold waves of death divide,
    And land us safe in heaven.

FOR SOCIAL AND PRIVATE WORSHIP.

244

ALL glorious Saviour, source of
    To thee we raise our cry; [grace,
Unveil the beauties of thy face,
    To every waiting eye.
2 Make known thy power, victorious
    Subdue each stubborn will; [King,
  Then sovereign grace we'll join to sing,
    On Zion's sacred hill.

245

MAJESTIC sweetness sits enthroned
    On my Redeemer's brow;
His head with radiant glories crowned,
    His lips with grace o'erflow.
2 He saw me plunged in deep distress,
    He flew to my relief;
  For me he bore the shameful cross,
    And carried all my grief.
3 To him I owe my life, and breath,
    And all the joys I have:
  He makes me triumph over death,
    And saves me from the grave.

4 To heaven, the place of his abode,
    He brings my weary feet;
  Shows me the glories of my God,
    And makes my joys complete.

246

JESUS, in sickness and in pain,
    Be near to succor me,
My sinking spirit still sustain;
    To thee I turn, to thee.
2 When cares and sorrows thicken round,
    And nothing bright I see,
  In thee alone can help be found;
    To thee I turn, to thee.
3 Should strong temptations fierce assail,
    As if to ruin me,
  Then in thy strength will I prevail,
    While still I turn to thee.
4 When past transgressions fearful rise
    Before my memory,
  I'll plead thy perfect sacrifice,
    And turn to thee, to thee.
5 Through all my pilgrimage below,
    Whate'er my lot may be,
  In joy or sadness, weal or woe,
    Jesus, I'll turn to thee.

247   *For Children only.*

DEAR Saviour, ever at my side,
    How loving thou must be,
To leave thy home in heaven to guard
    A little child like me.
2 Thy beautiful and shining face
    I see not, tho' so near:
  The sweetness of thy soft, low voice,
    I am too deaf to hear.
3 But I have felt thee in my thoughts,
    Fighting with sin for me;
  And when my heart loves God, I know
    The sweetness is from thee.
4 And when I pray, thou prayest too;
    Thy prayer is all for me;
  But when I sleep, thou sleepest not,
    But watchest patiently.
5 Then for thy sake, dear Saviour, now
    More humble will I be;
  And as thou lov'st me day by day,
    I ever will love thee.
6 And thou in life's last hour wilt give
    A fresh supply of grace,
  And afterwards wilt let me see
    Thy beautiful, bright face.

PETERBORO. C. M.

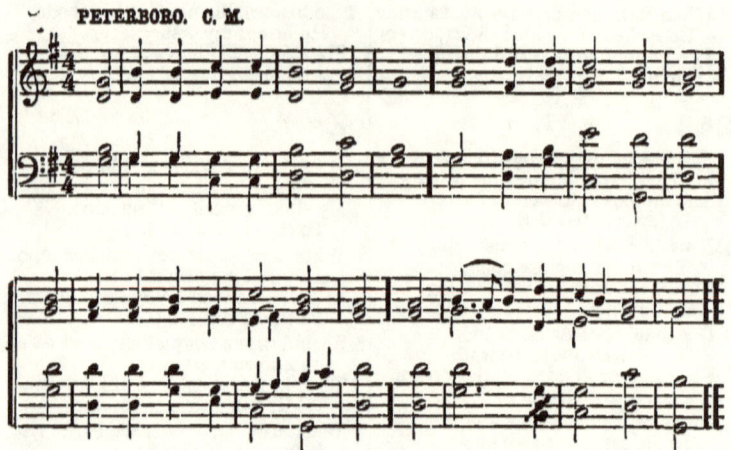

248   I.

IN vain we seek for peace with God
By methods of our own:
Nothing, O Saviour! but thy blood
Can bring us near the throne.

2 The threatenings of the broken law
Impress the soul with dread:
If God his sword of vengeance draw,
It strikes the spirit dead.

3 But thine illustrious sacrifice
Hath answered these demands;
And peace and pardon from the skies
Are offered by thy hands.

4 'Tis by thy death, we live, O Lord!
'Tis on thy cross we rest:
Forever be thy love adored,
Thy name forever blessed.

249   I.

THE Lord himself, the mighty Lord,
Vouchsafes to be my guide;
The shepherd, by whose constant care
My wants are all supplied.

2 In tender grass he makes me feed,
And gently there repose;
Then leads me to cool shades, and where
Refreshing water flows. [

3 He does my wandering soul reclaim,
And, to his endless praise,
Instruct with humble zeal to walk
In his most righteous ways.

4 I pass the gloomy vale of death,
From fear and danger free;
For there his aiding rod and staff
Defend and comfort me.

5 Since God doth thus his wondrous love
Through all my life extend,
That life to him I will devote,
And in his temple spend.

250   II.

GREAT is the Lord; his works of might
Demand our noblest songs; [
Let his assembled saints unite
Their harmony of tongues.

2 Great is the mercy of the Lord,
He gives his children food;
And, ever mindful of his word,
He makes his promise good.

3 His Son, the great Redeemer, came
To seal his covenant sure;
Holy and reverend is his name,
His ways are just and pure.

4 They that would grow divinely wise,
Must with his fear begin;
Our fairest proof of knowledge lies
In hating every sin.

251

SWEET is the memory of thy grace,
My God, my heavenly King;
Let age to age thy righteousness
In sounds of glory sing.

2 God reigns on high, but ne'er confines
His goodness to the skies;
Through the whole earth his bounty shines,
And every want supplies. [shines,

3 With longing eyes thy creatures wait
On thee for daily food;
Thy liberal hand provides their meat,
And fills their mouths with good.

4 How kind are thy compassions, Lord!
How slow thine anger moves!
But soon he sends his pardoning word
To cheer the souls he loves.

5 Creatures, with all their endless race,
Thy power and praise proclaim;
But saints, that taste thy richer grace,
Delight to bless thy name.

For Social and Private Worship.

252

LORD, I approach the mercy-seat,
Where thou dost answer prayer;
There humbly fall before thy feet,
For none can perish there.

2 Thy promise is my only plea;
With this I venture nigh:
Thou callest burdened souls to thee,
And such, O Lord, am I.

3 Bowed down beneath a load of sin,
By Satan sorely pressed,
By war without, and fear within,
I come to thee for rest.

4 Be thou my shield and hiding-place;
That, sheltered near thy side,
I may my fierce accuser face,
And tell him thou hast died.

5 Oh, wondrous love!—to bleed and die,
To bear the cross and shame,
That guilty sinners, such as I,
Might plead thy gracious name.

253

SOVEREIGN of all the worlds on high,
Allow our humble claim; [high,
Nor while poor worms would raise their
Disdain a Father's name. [heads,

2 Our Father God! how sweet the sound!
How tender and how dear!
Not all the melody of heaven
Could so delight the ear.

3 Come, sacred Spirit, seal the name
On my expanding heart;
And show, that in Jehovah's grace
I share a filial part.

4 Cheered by a signal so divine,
Unwavering I believe;
Thou knowest I, Abba, Father, cry,
Nor can thy word deceive.

254

ONCE more, my soul, the rising day
Salutes thy waking eyes;
Once more, my voice, thy tribute pay
To him that rules the skies.

2 'Tis he supports my mortal frame,
My tongue shall speak his praise;
My sins would rouse his wrath to flame,
And yet his wrath delays.

3 Great God, let all my hours be thine,
Whilst I enjoy the light;
Then shall my sun in smiles decline,
And bring a pleasant night.

255

DREAD Sovereign, let my evening,
Like holy incense rise! [song
Assist the offerings of my tongue,
To reach the lofty skies.

2 Through all the dangers of the day,
Thy hand was still my guard;
And still to drive my wants away,
Thy mercy stood prepared.

3 Perpetual blessings from above,
Encompassed me around;
But O! how few returns of love
Has my Creator found!

4 What have I done for him who died
To save my wretched soul?
How are my follies multiplied,
Fast as my minutes roll!

5 Lord, with this guilty heart of mine,
To thy dear cross I flee,
And to thy grace my soul resign,
To be renewed by thee.

6 Sprinkled afresh with pardoning blood,
I'll lay me down to rest,
As in the embraces of my God,
Or on my Saviour's breast.

HYMNS 256, 257, 258.

PHUVAH. C. M.

256 I.

I LOVE the Lord; he heard my cries,
  And pitied every groan;
Long as I live, when troubles rise,
  I'll hasten to his throne.

2 I love the Lord: he bowed his ear,
  And chased my griefs away;
O! let my heart no more despair
  While I have breath to pray.

3 The Lord beheld me sore distressed,
  He bade my pains remove;
Return, my soul, to God thy rest,
  For thou hast known his love.

4 My God hath saved my soul from death,
  And dried my falling tears;
Now to his praise I'll spend my breath,
  And my remaining years.

257 I.

MY God, what gentle cords are thine,
  How soft, and yet how strong!
While power, and truth, and love com- [bine,
  To draw our souls along.

2 Thou saw'st us crushed beneath the [yoke
  Of Satan and of sin;
Thy hand the iron bondage broke,
  Our worthless hearts to win.

3 The guilt of twice ten thousand sins
  One offering takes away;
And grace, when first the war begins,
  Secures the crowning day.

4 Comfort through all this vale of tears,
  In rich profusion flows,
And glory of unnumbered years
  Eternity bestows.

5 Drawn by such cords, we onward move,
  Till round thy throne we meet;
And captives in the chains of love,
  Embrace our conqueror's feet.

258 II.

AWAKE, ye saints, to praise your [King,
  Your sweetest passions raise;
Your pious pleasure, while you sing,
  Increasing with the praise.

2 Great is the Lord, and works unknown
  Are his divine employ;
But still his saints are near the throne,
  His treasure and his joy.

3 Heaven, earth, and sea confess his hand;
  He bids the vapors rise;
Lightning and storm, at his command,
  Sweep through the sounding skies.

4 Ye nations, know the living God,
  Serve him with faith and fear;
He makes the churches his abode,
  And claims your honors there.

259
II.

FATHER, how wide thy glory shines!
How high thy wonders rise! [signs,
Known through the earth by thousand
By thousands through the skies.

2 But when we view thy strange design,
To save rebellious worms;
Where vengeance and compassion join
In their divinest forms;—

3 Our thoughts are lost in reverent awe;
We love, and we adore:
The first archangel never saw
So much of God before.

4 Now the full glories of the Lamb
Adorn the heavenly plains;
Bright seraphs learn Immanuel's name,
And try their choicest strains.

5 O may I bear some humble part,
In that immortal song!
Wonder and joy shall tune my heart,
And love command my tongue.

For Social and Private Worship.
260

O! FOR a heart to praise my God,
A heart from sin set free;
A heart that always feels thy blood,
So freely shed for me.

2 A heart resigned, submissive, meek,
My great Redeemer's throne;
Where only Christ is heard to speak;
Where Jesus reigns alone:

3 A heart in every thought renewed,
And full of love divine;
Holy, and right, and pure, and good,
A copy, Lord, of thine.

261

I'M not ashamed to own my Lord,
Nor to defend his cause,
Maintain the honor of his word,
The glory of his cross.

2 Jesus, my God, I know his name,
His name is all my trust;
Nor will he put my soul to shame,
Nor let my hope be lost.

3 Firm as his throne his promise stands,
And he can well secure
What I've committed to his hands,
Till the decisive hour.

4 Then will he own my worthless name,
Before his Father's face,
And in the new Jerusalem,
Appoint my soul a place.

262

OPPRESSED with fear, oppressed
with grief,
To God I breathed my cry;
His mercy brought divine relief,
And wiped my tearful eye.

2 His mercy chased the shades of death,
And snatched me from the grave;
O may his praise employ that breath
Which mercy deigns to save.

3 Come, O ye saints, your voices raise
To God in grateful songs;
And let the memory of his grace
Inspire your hearts and tongues.

4 Its deepest gloom when sorrow spreads
And light and hope depart;
His smile celestial morning sheds,
And joy revives the heart.

5 Then let my utmost glory be,
To raise thy honors high;
Nor let my gratitude to thee,
In guilty silence die.

6 To thee, my gracious God, I raise
My thankful heart and tongue;
O be thy goodness and thy praise
My everlasting song.

263

THERE is a house not made with
Eternal and on high; [hands
And here my spirit, waiting, stands,
Till God shall bid it fly.

2 Shortly this prison of my clay
Must be dissolved and fall;
Then, O my soul, with joy obey
Thy heavenly Father's call.

3 'Tis he, by his almighty grace,
That forms thee fit for heaven;
And, as an earnest of the place,
Has his own Spirit given.

4 We walk by faith of joys to come;
Faith lives upon his word;
But while the body is our home,
We're absent from the Lord.

5 'Tis pleasant to believe thy grace,
But we would rather see;
We would be absent from the flesh,
And present, Lord, with thee.

STEPHENS. C. M.

264   I.

THOU art the Way: to thee alone
From sin and death we flee;
And he who would the Father seek,
Must seek him, Lord, by thee.

2 Thou art the Truth: thy word alone
True wisdom can impart;
Thou only can'st instruct the mind,
And purify the heart.

3 Thou art the Life; the rending tomb
Proclaims thy conquering arm;
And those who put their trust in thee,
Nor death nor hell shall harm.

4 Thou art the Way, the Truth, the Life:
Grant us that Way to know,
That Truth to keep, that Life to win,
Whose joys eternal flow.

265   II.

YE humble souls, approach your God
With songs of sacred praise;
For he is good, supremely good,
And kind are all his ways.

2 All nature owns his guardian care,
In him we live and move;
But nobler benefits declare
The wonders of his love.

3 He gave his Son, his only Son,
To ransom rebel worms; [known,
'Tis here he makes his goodness
In its diviner forms.

4 To this dear refuge, Lord, we come,
'Tis here our hope relies;
A safe defence, a peaceful home,
When storms of trouble rise.

5 Thine eye beholds, with kind regard,
The souls who trust in thee;
Their humble hope thou wilt reward
With bliss divinely free.

6 Great God, to thine almighty love,
What honors shall we raise!
Not all the angelic songs above
Can render equal praise.

266   II.

TO our almighty Maker, God,
New honors be addressed;
His great salvation shines abroad,
And makes the nations blest.

2 To Abraham first he spoke the word,
And taught his numerous race;
The Gentiles own him sovereign Lord,
And learn to trust his grace.

3 Let the whole earth his love proclaim
With all her different tongues;
And spread the honor of his name
In melody and songs.

267
II.

SONGS of immortal praise belong
 To my almighty God;
He has my heart, and he my tongue,
 To spread his name abroad.

2 How great the works his hands have
 How glorious in our sight! [wro't!
And men in every age have sought
 His wonders with delight.

3 When he redeemed his chosen sons,
 He fixed his covenant sure;
The orders that his lips pronounce
 To endless years endure.

4 Nature and time, and earth and skies,
 Thy heavenly skill proclaim;
What shall we do to make us wise,
 But learn to read thy name?

FOR SOCIAL AND PRIVATE WORSHIP.

268

O THOU, whose tender mercy hears
 Contrition's humble sigh;
Whose hand indulgent wipes the tears
 From sorrow's weeping eye:

2 See, low before thy throne of grace,
 A wretched wanderer mourn;
Hast thou not bid me seek thy face?
 Hast thou not said—Return?

3 Absent from thee, my Guide, my Light,
 Without one cheering ray;
Through dangers, fears, and gloomy
 How desolate my way! [night,

4 O! shine on this benighted heart:
 With beams of mercy shine!
And let thy healing voice impart
 A taste of joys divine.

269

ETERNAL source of light and grace,
 We hail thy sacred name;
Through every year's revolving round,
 Thy goodness is the same.

2 On us, all worthless as we are,
 It wondrous mercy pours;
Sure as the heavens' established course,
 And plenteous as the showers.

3 Inconstant service we repay,
 And treacherous vows renew;
False as the morning's fleeting cloud,
 And transient as the dew.

4 In flowing tears our guilt we mourn,
 And loud implore thy grace,
To bear our feeble footsteps on,
 In all thy righteous ways.

5 Armed with this energy divine,
 Our souls shall steadfast move;
And with increasing transports press
 On to thy courts above.

270

THRO' sorrow's night and danger's
 Amid the deepening gloom, [path,
We, soldiers of an injured King,
 Are marching to the tomb.

2 There, when the turmoil is no more,
 And all our powers decay,
Our cold remains, in solitude,
 Shall sleep the years away.

3 Our labours done, securely laid
 In this our last retreat,
Unheeded, o'er our silent dust,
 The storms of life shall beat.

4 Then love's soft light o'er every eye
 Shall shed its mildest rays,
And the long silent dust shall burst,
 With shouts of endless praise.

271

GOD moves in a mysterious way,
 His wonders to perform;
He plants his footsteps in the sea,
 And rides upon the storm.

2 Deep in unfathomable mines
 Of never failing skill,
He treasures up his bright designs,
 And works his sovereign will.

3 Ye fearful saints, fresh courage take;
 The clouds ye so much dread
Are big with mercy, and shall break
 In blessings on your head.

4 Judge not the Lord by feeble sense,
 But trust him for his grace;
Behind a frowning providence,
 He hides a smiling face.

5 His purposes will ripen fast,
 Unfolding every hour:
The bud may have a bitter taste,
 But sweet will be the flower.

6 Blind unbelief is sure to err,
 And scan his work in vain;
God is his own interpreter,
 And he will make it plain.

TALLIS. C. M.

272 I.

NOW shall my solemn vows be paid
   To that almighty Power,
That heard the long requests I made,
   In my distressful hour.

2 My lips and cheerful heart prepare
   To make his mercies known;
Come, ye that fear my God, and hear
   The wonders he has done.

3 If sin lay covered in my heart,
   While prayer employed my tongue:
The Lord had shown me no regard,
   Nor I his praises sung.

4 But God (his name be ever blest)
   Has set my spirit free;
Nor turned from him my poor request,
   Nor turned his heart from me.

273 I.

THOU art my portion, O my God;
   Soon as I know thy way,
My heart makes haste to obey thy
   And suffers no delay.   [word,

2 I choose the path of heavenly truth,
   And glory in my choice;
Not all the riches of the earth
   Could make me so rejoice.

3 The testimonies of thy grace
   I set before my eyes;
Thence I derive my daily strength,
   And there my comfort lies.

4 If once I wander from thy path,
   I think upon my ways,
Then turn my feet to thy commands,
   And trust thy pardoning grace.

274 I.

MY God, accept my heart this day,
   And make it always thine,—
That I from thee no more may stray,
   No more from thee decline.

2 Before the cross of him who died,
   Behold, I prostrate fall:
Let every sin be crucified,—
   Let Christ be all in all!

3 Anoint me with thy heavenly grace,
   Adopt me for thine own,—
That I may see thy glorious face,
   And worship at thy throne!

4 May the dear blood once shed for me,
   My blest atonement prove,—
That I from first to last may be
   The purchase of thy love!

5 Let every thought, and work, and word,
   To thee be ever given,—
Then life shall be thy service, Lord,
   And death the gate of heaven.

HYMNS 275, 276, 277, 278, 279.   275

275   II.

THROUGH all the changing scenes
In trouble and in joy,   [of life,
The praises of my God shall still
My heart and tongue employ.
2 My soul shall make her boast in him,
And celebrate his fame;
Come, magnify the Lord with me,
With me exalt his name.
3 The hosts of God encamp around
The dwellings of the just;
Deliverance he affords to all
Who on his succor trust.
4 O! make but trial of his love;
Experience will decide,
How blest they are, and only they,
Who in his truth confide.
5 Fear him, ye saints, and you will then
Have nothing else to fear;
Come, make his service your delight;
He'll make your wants his care.

276   II.

ARISE, O King of grace, arise,
And enter to thy rest;   [eyes,
Lo! thy church waits with longing
Thus to be owned and blest.
2 Enter, with all thy glorious train,
Thy Spirit and thy word;
All that the ark did once contain
Could no such grace afford.
3 Here, mighty God, accept our vows,
Here let thy praise be spread;
Bless the provisions of thy house,
And fill thy poor with bread.
4 Here let the son of David reign,
Let God's Anointed shine;
Justice and truth his court maintain,
With love and power divine.
5 Here let him hold a lasting throne,
And as his kingdom grows,
Fresh honors shall adorn his crown,
And shame confound his foes.

FOR SOCIAL AND PRIVATE WORSHIP.
DOXOLOGY.

TO Father, Son, and Holy Ghost,
The God whom we adore,
Be glory as it was, is now
And shall be evermore.

277

COME, thou Desire of all thy saints,
Our humble strains attend;
While with our praises and complaints,
Low at thy feet we bend.
2 When we thy wondrous glories hear,
And all thy sufferings trace,
What sweetly awful scenes appear,
What rich unbounded grace!
3 How should our songs like those above,
With warm devotion rise!
How should our souls, on wings of
Mount upward to the skies!   [love,
4 Come, Lord, thy love alone can raise
In us the heavenly flame;
Then shall our lips resound thy praise,
Our hearts adore thy name.
5 Dear Saviour, let thy glory shine,
And fill thy dwellings here,
Till life, and love, and joy divine,
And heaven on earth appear.

278

IN every trouble, sharp and strong,
My soul to Jesus flies;
My anchor-hold is firm in him,
When swelling billows rise.
2 His comforts bear my spirits up,
I trust a faithful God;
The sure foundation of my hope
Is in a Saviour's blood.
3 Loud hallelujahs sing, my soul,
To thy Redeemer's name:
In joy, in sorrow, life and death,
His love is still the same.

279

LORD, when I count thy mercies
They strike me with surprise; [o'er,
Not all the sands that spread the shore,
To equal numbers rise.
2 My flesh with fear and wonder stands,
The product of thy skill;
And hourly blessings from his hands
Thy thoughts of love reveal.
3 These on my heart by night I keep;
How kind, how dear to me!
O! may the hour that ends my sleep
Still find my thoughts with thee.

WARWICK. C. M.

280   I.

MY soul, how lovely is the place
  To which thy God resorts!
'Tis heaven to see his smiling face,
  Though in his earthly courts.

2 There the great Monarch of the skies
  His saving power displays,
And light breaks in upon our eyes,
  With kind and quickening rays.

3 With his rich gifts the heavenly Dove
  Descends and fills the place,
While Christ reveals his wondrous love,
  And sheds abroad his grace.

4 There, mighty God, thy words declare
  The secrets of thy will;
And still we seek thy mercies there,
  And sing thy praises still.

281   I.

THOU lovely Source of true delight,
  Whom I, unseen, adore;
Unveil thy beauties to my sight,
  That I may love thee more.

2 Thy glory o'er creation shines;
  But in thy sacred word,
I read in fairer, brighter lines,
  My bleeding, dying Lord.

3 'Tis here, whene'er my comforts droop,
  And sins and sorrows rise,
Thy love, with cheerful beams of hope,
  My fainting heart supplies.

4 Jesus, my Lord, my life, my light,
  O come, with blissful ray;
Break radiant through the shades of night,
  And chase my fears away.

5 Then shall my soul with rapture trace
  The wonders of thy love;
But the full glories of thy face
  Are only known above.

282   II.

I'LL speak the honors of my King,
  His form divinely fair;
None of the sons of mortal race
  May with the Lord compare.

2 Sweet is thy speech, and heavenly grace
  Upon thy lips is shed;
Thy God, with blessings infinite,
  Hath crowned thy sacred head.

3 Gird on thy sword, victorious Prince,
  Ride with majestic sway;
Thy terror shall strike thro' thy foes,
  And make the world obey.

4 Thy throne, O God, for ever stands,
  Thy word of grace shall prove
A peaceful sceptre in thy hands,
  To rule thy saints by love.

5 Justice and truth attend thee still,
   But mercy is thy choice:
   And God, thy God, thy soul shall fill
   With most peculiar joys.

283   II.

MY Saviour, my almighty Friend,
   When I begin thy praise,
Where will the glowing numbers end,
   The numbers of thy grace?

2 Thou art my everlasting trust,
   Thy goodness I adore;
   And since I knew thy graces first,
   I speak thy glories more.

3 How will my lips rejoice to tell
   The victories of my King;
   My soul, redeemed from sin and hell,
   Shall thy salvation sing.

4 My tongue shall all the day proclaim
   My Saviour and my God;
   His death has brought my foes to shame,
   And saved me by his blood.

5 Awake, awake, my tuneful powers;
   With this delightful song
   I'll entertain the darkest hours,
   Nor think the season long.

FOR SOCIAL AND PRIVATE WORSHIP.

284

HOLY and reverend is the name
   Of our eternal King:
Thrice holy Lord! the angels cry;
   Thrice holy! let us sing.

2 Thou holy God! preserve our souls
   From all pollution free;
   The pure in heart are thy delight,
   And they thy face shall see.

285

JESUS, I love thy charming name,
   'Tis music to mine ear;
Fain would I sound it out so loud,
   That earth and heaven should hear.

2 Yes, thou art precious to my soul,
   My joy, my hope, my trust;
   Jewels, to thee, are gaudy toys,
   And gold is sordid dust.

3 All my capacious powers can wish,
   In thee most richly meet;
   Nor to mine eyes is light so dear,
   Nor friendship half so sweet.

4 Thy grace still dwells upon my heart,
   And sheds its fragrance there;
   The noblest balm of all its wounds,
   The cordial of its care.

5 I'll speak the honors of thy name
   With my last, laboring breath.
   Then speechless, clasp thee in my arms,
   The antidote of death.

286

LORD, in the morning thou shalt hear
   My voice ascending high;
To thee will I direct my prayer,
   To thee lift up mine eye:

2 Up to the hills where Christ is gone
   To plead for all his saints,
   Presenting at his Father's throne
   Our songs and our complaints.

3 Thou art a God before whose sight
   The wicked shall not stand;
   Sinners shall ne'er be thy delight,
   Nor dwell at thy right hand.

4 But to thy house will I resort,
   To taste thy mercies there;
   I will frequent thy holy court,
   And worship in thy fear.

5 O may thy Spirit guide my feet
   In ways of righteousness!
   Make every path of duty straight
   And plain before my face.

287

THERE is an hour of peaceful rest,
   To mourning wanderers given:
There is a joy for souls distressed,
   A balm for every wounded breast,
   'Tis found above—in heaven.

2 There is a home for weary souls,
   By sin and sorrow driven; [shoals,
   When tossed on life's tempestuous
   Where storms arise and ocean rolls,
   And all is drear but heaven.

3 There faith lifts up her cheerful eye,
   To brighter prospects given;
   And views the tempest passing by,
   The evening shadows quickly fly,
   And all serene is heaven.

4 There fragrant flowers immortal
   And joys supreme are given; [bloom,
   There rays divine disperse the gloom;
   Beyond the confines of the tomb,
   Appears the dawn of heaven.

HYMNS 288, 289, 290, 291.

YORK. C. M.

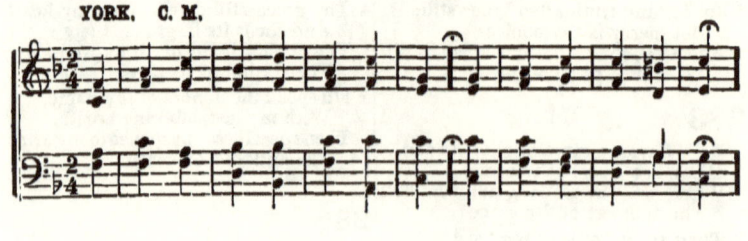

288 I.

SALVATION! O the joyful sound;
  'Tis pleasure to our ears;
A sovereign balm for every wound,
  A cordial for our fears.

2 Buried in sorrow and in sin,
    At hell's dark door we lay;
  But we arise, by grace divine,
    To see a heavenly day.

3 Salvation! let the echo fly
    The spacious earth around;
  While all the armies of the sky
    Conspire to raise the sound.

289 I.

BLEST are the undefiled in heart,
  Whose ways are right and clean;
Who never from thy law depart,
  But flee from every sin.

2 Blest are the men that keep thy word,
    And practice thy commands; [Lord,
  With their whole heart they seek the
    And serve thee with their hands.

3 Great is their peace who love thy law;
    How firm their souls abide!
  Nor can a bold temptation draw
    Their steady feet aside.

4 Then shall my heart have inward joy,
    And keep my face from shame,
  When all thy statutes I obey,
    And honor all thy name.

290 II.

SING, ye redeemed of the Lord,
  Your great Deliverer sing;
Pilgrims for Zion's city bound,
  Be joyful in your King.

2 A hand divine shall lead you on
    Through all the blissful road,
  Till to the sacred mount you rise,
    And see your smiling God.

3 The garlands of immortal joy
    Shall bloom on every head,
  While sorrow, sighing, and distress,
    Like shadows all are fled.

4 March on in your Redeemer's strength,
    Pursue his footsteps still;
  And let the prospect cheer your eye,
    While laboring up the hill.

291 II.

WITH songs and honors sounding
  Address the Lord on high; [loud,
Over the heavens he spreads his cloud,
  And waters veil the sky.

2 He gives the grazing ox his meat,
   He hears the ravens cry;
   But man, who tastes his finest wheat,
   Should raise his honors high.
3 His steady counsels change the face
   Of the declining year;
   He bids the sun cut short his race,
   And wintry days appear.
4 He sends his word, and melts the snow,
   The fields no longer mourn;
   He calls the warmer gales to blow,
   And bids the spring return.
5 The changing wind, the flying cloud,
   Obey his mighty word;
   With songs and honors sounding loud,
   Praise ye the sovereign Lord.

FOR SOCIAL AND PRIVATE WORSHIP.

292

ETERNAL Father, God of love,
   To thee our hearts we raise;
   Thy all-sustaining power we prove,
   And gladly sing thy praise.
2 Thine, wholly thine, oh, let us be!
   Our sacrifice receive;
   Made, and preserved, and saved by thee,
   To thee ourselves we give.
3 Come, Holy Ghost! the Saviour's love
   Shed in our hearts abroad;
   So shall we ever live and move,
   And be, with Christ, in God.

293

MY God, I love thee—not because
   I hope for heaven thereby;
   Nor yet because, if I love not,
   I must forever die.
2 Thou, oh my Jesus, thou didst me
   Upon the cross embrace;
   For me didst bear the nails and spear,
   And manifold disgrace;
3 And griefs and torments numberless,
   And sweat of agony;
   E'en death itself;—and all for one
   Who was thine enemy.
4 I love thee, blessed Jesus Christ,
   Not seeking a reward;—
   But as thyself hast loved me,
   O ever loving Lord!
5 E'en so I love thee, and will love,
   And in thy praise will sing;

Only because thou art my God,
And my eternal King.

294

MY God! the covenant of thy love
   Abides for ever sure;
   And in its matchless grace I feel
   My happiness secure.
2 Since thou, the everlasting God,
   My Father art become,
   Jesus my Guardian and my Friend,
   And heaven my final home,—
3 I welcome all thy sovereign will,
   For all that will is love;
   And when I know not what thou dost,
   I wait the light above.
4 Thy covenant in the darkest gloom
   Shall heavenly rays impart,
   And when my eyelids close in death,
   Sustain my fainting heart.

295

YE trembling souls, dismiss your fears,
   Be mercy all your theme;
   Mercy, which like a river flows
   In one perpetual stream.
2 Fear not the powers of earth, and hell;
   God will those powers restrain;
   His arm shall all their rage repel,
   And make their efforts vain.
3 Fear not the want of outward good;
   For his he will provide;
   Grant them supplies of daily food,
   And give them heaven beside.
4 Fear not that he will e'er forsake,
   Or leave his work undone;
   He's faithful to his promises,
   And faithful to his Son.

296

FREQUENT the day of God returns,
   To shed its quickening beams;
   And yet how slow devotion burns;
   How languid are its flames!
2 Accept our faint attempts to love;
   Our frailties, Lord, forgive:
   We would be like thy saints above,
   And praise thee while we live.
3 Increase, O Lord, our faith and hope,
   And fit us to ascend,
   Where the assembly ne'er breaks up,
   The Sabbath ne'er shall end.

HYMNS 297, 298, 299.

BADEA. S. M.

297 I.

NOT all the blood of beasts
On Jewish altars slain,
Could give the guilty conscience peace,
Or wash away the stain.

2 But Christ, the heavenly Lamb,
Takes all our sins away;
A sacrifice of nobler name,
And richer blood than they.

3 My faith would lay her hand
On that dear head of thine,
While like a penitent I stand,
And there confess my sin.

4 Believing, we rejoice
To see the curse remove;
We bless the Lamb with cheerful voice
And sing his bleeding love.

298 I.

THE Lord my Shepherd is,
I shall be well supplied;
Since he is mine, and I am his,
What can I want beside?

2 He leads me to the place
Where heavenly pasture grows,
Where living waters gently pass,
And full salvation flows.

3 If e'er I go astray,
He doth my soul reclaim,
And guides me in his own right way,
For his most holy name.

4 While he affords his aid,
I cannot yield to fear; [shade.
Tho' I should walk thro' death's dark
My Shepherd's with me there.

5 Amid surrounding foes
Thou dost my table spread,
My cup with blessings overflows,
And joy exalts my head.

6 The bounties of thy love
Shall crown my following days;
Nor from thy house will I remove,
Nor cease to speak thy praise.

299 I.

LIKE sheep we went astray,
And broke the fold of God;
Each wandering in a different way,
But all the downward road.

2 How dreadful was the hour
When God our wanderings laid,
And did at once his vengeance pour
Upon the Shepherd's head!

3 How glorious was the grace
When Christ sustained the stroke!
His life and blood the Shepherd pays
A ransom for the flock.

4 His honor and his breath
  Were taken both away;
  Joined with the wicked in his death,
  And made as vile as they.

300 II.

BEHOLD, what wondrous grace
  The Father has bestowed
On sinners of a mortal race,
  To call them sons of God.

2 'Tis no surprising thing
  That we should be unknown;
The Jewish world knew not their King,
  God's everlasting Son.

3 Nor doth it yet appear
  How great we must be made:
But when we see our Saviour here
  We shall be like our head.

4 A hope so much divine
  May trials well endure,
May purge our souls from sense and sin,
  As Christ the Lord is pure.

301 II.

HOW charming is the place
  Where my Redeemer God
Unveils the beauties of his face,
  And sheds his love abroad!

2 Not the fair palaces
  To which the great resort
Are once to be compared with this,
  Where Jesus holds his court.

3 Here on the mercy-seat,
  With radiant glory crowned,
Our joyful eyes behold him sit,
  And smile on all around.

4 Give me, O Lord, a place
  Within thy blest abode,
Among the children of thy grace,
  The servants of my God.

For Social and Private Worship.

302

JESUS, we look to thee.
  Thy promised presence claim;
Thou in the midst of us wilt be,
  Assembled in thy name.

2 Thy name salvation is,
  Which here we come to prove;
Thy name is life, and health, and
  And everlasting love.   [peace,

3 We meet, the grace to take
  Which thou hast freely given;
We meet on earth for thy dear sake,
  That we may meet in heaven.

4 O, may thy quickening voice
  The death of sin remove,
And bid our inmost souls rejoice
  In hope of perfect love.

303

DEAR Saviour, we are thine,
  By everlasting bands:
Our names, our hearts, we would re-
  And souls, into thy hands.   [sign,

2 Accepted for thy sake,
  And justified by faith,
We of thy righteousness partake,
  And find in thee our life.

3 To thee we still would cleave,
  With ever growing zeal;
If millions tempt us Christ to leave,
  O let them ne'er prevail.

4 Thy Spirit shall unite
  Our souls to thee, our head;
Shall form us to thy image bright,
  That we thy paths may tread.

5 Death may our souls divide
  From these abodes of clay;
But love shall keep us near thy side,
  Through all the gloomy way.

6 Since Christ and we are one,
  Why should we doubt or fear?
Since he in heaven has fixed his throne,
  He'll fix his members there.

304

MY spirit on thy care,
  Blest Saviour, I recline;
Thou wilt not leave me to despair,
  For thou art love divine.

2 In thee I place my trust;
  On thee I calmly rest;
I know thee good, I know thee just,
  And count thy choice the best.

3 Whate'er events betide,
  Thy will they all perform;
Safe in thy breast my head I hide,
  Nor fear the coming storm.

4 Let good or ill befall,
  It must be good for me,—
Secure of having thee in all,
  Of having all in thee.

BOYLSTON. S. M.

305 I.

MY soul, repeat his praise,
  Whose mercies are so great;
Whose anger is so slow to rise,
  So ready to abate.

2 High as the heavens are raised
  Above the ground we tread,
So far the riches of his grace
  Our highest thoughts exceed.

3 His power subdues our sins;
  And his forgiving love,
Far as the east is from the west,
  Doth all our guilt remove.

4 Our days are as the grass,
  Or like the morning flower:
If one sharp blast sweep o'er the field,
  It withers in an hour.

5 But thy compassions, Lord,
  To endless years endure;
And children's children ever find
  Thy words of promise sure.

306 I.

I HEAR thy word with love,
  And I would fain obey:
Send thy good Spirit from above
  To guide me, lest I stray.

2 O! who can ever find
  The errors of his ways?
Yet, with a bold, presumptuous mind
  I would not dare transgress.

3 Warn me of every sin,
  Forgive my secret faults;
And cleanse this guilty soul of mine,
  Whose crimes exceed my thoughts.

4 While with my heart and tongue
  I spread thy praise abroad;
Accept the worship and the song,
  My Saviour and my God.

307 II.

MY Saviour and my King,
  Thy beauties are divine;
Thy lips with blessings overflow,
  And every grace is thine.

2 Now make thy glory known;
  Gird on thy dreadful sword,
And ride in majesty to spread
  The conquests of thy word.

3 Strike through thy stubborn foes,
  Or make their hearts obey;
While justice, meekness, grace and truth,
  Attend thy glorious way.

4 Thy laws, O God! are right;
  Thy throne shall ever stand;
And thy victorious gospel prove
  A sceptre in thy hand.

DENNIS. S. M.

308   I.

O! BLESS the Lord, my soul,
  Let all within me join,
And aid my tongue to bless his name,
  Whose favors are divine.

2 O! bless the Lord, my soul,
    Nor let his mercies lie
  Forgotten in unthankfulness,
    And without praises die.

3 'Tis he forgives thy sins,
    'Tis he relieves thy pain,
  'Tis he that heals thy sicknesses,
    And makes thee young again.

4 He crowns thy life with love,
    When ransomed from the grave;
  He that redeemed my soul from hell
    Hath sovereign power to save.

309   I.

HOW heavy is the night
  That hangs upon our eyes,
Till Christ, with his reviving light,
  Over our souls arise!

2 Our guilty spirits dread
    To meet the wrath of heaven;
  But, in his righteousness arrayed,
    We see our sins forgiven;

3 Unholy and impure
    Are all our thoughts and ways;
  His hands infected nature cure,
    With sanctifying grace.

4 The powers of hell agree
    To hold our souls in vain;
  He sets the sons of bondage free,
    And breaks the accursed chain.

5 Lord, we adore thy ways
    To bring us near to God;
  Thy sovereign power, thy healing
    And thy atoning blood.   [grace,

310   II.

O LORD our God, arise,
  The cause of truth maintain;
And wide o'er all the peopled world
  Extend her blessed reign.

2 Thou Prince of Life, arise,
    Nor let thy glory cease;
  Far spread the conquests of thy grace,
    And bless the earth with peace.

3 Thou holy Ghost arise,
    Expand thy quickening wing,
  And o'er a dark and ruined world,
    Let light and order spring.

4 All on the earth, arise,
    To God the Saviour sing,   [heaven,
  From shore to shore, from earth to
    Let echoing anthems ring.

DOVER. S. M.

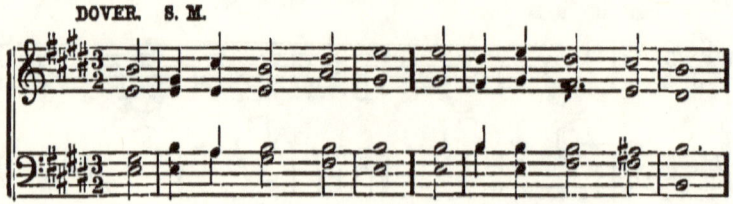

311 I.

BEHOLD, the morning sun
  Begins his glorious way;
His beams through all the nations run,
  And life and light convey.

2 But where the gospel comes,
  It spreads diviner light;
It calls dead sinners from their tombs,
  And gives the blind their sight.

3 How perfect is thy word!
  And all thy judgments just;
For ever sure thy promise, Lord,
  And men securely trust.

4 My gracious God, how plain
  Are thy directions given!
O! may I never read in vain,
  But find the path to heaven!

312 I.

BEHOLD the lofty sky
  Declares its Maker, God!
And all the starry works on high
  Proclaim his power abroad.

2 The darkness and the light
  Still keep their course the same;
While night to day, and day to night,
  Divinely teach his name.

3 In every different land,
  Their general voice is known;
They show the wonders of his hand,
  And orders of his throne.

4 Ye Christian lands, rejoice,
  Here he reveals his word;
We are not left to nature's voice
  To bid us know the Lord.

5 His statutes and commands
  Are set before our eyes;
He puts his gospel in our hands,
  Where our salvation lies.

313 II.

AWAKE, and sing the song
  Of Moses and the Lamb;
Wake, every heart and every tongue,
  To praise the Saviour's name.

2 Sing of his dying love,
  Sing of his rising power;
Sing how he intercedes above
  For those whose sins he bore.

3 Sing on your heavenly way,
  Ye ransomed sinners, sing;
Sing on, rejoicing every day
  In Christ, the eternal King.

4 Soon shall we hear him say,
  "Ye blessed children, come!"
Soon will he call us hence away,
  And take his wanderers home.

314
II.

GREAT is the Lord our God,
And let his praise be great;
He makes his churches his abode,
His most delightful seat.

2 These temples of his grace,
How beautiful they stand!
The honors of our native place,
And bulwarks of our land.

3 In Zion God is known
A refuge in distress;
How bright has his salvation shone!
How fair his heavenly grace!

4 Oft have our fathers told,
Our eyes have often seen,
How well our God secures the fold,
Where his own flocks have been.

5 In every new distress
We'll to his house repair,
Recall to mind his wondrous grace,
And seek deliverance there.

FOR SOCIAL AND PRIVATE WORSHIP.

DOXOLOGY.

GIVE to the Father praise,
Give glory to the Son,
And to the Spirit of his grace
Be equal honor done.

315

MY God, my life, my love;
To thee, to thee I call;
I cannot live if thou remove,
For thou art All in all.

2 The smilings of thy face,
How amiable they are!
'Tis heaven to rest in thine embrace,
And no where else but there.

3 Nor earth, nor all the sky,
Can one delight afford;
No, not a drop of real joy,
Without thy presence, Lord.

4 Thou art the sea of love,
Where all thy pleasures roll;
The circle where my passions move,
And centre of my soul.

5 To thee my spirits fly,
With infinite desire;
And yet how far from thee I lie!
Dear Jesus, raise me higher.

316

O LORD, our heavenly King,
Thy name is all divine;
Thy glories round the earth are spread,
And o'er the heavens they shine.

2 Lord, what is worthless man,
That thou shouldst love him so?
Next to thine angels he is placed,
And lord of all below. ·

3 How rich thy bounties are!
And wondrous are thy ways:
Of dust and worms thy power can
A monument of praise.   [frame

317

MY Maker and my King!
To thee my all I owe;
Thy sovereign bounty is the spring
Whence all my blessings flow.

2 Thou ever good and kind!
A thousand reasons move,
A thousand obligations bind
My heart to grateful love.

3 The creature of thy hand,
On thee alone I live;
My God, thy benefits demand
More praise than I can give.

4 Oh let thy grace inspire
My soul with strength divine;
Let all my powers to thee aspire,
And all my days be thine.

318

WELCOME, sweet day of rest,
That saw the Lord arise;
Welcome to this reviving breast,
And these rejoicing eyes.

2 The King himself comes near,
And feasts his saints to-day;
Here we may sit, and see him here,
And love and praise and pray.

3 One day amid the place
Where my dear God hath been
Is sweeter than ten thousand days
Of pleasurable sin.

4 My willing soul would stay
In such a frame as this,
And sit and sing herself away,
To everlasting bliss.

OLMUTZ. S. M.

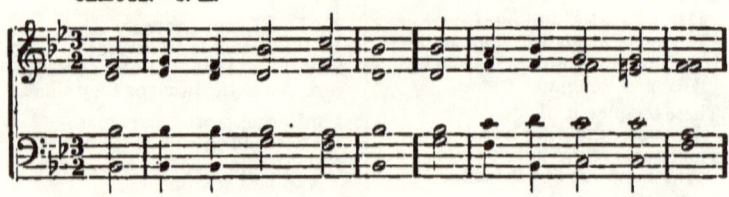

319   I.

WHEN overwhelmed with grief,
   My heart within me dies,
Helpless and far from all relief,
   To heaven I lift mine eyes.

2 O! lead me to the rock
   That's high above my head,
And make the covert of thy wings
   My shelter and my shade.

3 Within thy presence, Lord,
   For ever I'll abide;
Thou art the tower of my defence,
   The refuge where I hide.

4 Thou givest me the lot
   Of those that fear thy name;
If endless life be their reward,
   I shall possess the same.

320   I.

O! BLESSED souls are they
   Whose sins are covered o'er,
Divinely blest, to whom the Lord
   Imputes their guilt no more.

2 They mourn their follies past,
   And keep their hearts with care;
Their lips and lives without deceit
   Shall prove their faith sincere.

3 While I concealed my guilt,
   I felt the festering wound,
Till I confessed my sins to thee,
   And ready pardon found.

4 Let sinners learn to pray,
   Let saints keep near the throne;
Our help in times of deep distress,
   Is found in God alone.

321   II.

YOUR harps, ye trembling saints,
   Down from the willows take;
Loud to the praise of love divine,
   Bid every string awake.

2 Though in a foreign land,
   We are not far from home,
And nearer to our house above
   We every moment come.

3 His grace will, to the end,
   Stronger and brighter shine;
Nor present things, nor things to come,
   Shall quench the love divine.

4 When we in darkness walk,
   Nor feel the heavenly flame;
Then is the time to trust our God,
   And rest upon his name.

5 Soon shall our doubts and fears
   Subside, at his control:
His loving-kindness shall break thro'
   The midnight of the soul.

6 Blest is the man, O God,
   That stays himself on thee;
   Who waits for thy salvation Lord,
   Shall thy salvation see.

322   II.

TO bless thy chosen race,
   In mercy, Lord, incline;
And cause the brightness of thy face
On all thy saints to shine:—

2 That so thy wondrous way
   May through the world be known;
   While distant lands their tribute pay,
   And thy salvation own.

3 O let them shout and sing
   With joy and pious mirth;
   For thou, the righteous Judge and
   Shalt govern all the earth.   [King,

4 Let differing nations join
   To celebrate thy fame;
   Let all the world, O Lord, combine
   To praise thy glorious name.

For Social and Private Worship.

323

BLEST Comforter Divine,
   Whose rays of heavenly love
Amid our gloom and darkness shine,
And point our souls above;

2 Thou, who with "still small voice"
   Dost stop the sinner's way,
   And bid the mourning saint rejoice,
   Though earthly joys decay;

3 Thou, whose inspiring breath
   Can make the cloud of care,
   And e'en the gloomy vale of death,
   A smile of glory wear;

4 Thou, who dost fill the heart
   With love to all our race,
   Blest Comforter! to us impart
   The blessings of thy grace.

324

WHILE my Redeemer's near,
   My Shepherd and my Guide,
I bid farewell to anxious fear;
My wants are all supplied.

2 To ever fragrant meads,
   Where rich abundance grows,
   His gracious hand indulgent leads,
   And guards my sweet repose.

3 Dear Shepherd, if I stray,
   My wandering feet restore;
   To thy fair pastures guide my way,
   And let me rove no more.

325

BLEST be the tie that binds
   Our hearts in Christian love;
The fellowship of kindred minds
   Is like to that above.

2 Before our Father's throne
   We pour our ardent prayers:
   Our fears, our hopes, our aims are one,
   Our comforts and our cares.

3 We share our mutual woes,
   Our mutual burdens bear,
   And often for each other flows
   The sympathizing tear.

4 When we asunder part,
   It gives us inward pain;
   But we shall still be joined in heart,
   And hope to meet again.

5 This glorious hope revives
   Our courage by the way;
   While each in expectation lives,
   And longs to see the day.

6 From sorrow, toil, and pain,
   And sin we shall be free;
   And perfect love and friendship reign,
   Through all eternity.

326

O! FOR the death of those
   Who slumber in the Lord!
O be like theirs my last repose,
Like theirs my last reward!

2 Their bodies in the ground
   In silent hope may lie,
   Till the last trumpet's joyful sound
   Shall call them to the sky.

3 Their ransomed spirits soar,
   On wings of faith and love,
   To meet the Saviour they adore,
   And reign with him above.

4 With us their names shall live
   Through long succeeding years,
   Enbalmed with all our hearts can give,
   Our praises and our tears.

5 O for the death of those,
   Who slumber in the Lord!
   O be like theirs my last repose,
   Like theirs my last reward.

HYMN: 327, 328, 329.

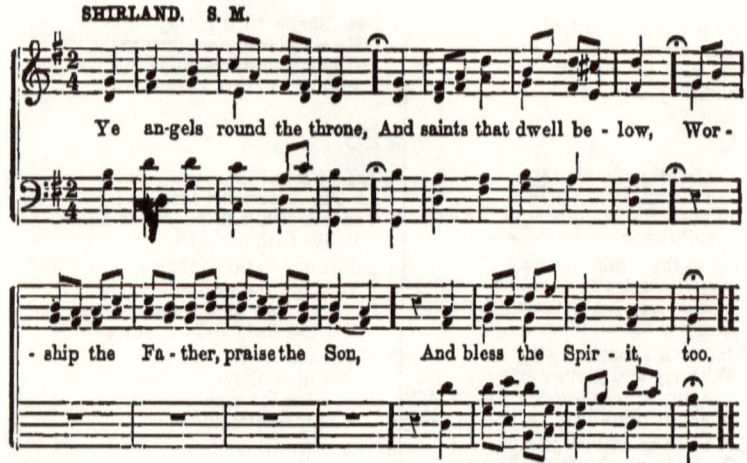

SHIRLAND. S. M.

Ye an-gels round the throne, And saints that dwell be-low, Wor-ship the Fa-ther, praise the Son, And bless the Spir-it, too.

327   I.

PREPARE me, gracious God,
  To stand before thy face;
Thy Spirit must the work perform,
  For it is all of grace.

2 In Christ's obedience clothe,
  And wash me in his blood:
So shall I lift my head with joy,
  Among the sons of God.

3 Do thou my sins subdue,
  Thy sovereign love make known;
The spirit of my mind renew,
  And save me in thy Son.

4 Let me attest thy power,
  Let me thy goodness prove,
Till my full soul can hold no more
  Of everlasting love.

328   II.

TO God, the only wise,
  Our Saviour and our King,
Let all the saints below the skies
  Their humble praises bring.

2 'Tis his almighty love,
  His counsel and his care,
Preserves us safe from sin and death,
  And every hurtful snare.

3 He will present our souls,
  Unblemished and complete,
Before the glory of his face,
  With joys divinely great.

4 Then all the chosen seed
  Shall meet around the throne;
Shall bless the conduct of his grace,
  And make his wonders known.

5 To our Redeemer God
  Wisdom and power belongs,
Immortal crowns of majesty,
  And everlasting songs.

329   II.

HOW beauteous are their feet
  Who stand on Zion's hill,
Who bring salvation on their tongues,
  And words of peace reveal!

2 How charming is their voice!
  How sweet their tidings are!
"Zion, behold thy Saviour King,
  He reigns and triumphs here."

3 How happy are our ears
  That hear this joyful sound,
Which kings and prophets waited for,
  And sought, but never found!

4 How blessed are our eyes
  That see this heavenly light!
Prophets and kings desired it long,
  But died without the sight.

5 The watchmen join their voice,
  And tuneful notes employ;
  Jerusalem breaks forth in songs,
  And deserts learn the joy.
6 The Lord makes bare his arm
  Through all the earth abroad:
  Let every nation now behold
  Their Saviour and their God.

FOR SOCIAL AND PRIVATE WORSHIP.

330

MINE eyes and my desire
  Are ever to the Lord,
I love to plead his promised grace
  And rest upon his word.
2 Turn, turn thee to my soul,
  Bring thy salvation near;
  When will thy hand release my feet
  Out of the deadly snare?
3 When shall the sovereign grace
  Of my forgiving God,
  Restore me from those dangerous ways
  My wandering feet have trod?
4 O! keep my soul from death,
  Nor put my hope to shame,
  For I have placed my only trust
  In my Redeemer's name.
5 With humble faith I wait
  To see thy face again;
  Of Israel it shall ne'er be said,
  He sought the Lord in vain.

331

NOT with our mortal eyes
  Have we beheld the Lord;
Yet we rejoice to hear his name,
  And love him in his word.
2 On earth we want the sight
  Of our Redeemer's face;
  Yet, Lord, our inmost thoughts delight
  To dwell upon thy grace.
3 And when we taste thy love,
  Our joys divinely grow,
  Unspeakable, like those above,
  And heaven begins below.

332

BLEST are the sons of peace,
  Whose hearts and hopes are one;
Whose kind designs to serve and please
  Through all their actions run.

2 Blest is the pious house
  Where zeal and friendship meet;
  Their songs of praise, their mingled vows
  Make their communion sweet.
3 Thus, when on Aaron's head
  They poured the rich perfume,
  The oil down to his raiment spread,
  And pleasure filled the room.
4 Thus, on the heavenly hills,
  The saints are blest above,
  Where joy, like morning dew, distils,
  And all the air is love.

333

GIVE to the winds thy fears;
  Hope on, be not dismayed:
God hears thy sighs and counts thy tears;
  God shall lift up thy head.
2 Through waves, and clouds, and storms,
  He gently clears the way;
  Wait thou his time: the darkest night
  Shall end in brightest day.
3 Far, far above thy thought
  His counsel shall appear,
  When fully he the work hath wrought,
  That caused thy needless fear.
4 What though thou rulest not!
  Yet heaven and earth and hell
  Proclaim—God sitteth on the throne,
  And ruleth all things well.

334

THE day is past and gone,
  The evening shades appear;
O may we all remember well,
  The night of death draws near.
2 We lay our garments by,
  Upon our beds to rest;
  So death will soon disrobe us all
  Of what is here possessed.
3 Lord, keep us safe this night,
  Secure from all our fears;
  May angels guard us while we sleep,
  Till morning light appears.
4 And when we early rise,
  And view the unwearied sun,
  May we set out to win the prize,
  And after glory run.
5 And when our days are past,
  And we from time remove,
  O may we in thy bosom rest,
  The bosom of thy love.

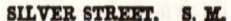

SILVER STREET. S. M.

335   I.

COME sound his praise abroad,
  And hymns of glory sing;
Jehovah is the sovereign God,
  The universal King.

2 He formed the deeps unknown;
  He gave the seas their bound;
The watery worlds are all his own;
  And all the solid ground.

3 Come, worship at his throne,
  Come, bow before the Lord;
We are his works, and not our own;
  He formed us by his word.

4 To-day attend his voice,
  Nor dare provoke his rod;
Come, like the people of his choice,
  And own your gracious God.

336   I.

COME, Holy Spirit, come;
  Let thy bright beams arise;
Dispel the darkness from our minds,
  And open thou our eyes.

2 Revive our drooping faith;
  Our doubts and fears remove;
And kindle in our breasts the flame
  Of never-dying love.

3 Convince us of our sin,
  Then lead to Jesus' blood;
And to our wondering view reveal
  The gracious love of God.

4 'Tis thine to cleanse the heart,
  To sanctify the soul,
To pour fresh life on every part,
  And new create the whole.

5 Dwell, therefore, in our hearts;
  Our minds from bondage free;
Then shall we know, and praise, and love
  The Father, Son, and Thee.

337   II.

COME, we that love the Lord,
  And let our joys be known;
Join in a song with sweet accord,
  And thus surround the throne.

2 The God that rules on high,
  And thunders when he please,
That rides upon the stormy sky,
  And manages the seas:

3 This awful God is ours,
  Our Father and our love;
He shall send down his heavenly powers
  To carry us above.

4 The men of grace have found
  Glory begun below:
Celestial fruits on earthly ground,
  From faith and hope may grow.

5 The hill of Zion yields
   A thousand sacred sweets,
   Before we reach the heavenly fields,
   Or walk the golden streets.
6 Then let our songs abound
   And every tear be dry; [ground,
   We're marching through Immanuel's
   To fairer worlds on high.

338 II.

THY name, almighty Lord,
   Shall sound through distant lands:
Great is thy grace and sure thy word:
Thy truth for ever stands.
2 Far be thine honor spread,
   And long thy praise endure,
   Till morning light and evening shade
   Shall be exchanged no more.

339 II.

FAR as thy name is known
   The world declares thy praise;
Thy saints, O Lord, before thy throne
Their songs of honor raise.
2 With joy thy people stand
   On Zion's chosen hill,
   Proclaim the wonders of thy hand,
   And counsels of thy will.
3 Let strangers walk around
   The city where we dwell,
   Compass and view thy holy ground,
   And mark the building well.
4 The orders of thy house,
   The worship of thy name,
   The cheerful songs, the solemn vows,
   Our blessedness proclaim.
5 The God we worship now
   Will guide us till we die;
   Will be our God while here below,
   And ours above the sky.

For Social and Private Worship.

340

GRACE! 'tis a charming sound,
   Harmonious to mine ear:
Heaven with the echo shall resound,
And all the earth shall hear.
2 Grace first contrived the way
   To save rebellious man;
   And all the steps *that* grace display,
   Which drew the wondrous plan.

3 Grace first inscribed my name
   In God's eternal book;
   'Twas grace that gave me to the Lamb,
   Who all my sorrows took.
4 Grace led my roving feet
   To tread the heavenly road;
   And new supplies each hour I meet,
   While pressing on to God.
5 Grace taught my soul to pray,
   And made my eyes o'erflow;
   'Twas grace that kept me to this day,
   And will not let me go.
6 Grace all the work shall crown,
   Through everlasting days;
   It lays in heaven the topmost stone,
   And well deserves the praise.

341

"FOR ever with the Lord!"
   Amen! so let it be:
Life from the dead is in that word:
'Tis immortality!
2 Here in the body pent,
   Absent from him I roam,
   Yet nightly pitch my moving tent
   A day's march nearer home.
3 My Father's house on high,
   Home of my soul! how near,
   At times, to faith's aspiring eye,
   Thy golden gates appear!
4 "For ever with the Lord!"
   Father, if 'tis thy will,
   The promise of thy gracious word,
   Ev'n here to me fulfil.
5 Be thou at my right hand;
   So shall I never fail:
   Uphold thou me and I shall stand;
   Help, and I shall prevail.
6 So, when my latest breath
   Shall rend the vail in twain,
   By death I shall escape from death,
   And life eternal gain.

342

WE lift our hearts to thee,
   Thou Day-star from on high:
The sun itself is but thy shade,
Yet cheers both earth and sky.
2 Oh, let thy rising beams
   Dispel the shades of night;
   And let the glories of thy love,
   Come like the morning light!

ST. MICHAEL. S. M.

343 I.

O! CEASE, my wandering soul,
  On restless wing to roam;
All the wide world to either pole,
  Has not for thee a home.

2 Behold the ark of God,
  Behold the open door;
Hasten to gain that dear abode,
  And rove, my soul, no more.

3 There, safe thou shalt abide,
  There, sweet shall be thy rest,
And every longing satisfied,
  With full salvation blest.

344 II.

STAND up, and bless the Lord,
  Ye people of his choice!
Stand up, and bless the Lord your God,
  With heart, and soul, and voice.

2 Though high above all praise,
  Above all blessing high,
Who would not fear his holy name,
  And laud, and magnify?

3 God is our strength and song,
  And his salvation ours;
Then be his love in Christ proclaimed,
  With all our ransomed powers.

4 Stand up, and bless the Lord,—
  The Lord your God, adore,
Stand up and bless his glorious name,
  Henceforth for evermore.

345 II.

LET every creature join
  To praise th' eternal God;
Ye heavenly hosts, the song begin,
  And sound his name abroad.

2 Thou sun with golden beams,
  And moon with paler rays,
Ye starry lights, ye twinkling flames,
  Shine to your Maker's praise.

3 He built those worlds above,
  And fixed their wondrous frame;
By his command they stand or move,
  And ever speak his name.

4 Ye vapors, when ye rise,
  Or fall in showers of snow, [skies,
Ye thunders, murmuring round the
  His power and glory show.

5 Wind, hail, and flaming fire,
  Agree to praise the Lord,
When ye in dreadful storms conspire
  To execute his word.

6 By all his works above
  His honors be expressed;
But saints that taste his saving love,
  Should sing his praises best.

346

II.

THE Lord, the sovereign King,
Hath fixed his throne on high;
O'er all the heavenly world he rules,
And all beneath the sky.

2 Ye angels great in might,
And swift to do his will,
Bless ye the Lord, whose voice ye hear,
Whose pleasure ye fulfil.

3 Let the bright hosts who wait
The orders of their King, [pray,
And guard his churches when they
Join in the praise they sing.

4 While all his wondrous works
Through his vast kingdom show
Their Maker's glory, thou, my soul,
Shalt sing his praises too.

For Social and Private Worship.

347

I LIFT my soul to God,
My trust is in his name;
Let not the foes that seek my blood
Still triumph in my shame.

2 From the first dawning light
Till evening shades arise,
For thy salvation, Lord, I wait,
With ever-longing eyes.

3 Remember all thy grace,
And lead me in thy truth:
Forgive the sins of riper days,
And follies of my youth.

4 The Lord is just and kind,
The meek shall learn his ways,
And every humble sinner find
The methods of his grace.

5 For his own goodness' sake
He saves my soul from shame;
He pardons, though my guilt be great,
Through my Redeemer's name.

348

MY God, permit my tongue
This joy to call thee mine;
And let my early cries prevail
To taste thy love divine.

2 My thirsty fainting soul
Thy mercy does implore:
Not travellers in desert lands
Can pant for water more.

3 Within thy churches, Lord,
I long to find my place,
Thy power and glory to behold,
And feel thy quickening grace.

4 Since thou hast been my help,
To thee my spirit flies,
And on thy watchful providence
My cheerful hope relies.

5 The shadow of thy wings
My soul in safety keeps;
I follow where my Father leads,
And he supports my steps.

349

COMMIT thou all thy griefs
And ways into his hands;
To his sure truth and tender care,
Who earth and heaven commands—

2 Who points the clouds their course,
Whom winds and seas obey;
He shall direct thy wandering feet,
He shall prepare thy way.

3 On God alone rely;
Then safe shalt thou go on:
Fix on his work thy steadfast eye;
Then shall thy work be done.

4 When he makes bare his arm,
What shall his aim withstand?
When he will save his friends from
Who, who shall stay his hand? [harm,

5 He hears thy softest prayer,
He girdeth thee with might;
His works the purest blessings are;
His ways, the purest light.

350

SWEET is the work, O Lord,
Thy glorious acts to sing,
To praise thy name, and hear thy word,
And grateful offerings bring.

2 Sweet at the dawning light,
Thy boundless love to tell;
And when approach the shades of
Still on the theme to dwell. [night,

3 Sweet, on this day of rest,
To join in heart and voice
With those who love and serve thee
And in thy name rejoice. [best,

4 To songs of praise and joy,
Be every Sabbath given,
That such may be our blest employ
Eternally in heaven.

ST. THOMAS. S. M.

351   I.

R AISE your triumphant songs
  To an immortal tune,
Let the wide earth resound the deeds
  Celestial grace has done.

2 Sing how eternal Love
  Its chief Beloved chose,
And bade him raise our wretched race
  From their abyss of woes.

3 His hand no thunder bears,
  Nor terror clothes his brow;
No bolts to drive our guilty souls
  To fiercer flames below.

4 'Twas mercy filled the throne,
  And wrath stood silent by,
When Christ was sent with pardons
  To rebels doomed to die.   [down,

5 Lord, we obey thy call;
  We lay an humble claim
To the salvation thou hast brought,
  And love and praise thy name.

352   II.

SEE what a living stone
  The builder's did refuse;
Yet God hath built his church thereon
  In spite of envious Jews.

2 The work, O Lord, is thine,
  And wondrous in our eyes:
This day declares it all divine,
  This day did Jesus rise.

3 This is the glorious day
  That our Redeemer made;
Let us rejoice, and sing, and pray;
  Let all the church be glad.

4 Hosanna to the King
  Of David's royal blood:
Bless him, ye saints; he comes to bring
  Salvation from your God.

5 We bless thine holy word,
  Which all this grace displays;
And offer on thine altar, Lord,
  Our sacrifice of praise.

353   II.

THE God Jehovah reigns,
  Let all the nation's fear;
Let sinners tremble at his throne,
  And saints be humble there.

2 Jesus the Saviour reigns,
  Let earth adore its Lord;
Bright cherubs his attendants stand,
  Swift to fulfil his word.

3 In Zion stands his throne,
  His honors are divine;   [known,
His church shall make his wonders
  For there his glories shine.

4 How holy is his name!
  How terrible his praise!
  Justice, and truth, and judgment join
  In all his works of grace.

354
II.

I LOVE thy kingdom, Lord,
  The house of thine abode;
  The church our blest Redeemer saved
  With his own precious blood.

2 I love thy church, O God!
  Her walls before thee stand,
  Dear as the apple of thine eye,
  And graven on thy hand.

3 If e'er to bless thy sons,
  My voice or hands deny,
  These hands let useful skill forsake,
  This voice in silence die.

4 If e'er my heart forget
  Her welfare or her woe,
  Let every joy this heart forsake,
  And every grief o'erflow.

5 For her my tears shall fall;
  For her my prayers ascend:
  To her my cares and toils be given,
  Till toils and cares shall end.

6 Beyond my highest joy
  I prize her heavenly ways;
  Her sweet communion, solemn vows,
  Her hymns of love and praise.

7 Jesus, thou Friend divine,
  Our Saviour and our King,
  Thy hand from every snare and foe
  Shall great deliverance bring.

8 Sure as thy truth shall last,
  To Zion shall be given
  The brightest glories earth can yield,
  And brighter bliss of heaven.

For Social and Private Worship.

355

MY soul, be on thy guard,
  Ten thousand foes arise;
  And hosts of sins are pressing hard,
  To draw thee from the skies.

2 O watch, and fight, and pray,
  The battle ne'er give o'er;
  Renew it boldly every day,
  And help divine implore.

3 Ne'er think the victory won,
  Nor once at ease sit down;

Thy arduous work will not be done
  Till thou hast got the crown.

4 Fight on, my soul, till death
  Shall bring thee to thy God;
  He'll take thee, at thy parting breath,
  Up to his blest abode.

356

TO God, in whom I trust,
  I lift my heart and voice;
  O let me not be put to shame,
  Nor let my foes rejoice.

2 Thy mercies and thy love,
  O Lord, recall to mind;
  And graciously continue still,
  As thou wast ever, kind.

3 Let all my youthful crimes
  Be blotted out by thee,
  And, for thy wondrous goodness' sake,
  In mercy think on me.

4 His mercy and his truth
  The righteous Lord displays,
  In bringing wandering sinners home,
  And teaching them his ways.

357

'TIS but a little while,
  And he shall come again,
  Who died that we might live, who
  That we with him may reign:

2 Then, O my Lord, prepare
  My soul for that glad day;
  O wash me in thy precious blood,
  And take my sins away!

358

AND must this body die,
  This mortal frame decay?
  And must these active limbs of mine
  Lie mouldering in the clay?

2 God my Redeemer lives,
  And often from the skies
  Looks down and watches all my dust,
  Till he shall bid it rise.

3 Arrayed in glorious grace
  Shall these vile bodies shine,
  And every shape and every face
  Look heavenly and divine.

4 These lively hopes we owe
  To Jesus' dying love;
  We would adore his grace below,
  And sing his power above.

NEWCOURT. L. P. M.

359 I.

I LOVE the volume of thy word;
What light and joy those leaves afford
To souls benighted and distressed!
Thy precepts guide my doubtful way,
Thy fear forbids my feet to stray,
Thy promise leads my heart to rest.

2 From the discoveries of thy law
The perfect rules of life I draw:
These are my study and delight:
Not honey so invites the taste,
Nor gold that hath the furnace passed
Appears so pleasing to the sight.

3 Thy threatenings wake my slumbering eyes,
And warn me where my danger lies;
But 'tis thy blessed gospel, Lord,
That makes my guilty concience clean,
Converts my soul, subdues my sin,
And gives a free, but large reward.

4 Who knows the errors of my thoughts?
My God, forgive my secret faults,
And from presumptuous sin restrain;
Accept my poor attempts of praise,
That I have read thy book of grace,
And book of nature, not in vain.

360 I.

O GOD—my gracious God—to thee
My morning prayers shall offered be;
For thee my thirsty soul doth pant!
My fainting flesh implores thy grace,
Within this dry and barren place,
Where I refreshing waters want.

2 O to my longing eyes once more
That view of glorious power restore,
Which thy majestic house displays!
Because to me thy wondrous love
Than life itself does dearer prove,
My lips shall always speak thy praise.

361 I.

THOU art the everlasting Son,
O Christ! and, high upon thy throne,
Thou art at the right hand of God,
And hast redeemed us by thy blood;
And heaven and earth are full of thee,
The glory of thy Majesty!

2 When all the sharpness of our death
Was overcome in thy last breath,
Then didst thou open wide heaven's door
To all believers evermore:
O Lamb of God! and thou wilt come,
To be our Judge, and take us home.

6 In thee we trust: we pray thee, Lord,
Remember thy most precious blood!
In honor may we numbered be
With all the noble company,
Who bow before thy mercy-seat,
And cast their treasures at thy feet.

362 II.

I'LL praise my Maker with my breath,
And when my voice is lost in death,
Praise shall employ my nobler powers:
My days of praise shall ne'er be past,
While life, and thought, and being last,
Or immortality endures.

2 Happy the man whose hopes rely
On Israel's God: he made the sky,
And earth, and seas, with all their train:
His truth forever stands secure;
He saves th' oppressed, he feeds the poor,
And none shall find his promise vain.

3 The Lord hath eyes to give the blind;
The Lord supports the sinking mind;
He sends the laboring conscience peace:
He helps the stranger in distress,
The widow and the fatherless,
And grants the prisoner sweet release.

4 He loves his saints, he knows them well,
But turns the wicked down to hell;
Thy God, O Zion, ever reigns:
Let every tongue, let every age,
In this exalted work engage;
Praise him in everlasting strains.

363 II.

LET all the earth her voices raise,
To sing the choicest psalm of praise,
To sing and bless Jehovah's name:
His glory let the heathen know,
His wonders to the nations show,
And all his saving works proclaim.

2 The heathen know thy glory, Lord,
The wondering nations read thy word;
But here Jehovah's name is known:
Nor shall our worship e'er be paid
To gods which mortal hands have made:
Our Maker is our God alone. [

3 He framed the globe, he built the sky,
He made the shining worlds on high,
And reigns complete in glory there;
His beams are majesty and light;
His beauties how divinely bright!
His temple how divinely fair!

4 Come the great day, the glorious hour,
When earth shall feel his saving power,
And barbarous nations fear his name.
Then shall the race of men confess
The beauty of his holiness,
And in his courts his grace proclaim.

FOR SOCIAL AND PRIVATE WORSHIP.

364

THOU hidden Source of calm repose,
Thou all-sufficient Love divine,
My help and refuge from my foes,
Secure I am while thou art mine:
And lo! from sin, and grief, and shame,
I hide me, Jesus, in thy name.

2 Thy mighty name salvation is,
And keeps my happy soul above:
Comfort it brings, and power, and peace,
And joy, and everlasting love:
To me, with thy great name, are given
Pardon, and holiness, and heaven.

3 Jesus, my all in all thou art;
My rest in toil, my ease in pain;
The healing of my broken heart;
In war, my peace; in loss, my gain;
My smile beneath the tyrant's frown;
In shame, my glory and my crown:

4 In want, my plentiful supply;
In weakness, my almighty power;
In bonds, my perfect liberty;
My light, in Satan's darkest hour;
In grief, my joy unspeakable;
My life in death, my all in all.

HYMNS 365, 366.

ARIEL. C. P. M.

365   I.

O! COULD I speak the matchless worth,
O! could I sound the glories forth,
  Which in my Saviour shine:
I'd soar and touch the heavenly strings,
And vie with Gabriel, while he sings,
  In notes almost divine.

2 I'd sing the precious blood he spilt,
  My ransom from the dreadful guilt
    Of sin and wrath divine:
  I'd sing his glorious righteousness,
  In which all-perfect, heavenly dress,
    My soul shall ever shine.

3 I'd sing the characters he bears,
  And all the forms of love he wears,
    Exalted on his throne;
  In loftiest songs of sweetest praise,
  I would to everlasting days
    Make all his glories known.

4 Soon the delightful day will come,
  When my dear Lord will call me home,
    And I shall see his face:
  Then, with my Saviour, Brother, Friend,
  A blest eternity I'll spend,
    Triumphant in his grace.

366   II.

O! ISRAEL, who is like to thee,
  A people saved and called to be
    Peculiar to the Lord!
Thy shield, he guards thee from the foe;
Thy sword, he fights thy battles too;
    Himself thy great reward.

2 Fear not, though many should oppose,
  For God is stronger than thy foes,
  And makes thy cause his own:
  The promised land before thee lies,
  Go and possess the glorious prize,
  Reserved for thee alone.

3 In glory there the King appears,
  He wipes away his people's tears,
  And makes their sorrows cease;
  From toil and strife they there repose,
  And dwell secure from all their foes,
  In everlasting peace.

4 Fair emblem of a better rest,
  Of which believers are possessed,
  Beyond material space;
  Methinks I see the heavenly shore,
  Where sin and sorrow are no more,
  And long to reach the place.

5 Nor shall I always absent be
  From him my soul desires to see,
  Within the realms of light.
  Ere long my Lord will rend the veil,
  And not a cloud shall then conceal
  His glory from my sight.

367 II.

BEGIN, my soul, th' exalted lay,
  Let each enraptured thought obey,
  And praise th' Almighty's name.
  Lo! heaven and earth, and seas and skies
  In one melodious concert rise,
  To swell th' inspiring theme.

2 Ye angels catch the thrilling sound;
  While all th' adoring thrones around
  His boundless mercy sing;
  Let every listening saint above
  Wake all the tuneful soul of love,
  And touch the sweetest string.

3 Let every element rejoice:
  Ye thunders, burst with awful voice,
  To him who bids you roll:
  His praise in softer notes declare,
  Each whispering breeze of yielding air,
  And breathe it to the soul.

4 Let saints, redeemed from death and hell,
  In louder, loftier numbers tell,
  The wonders of his grace:
  Beyond creation's utmost bounds;
  Above her noblest sweetest sounds,
  Declare Jehovah's praise.

For Social and Private Worship.

368

O THOU that hear'st the prayer of faith,
  Wilt thou not save a soul from death,
    That casts itself on thee?
  I have no refuge of my own,
  But fly to what my Lord hath done
    And suffered once for me.

2 Slain in the guilty sinner's stead,
  His spotless righteousness I plead,
    And his availing blood:
  That righteousness my robe shall be,
  That merit shall atone for me,
    And bring me near to God.

3 Then save me from eternal death,
  The Spirit of adoption breathe,
    His consolations send:
  By him some word of life impart,
  And sweetly whisper to my heart,—
    "Thy Maker is thy Friend."

4 The king of terrors then would be
  A welcome messenger to me,
    To bid me come away;
  Unclogged by earth, or earthly things,
  I'd mount, I'd fly, with eager wings,
    To everlasting day.

369

THE festal morn, my God, is come,
  That calls me to thy hallow'd dome,
    Thy presence to adore:
  My feet the summons shall attend,
  With willing steps thy courts ascend,
    And tread the sacred floor.

2 With joy shall I behold the day,
  That calls my thirsting soul away,—
    To dwell among the blest!
  For lo! my great Redeemer's power
  Unfolds the everlasting door,
    And leads me to his rest!

3 E'en now, to my expecting eyes,
  The heaven-built towers of Salem rise;
    E'en now, with glad survey,
  I view her mansions, that contain
  The angel forms, a beauteous train,
    And shine with cloudless day.

4 Hither, from earth's remotest end,
  Lo, the redeemed of God ascend,
    Their tribute hither bring;
  Here, crowned with everlasting joy,
  In hymns of praise their tongues em- [ploy,
    And hail th' immortal King.

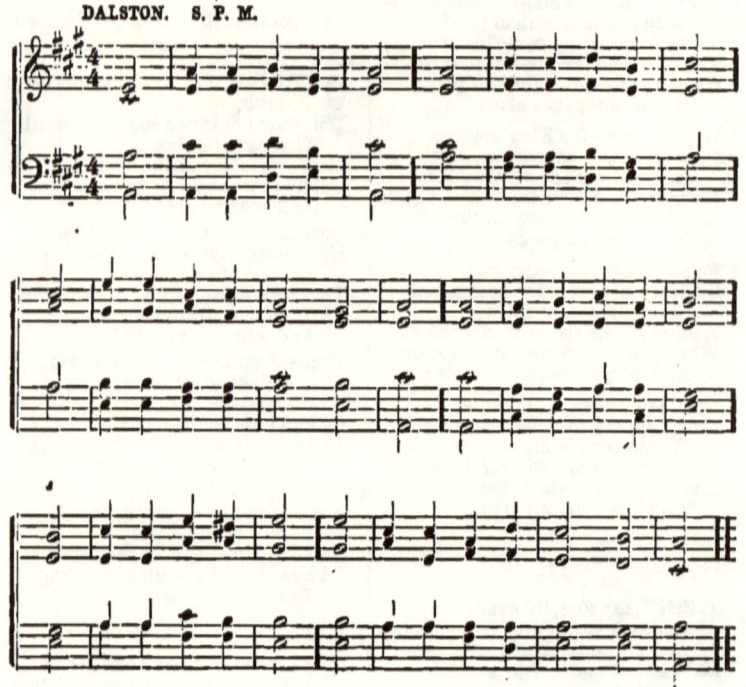

DALSTON. S. P. M.

370   I.

FATHER, thy Son hath died
   The sinner's death of woe;
Stooping in love from heaven to earth,
   Our curse to undergo,
     Upon the hateful tree:
   Give glory to thy Son, O Lord!

2 Father, thy Son hath poured
   His life-blood on this earth,
To cleanse away our guilt and stains,
   To give us second birth,
     From sin to set us free:
   Give glory to thy Son, O Lord!

3 Father, thy Son on earth
   No one to own him found:
He passed among the sons of men
   Rejected and disowned,
     That we received might be:
   Give glory to thy Son, O Lord!

4 Father, thy Son is king:
   Heaven's crown, and earth's is his!
For us, for us he bought the crown,
   For us he earned the bliss:
     Amen, so let it be!
   Give glory to thy Son, O Lord!

371   II.

THE Lord Jehovah reigns,
   And royal state maintains,
His head with awful glories crowned;
   Arrayed in robes of light,
   Begirt with sovereign might,
And rays of majesty around.

2 Upheld by thy commands,
　　The world securely stands,
　And skies and stars obey thy word;
　　Thy throne was fixed on high
　Ere stars adorned the sky :
　　Eternal is thy kingdom, Lord.

3 Let floods and nations rage,
　　And all their powers engage;
　Let swelling tides assault the sky;
　　The terrors of thy frown
　Shall beat their madness down;
　　Thy throne for ever stands on high.

4 Thy promises are true,
　　Thy grace is ever new,
　There fixed, thy church shall ne'er remove;
　　Thy saints with holy fear
　Shall in thy courts appear,
　　And sing thine everlasting love.

372 II.

HOW pleased and blest was I
　　To hear the people cry,
"Come, let us seek our God to-day!"
　　Yes, with a cheerful zeal
　We haste to Zion's hill,
　　And there our vows and honors pay.

2 Zion, thrice happy place,
　　Adorned with wondrous grace,
　And walls of strength embrace thee round:
　　In thee our tribes appear
　To pray, and praise, and hear
　　The sacred gospel's joyful sound.

3 There David's greater Son
　　Has fixed his royal throne;
　He sits for grace and judgment there:
　　He bids the saints be glad,
　He makes the sinners sad,
　　And humble souls rejoice with fear.

4 May peace attend thy gate,
　　And joy within thee wait,
　To bless the soul of every guest:
　　The man that seeks thy peace,
　And wishes thine increase,
　　A thousand blessings on him rest!

5 My tongue repeats her vows,
　　Peace to this sacred house!
　For here my friends and kindred dwell:
　　And since my glorious God
　Makes thee his blest abode,
　　My soul shall ever love thee well.

For Social and Private Worship.

373

FRIEND after friend departs;
　Who has not lost a friend?
There is no union here of hearts,
　That finds not here an end.
Were this frail world our final rest,
　Living or dying none were blest.

2 Beyond the flight of time,
　Beyond the reign of death,
There surely is some blessed clime
　Where life is not a breath;
Nor life's affections, transient fire,
　Whose sparks fly upward and expire.

3 There is a world above,
　Where parting is unknown:
A long eternity of love,
　Formed for the good alone;
And faith beholds the dying here,
　Translated to that glorious sphere.

4 Thus star by star declines,
　Till all are passed away,
As morning high and higher shines
　To pure and perfect day;
Nor sink those stars in empty night,
　But hide themselves in heaven's own light.

374

WHEN I can trust my all with God
　In trial's fearful hour—
Bow all resigned beneath his rod,
　And bless his sparing power:
A joy springs up amid distress,
A fountain in the wilderness.

2 An earthly mind, a faithless heart,
　Christ sees with pitying eye;
He will not let his grace depart,
　But—kind severity!—
He takes a hostage of our love,
To draw the parent's heart above.

3 There stands our child before the Lord,
　In royal vesture dressed;
A victor ere he drew the sword,
　Ere he had toiled, at rest.
No doubts this blessed faith bedim;
We know that Jesus died for him.

4 O blessed be the hand that gave;
　Still blessed when it takes;
Blessed be he who smites to save,
　Who heals the heart he breaks.
Perfect and true are all his ways,
Whom heaven adores, and death obeys.

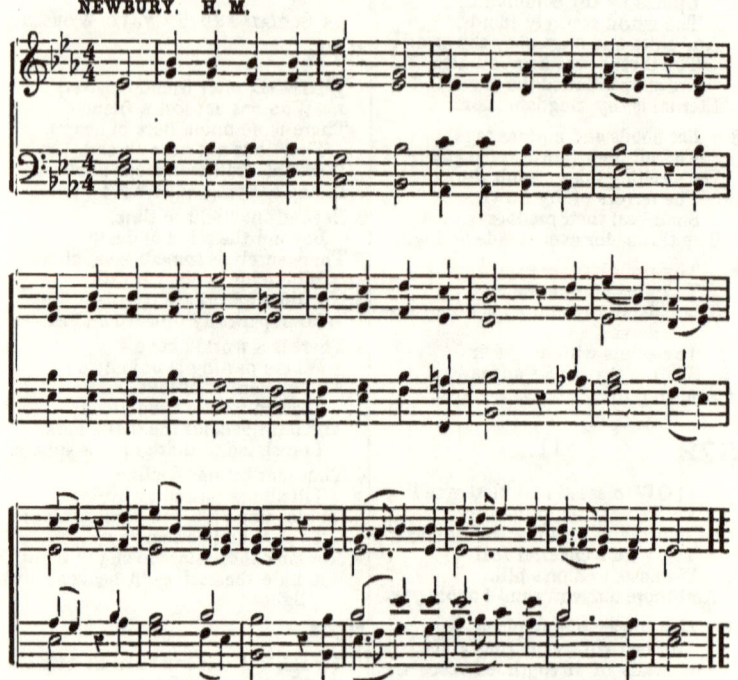

NEWBURY. H. M.

375   I.

WE give immortal praise
   To God the Father's love,
For all our comforts here,
   And all our hopes above;
He sent his own eternal Son,
To die for sins that man had done.

2 To God the Son belongs
   Immortal glory too,
Who saved us by his blood,
   From everlasting wo:
And now he lives, and now he reigns,
And sees the fruit of all his pains.

3 To God the Spirit, praise
   And endless worship give,
Whose new-creating power
   Makes the dead sinner live:
His work completes the great design,
And fills the soul with joy divine.

4 Almighty God, to thee,
   Be endless honors done,
The sacred Persons Three,
   The Godhead only One:
Where reason fails, with all her powers,
There faith prevails, and love adores.

376   II.

YES, the Redeemer rose,
   The Saviour left the dead;
And o'er our hellish foes
   High raised his conquering head;
In wild dismay, the guards around
Fall to the ground, and sink away.

2 Lo! the angelic bands
  In full assembly meet,
  To wait his high commands,
  And worship at his feet;
  Joyful they come, and wing their way
  From realms of day to Jesus' tomb.

3 All hail, triumphant Lord,
  Who sav'st us with thy blood!
  Wide be thy name adored,
  Thou rising, reigning God;
  With thee we rise, with thee we reign,
  And empires gain beyond the skies.

377   II.

REJOICE, the Lord is King,
  Your God and King adore;
  Mortals, give thanks and sing,
  And triumph evermore:
  Lift up the heart, lift up the voice,
  Rejoice aloud, ye saints, rejoice.

2 Rejoice, the Saviour reigns,
  The God of truth and love;
  When he had purged our stains,
  He took his seat above:
  Lift up the heart, lift up the voice,
  Rejoice aloud, ye saints, rejoice.

3 His kingdom cannot fail,
  He rules o'er earth and heaven;
  The keys of death and hell
  Are to our Jesus given;
  Lift up the heart, lift up the voice,
  Rejoice aloud, ye saints, rejoice.

4 Rejoice in glorious hope;
  Jesus the Judge shall come,
  And take his servants up
  To their eternal home:
  We soon shall hear th' archangel's voice,
  The trump of God shall sound, Rejoice.

378   II.

CHRIST is our Corner Stone;
  On him alone we build;
  With his true saints above
  The courts of heaven are filled.
  On his great love our hopes we place,
  Of present grace, and joys above.

2 O then with hymns of praise
  These hallowed courts shall ring;
  Our voices we will raise,
  The Three in One to sing,
  And thus proclaim in joyful song,
  Both loud and long, that glorious name.

3 Here, gracious God, do thou
  Forevermore draw nigh;
  Accept each faithful vow,
  And mark each suppliant sigh.
  In copious shower on all, we pray,
  Each holy day thy blessing pour!

4 Here may we gain from heaven
  The grace which we implore;
  And may that grace once given,
  Be with us evermore,
  Until that day, when all the blest
  To endless rest are called away.

379   II.

UPWARD I lift my eyes,
  From God is all my aid;
  The God that built the skies,
  And earth and nature made;
  God is the tower to which I fly;
  His grace is nigh in every hour.

2 My feet shall never slide,
  And fall in fatal snares,
  Since God, my guard and guide,
  Defends me from my fears.
  Those wakeful eyes that never sleep
  Shall Isreel keep when dangers rise.

3 Hast thou not given thy word
  To save my soul from death?
  And I can trust my Lord
  To keep my mortal breath:
  I'll go and come, nor fear to die,
  Till from on high thou call me home.

380   II.

O ZION, tune thy voice,
  And lift thy hands on high;
  Tell all the world thy joys,
  And shout salvation nigh;
  Cheerful in God, arise and shine,
  While rays divine stream all abroad.

2 He gilds thy mourning face
  With beams that cannot fade;
  His all-resplendent grace
  He pours around thy head:
  The nations round thy form shall view,
  With lustre new divinely crowned.

3 In honor to his name
  Reflect that sacred light,
  And loud that grace proclaim
  Which makes thy darkness bright:
  Pursue his praise till sovereign love
  In worlds above thy glory raise.

381 I.

COME, my Redeemer, come,
 And deign to dwell with me;
Come, and thy right assume,
 And bid thy rivals flee :
Come, my Redeemer, quickly come,
And make my heart thy lasting home.

2 Exert thy mighty power,
 And banish all my sin;
In this auspicious hour,
 Bring all thy graces in :
Come, my Redeemer, quickly come,
And make my heart thy lasting home.

3 Rule thou in every thought
 And passion of my soul,
Till all my powers are brought
 Beneath thy full control :
Come, my Redeemer, quickly come,
And make my heart thy lasting home.

4 Then shall my days be thine,
 And all my heart be love,
And joy and peace be mine,
 Such as are known above :
Come, my Redeemer, quickly come,
And make my heart thy lasting home.

382 I.

COME, every pious heart,
 That loves the Saviour's name,
Your noblest powers exert,
 To celebrate his fame :
Tell all above, and all below,
The debt of love to him you owe.

2 Such was his zeal for God,
  And such his love for you,
 He freely undertook
  What angels could not do:
 His mighty deeds of love and grace,
 All words exceed, and tho'ts surpass.
3 He left his starry crown,
  And laid his robes aside;
 On wings of love came down,
  And wept, and bled, and died:
 What he endured O! who can tell,
 To save our souls from death and hell!
4 From the dark grave he rose,
  The mansions of the dead;
 And thence his mighty foes,
  In glorious triumph led:
 Up thro' the sky the Conqueror rode,
 And reigns on high, the Saviour God.
5 Jesus, we ne'er can pay
  The debt we owe thy love,
 Yet tell us how we may,
  Our gratitude approve:
 Our hearts, our all, to thee we give;
 The gift, tho' small, thou wilt receive.

383

TO him that chose us first,
  Before the world began;
 To him that bore the curse,
  To save rebellious man:
 To him that formed our hearts anew,
 Are endless praise and glory due.
2 The Father's love shall run
  Through our immortal songs:
 We bring to God the Son
  Hosannas on our tongues:
 Our lips address the Spirit's name
 With equal praise, and zeal the same.
3 Let every saint above,
  And angel round the throne,
 For ever bless and love
  The sacred Three in One:
 Thus heaven shall raise his honors high
 When earth and time grow old and die.

384 II.

LORD of the worlds above,
  How pleasant and how fair
 The dwellings of thy love,
  Thy earthly temples are!
 To thine abode my heart aspires,
 With warm desires, to see my God.
2 O happy souls that pray,
  Where God appoints to hear!

O happy men that pay
  Their constant service there!
 They praise thee still; and happy they,
 That love the way to Zion's hill.
3 They go from strength to strength,
  Through this dark veil of tears,
 Till each arrives at length,
  Till each in heaven appears;
 O glorious seat, when God our King
 Shall thither bring our willing feet!
4 The Lord his people loves;
  His hand no good withholds
 From those his heart approves;
  From pure and pious souls:
 Thrice happy he, O God of hosts,
 Whose spirit trusts alone in thee.

FOR SOCIAL AND PRIVATE WORSHIP.

385

THY works, not mine, O Christ!
  Speak gladness to this heart;
 They tell me all is done;
  They bid my fear depart:
 To whom, save thee who canst alone
 For sin atone, Lord! shall I flee.
2 Thy tears, not mine, O Christ,
  Have wept my guilt away;
 And turned this night of mine
  Into a blessed day:
 To whom, save thee, &c.
3 Thy wounds, not mine, O Christ,
  Can heal my bruised soul;
 Thy stripes, not mine, contain
  The balm that makes me whole:
 To whom, save thee, &c.
4 Thy cross, not mine, O Christ,
  Has borne the awful load
 Of sins that none could bear
  But the incarnate God:
 To whom, save thee, &c.
5 Thy death, not mine, O Christ,
  Has paid the ransom due;
 Ten thousand deaths like mine
  Would have been all too few:
 To whom, save thee, &c.
6 Thy righteousness alone
  Can clothe and beautify;
 I wrap it round my soul
  In this I'll live and die:
 To whom, save thee, &c.

AUTUMN. 8s & 7s, Double.

386 II.

PRAISE to thee, thou great Creator!
  Praise to thee from every tongue:
Join, my soul, with every creature,
  Join the universal song.
Father, Source of all compassion,
  Pure, unbounded grace is thine:
Hail the God of our salvation!
  Praise him for his love divine.

2 For ten thousand blessings given,
    For the hope of future joy, [heaven,
  Sound his praise through earth and
    Sound Jehovah's praise on high.
  Joyfully on earth adore him,
    Till in heaven our song we raise;
  There, enraptured, fall before him,
    Lost in wonder, love, and praise.

FOR SOCIAL AND PRIVATE WORSHIP.

387

JESUS! who on Calv'ry's mountain
  Poured thy precious blood for me,
Wash me in its flowing fountain,
  That my soul may spotless be.
I have sinned, but, oh, restore me;
  For, unless thou smile on me,

Dark is all the world before me,
  Darker yet eternity!

2 In thy word I hear thee saying,
    "Come, and I will give you rest;"
  Glad the gracious call obeying,
    See, I hasten to thy breast.
  Grant, oh, grant thy Spirit's teaching,
    That I may not go astray,
  Till, the gate of heaven reaching,
    Earth and sin are passed away!

388

SAVIOUR, breathe an evening bless-
  Ere repose our spirits seal: [ing,
Sin and want we come confessing,
  Thou canst save and thou canst heal.
Though destruction walk around us,
  Though the arrow near us fly,
Angel-guards from thee surround us,
  We are safe if thou art nigh.

2 Though the night be dark and dreary,
    Darkness cannot hide from thee;
  Thou art he who, never weary,
    Watchest where thy people be. [us,
  Should swift death this night o'ertake
    And our couch become our tomb,
  May the morn in heaven awake us,
    Clad in light and deathless bloom.

FOUNT. 8s & 7s, Double.

FOR SOCIAL AND PRIVATE WORSHIP.

389

COME, thou fount of every blessing,
  Tune my heart to sing thy grace;
Streams of mercy never ceasing
  Call for songs of loudest praise.
Teach me some melodious sonnet,
  Sung by flaming tongues above;
Praise the mount—O fix me on it,
  Mount of God's unchanging love.

2 Here I raise my Ebenezer,
  Hither by thy help I'm come;
And I hope by thy good pleasure,
  Safely to arrive at home.
Jesus sought me when a stranger,
  Wandering from the fold of God;
He, to rescue me from danger,
  Interposed with precious blood.

3 O to grace how great a debtor,
  Daily I'm constrained to be!
Let that grace, Lord, like a fetter,
  Bind my wandering heart to thee.
Prone to wander, Lord, I feel it;
  Prone to leave the God I love;
Here's my heart, Lord, take and seal it,
  Seal it from thy courts above.

390

JESUS, I my cross have taken,
  All to leave and follow thee;
Naked, poor, despised, forsaken,
  Thou from hence my All shalt be:
Let the world neglect and leave me;
  They have left my Saviour too;
Human hopes have oft deceived me;
  Thou art faithful, thou art true.

2 Perish, earthly fame and treasure,
  Come, disaster, scorn and pain:
In thy service, pain is pleasure;
  With thy favor, loss is gain:
O 'tis not in grief to harm me,
  While thy bleeding love I see;
O 'tis not in joy to charm me,
  When that love is hid from me.

391

LORD, dismiss us with thy blessing,
  Fill our hearts with joy and peace;
Let us each, thy love possessing,
  Triumph in redeeming grace;
O refresh us,
  Traveling through this wilderness.

2 Thanks we give and adoration,
  For thy Gospel's joyful sound;
May the fruits of thy salvation
  In our hearts and lives abound;
May thy presence
  With us evermore be found.

3 So, whene'er the signal's given,
  Us from earth to call away;
Borne on angel's wings to heaven,
  Glad to leave our cumbrous clay,
May we, ready,
  Rise and reign in endless day.

HYMNS 392, 393.

GREENVILLE. 8s & 7s, Double.

392 I.

COME, thou long expected Jesus,
　Born to set thy people free;
From our fears and sins release us,
　Let us find our rest in thee:
Israel's Strength and Consolation,
　Hope of all the saints thou art;
Dear Desire of every nation,
　Joy of every longing heart.

2 Born, thy people to deliver;
　Born a child, and yet a King;
Born to reign in us for ever,
　Now thy precious kingdom bring:
By thine own eternal Spirit,
　Rule in all our hearts alone;
By thine all-sufficient merit,
　Raise us to thy glorious throne.

393 I.

LOVE divine, all love excelling,
　Joy of heaven to earth come down;
Fix in us thy humble dwelling,
　All thy faithful mercies crown.
Jesus, thou art all compassion,
　Pure unbounded love thou art;
Visit us with thy salvation,
　Enter every longing heart.

2 Breathe, O breathe thy loving Spirit
　Into every troubled breast;
Let us all in thee inherit,
　Let us find thy promised rest:
Take away the love of sinning,
　Alpha and Omega be,
End of faith, as its beginning,
　Set our hearts at liberty.

HYMNS 394, 395, 396, 397.   309

3 Come, almighty to deliver,
    Let us now thy life receive,
  Suddenly return, and never
    Never more thy temples leave.
  Thee we would be always blessing,
    Serve thee as thine hosts above;
  Pray, and praise thee without ceasing,
    Glory in thy precious love.

4 Finish then thy new creation,
    Pure, unspotted may we be:
  Let us see our whole salvation
    Perfectly secured by thee:
  Changed from glory into glory,
    Till in heaven we take our place;
  Till we cast our crowns before thee,
    Lost in wonder, love and praise.

394   II.

GENTLY, Lord, O! gently lead us,
    Through this lonely vale of tears;
  Thro' the changes thou'st decreed us,
    Till our last great change appears.
  When temptation's darts assail us,
    When in devious paths we stray,
  Let thy goodness never fail us,
    Lead us in thy perfect way.

2 In the hour of pain and anguish,
    In the hour when death draws near,
  Suffer not our hearts to languish,
    Suffer not our souls to fear.
  And when mortal life is ended,
    Bid us in thine arms to rest,
  Till by angel bands attended,
    We awake among the blest.

395   II.

GLORIOUS things of thee are spoken,
    Zion, city of our God;
  He whose word cannot be broken,
    Formed thee for his own abode:
  On the Rock of Ages founded,
    What can shake thy sure repose?
  With salvation's walls surrounded,
    Thou may'st smile at all thy foes.

2 See the streams of living waters
    Springing from eternal love,
  Well supply thy sons and daughters,
    And all fear of want remove.
  Who can faint while such a river
    Ever flows their thirst to assuage;
  Grace, which like the Lord, the giver,
    Never fails from age to age?

3 Round each habitation hovering,
    See the clouds and fire appear,
  For a glory and a covering,
    Showing that the Lord is near:
  Thus deriving from their banner,
    Light by night, and shade by day;
  Safe they feed upon the manna [pray.
  Which he gives them when they

FOR SOCIAL AND PRIVATE WORSHIP.

396

CALL Jehovah thy salvation,
    Rest beneath th' Almighty's shade;
  In his secret habitation
    Dwell, and never be dismayed!
  There no tumult can alarm thee,
    Thou shalt dread no hidden snare;
  Guile nor violence can harm thee,
    In eternal safeguard there.

2 Thee,tho' winds and waves are swelling,
    God, thy Hope, shall bear thro' all;
  Plague shall not co..ne nigh thy dwell-
    Thee no evil shall befall.   [ing,
  He shall charge his angel legions
    Watch and ward o'er thee to keep,
  Tho' thou walk thro' hostile regions,
    Though in desert wilds thou sleep.

3 Since, with firm and pure affection,
    Thou on God hast set thy love,
  With the wings of his protection
    He shall shield thee from above.
  Thou shalt call on him in trouble,
    He will hearken, he will save,
  Here, for grief reward thee double,
    Crown with life beyond the grave.

397   *For Children only.*

TAKE my heart, O Father! take it;
    Make and keep it all thine own:
  Let thy Spirit melt and break it;
    Turn to flesh this heart of stone.
  Heavenly Father, deign to mould it
    In obedience to thy will;
  And, as passing years unfold it,
    Keep it meek and childlike still.

2 Father, make it pure and lowly,
    Peaceful, kind, and far from strife,
  Turning from the paths unholy
    Of this vain and sinful life.
  May the blood of Jesus heal it,
    And its sins be all forgiven:
  Holy Spirit, take and seal it;
    Guide it in the path to heaven.

HYMNS 398, 399, 400.

SICILIAN HYMN. 8s & 7s, or 8s, 7s, & 4s.

398 I.

CROWN his head with endless blessing,
  Who, in God the Father's name,
With compassions never ceasing,
  Comes salvation to proclaim.

2 Lo! Jehovah, we adore thee;
  Thee, our Saviour; thee, our God!
From his throne his beams of glory
  Shine through all the world abroad.

3 Jesus, thee our Saviour hailing,
  Thee, our God, in praise we own;
Highest honors, never failing,
  Rise eternal round thy throne.

4 Now, ye saints, his power confessing,
  In your grateful strains adore;
For his mercy, never ceasing,
  Flows, and flows for evermore.

399 I.

SAVIOUR, who thy flock art feeding
  With the shepherd's kindest care;
All the feeble gently leading,
  While the lambs thy bosom share;

2 Now, these little ones receiving,
  Fold them in thy gracious arm;
There we know, thy word believing,
  Only there secure from harm,

3 Never, from thy pasture roving,
  Let them be the lion's prey;
Let thy tenderness, so loving,
  Keep them all life's dangerous way.

4 Then within thy fold eternal
  Let them find a resting place;
Feed in pastures ever vernal;
  Drink the rivers of thy grace.

400 II.

LORD of every land and nation,
  Ancient of eternal days,
Sounded through the wide creation,
  Be thy just and awful praise.

2 For the grandeur of thy nature,
  Grand beyond a seraph's thought;
For created works of power,
  Works with skill and kindness wrought;

3 For thy providence, that governs
  Thro' thine empire's wide domain;
Wings an angel, guides a sparrow;
  Blessed be thy gentle reign.

4 But thy rich, thy free redemption,
  Dark through brightness all along;
Thought is poor, and poor expression:
  Who can sing that awful song?

5 Brightness of the Father's glory,
  Shall thy praise unuttered lie?
Fly, my tongue, such guilty silence;
  Sing the Lord, who came to die.

6 Did the angels sing thy coming?
 Did the shepherds learn their lays?
 Shame would cover me ungrateful,
 Should my tongue refuse to praise.

7 From the highest throne in glory!
 To the cross of deepest woe!
 All to ransom guilty captives!
 Flow, my praise, for ever flow.

8 Go, return, immortal Saviour,
 Leave thy footstool, take thy throne;
 Thence return, and reign for ever;
 Be the kingdom all thy own.

401   II.

JESUS hail, enthroned in glory,
 There forever to abide;
 All the heavenly hosts adore thee,
 Seated at thy Father's side.

2 There for sinners thou art pleading,
 There thou dost our place prepare;
 Ever for us interceding,
 Till in glory we appear.

3 Worship, honor, power and blessing,
 Thou art worthy to receive:
 Loudest praises without ceasing,
 Meet it is for us to give.

402   II.

ZION'S King shall reign victorious,
 All the earth shall own his sway;
 He will make his kingdom glorious,
 He shall reign through endless day.

2 See the ancient idols falling,
 Worshiped once, but now abhorred,
 Men on Zion's King are calling,
 Zion's King by all adored.

3 Then shall Israel all be saved,
 War and tumult then shall cease,
 While the greater Son of David
 Rules a conquered world in peace.

4 Mighty King thine arm revealing,
 Now thy glorious cause maintain;
 Bring the nations help and healing,
 Make them subject to thy reign!

5 Angels in their lofty station,
 Praise thy name, thou only wise;
 O let earth, with emulation,
 Join the triumph of the skies.

403   II.

GUIDE me, O thou great Jehovah,
 Pilgrim through this barren land;
 I am weak, but thou art mighty,
 Hold me with thy powerful hand:
  Bread of heaven,
 Feed me, till I want no more.

2 Open now the crystal fountain
 Whence the healing streams do flow,
 Let the fiery cloudy pillar
 Lead me all my journey through:
  Strong Deliverer,
 Be thou still my strength and shield.

3 When I tread the verge of Jordan,
 Bid my anxious fears subside:
 Death of death, and hell's destruction,
 Land me safe on Canaan's side;
  Songs of praises
 I will ever give to thee.

For Social and Private Worship.

404   *For Children Only.*

SAVIOUR, while my heart is tender,
 I would yield that heart to thee;
 All my powers to thee surrender,
 Thine and only thine to be.

2 Take me, now, Lord Jesus, take me,
 Let my youthful heart be thine:
 Thy devoted servant make me;
 Fill my soul with love divine.

3 May this solemn dedication
 Never once forgotten lie;
 Let it know no revocation,
 Published and confirmed on high.

4 Thine I am, O Lord, for ever,
 To thy service set apart;
 Suffer me to leave thee never;
 Seal thine image on my heart.

405

TARRY with me, O my Saviour!
 For the day is passing by;
 See! the shades of evening gather,
 And the night is drawing nigh.

2 Feeble, trembling, fainting, dying,
 Lord, I cast myself on thee;
 Tarry with me through the darkness;
 While I sleep, still watch by me.

3 Tarry with me, O my Saviour!
 Lay my head upon thy breast;
 Till the morning; then awake me—
 Morning of eternal rest!

TRUST. 8s & 7s.

406 I.

HAIL, thou once despised Jesus!
  Hail, thou Galilean King!
Thou didst suffer to release us;
  Thou didst free salvation bring.

2 Hail, thou agonizing Saviour,
    Bearer of our sin and shame!
  By thy merits we find favor,
    Life is given through thy name.

3 Paschal Lamb, by God appointed,
    All our sins on thee were laid;
  By almighty love anointed,
    Thou hast full atonement made.

4 All thy people are forgiven,
    Through the virtue of thy blood;
  Opened is the gate of heaven;
    Peace is made 'twixt man and God.

407 I.

LIGHT of those whose dreary dwell-
  Borders on the shades of death! [ing
Rise on us, thyself revealing,
  Rise and chase the clouds beneath.

2 Thou, of heaven and earth Creator!
    In our deepest darkness rise;
  Scatter all the night of nature;
    Pour the day upon our eyes.

3 Still we wait for thine appearing;
    Life and joy thy beams impart,
  Chasing all our fears, and cheering
    Every poor, benighted heart.

4 By thine all-sufficient merit,
    Every burdened soul release;
  Every weary, wandering spirit,
    Guide into thy perfect peace.

408 I.

HARK! what mean those holy voices,
  Sweetly sounding through the skies!
Lo! the angelic host rejoices,
  Heavenly hallelujahs rise.

2 Listen to the wondrous story
    Which they chant in hymns of joy;
  Glory in the highest, glory!
    Glory be to God most high!

3 Peace on earth, good will from heaven,
    Reaching far as man is found;
  Souls redeemed and sins forgiven,
    Loud our golden harps shall sound.

4 Christ is born, the great Anointed,
    Heaven and earth his praises sing;
  O! receive, whom God appointed,
    For your Prophet, Priest, and King.

5 Hasten mortals to adore him,
    Learn his name and taste his joy;
  Till in heaven ye sing before him,
    Glory be to God most high!

409 II.

1 LO! the Lord Jehovah liveth!
He's my rock, I bless his name:
He, my God, salvation giveth;
All ye lands, exalt his fame.

2 O'er his enemies exalted,
See the great Redeemer rise!
Though by powers of hell assaulted,
God supports him to the skies.

3 God, Messiah's cause maintaining,
Shall his righteous throne extend:
O'er the world the Saviour reigning,
Earth shall at his footstool bend.

FOR SOCIAL AND PRIVATE WORSHIP.

410

1 ONE there is, above all others
Well deserves the name of Friend;
His is love beyond a brother's,
Costly, free, and knows no end.

2 Which of all our friends, to save us,
Could or would have shed his blood?
But this Saviour died to have us
Reconciled in him to God.

3 When he lived on earth abased,
Friend of sinners was his name;
Now above all glory raised,
He rejoices in the same.

4 O! for grace our hearts to soften;
Teach us, Lord, at length to love;
We, alas! forget too often
What a friend we have above.

411

1 SWEET the moment, rich in blessing,
Which before the cross I spend,
Life, and health, and peace possessing,
From the sinner's dying friend.

2 Here I'll sit forever viewing
Mercy stream in streams of blood,
Precious drops, my soul bedewing,
Plead and claim my peace with God.

3 Here it is I find my heaven,
While upon the cross I gaze;
Love I much? I'm much forgiven,
I'm a miracle of grace.

4 Love and grief my heart dividing,
With my tears his feet I bathe;
Constant still in faith abiding,
Life deriving from his death.

412

1 KNOW, my soul, thy full salvation;
Rise o'er sin, and fear, and care;
Joy to find in every station
Something still to do or bear:

2 Think what Spirit dwells within thee;
Think what Father's smiles are thine;
Think that Jesus died to win thee:
Child of heaven, canst thou repine?

3 Haste thee on from grace to glory,
Armed by faith, and winged by prayer;
Heaven's eternal day before thee—
God's own hand shall guide thee there.

4 Soon shall close thine earthly mission,
Soon shall pass thy pilgrim days;
Hope shall change to glad fruition,
Faith to sight, and prayer to praise.

413

1 DREAD Jehovah! God of nations!
From thy temple in the skies,
Hear thy people's suplications,
Now for their deliverance rise.

2 Lo! with deep contrition turning,
Humbly at thy feet we bend;
Hear us, fasting, praying, mourning,
Hear us, spare us, and defend.

3 Tho' our sins, our hearts confounding,
Long and loud for vengeance call,
Thou hast mercy more abounding,
Jesus' blood can cleanse them all.

4 Let that love veil our transgressions,
Let that blood our guilt efface:
Save thy people from oppression,
Save from spoil thy holy place.

414 *For Children Only.*

1 JESUS, tender Shepherd, hear us;
Bless thy little lambs to-night:
Thro' the darkness be thou near us;
Keep us safe till morning light.

2 All this day thy hand has led us,
And we thank thee for thy care;
Thou hast clothed us, warned us, fed us,
Listen to our evening prayer. [

3 May our sins be all forgiven;
Bless the friends we love so well:
Take us, when we die, to heaven;
Happy there with thee to dwell.

ZION. 8s, 7s, & 4.

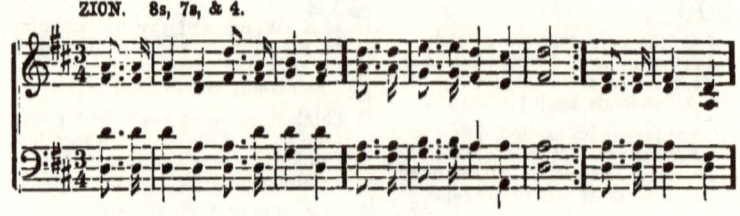

415   I.

ANGELS, from the realms of glory,
  Wing your flight o'er all the earth,
Ye who sang creation's story,
  Now proclaim Messiah's birth;
    Come and worship,
  Worship Christ the new-born King.

2 Shepherds, in the field abiding,
  Watching o'er your flocks by night,
God with man is now residing,
  Yonder shines the infant-light;
    Come and worship,
  Worship Christ the new-born King.

3 Sages, leave your contemplations,
  Brighter visions beam afar;
Seek the great Desire of nations;
  Ye have seen his natal star;
    Come and worship,
  Worship Christ the new-born King.

4 Saints, before the altar bending,
  Watching long in hope and fear,
Suddenly the Lord, descending,
  In his temple shall appear;
    Come and worship,
  Worship Christ the new-born King.

416   II.

ON the mountain's top appearing,
  Lo! the sacred herald stands,
Welcome news to Zion bearing—
  Zion, long in hostile lands:
    Mourning captive,
  God himself will loose thy bands.

2 Has thy night been long and mournful?
  Have thy friends unfaithful proved?
Have thy foes been proud and scornful?
  By thy sighs and tears unmoved?
    Cease thy mourning;
  Zion still is well beloved.

3 God, thy God, will now restore thee:
  He himself appears thy Friend;
All thy foes shall flee before thee;
  Here their boasts and triumphs end:
    Great deliverance
  Zion's King will surely send.

4 Peace and joy shall now attend thee:
  All thy warfare now is past;
God thy Saviour will defend thee;
  Victory is thine at last:
    All thy conflicts
  End in everlasting rest.

417   II.

O'ER the realms of pagan darkness,
  Let the eye of pity gaze;
See the kindreds of the people,
  Lost in sin's bewildering maze:
    Darkness brooding,
On the face of all the earth.

2 Light of them who sit in error,
  Rise and shine, thy blessings bring;
Light, to lighten all the Gentiles,
  Rise with healing in thy wing,
    To thy brightness
Let all kings and nations come.

3 Let the heathen, now adoring
  Idol-gods of wood and stone,
Come, and worshiping before him
  Serve the living God alone.
    Let thy glory
Fill the earth, as floods the sea.

4 Thou, to whom all power is given,
  Speak the word; at thy command,
Let the company of heralds
  Spread thy name from land to land:
    Lord, be with them,
Always, till time's latest end.

418   II.

CHRISTIAN! see—the orient morn-
  Breaks along the heathen sky; [ing
Lo! th' expected day is dawning—
  Glorious day-spring from on high:
    Hallelujah!
Hail the day-spring from on high!

2 Heathen at the sight are singing;
  Morning wakes the tuneful lays;
Precious offerings they are bringing,—
  First-fruits of more perfect praise:
    Hallelujah!—
Hail the day-spring from on high!

3 Zion's Sun! salvation beaming,
  Gilding now the radiant hills,—
Rise and shine, till brighter gleamings,
  All the world thy glory fills:
    Hallelujah!
Hail the day-spring from on high!

4 Lord of every tribe and nation!
  Spread thy truth from pole to pole,
Spread the light of thy salvation,
  Till it shine on every soul:
    Hallelujah!
Hail the day-spring from on high!

419   II.

LO! he comes, with clouds descend-
  Once for favored sinners slain; [ing,
Thousand thousand saints attending,
  Swell the triumph of his train;
    Hallelujah!
Jesus comes, and comes to reign.

2 Every eye shall now behold him,
  Robed in dreadful majesty;
Those who set at naught, and sold him,
  Pierced and nailed him to the tree,
    Deeply wailing,
Shall the true Messiah see.

3 Every island, sea and mountain,
  Heaven and earth shall flee away;
All who hate him must, confounded,
  Hear the trump proclaim the day:
    "Come to judgment!
Come to judgment! come away."

4 Now redemption, long expected,
  See, in solemn pomp appear:
All his saints by man rejected,
  Now shall meet him in the air
    Hallelujah!
See the day of God appear.

5 Mighty King, let all adore thee,
  High on thine eternal throne;
Saviour, take the power and glory,
  Claim the kingdom for thine own!
    O come quickly,
Hallelujah! come, Lord, come.

MARTYN. 7s, Double.

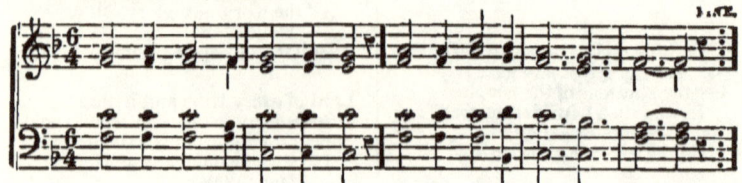

420 I.

JESUS, lover of my soul,
  Let me to thy bosom fly,
While the raging billows roll,
  While the tempest still is high.
Hide me, O my Saviour, hide,
  Till the storm of life is past;
Safe into the haven guide;
  O receive my soul at last.

2 Other refuge have I none,
  Hangs my helpless soul on thee;
Leave, ah! leave me not alone,
  Still support and comfort me;
All my trust on thee is staid,
  All my help from thee I bring;
Cover my defenceless head,
  With the shadow of thy wing.

3 Thou, O Christ, art all I want;
  All in all in thee I find;
Raise the fallen, cheer the faint,
  Heal the sick and lead the blind:
Just and holy is thy name,
  I am all unrighteousness;
Vile and full of sin I am,
  Thou art full of truth and grace.

4 Plenteous grace with thee is found,
  Grace to pardon all my sin;
Let the healing streams abound,
  Make and keep me pure within.

Thou of life the fountain art,
  Freely let me take of thee:
Spring thou up within my heart,
  Rise to all eternity.

421 II.

HOLY, holy, holy Lord [earth
  God of Hosts! when heaven and
Out of darkness, at thy word
  Issued into glorious birth,
All thy works before thee stood,
  And thine eye beheld them good;
While they sung with sweet accord,
  Holy, holy, holy Lord.

2 Holy, holy, holy! thee,
  One Jehovah evermore,
Father, Son, and Spirit! we,
  Dust and ashes, would adore:
Lightly by the world esteemed,
  From that world by thee redeemed,
Sing we here with glad accord,
  Holy, holy, holy Lord!

3 Holy, holy, holy! all   [sing,
  Heaven's triumphant choir shall
While the ransomed nations fall
  At the footstool of their King:
Then shall saints and seraphim,
  Harps and voices, swell one hymn,
Blending in sublime accord,
  Holy, holy, holy Lord!

422

HARK! the song of Jubilee;
 Loud as mighty thunders roar,
Or the fullness of the sea,
 When it breaks upon the shore :
Hallelujah! for the Lord,
 God omnipotent, shall reign;
Hallelujah! let the word
 Echo round the earth and main.

2 Hallelujah! hark! the sound,
 From the centre to the skies,
Wakes above, beneath, around,
 All creation's harmonies:
See Jehovah's banner's furled,
 Sheathed his sword: he speaks—'tis
And the kingdoms of this world [done,
 Are the kingdoms of his Son.

3 He shall reign from pole to pole,
 With illimitable sway;
He shall reign, when like a scroll
 Yonder heavens have passed away:
Then the end;—beneath his nod,
 Man's last enemy shall fall;
Hallelujah! Christ is God,
 God in Christ is all in all.

FOR SOCIAL AND PRIVATE WORSHIP.

423

PEOPLE of the living God,
 I have sought the world around,
Paths of sin and sorrow trod,
 Peace and comfort nowhere found :
Now to you my spirit turns,
 Turns a fugitive unblest;
Brethren, where your altar burns,
 O! receive me into rest.

2 Lonely, I no longer roam,
 Like the cloud, the wind, the wave;
Where you dwell shall be my home,
 Where you die shall be my grave.
Mine the God whom you adore,
 Your Redeemer shall be mine ;
Earth shall fill my soul no more,
 Every idol I resign.

3 Tell me not of gain or loss,
 Ease, enjoyment, pomp or power,
Welcome poverty and cross,
 Shame, reproach, affliction's hour:
"Follow me;" I know thy voice;
 Jesus, Lord, thy steps I see;
Now I take thy yoke, by choice;
 Light thy burden now to me.

424

WATCHMAN, tell us of the night,
 What its signs of promise are.
Traveller, o'er yon mountain's height,
 See that glory-beaming star.
Watchman, does its beauteous rays
 Aught of hope or joy foretell ?
Traveller, yes, it brings the day,
 Promised day of Israel.

2 Watchman tell us of the night ;
 Higher yet that star ascends.
Traveller, blessedness and light,
 Peace and truth, its course portends.
Watchman, will its beams alone
 Gild the spot that gave them birth ?
Traveller, ages are its own,
 See it bursts o'er all the earth.

3 Watchman, tell us of the night,
 For the morning seems to dawn.
Traveller, darkness takes its flight,
 Doubt and terror are withdrawn.
Watchman, let thy wanderings cease ;
 Hie thee to thy quiet home.
Traveller, lo! the Prince of peace,
 Lo! the Son of God is come.

425

WHILE with ceaseless course the sun
 Hasted through the former year,
Many souls their race have run,
 Never more to meet us here ;
Fixed in their eternal state,
 They have done with all below ;
We a little longer wait,
 But how little none can know.

2 As the winged arrow flies
 Speedily the mark to find ;
As the lightning from the skies
 Darts, and leaves no trace behind :
Swiftly thus our fleeting days
 Bear us down life's rapid stream;
Upward, Lord, our spirits raise;
 All below is but a dream.

3 Thanks for mercies past receive,
 Pardon of our sins renew ;
Teach us henceforth how to live
 With eternity in view.
Bless thy word to young and old,
 Fill us with a Saviour's love ;
And when life's short tale is told
 May we dwell with thee above.

M'ILVAINE. 7s.

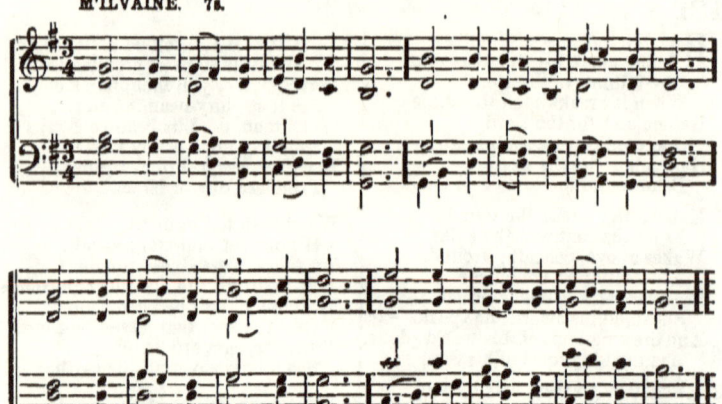

426   I.

BOUNDLESS glory, Lord, be thine;
Thou hast made the darkness shine:
Thou hast sent a cheering ray;
Thou hast turned our night to day.

2 Darkness long involved us round,
Till we knew the joyful sound:
Then our darkness fled away,
Chased by truth's effulgent ray.

3 They are blest, and none beside,
They who in the truth abide;
Clear the light that marks their way
Leading to eternal day.

4 Guide us, Saviour, through the road,
Till we reach the saint's abode;
Till we see thee throned above,
As thou art, the God of love.

427   II.

HARK! the herald angels say,
Christ the Lord is risen to-day;
Raise your joys and triumphs high,
Let the glorious tidings fly.

2 Love's redeeming work is done,
Fought the fight, the battle won;
Lo! the sun's eclipse is o'er,
Lo! he sets in blood no more.

3 Vain the stone, the watch, the seal;
Christ has burst the gates of hell:
Death in vain forbids him rise,
Christ has opened Paradise.

4 Lives again our glorious King;
Where, O death, is now thy sting?
Once he died our souls to save:
Where's thy victory, boasting grave?

5 What though once we perished all,
Partners of our parent's fall?
Second life we now receive,
And in Christ forever live.

6 Hail! thou dear almighty Lord,
Hail! thou great incarnate Word,
Hail! thou suffering Son of God,
Take the trophies of thy blood.

428   II.

LORD of hosts, how lovely fair,
E'en on earth thy temples are;
Here thy waiting people see
Much of heaven, and much of thee.

2 From thy gracious presence flows
Bliss that softens all our woes;
While thy Spirit's holy fire
Warms our hearts with pure desire.

3 Here we supplicate thy throne,
Here thou makest thy glories known;
Here we learn thy righteous ways,
Taste thy love, and sing thy praise.

4 Thus with sacred songs of joy,
  We our happy lives employ;
  Love and long to love thee more,
  Till from earth to heaven we soar.

429
II.

HOLY, holy, holy Lord,
  Be thy glorious name adored!
Lord, thy mercies never fail;
Hail, celestial Goodness, hail!

2 Though unworthy, Lord, thine ear,
  Deign our humble songs to hear:
  Purer praise we hope to bring,
  When around thy throne we sing.

3 While on earth ordained to stay,
  Guide our footsteps in thy way,
  Till we come to dwell with thee,
  Till we all thy glory see.

4 Then with angel-harps again;
  We will wake a nobler strain;
  There, in joyful songs of praise,
  Our triumphant voices raise.

FOR SOCIAL AND PRIVATE WORSHIP.

430

LORD, we come before thee now,
  At thy feet we humbly bow;
O do not our suit disdain;
Shall we seek thee, Lord, in vain?

2 Lord, on thee our souls depend;
  In compassion now descend;
  Fill our hearts with thy rich grace;
  Tune our lips to sing thy praise.

3 In thine own appointed way,
  Now we seek thee, here we stay;
  Lord, we know not how to go,
  Till a blessing thou bestow.

4 Send some message from thy word
  That may joy and peace afford;
  Let thy Spirit now impart
  Full salvation to each heart.

431

JESUS, all-atoning Lamb,
  Thine, and only thine, I am:
Take my body, spirit, soul;
Only thou possess the whole.

2 Thou my one thing needful be;
  Let me ever cleave to thee;
  Let me choose the better part:
  Let me give thee all my heart.

3 Whom have I on earth below?
  Thee, and only thee, I know:
  Whom have I in heaven but thee?
  Thou art all in all to me.

432

TO thy pastures fair and large,
  Heavenly Shepherd, lead thy charge,
And my couch with tenderest care,
'Mid the springing grass prepare.

2 When I faint with summer's heat,
  Thou shalt guide my weary feet
  To the streams that, still and slow,
  Through the verdant meadows flow.

3 Safe the dreary vale I tread,
  By the shades of death o'erspread,
  With thy rod and staff supplied,
  This my guard—and that my guide.

4 Constant to thy latest end,
  Thou my footsteps shall attend;
  And shalt bid thy hallowed dome
  Yield me an eternal home.

433

SOVEREIGN Ruler of the skies,
  Ever gracious, ever wise!
All my times are in thy hand,
All events at thy command.

2 Times of sickness, times of health,
  Times of penury and wealth;
  Times of trial and of grief;
  Times of triumph and relief;

3 Times the tempter's power to prove;
  Times to taste a Saviour's love;
  All must come, and last, and end,
  As shall please my heavenly Friend.

4 Thee at all times will I bless;
  Having thee, I all possess;
  How can I bereaved be
  Since I cannot part with thee!

434

SOFTLY now the light of day
  Fades upon my sight away;
Free from care, from labor free,
Lord, I would commune with thee.

2 Soon, for me, the light of day
  Shall for ever pass away:
  Then, from sin and sorrow free,
  Take me, Lord, to dwell with thee.

PLEYEL'S HYMN. 7s.

435   I.

1 GOD with us! O glorious name!
  Let it shine in endless fame:
  God and man in Christ unite;
  O mysterious depth and height!

2 God with us! the eternal Son
  Took our soul, our flesh and bone:
  Now, ye Saints, his grace admire,
  Swell the song with holy fire.

3 God with us! but tainted not
  With the first transgressor's blot;
  Yet did he our sins sustain,
  Bear the guilt, the curse, the pain.

4 God with us! O wondrous grace!
  Let us see him face to face:
  That we may Immanuel sing,
  As we ought, our God and King.

436   I.

1 HARK! the herald angels sing,
  Glory to the new-born King!
  Peace on earth and mercy mild,
  God and sinners reconciled.

2 Joyful, all ye nations rise,
  Join the triumphs of the skies,
  With the angelic host proclaim,
  "Christ is born in Bethlehem!"

3 Christ, by highest heaven adored,
  Christ, the everlasting Lord;
  Late in time behold him come,
  Offspring of a virgin's womb.

4 Veiled in flesh, the Godhead see,
  Lo! the incarnate Deity!
  Pleased as man with men to appear,
  Jesus, our Immanuel here.

5 Mild, he lays his glory by,
  Born, that man no more may die;
  Born to raise the sons of earth,
  Born to give them second birth.

6 Come, Desire of nations, come,
  Fix in us thy humble home;
  Rise, the woman's conquering Seed,
  Bruise in us the serpent's head.

437   I.

1 GRACIOUS Spirit! Love divine,
  Let thy light within me shine;
  All my guilty fears remove,
  Fill me full of heaven and love.

2 Speak thy pardoning grace to me,
  Set the burdened sinner free;
  Lead me to the Lamb of God,
  Wash me in his precious blood.

3 Life and peace to me impart,
  Seal salvation on my heart;
  Breathe thyself into my breast,
  Earnest of immortal rest.

4 Let me never from thee stray,
　Keep me in the narrow way;
　Fill my soul with joy divine,
　Keep me, Lord, forever thine.

438　II.

LO! the stone is rolled away,
　Death yields up his mighty prey;
Jesus, rising from the tomb,
Scatters all its fearful gloom.

2 Praise him, ye celestial choirs,
　Praise and sweep your golden lyres;
　Praise him in the noblest songs,
　From ten thousand thousand tongues.

3 Every note with rapture swell,
　And the Saviour's triumph tell;
　Where, O death, is now thy sting?
　Where thy terrors, vanquished king?

4 Let Immanuel be adored,
　Ransom, Mediator, Lord!
　To creation's utmost bound
　Let the eternal praise resound.

439　II.

WAKE the song of jubilee,
　Let it echo o'er the sea!
Now is come the promised hour;
Jesus reigns with glorious power!

2 All ye nations, join and sing,
　Praise your Saviour, praise your King,
　Let it sound from shore to shore,—
　"Jesus reigns for evermore!"

3 Hark! the desert lands rejoice;
　And the islands join their voice;
　Joy! the whole creation sings,—
　"Jesus is the King of kings!"

440　II.

ALL ye nations, praise the Lord!
　All ye lands, your voices raise;
Heaven and earth with loud accord,
　Praise the Lord—for ever praise!

2 For his truth and mercy stand,
　Past, and present, and to be,
Like the years of his right hand,
　Like his own eternity.

441　II.

HAIL the day that sees him rise,
　Glorious, to his native skies!
Christ, awhile to mortals given,
Enters now the gates of heaven.

2 There the glorious triumph waits;
　Lift your heads, eternal gates!
　Christ hath vanquished death and sin;
　Take the King of glory in.

3 See, the heaven its Lord receives!
　Yet he loves the earth he leaves:
　Though returning to his throne,
　Still he calls mankind his own.

4 Still for us he intercedes,
　His prevailing death he pleads;
　Near himself prepares our place,
　Great Fore-runner of our race.

442　II.

CHILDREN of the heavenly King,
　As ye journey sweetly sing:
Sing your Saviour's worthy praise,
Glorious in his works and ways.

2 Ye are traveling home to God,
　In the way the fathers trod;
　They are happy now, and ye
　Soon their happiness shall see.

3 Shout ye little flock, and blest,
　Soon you'll enter into rest;
　There your seat is now prepared,
　There your kingdom and reward.

4 Fear not, brethren, joyful stand
　On the borders of your land;
　Jesus Christ, our Father's Son,
　Bids us undismayed go on.

5 Lord, submissive make us go,
　Gladly leaving all below;
　Only thou our leader be,
　And we still will follow thee.

FOR SOCIAL AND PRIVATE WORSHIP.

443

FOR the mercies of the day,
　For this rest upon our way,
Thanks to thee alone be given,
Lord of earth and King of heaven.

2 Let these earthly Sabbaths prove
　Fore-tastes of our joys above;
　While their steps thy children bend
　To the rest which knows no end.

TOPLADY. 7s, 6 lines.

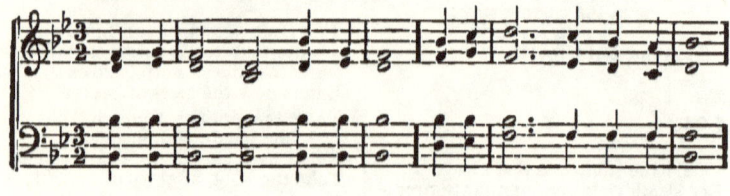

444   I.

ROCK of ages, cleft for me,
  Let me hide myself in thee;
Let the water and the blood,
From thy wounded side which flowed,
Be of sin the double cure:
Cleanse me from its guilt and power.

2 Not the labor of my hands
  Can fulfil the law's demands;
  Could my zeal no respite know,
  Could my tears for ever flow,
  All for sin could not atone,
  Thou must save, and thou alone.

3 Nothing in my hand I bring,
  Simply to thy cross I cling;
  Naked, come to thee for dress,
  Helpless, look to thee for grace;
  Vile, I to the fountain fly,
  Wash me, Saviour, or I die.

4 While I draw this fleeting breath,
  When my heart-strings break in death,
When I soar to worlds unknown,
See thee on thy judgment-throne,
Rock of ages, cleft for me,
Let me hide myself in thee.

445   II.

GOD of mercy, God of grace!
  Show the brightness of thy face:
Shine upon us, Saviour! shine;
Fill thy church with light divine;
And thy saving health extend
To the earth's remotest end.

2 Let the people praise thee, Lord!
  Be by all that live adored:
  Let the nations shout and sing,
  Glory to their Saviour King;
  At thy feet their tribute pay,
  And thy holy will obey.

3 Let the people praise thee, Lord!
  Earth shall then her fruits afford;
  God to man his blessing give,
  Man to God devoted live;

All below, and all above,
One in joy, and light, and love.

446
II.

BREAD of heaven, on thee I feed,
For thy flesh is meat indeed ;
Ever may my soul be fed,
With the true and living Bread :
Day by day with strength supplied,
Through the life of him that died.

2 Vine of heaven, thy blood supplies
This blest cup of sacrifice ;
'Tis thy wounds my healing give ;
To thy cross I look and live :
Thou, my life, O let me be
Rooted, grounded, built on thee.

FOR SOCIAL AND PRIVATE WORSHIP.

447

SON of God! to thee I cry :
By the holy mystery
Of thy dwelling here on earth,
By thy pure and holy birth,
Hear, oh, hear my lowly plea :
Manifest thyself to me !

2 Lamb of God! to thee I cry :
By thy bitter agony,
By thy pangs to us unknown,
By thy spirit's parting groan,
Hear, oh, hear my lowly plea :
Manifest thyself to me !

3 Prince of Life ! to thee I cry :
By thy glorious majesty,
By thy triumph o'er the grave,
Meek to suffer, strong to save,
Hear, oh, hear my fervid plea :
Manifest thyself to me !

448

RISE, my soul, and stretch thy wings,
Thy better portion trace ;
Rise from transitory things,
Towards heaven thy native place :
Sun and moon and stars decay ;
Time shall soon this earth remove :
Rise, my soul, and haste away,
To seats prepared above.

2 Rivers to the ocean run,
Nor stay in all their course ;
Fire ascending seeks the sun ;
Both speed them to their source :
So a soul that's born of God,
Pants to view his glorious face,
Upward tends to his abode,
To rest in his embrace.

3 Cease, ye pilgrims, cease to mourn ;
Press onward to the prize ;
Soon our Saviour will return ;
Triumphant in the skies.
Yet a season, and you know,
Happy entrance will be given ;
All our sorrows left below,
And earth exchanged for heaven.

449

CHRIST, whose glory fills the skies,
Christ, the true, the only Light,
Sun of righteousness, arise,
Triumph o'er the shades of night ;
Day-spring from on high, be near,
Day-star in my heart appear.

2 Dark and cheerless is the morn,
If thy light be hid from me ;
Joyless is the day's return,
Till thy mercy's beams I see—
Till they inward light impart,
Peace and gladness to my heart.

3 Visit then this soul of mine,
Pierce the gloom of sin and grief,
Fill me, O thou light divine,
Scatter all my unbelief ;
More and more thyself display,
Shining to the perfect day.

450

SAFELY through another week,
God has brought us on our way ;
Let us now a blessing seek,
On th' approaching Sabbath-day :
Day of all the week the best,
Emblem of eternal rest.

2 While we seek supplies of grace,
Through the dear Redeemer's name,
Show thy reconciled face,
Take away our sin and shame :
From our worldly cares set free,
May we rest this night in thee.

3 When the morn shall bid us rise,
Let us feel thy presence near ;
May thy glory meet our eyes,
When we in thy house appear :
There afford us, Lord, a taste
Of our everlasting feast.

4 May the gospel's joyful sound
Conquer sinners, comfort saints ;
Make the fruits of grace abound,
Bring relief from all complaints :
Such let all our Sabbaths prove
Till we join the church above.

451   I.

O SACRED Head, now wounded,
    With grief and shame weigh'd down!
Now scornfully surrounded
    With thorns—thine only crown!
O sacred Head, what glory!
    What bliss, till now, was thine!
Yet, though despised and gory,
    I joy to call thee mine.

2 How art thou pale with anguish,
    With sore abuse and scorn!
How does that visage languish
    Which once was bright as morn!
Thy grief and thy compassion
    Were all for sinners' gain;
Mine, mine was the transgression,
    But thine the deadly pain.

3 What language shall I borrow
    To thank thee dearest Friend,
For this thy dying sorrow,—
    Thy pity without end!
Lord, make me thine for ever,
    Nor let me faithless prove;
O let me never, never
    Abuse such dying love.

4 And when I am departing,
    O part not thou from me;
When mortal pangs are darting,
    Come, Lord, and set me free!
These eyes new faith receiving,
    From Jesus shall not move,
For he who dies believing,
    Dies safely, through thy love.

452 II.

HAIL to the Lord's Anointed!
  Great David's greater Son!
Hail, in the time appointed,
  His reign on earth begun!
He comes to break oppression,
  To set the captive free;
To take away transgression,
  And rule in equity.

2 He comes with succor speedy
    To those who suffer wrong;
  To help the poor and needy,
    And bid the weak be strong;
  To give them songs for sighing,
    Their darkness turn to light,
  Whose souls, condemned and dying,
    Were precious in his sight.

3 Kings shall fall down before him,
    And gold and incense bring:
  All nations shall adore him,
    His praise all people sing.
  For him shall prayer unceasing,
    And daily vows ascend;
  His kingdom still increasing,
    A kingdom without end.

4 O'er every foe victorious,
    He on his throne shall rest,
  From age to age more glorious,
    All-blessing and all-blest;
  The tide of time shall never
    His covenant remove;
  His name shall stand for ever,
    That name to us is—LOVE.

453 II.

FROM Greenland's icy mountains,
  From India's coral strand;
Where Afric's sunny fountains
  Roll down their golden sand;
From many an ancient river,
From many a palmy plain,
They call us to deliver
Their land from error's chain.

2 What, though the spicy breezes
    Blow soft o'er Ceylon's isle,
  Though every prospect pleases,
    And only man is vile;
  In vain with lavish kindness,
    The gifts of God are strown;
  The heathen, in his blindness,
    Bows down to wood and stone.

3 Shall we, whose souls are lighted
    With wisdom from on high,
  Shall we, to men benighted,
    The lamp of life deny?

Salvation! O salvation!
  The joyful sound proclaim,
Till earth's remotest nation
  Has learned Messiah's name.

4 Waft, waft, ye winds, his story,
    And you, ye waters, roll,
  Till like a sea of glory,
    It spreads from pole to pole;
  Till o'er our ransomed nature,
    The Lamb for sinners slain,
  Redeemer, King, Creator,
    In bliss returns to reign.

454 II.

GOD is my strong salvation,
  What foe have I to fear?
In darkness and temptation,
  My light, my help is near:
Though hosts encamp around me,
  Firm to the fight I stand:
What terror can confound me,
  With God at my right hand?

2 Place on the Lord reliance,
    My soul, with courage wait:
  His truth be thine affiance,
    When faint and desolate:
  His might thine heart shall strengthen,
    His love thy joy increase;
  Mercy thy days shall lengthen,
    "The Lord will give thee peace."

455 II.

FOR thee, O dear, dear Country,
  Mine eyes their vigils keep;
For very love beholding
  Thy happy name they weep:
The mention of thy glory
  Is unction to the breast,
It brings us joy in sorrow,
  And love, and life, and rest.

2 There is the throne of David,
    And there, from toil released,
  The shout of them that triumph,
    The song of them that feast:
  There those who, thro' their Leader,
    Have conquered in the fight,
  For ever and for ever
    Are clad in robes of white.

3 Their breasts are filled with gladness,
    Their tongues the gladness prove,
  Their one and only anthem,
    The dear Redeemer's love.
  There we our King and Portion,
    In fulness of his grace,
  Shall soon behold for ever,
    And worship face to face!

AMERICA. 6s & 4s.

456 I.

COME, thou almighty King,
  Help us thy name to sing,
    Help us to praise.
Father all glorious,
O'er all victorious,
Come, and reign over us,
    Ancient of Days.

2 Come, thou incarnate Word,
Gird on thy mighty sword;
    Our prayer attend.
Come, and thy people bless,
And give thy word success;
Spirit of holiness,
    On us descend.

3 Come, Holy Comforter,
Thy sacred witness bear,
    In this glad hour.
Thou, who almighty art,
Now rule in every heart,
And ne'er from us depart,
    Spirit of power.

4 To the great One in Three
The highest praises be,
    Hence evermore.
His sovereign majesty
May we in glory see,
And to eternity
    Love and adore.

457 I.

COME, Holy Ghost,—in love
  Shed on us from above
Thine own bright ray!
Divinely good thou art;
Thy sacred gifts impart
To gladden each sad heart:
    Oh, come to-day!

2 Come, Light serene and still,
Our inmost bosoms fill;
    Dwell in each breast:
We know no dawn but thine;
Send forth thy beams divine,
On our dark souls to shine,
    And make us blest!

3 Exalt our low desires;
Extinguish passion's fires;
    Heal every wound:
Our stubborn spirits bend;
Our icy coldness end;
Our devious steps attend,
    While heavenward bound.

4 Come, all the faithful bless;
Let all, who Christ confess,
    His praise employ:
Give virtue's rich reward;
Victorious death accord,
And, with our glorious Lord,
    Eternal joy.

458 I.

SHEPHERD of tender youth,
  Guiding in love and truth
Through devious ways—
Christ our triumphant King,
We come thy name to sing,

And here our children bring,
  To shout thy praise.
2 Thou art our holy Lord,
  O all-subduing Word,
    Healer of strife:
  Thou didst thyself abase,
  That from sin's deep disgrace
  Thou mightest save our race,
    And give us life.
3 Ever be near our side,
  Our Shepherd and our Guide,
    Our staff and song;
  Jesus, thou Christ of God,
  By thine enduring word
  Lead us where thou hast trod;
    Make our faith strong.
4 So now, and till we die,
  Sound we thy praises high,
    And joyful sing:
  Let all the holy throng,
  Who to thy church belong,
  Unite and swell the song
    To Christ our King!

459 II.

GLORY to God on high!
  Let earth and skies reply,
    Praise ye his name;
  His love and grace adore,
  Who all our sorrows bore:
  Sing loud for evermore,
    Worthy the Lamb.
2 Jesus, our Lord and God,
  Bore sin's tremendous load,
    Praise ye his name;
  Tell what his arm has done,
  What spoils from death he won:
  Sing his great name alone,
    Worthy the Lamb.
3 While they around the throne
  Cheerfully join in one,
    Praising his name;
  Those who have felt his blood,
  Sealing their peace with God,
  Sound his dear fame abroad,
    Worthy the Lamb.
4 Join, all ye ransomed race,
  Our holy Lord to bless;
    Praise ye his name;
  In him we will rejoice,
  And make a joyful noise,
  Shouting with heart and voice,
    Worthy the Lamb.

460 II.

THOU, whose almighty word
  Chaos and darkness heard,
    And took their flight,
  Hear us, we humbly pray,
  And, where the gospel day
  Sheds not its glorious ray,
    "Let there be light."
2 Thou, who didst come to bring,
    On thy redeeming wing,
      Healing and sight,
  Health to the sick in mind,
  Sight to the inly blind,
  Oh, now to all mankind
    "Let there be light."
3 Spirit of truth and love,
  Life-giving, Holy Dove,
    Speed forth thy flight;
  Move on the water's face,
  Bearing the lamp of grace;
  And in earth's darkest place
    "Let there be light."

FOR SOCIAL AND PRIVATE WORSHIP.

461

MY faith looks up to thee,
  Thou Lamb of Calvary,
    Saviour divine:
  Now hear me while I pray;
  Take all my guilt away;
  O let me from this day
    Be wholly thine.
2 May thy rich grace impart
  Strength to my fainting heart,
    My zeal inspire:
  As thou hast died for me,
  O may my love to thee,
  Pure, warm, and changeless be—
    A living fire.
3 While life's dark maze I tread,
  And griefs around me spread,
    Be thou my guide;
  Bid darkness turn to day,
  Wipe sorrow's tears away,
  Nor let me ever stray
    From thee aside.
4 When ends life's transient dream,
  When death's cold, sullen stream
    Shall o'er me roll;
  Blest Saviour, then, in love,
  Fear and distrust remove;
  O bear me safe above—
    A ransomed soul.

WAREHAM. 11s & 8s.

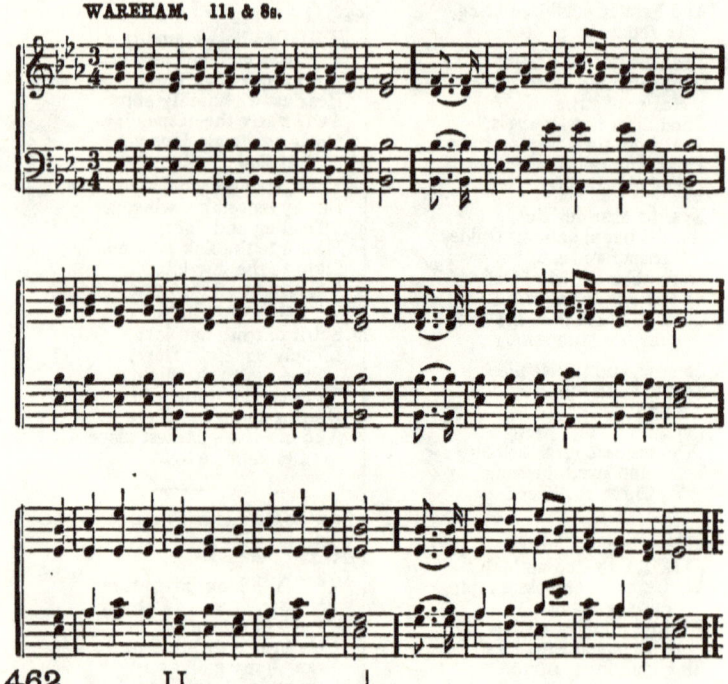

462   II.

O THOU, in whose presence my soul takes delight,
On whom in affliction I call; [night,
My comfort by day, and my song in the
My hope, my salvation, my all.

2 O, why should I wander, an alien from
Or cry in the desert for bread? [thee,
Thy foes will rejoice when my sorrows
    they see,
And smile at the tears I have shed.

3 Ye daughters of Zion, declare, have
    you seen,
The star that on Israel shone?
Say, if in your tents my Beloved has been,
And where with his flock he has gone.

4 His voice, as the sound of the dulcimer
    sweet,
Is heard thro' the shadows of death;
The cedars of Lebanon bow at his feet,
The air is perfumed with his breath.

For Social and Private Worship.

463   *For Children only.*

I THINK, when I read that sweet story
    of old,
When Jesus was here among men,
How he called little children as lambs to
    his fold, [then.
I should like to have been with them

2 I wish that his hands had been placed
    on my head, [me,
That his arm had been thrown around
And that I might have seen his kind look
    when he said,
"Let the little ones come unto me."

3 Yet still to his footstool in prayer I may
    go,
And ask for a share in his love;
And if I thus earnestly seek him below,
    I shall see him and hear him above.

LYONS. 10s & 11s.

464 II.

OH, worship the King, all-glorious above; [love!
Oh, gratefully sing his power and his
Our Shield and Defender, the Ancient of Days,
Pavilioned in splendor, and girded with praise.

2 Oh, tell of his might, oh, sing of his grace,
Whose robe is the light, whose canopy space!
His chariots of wrath the deep thunderclouds form,
And dark is his path on the wings of the storm.

3 Frail children of dust, and feeble as frail,
In thee do we trust, nor find thee to fail;
Thy mercies how tender! how firm to the end!
Our Maker, Defender, Redeemer, and Friend.

465 II.

YE servants of God, your Master proclaim,
And publish abroad his wonderful name:
The name all-victorious of Jesus extol:
His kingdom is glorious, he rules over all.

2 God ruleth on high, almighty to save;
And still he is nigh—his presence we have:
The great congregation his triumph shall sing,
Ascribing salvation to Jesus our King.

3 Then let us adore, and give him his right,
All glory and power, and wisdom and might,
All honor and blessing, with angels above,
And thanks never ceasing, for infinite love.

PORTUGUESE HYMN. 11s.

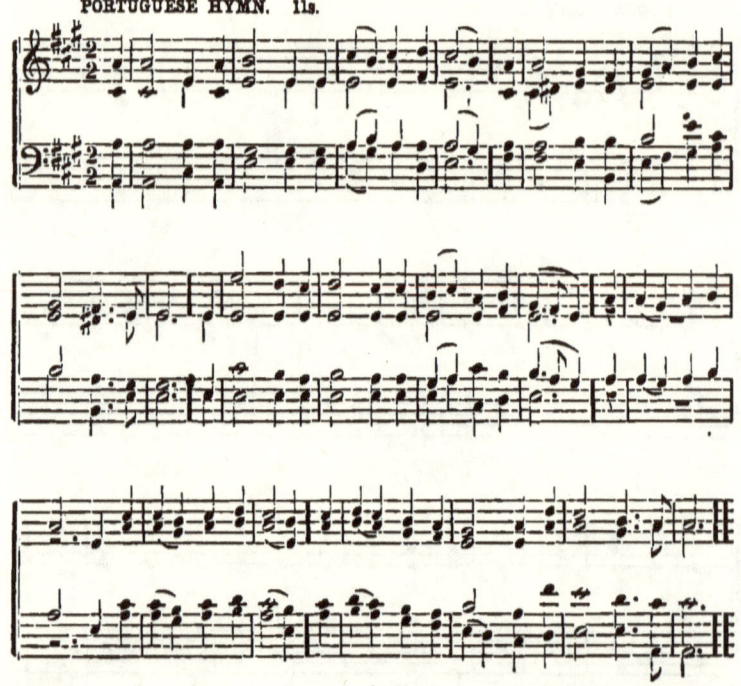

466   I.

THE Lord is my Shepherd, no want
   shall I know,   [rest;
I feed in green pastures, safe-folded I
He leadeth my soul where the still waters
   flow,
Restores me when wandering, redeems
   when oppressed.
2 Thro' the valley and shadow of death
   tho' I stray,   [fear,
Since thou art my guardian, no evil I
Thy rod shall defend me, thy staff be my
   stay,
No harm can befall, with my Comforter
   near.
3 Let goodness and mercy, my bountiful
   God,
Still follow my steps till I meet thee
   above: [trod,
I seek, by the path which my forefathers
Through the land of their sojourn thy
   kingdom of love.

467   I.

BRIGHTEST and best of the sons of
   the morning!
Dawn on our darkness and lend us
   thine aid;
Star of the east, the horizon adorning,
Guide where our infant Redeemer is
   laid.

2 Cold on his cradle the dew-drops are
   shining;
Low lies his head with the beasts of
   the stall;
Angels adore him in slumber reclining,
Maker, and Monarch, and Saviour of
   all.

3 Say, shall we yield him, in costly devotion?
Odors of Edom, and offerings divine?
Gems of the mountain, and pearls of the
   ocean,
Myrrh from the forest, or gold from the
   mine?

4 Vainly we offer each ample oblation,
Vainly with gold would his favor
   secure;
Richer by far is the heart's adoration,
Dearer to God are the prayers of the
   poor.

468 I.

HITHER, ye faithful, haste with songs of triumph,
To Bethlehem go, the Lord of life to meet;
To you this day is born a Prince and Saviour;
O come, and let us worship at his feet.

2 O Jesus, for such wondrous condescension,
Our praise and reverence are an offering meet;
Now is the Word made flesh, and dwells among us;
O come, and let us worship at his feet.

3 Shout his almighty name, ye choirs of angels,
Let the celestial courts his praise repeat:
Unto our God be glory in the highest;
O come, and let us worship at his feet.

469 I.

COME, ye disconsolate, where'er ye languish,
Come to the mercy-seat, fervently kneel,
Here bring your wounded hearts, here tell your anguish;
Earth has no sorrows that heaven cannot heal.

2 Joy of the desolate, Light of the straying,
Hope of the penitent, fadeless and pure,
Here speaks the Comforter, in mercy saying,
Earth has no sorrows that heaven cannot cure.

3 Here see the bread of life; see waters flowing
Forth from the throne of God, boundless in love:
Come to the feast prepared; come, ever knowing,
Earth has no sorrows, but heaven can remove.

470 II.

DAUGHTER of Zion, awake from thy sadness; [no more;
Awake, for thy foes shall oppress thee
Bright o'er thy hills dawns the day-star of gladness,
Arise, for the night of thy sorrow is o'er.

2 Daughter of Zion, the Power that hath saved thee,
Extolled with the harp and the timbrel should be;

Shout, for the foe is destroyed that enslaved thee,
Th' oppressor is vanquished, and Zion is free.

FOR SOCIAL AND PRIVATE WORSHIP.

471

I WOULD not live alway: I ask not to stay
Where storm after storm rises dark o'er the way;
The few lurid mornings that dawn on us here,
Are enough for life's woes, full enough for its cheer.

2 I would not live alway, thus fettered by sin;
Temptation without and corruption within:
E'en the rapture of pardon is mingled with fears,
And the cup of thanksgiving with penitent tears.

3 I would not live alway; no—welcome the tomb,
Since Jesus hath lain there I dread not its gloom;
There, sweet be my rest, till he bid me arise,
To hail him in triumph descending the skies.

4 Who, who would live alway, away from his God;
Away from yon heaven, that blissful abode,
Where the rivers of pleasure flow o'er the bright plains,
And the noontide of glory eternally reigns;

5 Where the saints of all ages in harmony meet,
Their Saviour and brethren transported to greet;
While the anthems of rapture unceasingly roll,
And the smile of the Lord is the feast of the soul.

472

NEARER, my God, to thee, nearer to thee!
E'en tho' it be a cross that raiseth me;
Still all my song shall be,
Nearer, my God, to thee, nearer to thee.

HYMN 473.

A SAVIOUR EVER NEAR.

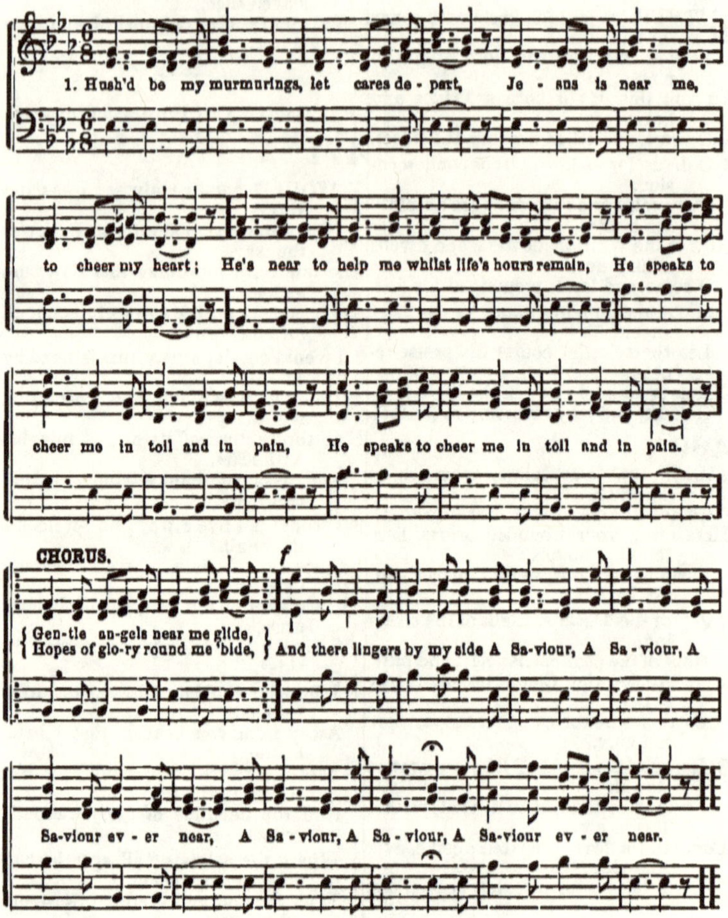

1. Hush'd be my murmurings, let cares depart, Jesus is near me, to cheer my heart; He's near to help me whilst life's hours remain, He speaks to cheer me in toil and in pain, He speaks to cheer me in toil and in pain.

CHORUS.

Gentle angels near me glide, Hopes of glory round me 'bide, And there lingers by my side A Saviour, A Saviour, A Saviour ever near, A Saviour, A Saviour, A Saviour ever near.

473   For Social and Private Worship.

2 Why should I languish—why should I fear?
In sorrow and anguish he's ever near;
Sleeping or waking—in pleasure or pain,
Roaming or resting, he'll near me remain.
  Chorus.—Gentle angels, &c.

3 Scenes that will vanish smile on me now,
Joys of a moment play round my brow,
But soon in heaven he'll meet me again,
There'll end my sorrow, and there'll end my pain.
  Chorus.—Gentle angels, &c.

CHILDREN IN HEAVEN.

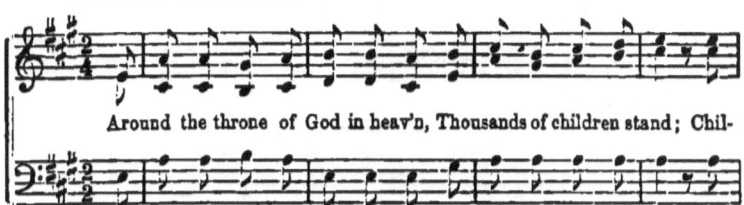

Around the throne of God in heav'n, Thousands of children stand; Chil-

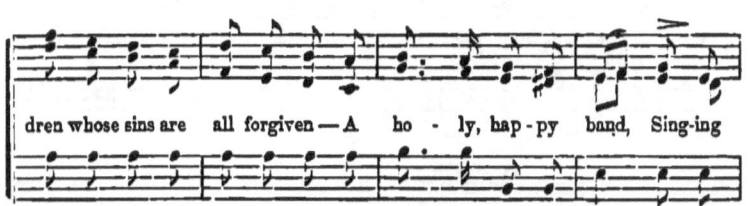

dren whose sins are all forgiven—A ho - ly, hap-py band, Sing-ing

glo - ry, glo - ry, glo - ry be to God on high.

474 *For Children Only.*

2 In flowing robes of spotless white,
    See every one arrayed;
  Dwelling in everlasting light,
    And joys that never fade.
            Singing, &c.

3 What bro't them to that world above?
    That heaven so bright and fair,
  Where all is peace, and joy, and love—
    How came those children there?
            Singing, &c.

4 Because the Saviour shed his blood,
    To wash away their sin:
  Bathed in that pure and precious flood,
    Behold them white and clean!
            Singing, &c,

5 On earth they sought the Saviour's
    On earth they loved his name;[grace,
  So now they see his blessed face,
    And stand before the Lamb.
            Singing, &c.

HYMN 475.

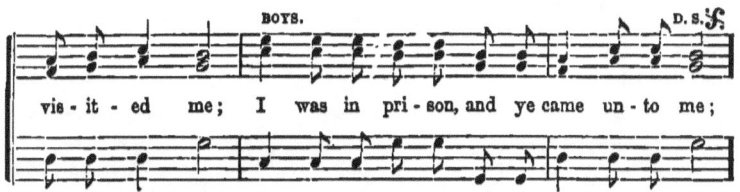

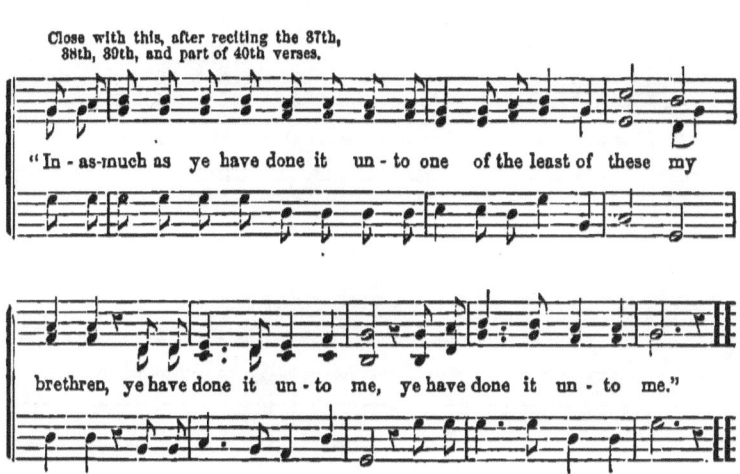

475   *Charity Hymn for Children.*—MATT. XXV, 34–40.

37 Then shall the righteous answer him, saying:
Lord, when saw we thee an hungered, and fed thee?
Or thirsty, and gave thee drink?

38 When saw we thee a stranger, and took thee in?
Or naked, and clothed thee?

39 Or when saw we thee sick, or in prison, and came unto thee?

40 And the King shall answer, and say unto them:
Verily I say unto you, Inasmuch, &c.

REST FOR THE WEARY.

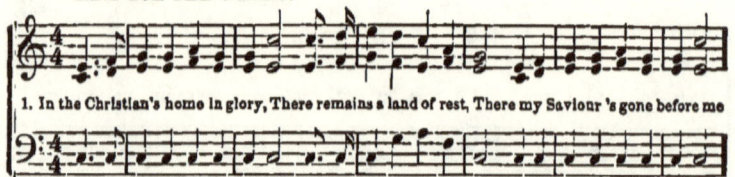

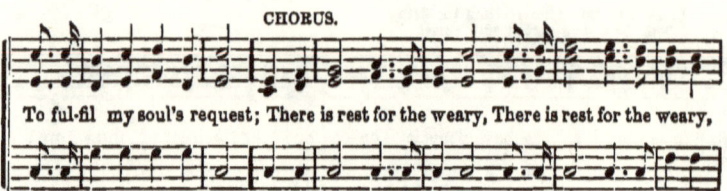

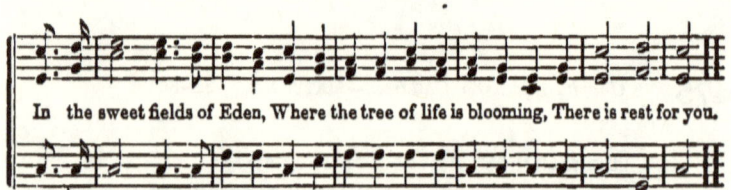

476   For Social and Private Worship.

2 He is fitting up my mansion,
   Which eternally shall stand,
For my stay shall not be transient
   In that holy, happy land.
     There is rest, &c.

3 Pain nor sickness ne'er shall enter,
   Grief nor woe my lot shall share;
But in that celestial centre,
   I a crown of life shall wear.
     There is rest, &c.

4 Death itself shall then be vanquished,
   And his sting shall be withdrawn;
Shout for gladness, O ye ransomed,
   Hail with joy the rising morn.
     There is rest, &c.

5 Sing, O sing, ye heirs of glory;
   Shout your triumph as you go;
Zion's gates will open for you,
   You shall find an entrance through.
     There is rest, &c.

HYMN 477.   337

SAVIOUR, LIKE A SHEPHERD LEAD US.

1. Sa-viour like a shepherd lead us, Much we need thy tenderest care,
In thy pleasant pas-tures feed us, For our use thy folds pre-pare.
Blessed Je-sus, Blessed Je-sus, Thou hast bought us—thine we are;
Blessed Je-sus, Blessed Je-sus, Thou hast bought us—thine we are.

477.   *For Children only.*

2 Thou hast promised to receive us,
    Poor and sinful though we be;
  Thou hast mercy to relieve us,
    Grace to cleanse, and power to free:
      Blessed Jesus,
  Let us early turn to thee.

3 Early let us seek thy favor;
    Early let us learn thy will;
  Do thou, Lord, our only Saviour,
    With thy love our bosoms fill:
      Blessed Jesus,
  Thou hast loved us,—love us still.

HYMN 478.

SWEET HOUR OF PRAYER.

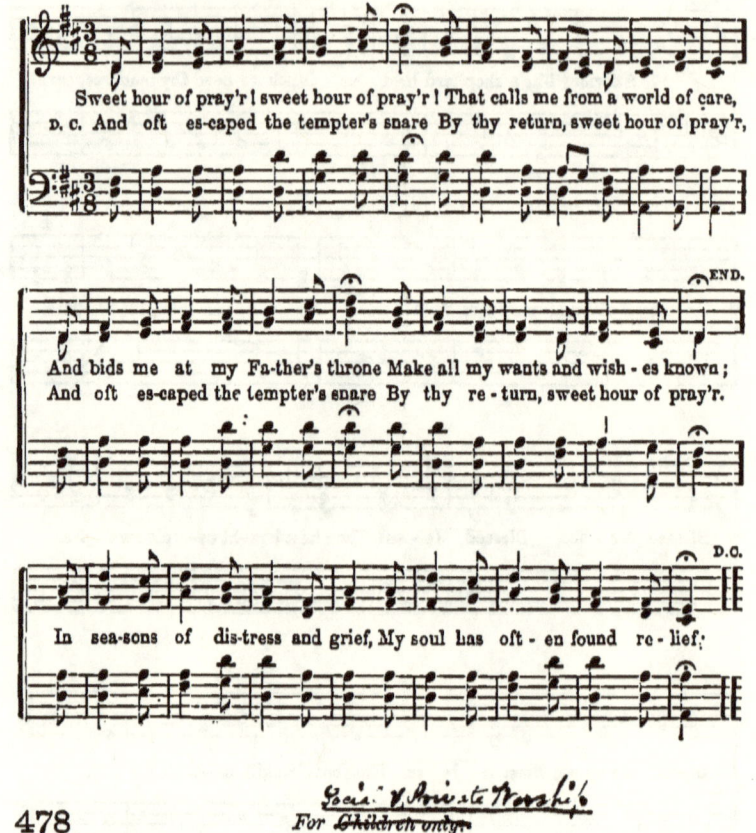

478

2 Sweet hour of prayer! sweet hour of prayer!
Thy wings shall my petition bear
To him whose truth and faithfulness
Engage the waiting soul to bless;
And since he bids me seek his face,
Believe his word and trust his grace,
I'll cast on him my every care,
And wait for thee, sweet hour of prayer!

3 Sweet hour of prayer! sweet hour of prayer!
May I thy consolation share;
Till from Mount Pisgah's lofty height,
I view my home, and take my flight:
This robe of flesh I'll drop, and rise
To seize the everlasting prize;
And shout, while passing through the air,
Farewell, farewell, sweet hour of prayer.

HYMN 479.

THAT BEAUTIFUL LAND.

A beau-ti-ful land by faith I see, A land of rest, from sor-row free, The home of the ransomed, bright, and fair, And beau-ti-ful an-gels, too, are there.

CHORUS.
Will you go? Will you go? Go to that beau-ti-ful land with me?

May be repeated at pleasure. pp
Will you go? Will you go? Go to that beau-ti-ful land?

479 For

2 That beautiful land, the City of Light,
It ne'er has known the shades of night,
The glory of God, the light of day,
Hath driven the darkness far away.
  Will you go? &c.

3 In vision I see its streets of gold;
Its beautiful gates I too behold;
The river of life, the crystal sea,
The ambrosial fruit of life's fair tree.
  Will you go, &c.

4 The heavenly throng, arrayed in white,
In rapture range the plains of light,
And in one harmonious choir they praise
Their glorious Saviour's matchless grace.
  Will you go? &c.

HYMN 480.

THE LOVE OF JESUS.

1. I know 'tis Jesus loves my soul, And

makes the wound-ed spi-rit whole; My na-ture is by

sin de-filed, Yet Jesus loves a lit-tle child.

480 *For Children only.*

2 How kind is Jesus, O how good!
'Twas for my soul he shed his blood;
For children's sake he was reviled,
For Jesus loves a little child.

3 To me may Jesus now impart,
Although so young, a gracious heart;
Alas! I'm oft by sin defiled,
Yet Jesus loves a little child.

HYMN 481.

THE SHINING SHORE.

My days are glid-ing swift-ly by, And I, a pil-grim stranger, Would not de-tain them as they fly—Those hours of toil and dan-ger. For O, we stand on Jor-dan's strand, Our friends are pass-ing o-ver, And just be-fore, the shining shore We may al-most dis-cov-er.

481 *For Children only.*

2 Our absent king the watchword gave,—
 "Let every lamp be burning;"
 We look afar, across the wave,
 Our distant home discerning:
  For now, &c.

3 Should coming days be dark and cold,
 We will not yield to sorrow,

For hope will sing, with courage bold,
 "There's glory on the morrow:"
  For now, &c.

4 Let storms of woe in whirlwinds rise,
 Each cord on earth to sever,—
 There, bright and joyous in the skies—
 There—is our home for ever:
  For now, &c.

WHEN, HIS SALVATION BRINGING.

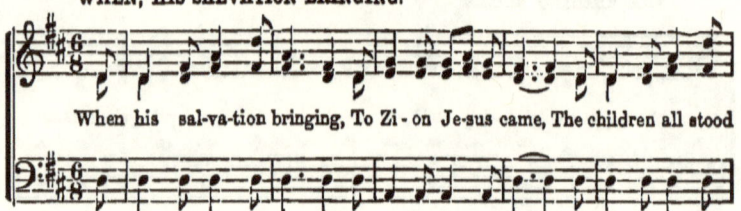

When his salvation bringing, To Zi-on Jesus came, The children all stood

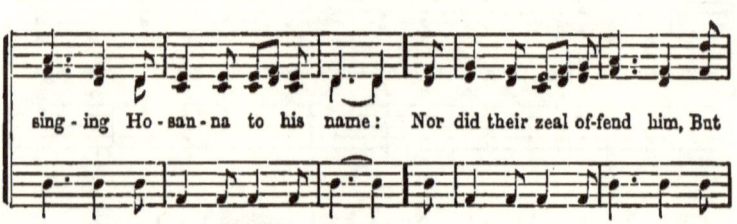

singing Hosanna to his name: Nor did their zeal offend him, But

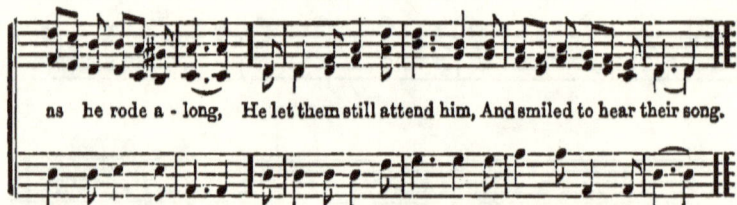

as he rode along, He let them still attend him, And smiled to hear their song.

482 *For Children only.*

2 And since the Lord retaineth
   His love for children still,
Though now as King he reigneth
   On Zion's heavenly hill:
We'll flock around his banner,
   Who sits upon the throne;
And cry aloud, "Hosanna
   To David's royal Son."

3 For should we fail proclaiming
   Our great Redeemer's praise,
The stones, our silence shaming,
   Might well hosannas raise.
But shall we only render
   The tribute of our words?
No; while our hearts are tender,
   They too shall be the Lord's.

483 *For Children only.*

WE bring no glittering treasures,
   No gems from earth's deep mine;
We come, with simple measures,
   To chant thy love divine.
O Lord, thy favors sharing,
   Our voice of thanks we raise;
Father, accept our offering,
   Our song of grateful praise.

2 Saviour, bestow thy blessing;
   Oh, teach us how to pray;
That each, thy fear possessing,
   May tread life's onward way.
Then, where the pure are dwelling,
   We'll hope to meet again;
And, sweeter numbers swelling,
   We'll join to praise thy name.

INDEX OF THE HYMNS.

	PAGE.
A beautiful land by faith I see	339
A glory gilds the sacred page	232
Alas, and did my Saviour bleed	241
All glorious Saviour, Source of grace	267
All hail the power of Jesus' name	253
All praise to thee, eternal Lord	216
All ye nations, praise the Lord	321
And must this body die	295
Angels from the realms of glory	314
Arise, my soul, my joyful powers	240
Arise, O King of grace, arise	275
Around the throne of God in heaven	333
At thy command, our dearest Lord	237
Awake, and sing the song	264
Awake, my soul, and with the sun	215
Awake, my soul, in joyful lays	237
Awake, my soul, stretch every nerve	251
Awake, ye saints, to praise your King	270
Away from every mortal care	217
Before Jehovah's awful throne	230
Begin, my soul, the exalted lay	209
Behold the glories of the Lamb	262
Behold, the lofty sky	234
Behold the morning sun	264
Behold, the mountain of the Lord	259
Behold, the sin-atoning Lamb	234
Behold, what wondrous grace	261
Beneath a num'rous train of ills	215
Blessed be the Lord, who heard my prayer	210
Bless, O my soul, the living God	224
Blest are the sons of peace	269
Blest are the souls who hear and know	248
Blest are the undefiled in heart	273
Blest be the tie that binds	267
Blest Comforter divine	267
Blest is the man, forever blest	218
Blest morning, whose first dawning light	255
Boundless glory, Lord, be thine	318
Bread of heav'n, on thee I feed	323
Brightest and best of the sons of the morning	330
Buried in shadows of the night	220
Call Jehovah thy salvation	309
Children of the heavenly King	321
Christian, see the orient morning	315
Christ is our corner stone	303
Christ, whose glory fills the skies	323
Come, dearest Lord, who reign'st above	211
Come, every pious heart	304
Come, gracious Lord, descend and dwell	219
Come, gracious Spirit, heavenly Dove	238
Come, Holy Ghost, in love	336
Come, Holy Spirit, calm my mind	271
Come, Holy Spirit, heavenly Dove	263
Come, Holy Spirit, come	290
Come, let our hearts and voices join	261
Come, let us join our cheerful songs	257
Come, let us join our friends above	267

	PAGE.
Come, let us lift our joyful eyes	255
Come, Lord, and warm each languid heart	263
Come, my Redeemer, come	304
Come, O Creator Spirit, blest	210
Come, sound his praise abroad	290
Come, thou almighty King	326
Come, thou Desire of all thy saints	275
Come, thou fount of every blessing	307
Come, thou long-expected Jesus	308
Come, we that love the Lord	290
Come, weary souls, with sins distress'd	223
Come, ye disconsolate, where'er ye languish	331
Come, ye that love the Saviour's name	249
Commit thou all thy griefs	293
Crown his head with endless blessing	310
Daughter of Zion, awake from thy sadness	331
Daughter of Zion, from the dust	251
Dearest of all the names above	243
Dear Refuge of my weary soul	247
Dear Saviour, ever at my side	267
Dear Saviour, we are thine	281
Dear Shepherd of thy people, hear	259
Descend from heav'n, immortal Dove	209
Didst thou, dear Jesus, suffer shame	259
Dismiss us with thy blessing, Lord	231
Dread Jehovah, God of nations	313
Dread Sovereign, let my evening song	269
Early, my God, without delay	256
Enthroned on high, almighty Lord	264
Ere the blue heavens were stretched	214
Eternal Father, God of love	279
Eternal Source of every joy	235
Eternal source of light and grace	273
Eternal Spirit, we confess	247
Far as thy name is known	291
Farewell, ye transitory things	226
Father, how wide thy glory shines	271
Father, I sing thy wondrous grace	260
Father of all, whose love profound	221
Father of mercies, God of love	216
Father of mercies, in thy word	264
Father of peace and God of love	260
Father, thy Son hath died	300
Father, whate'er of earthly bliss	265
Firm as the earth thy gospel stands	257
Forever blessed be the Lord	262
Forever with the Lord	291
Forgiveness! 'tis a joyful sound	299
For thee, O dear, dear country	325
For the mercies of the day	321
Frequent the day of God returns	279
Friend after friend departs	301
From all that dwell below the skies	280
From deep distress and troubled tho'ts	222
From every stormy wind that blows	239
From Greenland's icy mountains	325

INDEX OF THE HYMNS.

	Page
From thee, my God, my joys shall rise	251
Gently, Lord, O gently lead us	309
Give thanks to God, he reigns above	227
Give to our God immortal praise	208
Give to the Father praise	285
Give to the winds thy fears	289
Glorious things of thee are spoken	309
Glory to God on high	327
Glory to God the Father's name	250
Glory to thee, my God, this night	215
God in his earthly temple lays	237
God in the gospel of his Son	220
God is my strong salvation	325
God is our refuge, tried and prov'd	266
God is the refuge of his saints	238
God moves in a mysterious way	273
God, my supporter and my hope	265
God of mercy, God of grace	322
God of our life, thy various praise	264
God with us! O glorious name	310
Grace! 'tis a charming sound	291
Gracious Spirit, love divine	320
Great God, attend while Zion sings	232
Great God, before thy mercy seat	259
Great God, indulge my humble claim	234
Great God, to thee my evening song	218
Great God, we sing thy mighty hand	209
Great God, whose universal sway	229
Great is the Lord; whose works of might	268
Great is the Lord our God	285
Great Shepherd of thine Israel	210
Great One in three, great Three in one	237
Guide me, O thou great Jehovah	311
Hail the day that sees him rise	321
Hail, thou once despised Jesus	312
Hail to the Lord's Anointed	325
Happy the church, thou sacred place	211
Hark, the glad sound, the Saviour comes	252
Hark, the herald angels say	318
Hark the herald angels sing	320
Hark, the song of Jubilee	317
Hark, what mean those holy voices	312
Here at thy cross incarnate God	226
He that hath made his refuge God	211
High in the heavens, eternal God	236
Hither, ye faithful, haste with songs of triumph	330
Holy and reverend is the name	277
Holy, holy, holy Lord, be thy glorious	319
Holy, holy, holy Lord God of hosts	316
Hosanna with a cheerful sound	265
How beauteous are their feet	288
How blest the righteous, when he dies	213
How charming is the place	281
How did my heart rejoice to hear	263
How glorious is the sacred place	257
How heavy is the night	285
How large the promise, how divine	240
How pleasant, how divinely fair	229
How pleased and blest was I	301
How precious is the book divine	245
How sweet the name of Jesus sounds	254
Hush'd be my murmurings, let cares depart	332
I hear thy word with love	292
I know 'tis Jesus loves my soul	340
I lift my soul to God	293
I'll praise my Maker with my breath	297
I'll speak the honors of my king	276
I love the Lord; he heard my cries	276
I love the volume of thy word	296
I love thy kingdom, Lord	295
I love to steal awhile away	241
I'm not ashamed to own my Lord	271
In all my vast concerns with thee	259
In every trouble, sharp and strong	275
In the Christian's home in glory	336
In vain we seek for peace with God	268
I send the joys of earth away	215
I thank the goodness and the grace	255
I think when I read that sweet	329
I waited patient for the Lord	258
I would not live alway, I ask not to stay	331
Jehovah reigns, he dwells in light	233

	Page
Jehovah reigns, his throne is high	233
Jerusalem, my happy home	249
Jesus, all-atoning Lamb	319
Jesus, and shall it ever be	283
Jesus, engrave it on my heart	225
Jesus, hail, enthroned in glory	311
Jesus, I love thy charming name	277
Jesus, I my cross have taken	307
Jesus, in sickness and in pain	267
Jesus, lover of my soul	316
Jesus, my Saviour, bind me fast	347
Jesus shall reign where'er the sun	229
Jesus, tender Shepherd, hear us	318
Jesus, the spring of joys divine	216
Jesus, the very thought of thee	260
Jesus, we look to thee	281
Jesus, where'er thy people meet	225
Jesus, who on Calvary's mountain	306
Join, all who love the Saviour's name	213
Joy to the world, the Lord is come	246
Just are thy ways, and true thy word	212
Just as I am, without one plea	218
Know, my soul, thy full salvation	313
Let all the earth her voices raise	297
Let everlasting glories crown	222
Let every creature join	292
Let me but hear my Saviour say	211
Let them neglect thy glory, Lord	256
Let Zion in her king rejoice	215
Let Zion praise the mighty God	227
Like sheep we went astray	290
Light of those whose dreary dwelling	312
Lo, he comes with clouds descending	315
Long as I live I'll bless thy name	261
Lord, dismiss us with thy blessing	307
Lord, bow mysterious are thy ways	289
Lord, I approach the mercy seat	269
Lord, I have made thy word my choice	240
Lord, I will bless thee all my days	224
Lord, in the morning thou shalt hear	277
Lord, in thy great, thy glorious name	237
Lord, look upon a little child	223
Lord of every land and nation	310
Lord of hosts, how lovely, fair	316
Lord of the worlds above	308
Lord, thou hast heard thy servant cry	246
Lord, thou wilt hear me when I pray	243
Lord, we come before thee now	319
Lord, what is man that he sh'ld prove	214
Lord, when I count thy mercies o'er	275
Lord, when thou didst ascend on high	213
Lo, the Lord Jehovah liveth	313
Lo, the stone is rolled away	321
Love divine, all love excelling	306
Lo, what a cloud of witnesses	263
Lo, what a glorious sight appears	253
Majestic sweetness sits enthroned	267
Mine eyes and my desire	269
My days are gliding swiftly by	341
My dear Redeemer and my Lord	229
My faith looks up to thee	227
My God, accept my early vows	225
My God, accept my heart this day	274
My God, how endless is thy love	221
My God, I love thee, not because	270
My God, in whom are all the springs	217
My God, my Father! blissful name	255
My God, my King, thy various praise	219
My God, my life, my love	265
My God, permit me not to be	217
My God, permit my tongue	299
My God, the covenant of thy love	279
My God, the spring of all my joys	251
My God, what gentle cords are thine	270
My Maker and my King	265
My never ceasing song shall show	242
My Saviour and my King	232
My Saviour, let me hear thy voice	259
My Saviour, my almighty Friend	277
My Shepherd is the living Lord	230
My soul, be on thy guard	266
My soul, how lovely is the place	276
My soul repeat his praise	262

INDEX OF THE HYMNS.

	PAGE
My soul, thy great Creator praise	222
My spirit looks to God alone	228
My spirit on thy care	281
My times of sorrow and of joy	247
Nature with open volume stands	226
Nearer, my God, to thee	831
No more, my God, I boast no more	219
Not all the blood of beasts	280
Not to the terrors of the Lord	254
Not with our mortal eyes	289
Now at the Lamb's high royal feast	231
Now be my heart inspired to sing	211
Now let our cheerful eyes survey	241
Now, O my soul, forever praise	250
Now shall my solemn vows be paid	274
Now to the Lord a noble song	235
Now to the Lord that makes us know	212
O all ye nations praise the Lord	249
O, blessed souls are they	286
O bless the Lord, my soul	283
O cease, my wandering soul	292
O Christ, our King, Creator, Lord	234
O Christ, with each returning morn	231
O could I speak the matchless worth	296
O'er the realms of pagan darkness	315
O for a closer walk with God	243
O for a heart to praise my God	271
O for a shout of sacred joy	253
O for a thousand tongues to sing	266
O for the death of those	287
O God, my gracious God, to thee	296
O God of Bethel, by whose hand	265
O God of mercy, hear my call	246
O God, thou art my God alone	225
O how I love thy holy law	262
O Israel, who is like to thee	298
O Lord, I would delight in thee	245
O Lord, our God, arise	283
O Lord, our heavenly king	285
Once more, my soul, the rising day	269
One there is above all others	313
On Jordan's stormy banks I stand	253
On the mountain's top appearing	314
Oppressed with fear, oppressed with grief	271
O praise the Lord, for he is good	248
O sacred head, now wounded	224
O Sun of righteousness, arise	221
O Sun of righteousness divine	231
O that I knew the secret place	247
O that the Lord would guide my ways	258
O thou, in whose presence my soul takes delight	326
O thou that hear'st the prayer of faith	299
O thou that hear'st when sinners cry	258
O thou, to whose all searching sight	219
O thou, true Life of all that live	219
O thou who driest the mourner's tear	261
O thou, whose hand the kingdom sways	232
O thou, whose tender mercy hears	273
Our God, our help in ages past	258
Our land, O Lord, with songs of praise	263
Out of the deeps of long distress	246
O worship the King, all glorious above	329
O Zion, tune thy voice	308
People of the living God	317
Plunged in a gulf of dark despair	246
Praise, everlasting praise be paid	214
Praise to thee, thou great Creator	306
Praise to the Lord for all the host	257
Praise waits in Zion, Lord, for thee	256
Praise ye the Lord, exalt his name	208
Prepare me, gracious God	288
Pure Light of light, eternal day	227
Raise your triumphant songs	204
Rejoice, the Lord is king	308
Rejoice, ye saints, rejoice and praise	209
Rise, my soul, and stretch thy wings	326
Rock of ages, cleft for me	322
Safely through another week	323
Salvation is forever nigh	228
Salvation! O the joyful sound	278
Saviour, breathe an evening blessing	306

	PAGE
Saviour, like a shepherd lead us	337
Saviour, while my heart is tender	311
Saviour, who thy flock art feeding	310
See what a living stone	294
Shepherd of tender youth	327
Shew pity, Lord, O Lord forgive	218
Shine, mighty God, on Zion shine	249
Sing to the Lord, ye distant lands	250
Sing, ye redeemed of the Lord	278
Softly now the light of day	319
Songs of immortal praise belong	273
Son of God, to thee I cry	323
Sovereign of all the worlds on high	269
Sovereign ruler of the skies	319
Stand up, and bless the Lord	292
Sure the blest Comforter is nigh	230
Sweet hour of prayer! sweet hour of	338
Sweet is the memory of thy grace	269
Sweet is the work, my God, my King	220
Sweet is the work, O Lord	293
Sweet peace of conscience, heavenly guest	209
Sweet the moments, rich in blessing	313
Swift as declining shadows pass	235
Take my heart, O Father take it	309
Tarry with me, O my Saviour	311
Th' Almighty reigns, exalted high	227
The day is past and gone	289
The day of wrath, that dreadful day	231
Thee we adore, eternal Lord	235
Thee will I love, O Lord, my strength	212
The festal morn, my God, is come	299
The God Jehovah reigns	294
The God of mercy be adored	252
The God of my salvation lives	229
The heavens declare thy glory, Lord	236
The hour of my departure 's come	223
The Lord descended from above	242
The Lord himself, the mighty Lord	268
The Lord, how wondrous are his ways	224
The Lord is my Shepherd, no want shall	330
The Lord Jehovah reigns	300
The Lord my Shepherd is	280
The Lord of glory is my light	242
The Lord, the sovereign King	293
Then shall the King say unto them on	334
The praise of Zion waits for thee	228
The promise of my Father's love	264
There is a fountain filled with blood	255
There is a house not made with hands	271
There is a land of pure delight	251
There is an hour of peaceful rest	277
The Saviour! O what endless charms	276
Thine earthly Sabbaths, Lord, we love	209
This is the day the Lord hath made	241
Thou art my portion, O my God	274
Thou art the everlasting Son	297
Thou art the Way, to thee alone	272
Though now the nations sit beneath	217
Thou hidden Source of calm repose	297
Thou lovely Source of true delight	276
Thou loving Maker of mankind	225
Thou only Sovereign of my heart	238
Thou, whom my soul admires above	228
Thou, whose almighty word	327
Through all the changing scenes of life	275
Through endless years thou art the same	245
Through every age, eternal God	228
Through sorrow's night and danger's path	273
Thus far the Lord has led me on	221
Thy mercies fill the earth, O Lord	244
Thy name, almighty Lord	261
Thy way, O God, is in the sea	243
Thy works, not mine, O Christ	305
'Tis but a little while	295
'Tis by the faith of joys to come	211
'Tis by thy strength the mountains stand	245
To bless thy chosen race	267
To Father, Son, and Holy Ghost	275
To God, in whom I trust	205
To God the Father, God the Son	290
To God, the great, the ever blest	232
To God, the only wise	288
To him that chose us first	305
To our almighty Maker, God	272
To thee, my God, whose presence fills	263

INDEX OF THE HYMNS.

	Page
To thy pastures, fair and large	319
To us a child of hope is born	252
Triumphant Zion, lift thy head	233
Unveil thy bosom, faithful tomb	217
Up to the hills I lift mine eyes	221
Upward I lift mine eyes	308
Wake the song of Jubilee	321
Watchman, tell us of the night	317
We are but young, yet we may sing	213
We bless the Prophet of the Lord	240
We bring no glittering treasures	342
We give immortal praise	302
Welcome, sweet day of rest	285
We lift our hearts to thee	291
We praise and bless thee, gracious Lord	254
What shall I render to my God	242
What sinners value, I resign	221
When all thy mercies, O my God	261
When God revealed his gracious name	244
When his salvation bringing	342
When I can read my title clear	248
When I can trust my all with God	301
When I survey the wondrous cross	226
When marshalled on the nightly plain	235
When overwhelmed with grief	296
When sins and fears prevailing rise	230
While my Redeemer's near	287
While with ceaseless course the sun	317
Whilst thee I seek, protecting Power	257
Whom have we, Lord, in heaven but thee	243
Who shall ascend thy heavenly place	218
Why do we mourn departing friends	247
Why droops my soul with grief oppressed	217
Why should we start, and fear to die	223
With all my powers of heart and tongue	206
With songs and honors sounding loud	278
Ye humble souls, approach your God	272
Ye servants of God, your Master proclaim	329
Yes, the Redeemer rose	302
Ye trembling souls, dismiss your fears	279
Your harps, ye trembling saints	286
Zion's King shall reign victorious	311

CLASSIFICATION OF THE HYMNS.

The Figures are the Numbers of the Hymns.

FOR PUBLIC WORSHIP.

I. For the First Part of the Service: Humiliation.

GOD: IN CONDESCENSION:
  His Mercy: 1, 28, 71, 72, 104, 159, 305.

CHRIST: IN HUMILIATION:
  His Advent: 184, 185, 392, 398.
  His Incarnation: 26, 34, 408, 415, 435, 436, 467, 468.
  His Sufferings and Death; 79, 112, 113, 160, 217, 299, 370, 406, 451.
    The Only Saviour: 35, 54, 62, 248, 264.
  His Offices: 135, 264.
  His Love for Us: 241.
    Formed and Dwelling in Us: 191, 381, 392, 393.

THE HOLY GHOST: GOD DWELLING IN US:
  For Sanctification: 36, 129, 216, 231, 306, 327, 336, 457.
  For Illumination: 129, 457.
  For Comfort: 10, 437.

THE HOLY TRINITY: THE GOD OF SALVATION: 175, 183, 201, 375, 383, 456.

THE MEANS OF GRACE: PRAISED AND DESIRED:
  The House of God and its Ordinances: 53, 89, 114, 143, 200, 280, 335, 360, 469.
  The Word of God: 52, 121, 128, 136, 152, 186, 208, 224, 273, 289, 311, 312, 359.

COMFORTABLE EXPERIENCE OF:
  Deliverance of the Soul: 9, 18, 70, 87, 151, 167, 207, 223, 256, 257, 272, 288, 308, 309, 426.
  Forgiveness: 37, 44, 61, 71, 120, 199, 257, 320.
  Faith in Christ, our Righteousness: 80, 297, 299, 351, 392; 444.
  Salvation by Grace: 37, 43, 72, 81, 88, 168, 176, 288, 309.
  Grateful Self-Consecration: 79, 114, 144, 216, 232, 274, 382.
  Love and Prayer to Christ: 78, 113, 192, 218, 240, 241, 281, 361, 365, 407 451, 458.
  Rest in God and Christ: 95, 249, 298, 319, 343, 351, 420, 458, 466.
  Trust in the Promises: 27, 128, 232.

FOR SPECIAL OCCASIONS:
  Baptism: 137, 176, 399, 458.
  Reception to the Communion: 144, 176, 274.
  Public Fast: 11, 73, 130.

II. For the Second Part of the Service: Exaltation.

GOD: IN GLORY:
  His Sovereignty: 63, 97, 107, 363, 371.
  His Eternity: 155, 209.
  His Power: 108, 154.
  His Goodness: 84, 170, 220, 250, 251, 265, 291, 362, 464.
  His Faithfulness: 3, 145, 328.
  His Mighty Works—Of Providence: 29, 108, 154, 291. Of Grace: 3, 219, 250, 258, 267.
  His Heavenly Beauty and Majesty: 464.
  Perfectly Revealed in Christ: 116, 259, 265, 400.
  The Refuge of his People: 20, 38, 55, 82, 105, 107, 122, 242, 275, 379, 454.

CHRIST: IN EXALTATION:
  His Resurrection: 139, 352, 376, 427, 438.
  His Ascension: 21, 188, 409, 441.
    The Perfect Revelation of God: 116, 259, 265, 400.
    Sitting at the Right Hand of God: 401.
  His Messianic Glory and Work: 153, 171, 282, 307, 329, 371, 400, 409, 432.
  His Universal Kingdom: 91, 92, 108, 169, 177, 187, 188, 353, 377, 402, 465.
  His Loveliness and Beauty: 14, 282.
  •His Second Coming to Judgment: 419.

CLASSIFICATION OF THE HYMNS. 349

The Lamb praised in Heaven: 202, 225, 259, 401, 459, 405.
Glory of the New Covenant; 193, 194, 329.

THE CHURCH:

The Habitation of God: 2, 12, 123, 189, 226, 276, 314, 395.
The Bride of Christ: 64, 462.
Her Glory: 123, 203, 380.
Her Safety: 12, 203, 314, 354, 395.
Delivered and Spreading: 39, 106, 172, 179, 210, 310, 322, 363, 380, 402, 416, 417, 418, 445, 453, 460.
Triumphant: 109, 329, 470.
Universal Praise to God: 96, 115, 170, 172, 173, 260, 338, 345, 346, 367, 386, 421.
" " to Christ: 187, 188, 202, 439, 440.
The Consummation: 189, 422, 439.

THE COMMUNION OF SAINTS: 193, 204, 243.

EXALTED EXPERIENCE OF:

Desire to and Delight in the Church and Ordinances: 64, 90, 226, 276, 301, 314, 339, 354, 372, 384, 428, 462.
Security: 13, 20, 55, 82, 84, 105, 107, 122, 138, 242, 275, 314, 321, 328, 379, 454.
Freedom and Sonship: 194, 300, 337.
Priesthood and Kingship: 19, 145, 225, 376.
Joy and Triumph: 97, 178, 219, 258, 283, 328, 344, 377.
Pilgrimage: 84, 90, 204, 228, 243, 290, 313, 321, 337, 366, 394, 395, 403, 429, 442.
Anticipation of Heaven: 4, 56, 174, 178, 189, 300, 366, 429, 455.

FOR SPECIAL OCCASIONS:

The Communion, or the Preparatory Service, 64, 98, 124, 446, 462.
Public Thanksgiving: 83, 118, 227, 291.
New Year: 5, 233.
Dedication of a Church; 276, 378.
Instalment of a Pastor: 329.
Ordination of a Minister, Elder, or Deacon: 10.

FOR SOCIAL AND FAMILY WORSHIP.

PENITENTIAL: 45, 66, 141, 161, 215, 268, 209, 308, 419.

SUPPLICATORY:

For Gospel Comfort: 8, 15, 49, 100, 125, 162, 163, 244, 252, 268, 330, 347, 356, 368, 387.

For Revival: 58, 229, 230, 277.
For Heavenly Mind: 41, 65, 94, 99, 148, 164, 235, 260, 269.
For Guidance: 48, 237, 461.
For Christ in Us: 49, 447, 449.
For the Holy Ghost: 99, 230, 323.

BELIEVING:

In Christ, as our Atonement: 46, 47, 66, 75, 147, 196, 252, 364, 411, 461.
" " as a Faithful Friend: 6, 75, 111, 132, 140, 221, 246, 261, 364, 410.
In the Holy Ghost: 85, 134.

DEDICATORY: 31, 141, 181, 212, 292, 303, 317, 355, 390, 412, 423, 431.

TRUSTFUL AND PEACEFUL:

In God's Omniscience: 214.
In the Covenant: 30, 118, 140, 205, 261, 294, 295.
In Christ's Strength: 17, 125, 146, 246, 396.
In Christ's Presence and Love: 93, 132, 213, 221, 230, 324, 432.
Under Privation and Troubles: 30, 157, 165, 246, 278, 295, 349, 433.
Amid Changes and Darkness of Providence: 118, 133, 158, 195, 206, 271, 304, 333, 433.
In Union with Christ: 303.

CONSOLATORY AND HOPEFUL:

For this Life: 133, 222, 333, 349.
For the Life Everlasting: 263, 270, 303, 357, 358.
In view of Death (Funereal): 25, 65, 166, 270, 326, 358.

HYMNS OF LOVE:

To God: 76, 236.
To Christ: 22, 93, 110, 111, 146, 180, 285, 293, 315, 331, 364.
To One Another: 325, 332.
To the Church and Ordinances: 131, 348.
To the Word of God: 156, 234.

OF GRATITUDE AND PRAISE:

To God: 50, 262, 316, 317, 389.
To Christ: 127, 245.

OF JOY:

In Salvation by Grace: 340, 411.
In the Resurrection of Christ: 197.
In Adoption: 195, 253, 294.
In Christian Fellowship: 325.
In the Spread of the Gospel: 424.
In the Hope of Glory: 7, 16, 149, 158, 182, 190, 263, 287, 341, 412, 448, 471.

CLASSIFICATION OF THE HYMNS. 351

TRINITARIAN HYMNS:
  Of Prayer: 57, 284, 292.
  Of Praise: 126.

FOR SPECIAL OCCASIONS:
  Opening of Worship: 40, 74, 99, 211, 229, 244, 277, 302, 430, 478,
  Close of Worship: 40, 101, 301.
  Morning: 32, 59, 77, 102, 238, 254, 286, 342, 449.
  Evening: 28, 33, 51, 59, 60, 142, 150, 255, 279, 334, 388, 434.
  Saturday Evening: 450.
  The Lord's Day: 350.
  "   "   "   Morning: 197, 286, 318, 369.
  "   "   "   Evening: 296, 448.
  New Year: 425.

FOR CHILDREN: 24, 67, 198, 247, 397, 404, 414, 468, 473, 474, 475, 476, 477, 478, 479, 480, 481, 482, 483.

DOXOLOGIES—*on pages:* 215, 230, 275, 285.

FOR PRIVATE DEVOTION ONLY.

IN CONVICTION—Coming to Christ: 385.
IN SPIRITUAL RELIEF—The Star of Bethlehem: 119.
IN TROUBLE—Resignation: 472. Supplication: 239.
IN BEREAVEMENT—Of a Friend: 373. Of a Child: 374.
IN WAKEFULNESS AT NIGHT: 86
IN DEATH: 42, 68, 69, 103, 405.

CONTENTS OF THE BOOK OF WORSHIP.

ORDER OF DIVINE SERVICES ....Page 3
    Morning Service of the Lord's Day 5
    Evening Service   "   "   13
    The Communion of the Lord's Supper 20
    The Order for the Administration of Baptism 26
    The Form of Receiving Adult Persons to the Communion ... 28
    The Order for the Solemnizing of Marriage 30
    The Order for the Burial of the Dead 32
    The Office for the Ordination and Instalment of Elders
        and Deacons 35
THE PSALTER 39
THE HYMNS 205
    Index of the Hymns 343
    Classification of the Hymns 347